Federal Tax Policy

Studies of Government Finance

TITLES PUBLISHED

Federal Fiscal Policy in the Postwar Recessions, by Wilfred Lewis, Jr.

Federal Tax Treatment of State and Local Securities, by David J. Ott and Allan H. Meltzer.

Federal Tax Treatment of Income from Oil and Gas, by Stephen L. McDonald.

Federal Tax Treatment of the Family, by Harold M. Groves.

The Role of Direct and Indirect Taxes in the Federal Revenue System, John F. Due, Editor. A Report of the National Bureau of Economic Research and the Brookings Institution (Princeton University Press).

The Individual Income Tax, by Richard Goode.

Federal Tax Treatment of Foreign Income, by Lawrence B. Krause and Kenneth W. Dam.

Measuring Benefits of Government Investments, Robert Dorfman, Editor.

Federal Budget Policy, by David J. Ott and Attiat F. Ott.

Financing State and Local Governments, by James A. Maxwell.

Essays in Fiscal Federalism, Richard A. Musgrave, Editor.

Economics of the Property Tax, by Dick Netzer.

A Capital Budget Statement for the U.S. Government, by Maynard S. Comiez.

Foreign Tax Policies and Economic Growth, E. Gordon Keith, Editor. A Report of the National Bureau of Economic Research and the Brookings Institution (Columbia University Press).

Defense Purchases and Regional Growth, by Roger E. Bolton.

Federal Budget Projections, by Gerhard Colm and Peter Wagner. A Report of the National Planning Association and the Brookings Institution.

Corporate Dividend Policy, by John A. Brittain.

Federal Estate and Gift Taxes, by Carl S. Shoup.

Federal Tax Policy, by Joseph A. Pechman.

Federal Tax Policy

JOSEPH A. PECHMAN

Studies of Government Finance

THE BROOKINGS INSTITUTION

WASHINGTON, D.C.

THE BROOKINGS INSTITUTION is an independent organization devoted to nonpartisan research, education, and publication in economics, government, foreign policy, and the social sciences generally. Its principal purposes are to aid in the development of sound public policies and to promote public understanding of issues of national importance.

The Institution was founded December 8, 1927, to merge the activities of the Institute for Government Research, founded in 1916, the Institute of Economics, founded in 1922, and the Robert Brookings Graduate School of Economics and Government, founded in 1924.

The general administration of the Institution is the responsibility of a self-perpetuating Board of Trustees. The trustees are likewise charged with maintaining the independence of the staff and fostering the most favorable conditions for creative research and education. The immediate direction of the policies, program, and staff of the Institution is vested in the President, assisted by the division directors and an advisory council, chosen from the professional staff of the Institution.

In publishing a study, the Institution presents it as a competent treatment of a subject worthy of public consideration. The interpretations and conclusions in such publications are those of the author or authors and do not purport to represent the views of the other staff members, officers, or trustees of the Brookings Institution.

BOARD OF TRUSTEES

Foreword

RECENT ECONOMIC DEVELOPMENTS and congressional action have stimulated new interest in taxation as an instrument of national policy. Between 1961 and 1965, taxation was used to help restore full employment and raise the rate of economic growth. More recently, tax policy has been in the forefront of discussions of methods to restrain aggregate demand to prevent inflation.

Perhaps the major tax event of the last several years was the passage of the Revenue Act of 1964. This was the largest tax cut in history; it was deliberately planned and put into effect when the federal budget was in deficit; and it involved many of the most complicated features of the tax laws. The success of the 1964 Act is widely acknowledged to have had a profound influence on the development of tax policy as a tool for achieving the nation's objectives.

The use of taxation as a policy instrument remains highly controversial. The purpose of this volume is to explain the major issues so that the interested citizen may better understand, and contribute to, the public discussion. He should be reminded, however, that this is one economist's interpretation of professional opinion in this difficult area of public policy. Conflicting points of view are presented, but their proponents will not necessarily agree with the author's interpretation and evaluation. Moreover, in the interest of brevity, the discussion sometimes omits details that others might regard as important. For further information and different points of view, the reader should refer to the extensive literature cited in the bibliographical notes at the end of the book.

The volume is part of the Brookings series of Studies of Government Finance, a special program of research and education in taxation and government expenditures at the federal, state, and local levels, sponsored by the National Committee on Government Finance. It is one of three publications in this series that are primarily educational. The other two are *Federal Budget Policy,* by David J. and Attiat F. Ott of Southern Methodist University, and *Financing State and Local Governments,* by James A. Maxwell of Clark University.

The study was prepared by Joseph A. Pechman, Director of Economic Studies at the Brookings Institution and Executive Director of Studies of Government Finance. The author owes a special debt of gratitude for the assistance he received from Charles B. Saunders, Jr., whose editorial skills added greatly to the clarity of exposition, and Andrew T. Williams, who painstakingly assembled the factual and statistical materials in the volume. He is also grateful to Attiat F. Ott, who assisted in the preparation of Chapters 2, 3, 5, and 7; Barbara P. Haskins, who did the final editing of the volume and saw it through the various stages of publication; Evelyn P. Fisher, who carefully reviewed the manuscript for accuracy and consistency; Adele Garrett, who indexed the volume; and Marcia Appel, who acted as secretary for the project and supervised the typing of the manuscript. Lillian I. Buck and Judith Johnson helped with the charts and tables, and Fred Powell of Executive Art Studios prepared the charts in final form.

The author also wishes to acknowledge the assistance of many professional experts who read the manuscript in draft and offered numerous suggestions. The Reading Committee, consisting of Boris I. Bittker, Richard Goode, Arnold C. Harberger, and Dan Throop Smith, commented on the entire manuscript. So did Harvey E. Brazer, George F. Break, Samuel B. Chase, Jr., Morton Cohen, Edward F. Denison, Harold M. Groves, Edwin T. Haefele, Oscar Lurie, and Lawrence H. Seltzer. The author also received helpful comments on one or more chapters from Gerard M. Brannon, Benjamin Bridges, Jr., John A. Brittain, William M. Capron, Wilbur J. Cohen, Samuel M. Cohn, John Copeland, John F. Due, L. Laszlo Ecker-Racz, Gary Fromm, Bert G. Hickman, Herbert E. Klarman, Robert J. Lampman, Wilfred Lewis, Jr., James A. Maxwell, Ida C.

Merriam, Herbert C. Morton, Oliver Oldman, Dorothy P. Rice, Richard E. Slitor, Carl S. Shoup, James L. Sundquist, Stanley S. Surrey, Burton A. Weisbrod, Anita Wells, David Westfall, Melvin I. White, and Laurence N. Woodworth.

The National Committee on Government Finance was established in 1960 by the trustees of the Brookings Institution to supervise a comprehensive program of studies on taxation and government expenditures. The program sponsored by the National Committee is supported with funds provided by the Ford Foundation.

The views expressed in this study are those of the author and are not presented as the views of the National Committee on Government Finance or its Advisory Committee, or the staff members, officers, or trustees of the Brookings Institution, or the Ford Foundation.

Robert D. Calkins
President

June 1966
Washington, D. C.

Studies of Government Finance

Studies of Government Finance is a special program of research and education in taxation and government expenditures at the federal, state, and local levels. These studies are under the supervision of the National Committee on Government Finance appointed by the trustees of the Brookings Institution, and are supported by a special grant from the Ford Foundation.

MEMBERS OF THE ADVISORY COMMITTEE

Contents

Foreword   vii

1. Introduction   1

     Features of the U.S. Tax System   1
     Goals of Taxation   5

2. Taxes and Economic Policy   7

     Stabilization Policy   10
         Impact of Expenditure and Tax Changes   10
         Built-in Stabilizers   12
         Expenditure vs. Tax Adjustments   13
     Policies To Promote Economic Growth   16
         Achieving Full Employment   16
         Raising the Growth Rate   21
         Automatic Budget Rules   24
         The "Debt Burden"   26
     Summary   28

3. The Tax Legislative Process   30

     Executive Preparation of a Tax Bill   33
     The Bill in Congress   35
         The Ways and Means Committee   36
         House Approval   39
         The Senate Finance Committee   39
         The Senate Debate   40
         The Bill in Conference   41
     Presidential Action   42

Improving the Process   43
    Representation of the Public Interest   43
    Consideration of Overall Fiscal Policies   45
    Accelerating Countercyclical Tax Action   46
Summary   48

4. The Individual Income Tax   50

Structure of the Federal Income Tax   52
    Adjusted Gross Income and Taxable Income   52
    Tax Rates   55
    Methods of Tax Payment   56
    The Final Tax Reconciliation   58
    Possible Modification of the Current Payment System   59
Economic Effects   60
    Role as Stabilizer   60
    Effect on Saving and Consumption   61
    Work and Investment Incentives   63
Structural Problems   64
    Personal Exemptions   65
    Personal Deductions   75
    The Family   81
    The Aged   84
    Earned Income   87
    Capital Gains and Losses   90
    State and Local Government Bond Interest   93
    Income Averaging   95
Summary   96

5. The Corporation Income Tax   98

Characteristics of the Tax   100
    The Tax Base   100
    Tax Rates   102
    Tax Payment   103
Shifting and Incidence of the Tax   103
    The Shifting Mechanism   104
    The Evidence   106
Economic Issues   109
    Investment and Saving   109
    Equity and Debt Finance   112
    Resource Allocation   113
    Built-in Flexibility   114
    Balance of Payments   115

Structural Problems 116
Capital Consumption Allowances 117
Allowances for the Minerals Industries 123
Multiple Surtax Exemptions 125
Financial Institutions 126
Tax-Exempt Organizations 129
Foreign Income 131
Integration of the Corporation and Individual Income Taxes 132
The Additional Burden on Dividends 133
Methods of Integration 134
The Value Added Tax as a Replacement for the Corporation Tax 138
Summary 139

6. Consumption Taxes 141
Issues in Excise Taxation 144
Economic Effects of Excise Taxes 144
Equity Considerations 149
A General Consumption Tax? 151
The General Sales Tax 151
The Value Added Tax 154
The Expenditure Tax 157
Consumption vs. Income Taxes 158
Summary 160

7. Payroll Taxes 162
Features of Payroll Taxes 166
Regressivity 166
Built-in Flexibility 168
Effect on Prices, Employment, and Wages 169
Personal and Public Saving 171
Financing Social Security 172
The Contributory System 172
Proposals for Reform 173
Financing Unemployment Insurance 175
Summary 176

8. Estate and Gift Taxes 178
Characteristics of the Two Taxes 180
The Estate Tax 181
The Gift Tax 181
The Tax Base 182

Structural Problems   183
    Transfers of Husbands and Wives   183
    Separate Taxation of Estates and Gifts   187
    Generation-Skipping Through Trusts   191
    Charitable Foundations   195
    Small Business and the Estate Tax   197
Alternatives to the Estate Tax   198
Summary   199

9. State and Local Taxes   201

The State-Local Tax Structure   203
    State Taxes   204
    Local Taxes   206
    State-Local Fiscal Performance, Capacity, and Effort   207
Major Issues   209
    Income Taxes vs. Sales Taxes   209
    Deductibility   211
    Tax Coordination   214
    State-Local Fiscal Relations   221
    Federal Aid   225

Summary   231

APPENDIX A.   Historical Summary of Major Federal
              Taxes   235

APPENDIX B.   Tax Bases of the Major Federal Taxes   255

APPENDIX C.   Statistical Tables   274

APPENDIX D.   Bibliographical Notes   299

Index   309

Text Tables

1-1 Federal, State, and Local Taxes and Other Revenues, by Major
    Source, Fiscal Year 1964   4
2-1 Effects of Built-in Stabilizers on the Federal Surplus, Postwar
    Recessions and Recoveries   14
3-1 Legislative History of Major Federal Tax Bills Enacted, and
    Revenue Gain or Loss, 1948-65   32
4-1 Comparison of Increases in Personal Income and the Federal
    Individual Income Tax Base, 1948-63   55
4-2 Federal Individual Income Tax Rates, 1966   56
4-3 Comparison of Federal Individual Income Tax Exemptions with
    Estimates of Incomes of Families of Different Size Correspond-
    ing to the Same Standard of Living   69
4-4 Comparison of Federal Individual Income Tax Exemptions with
    Estimated Family Budgets, 1964   70
5-1 Rates of Return and Debt-Capital Ratio, Manufacturing Corpo-
    rations, Selected Years, 1927-61   108
5-2 Comparison of the General Corporation Income Tax Rate and
    Effective Rate of Federal Taxes on Corporation Profits Before
    Tax and Before Capital Consumption Allowances, 1946-65   111
5-3 Comparison of Declines in Gross National Product, Federal
    Receipts, Federal Corporation Income Tax, and Undistributed
    Corporate Profits in Four Postwar Recessions   115
5-4 Comparison of Three Methods of Depreciation for a Ten-Year,
    $1,000 Asset   118
5-5 Use of Methods of Depreciation on Corporation Income Tax
    Returns, 1954, 1955, 1957, and 1960   119
5-6 Ratio of Annual Amounts of Depletion Claimed on Federal
    Corporation Tax Returns to Adjusted Basis Depletion, by
    Mineral Products, 1958-60   124
5-7 Additional Burden of the Corporation Income Tax on $100 of
    Corporation Income   133
5-8 Portion of the Additional Burden of the Corporation Income
    Tax Removed by the 4 Percent Dividend Received Credit   135
5-9 Portion of the Additional Burden of the Corporation Income
    Tax Removed by the Dividend Paid Deduction   136
5-10 Portion of the Additional Burden of the Corporation Income
    Tax Removed by Withholding Method   137
6-1 Federal Excise Tax Revenue Before and After the Enactment
    of the Excise Tax Reduction Act of 1965, by Major Source   145
6-2 Effective Rates of Federal Excise Taxes and Customs, 1954, and
    of a Hypothetical Wisconsin General Retail Sales Tax, 1956   150

7-1   Major Characteristics of the Social Insurance Programs as of
      July 1, 1966   164
7-2   Effective Rates of OASDHI Taxes and of Alternative Methods
      of Raising the Same Revenue, by 1960-61 Family Money
      Income Classes, with 1966 Tax Rates   167
7-3   Maximum Taxes on Employees and the Self-Employed Under
      the OASDI and Hospital Insurance Programs, 1966 and Later
      Years   168
8-1   Estate Taxes Paid by a Married Couple, by Net Estate Levels   185
8-2   Frequency of Gifts and Percentage of Wealth Transferred by Gift
      During Life Among Millionaire Decedents, 1945, 1951, 1957,
      and 1959   189
8-3   Frequency of Noncharitable Transfers in Trust and Percentage
      of Wealth Transferred in Trust by Millionaire Decedents,
      1945, 1951, 1957, and 1959   193
8-4   Timing of Next Estate Taxes on Outright and Trust Transfers
      of Millionaire Decedents, 1945, 1951, 1957, and 1959   194
9-1   Combined Federal and State Tax Liabilities for a Married Couple
      with Two Dependents in an Income and Sales Tax State, 1965   210
9-2   Net Impact of State Income Taxes Under (a) Federal Deducti-
      bility and (b) Federal and State Deductibility, at Illustrative
      Marginal Rates   212
9-3   Distribution of States by Ratios of Assessed Value to Sales Price
      of Real Property, 1956 and 1961   222

Charts

1-1   Receipts of Federal, State and Local Governments, 1929-65   2
2-1   Gross National Product, Actual and Potential, and Unemploy-
      ment Rate, 1955-65   8
2-2   Effect of Level of Activity on Federal Surplus or Deficit   17
2-3   Federal Deficits and Surpluses, Three Budget Concepts, 1948-65   18
2-4   Full Employment Surplus, National Income Accounts Basis,
      1955-65   21
2-5   Relation Between Net Federal Debt and Interest on Net Debt to
      the Gross National Product, 1942-65   27
4-1   Ratio of Taxable Individual Income to Personal Income, 1939-64   54
4-2   Influence of Various Provisions on Effective Rates of Federal
      Individual Income Tax, 1964 Act   66
4-3   History of Federal Individual Income Tax Exemptions in Current
      and 1939 Prices, 1913-65   68
4-4   Itemized Deductions as a Percentage of Adjusted Gross Income,
      Taxable and Nontaxable Federal Individual Returns, 1962   74
4-5   Ratio of Federal Tax Saving from Income Splitting for Married
      Couples to Tax of Single Persons at 1966 Rates   82

5-1 Percentage of Business Income Originating in the Corporate Sector, 1929-64   107

5-2 Property Income Share in Corporate Gross Product Less Indirect Taxes, 1922-29 and 1948-65   109

5-3 Effect of 7 Percent Investment Credit and Declining-Balance Depreciation on Rate of Return of Ten-, Fifteen-, and Twenty-Year Assets Yielding 10 Percent with Straight-Line Depreciation   122

6-1 Importance of Consumption Taxes and Customs in Selected Countries, 1961   142

7-1 Payroll Taxes as a Percentage of Gross National Product, Federal Cash Receipts, and Individual Income Tax Receipts, Fiscal Years 1948-65   163

8-1 Estate or Gift Taxes for Alternative Property Transfers During Life and at Death   188

9-1 Federal and State-Local Expenditures, Fiscal Years 1948-64   202

9-2 Sources of Growth of State-Local Revenue, 1954-64   204

9-3 Per Capita State-Local Revenue and Revenue Effort, by States, by Quintiles of State Personal Income Per Capita, 1964   208

9-4 Federal Aid to State-Local Governments, and State Aid to Local Governments, Selected Years, 1902-52, Annually, 1953-64   226

9-5 State-Local General Revenue from Own Sources and from Federal Grants, by States, by Quintiles of Personal Income Per Capita, 1964   228

Appendix Tables

A-1 History of Federal Individual Income Tax Exemptions and First and Top Bracket Rates   243

A-2 Federal Individual Income Tax Rate Schedules Under the Revenue Acts of 1944, 1945, 1948, 1950, 1951, and 1964   244

A-3 History of Federal Corporation Income Tax Rates   245

A-4 Marginal Rates of the Federal Corporation Income Tax Since 1942   245

A-5 Federal Excise Tax Rates on Selected Items as of December 31, Selected Years, 1913-69   246

A-6 History of Social Security and Railroad Retirement Tax Rates   250

A-7 History of Unemployment Tax Rates   251

A-8 Federal Estate Tax Rates and Rates of the State Tax Credit, 1942 to Date (1966)   252

A-9 History of Estate and Gift Tax Rates   253

A-10 History of Estate and Gift Tax Exemptions and Exclusions   254

B-1 Derivation of Adjusted Gross Income from Personal Income, 1963   260

B-2   Comparison of Personal Income and Adjusted Gross Income, 1939-64   261
B-3   Comparison of Total Adjusted Gross Income and Adjusted Gross Income Reported on Tax Returns, 1939-64   262
B-4   Derivation of the Individual Income Tax Base, 1946-63   263
B-5   Comparison of Personal Income and Taxable Income, 1939-64   264
B-6   Distribution of Taxable Income and Individual Income Tax, by Rate Brackets, 1963   265
B-7   Reconciliation of Corporation Profits Before Tax, Compiled Net Profits, and Taxable Income, 1962   266
B-8   Comparison of Corporation Profits Before Tax, Compiled Net Profits, and Taxable Income, 1939-63   267
B-9   Distribution of Corporation Taxable Income, by Rate Brackets, 1962   268
B-10 Number of Taxable Estate Tax Returns Filed as a Percentage of Adult Deaths, Selected Years, 1939-63   269
B-11 Number of Taxable Estate Tax Returns, Gross and Economic Estate, and Estate Tax Before and After Credits, Selected Years, 1939-63   270
B-12 Distribution of Taxable Estates, by Rate Brackets, 1963   271
B-13 Number of Taxable Gift Tax Returns, Total Gifts, Taxable Gifts, and Gift Tax, Selected Years, 1939-63   272
B-14 Distribution of Taxable Gifts, by Rate Brackets, 1963   273
C-1   Federal Receipts, Expenditures, Surpluses, or Deficits Under Three Budget Concepts, Fiscal Years 1929-65   274
C-2   Relationship of Federal, State, and Local Government Receipts to Gross National Product, 1929-65   275
C-3   Federal Receipts from the Public, by Source, 1934-65   276
C-4   Relationship of Direct and Indirect Taxes in Nine Countries to Gross National Product and to Total Tax Yield, 1961   278
C-5   Distribution of Taxes and Other Revenues by Major Source and Level of Government, Selected Years, 1902-64   279
C-6   Number and Amount of Standard and Itemized Deductions, Taxable and Nontaxable Federal Individual Income Tax Returns, 1944-63   280
C-7   Federal Individual Income Tax Liabilities, Prepayments, Final Balances of Tax Due and Overpayments, 1944-63   281
C-8   Number of Federal Individual Income Tax Returns by Type of Final Settlement, 1944-63   282
C-9   Distribution of Taxable Federal Individual Income Tax Returns and Tax Liabilities, 1941 and 1963   283
C-10 Influence of Various Provisions on Effective Rates of Individual Income Tax, Taxable Returns, 1964 Act   284

C-11 Itemized Deductions as a Percentage of Adjusted Gross Income, by Adjusted Gross Income Classes, Federal Individual Income Tax Returns with Itemized Deductions, 1962   285

C-12 Comparison of Federal Individual Income Tax Liabilities of Single Persons and Married Couples, 1965-66   286

C-13 Schedule of Transition to the Current Payment System for Corporations   287

C-14 Selected Ratios Relating to the Corporate Sector, 1929-64   288

C-15 Rates of Return Before and After Federal Income Tax, Manufacturing Corporations, 1927-41 and 1948-61   289

C-16 Sources and Uses of Funds, Nonfarm Nonfinancial Corporate Business, 1960-65   290

C-17 Assets of Selected Federal Trust Funds, Fiscal Years 1937-65   291

C-18 Number of Estate Tax Returns, Value of Estates, and Amount of Tax, by Gross Estate Classes, 1963   292

C-19 Number of Gift Tax Returns, and Amounts of Gifts and Gift Tax, by Taxable Gift Classes, 1963   293

C-20 General Expenditure of State and Local Governments, by Major Function, Fiscal Years 1954 and 1964   294

C-21 General Revenue of State and Local Governments, Fiscal Years 1954 and 1964   295

C-22 State and Local Government Debt, Fiscal Years 1954-64   296

C-23 Use of Major Tax Sources by the States, September 1, 1966   297

C-24 Top Bracket State Individual and Corporation Income Tax Rates Before and After Allowing for Federal and State Deductibility, as of September 1, 1966   298

CHAPTER 1

Introduction

FEDERAL, STATE, AND LOCAL government receipts now amount to slightly more than one-fourth of the gross national product. They are collected from a variety of taxes, as well as from fees, charges, and other miscellaneous receipts. The sources include almost the entire tax spectrum: income taxes, general and selective consumption taxes, payroll taxes, estate and gift taxes, and property taxes.

Despite the large amount of money collected—$187 billion in 1965—U.S. taxes are by no means the heaviest in the world. Most advanced European countries impose relatively higher taxes. In 1961, for example, taxes ranged between 30 and 35 percent of the gross national product in Germany, France, Italy, the Netherlands, Sweden, and the United Kingdom as compared with 27 percent in the United States (Appendix Table C-4).

Features of the U.S. Tax System

The most distinctive feature of the U.S. tax system is that it places great weight on the individual and corporation income taxes. These account for over 45 percent of total revenues (including social insurance taxes) of all levels of government. At the federal level, they account for over 60 percent (Appendix Table C-5).

1

CHART 1-1. Receipts of Federal, State and Local Governments, 1929–65

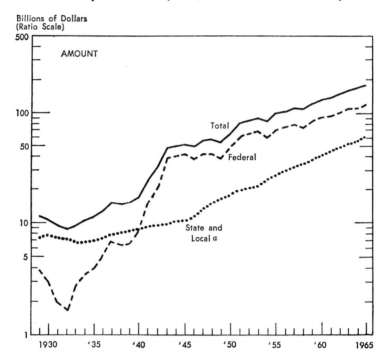

Billions of Dollars
(Ratio Scale)

AMOUNT

Total

Federal

State and
Local a

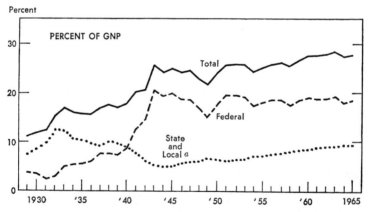

Percent

PERCENT OF GNP

Total

Federal

State
and
Local a

Source: Appendix Table C-2. Receipts are on a national income accounts basis.
a State and local receipts have been adjusted to exclude federal grants-in-aid.

2

A second distinction is that it is a federal system (Chart 1-1). The national and state governments have independent taxing powers, while the local governments derive their taxing powers from the state governments. There is duplication among the tax sources of the three governmental levels, especially between federal and state governments, but the tax structures differ markedly. The federal government relies primarily on income taxes, the states on consumption taxes, and the localities on real property taxes (Table 1-1).

Two-thirds of all taxes are collected by the federal government, but state and local taxes have been rising at a much more rapid rate during the past two decades. This reflects the rapid growth in demand for the public services that are operated and administered primarily by state and local governments. All governments finance most of their revenue needs from their own taxes. However, there is a well developed system of intergovernmental assistance, which transfers funds from higher to lower levels of government. Intergovernmental transfers have risen rapidly in recent years.

The broad outlines of the tax system have remained the same since World War II, when the federal government greatly expanded the coverage of the individual income tax and substantially increased corporation tax rates. Nevertheless, the structure has not been static—during the last twelve years, great changes have occurred at all levels of government. Federal income tax rates have been reduced substantially; depreciation allowances have been liberalized and an investment credit has been introduced to stimulate investment; practically all selective excise taxes other than the taxes on liquor and tobacco and the highway taxes have been reduced or eliminated; payroll tax rates have been raised; and numerous revisions have been made in the income tax bases. At the state and local levels, tax rates have been rising steadily. Traditional opposition to state income and sales taxes has broken down; more than half the states now have both. To alleviate the burden of the sales tax on the poor, the idea of a tax credit for state sales taxes against state income taxes (with refunds to those not subject to income tax) has begun to take hold. State and local governments have also been improving administration of the property tax, which continues to be the major revenue source for local governments.

These developments foreshadow continued change and evolu-

TABLE 1-1. Federal, State, and Local Taxes and Other Revenues, by Major Source, Fiscal Year 1964

Major Source	Revenues[a]	
	Amount (Billions of dollars)	Percentage of Total
Federal		
Individual income	48.4	42.6
Corporation income	23.6	20.7
Excises	13.9	12.2
Estate and gift	2.4	2.1
Payroll	23.6	20.8
Other	1.8	1.6
Total	113.6	100.0
State		
Individual income	3.3	13.1
Corporation income	1.6	6.2
Sales and excises	12.1	47.7
Estate and gift	0.6	2.4
Property	0.7	2.8
Other	7.0	27.7
Total	25.4	100.0
Local		
Property	20.6	77.5
Individual income	0.4	1.5
Sales and excises	1.7	6.2
Other	3.9	14.8
Total	26.6	100.0
State and Local		
Individual income	3.7	7.1
Corporation income	1.6	3.0
Sales and excises	13.8	26.5
Estate and gift	0.6	1.2
Property	21.3	41.0
Other	11.0	21.1
Total	52.0	100.0
All Levels		
Individual income	52.1	31.5
Corporation income	25.1	15.2
Sales and excises	27.7	16.7
Estate and gift	3.0	1.8
Payroll	23.6	14.2
Property	21.3	12.9
Other	12.8	7.7
Total	165.6	100.0

Sources: Worksheets of the Office of Business Economics; *Governmental Finances in 1964–65.* Figures are rounded and will not necessarily add to totals.

[a] Revenues are defined as receipts in the national income accounts less contributions for social insurance other than federal payroll taxes.

tion in the years ahead. Tax rates will be raised or lowered as domestic and international circumstances require. Reforms in federal individual and corporation income taxes will continue to be made. Consideration is being given to methods of alleviating the tax burden on low incomes and to integrating payroll taxes with the income tax. New interest is being shown in the federal estate and gift taxes. State and local finance will continue to be a major concern of policy at all levels of government.

The purpose of this book is to explain these and other emerging issues in federal taxation and to discuss alternative solutions. Chapter 2 examines the relation between taxation and economic growth and stability, and how tax policy fits into overall economic policy. Chapter 3 describes the tax legislative process, discusses its weaknesses, and suggests ways to improve it. Chapters 4 through 8 are devoted to the major federal tax categories: individual income tax, corporation income tax, consumption taxes, payroll taxes, and estate and gift taxes. Each chapter describes the basic features of the tax under review, recent changes in the law, and the problems yet unsolved. Chapter 9 analyzes the issues in state-local taxation that are relevant to federal policy.

Goals of Taxation

Taxation—the method by which a nation implements decisions to transfer resources from the private to the public sector—is a major instrument of social and economic policy. It has two goals: to distribute the cost of government fairly by income classes (vertical equity) and among people in approximately the same economic circumstances (horizontal equity); and to promote economic growth, stability, and efficiency. From these standpoints, the U.S. tax system is a source of both satisfaction and criticism. It is a progressive system, thus placing a proportionately greater burden on those who have greater ability to pay. It is also highly responsive to changes in business activity, and therefore exercises a powerful automatic stabilizing effect on private incomes and spending.

Some criticize the U.S. tax system because it is too progressive, others because it is not progressive enough. But there is a consensus in favor of at least *some* progression in the overall tax burden. Some believe that special provisions go too far toward promoting economic incentives, others believe that these provisions do not go far enough. Nonetheless, tax policy is generally regarded as a legitimate and useful device for promoting economic growth and stability, provided the particular measures chosen are effective means of accomplishing their objectives. Within these broad areas of agreement, there is considerable controversy regarding the relative emphasis to be placed on equity and economic objectives.

These issues involve difficult, technical questions of law, accounting, and economics. They are often obscured by lack of information, misunderstanding, and even misrepresentation. Yet they have important implications for the welfare of every citizen and for the vitality of the economy. This volume attempts to provide factual and analytical information that will help the reader make up his own mind. It was prepared in the belief that tax policy is too important to be left solely to the experts, and that taxation can and should be understood by the interested citizen.

CHAPTER 2

Taxes and Economic Policy

DURING MOST OF THE NATION'S HISTORY, federal budget policy was based on the rule that tax receipts should be roughly equal to annual expenditures. Declining receipts during a business contraction called for increasing taxes or reducing expenditures, while surpluses that developed during periods of prosperity called for lowering tax rates or increasing expenditures. This policy reduced private incomes when they were already falling, and raised them when they were rising. By aggravating fluctuations in purchasing power, the policy of annually balanced budgets accentuated economic instability.

In the 1930's, new concepts of budget policy emerged that emphasized the relationship of the federal budget to the performance of the economy. Adjustments in federal expenditures and taxes were to be made to reduce unemployment or to check inflation. Budget surpluses were to be used to restrain private spending during prosperity, deficits to stimulate spending during recessions. But variations in expenditures were expected to play a more active role than tax rate variations in counteracting fluctuations in private demand.

The current view is that private demand can be stimulated by reducing taxes as well as by increasing government expenditures.

CHART 2-1. Gross National Product, Actual and Potential, and Unemployment Rate, 1955–65

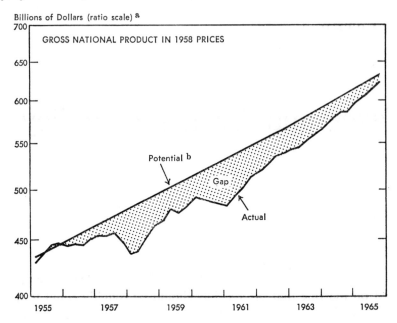

Billions of Dollars (ratio scale) [a]

GROSS NATIONAL PRODUCT IN 1958 PRICES

Potential [b]

Gap

Actual

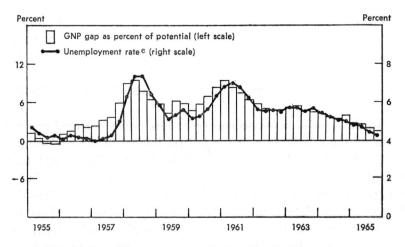

Percent   Percent

☐ GNP gap as percent of potential (left scale)

●—● Unemployment rate [c] (right scale)

Source: Reprinted from *Economic Report of the President*, January 1966, p. 41.

[a] Seasonally adjusted annual rates.

[b] Trend line of 3½% through middle of 1955 to 1962 IV; trend line of 3¾% thereafter.

[c] Unemployment as percent of civilian labor force; seasonally adjusted.

8

This view was regarded with skepticism by many people until the enactment of the Revenue Act of 1964. The economy had been operating at less than full employment levels since mid-1957, and the rate of economic growth had been disappointingly low. Despite increases in federal expenditures in 1961-63, unemployment remained high. The 1964 tax cut, amounting to $11.4 billion at an annual rate, triggered a substantial increase in consumer and business expenditures which contributed to a reduction in unemployment from 5.7 percent in 1963 to 4.5 percent in mid-1965. Continued growth in demand, spurred by a $1.75 billion cut in federal excise taxes in May and June 1965 and increased expenditures for the Vietnam conflict, reduced unemployment to 4.1 percent by the end of the year. The economic potency of tax cuts has thus been firmly established.

The purpose of this chapter is to explain how the fiscal actions of the government, including changes in expenditures and taxes, affect the level of economic activity and the rate of economic growth. Major emphasis will be placed on taxes, not because expenditures are less important but because the major focus of this volume is on taxation. It should also be noted that the growth and stability of the economy depend not only on fiscal decisions, but on many other government decisions which are outside the scope of this volume.

Fiscal economics is based on national income analysis as it has developed over the past thirty years. The essence of this analysis is that the level of expenditures depends on total output or gross national product (GNP), which in turn depends on the total spending of consumers, business, and government. At any given time, there is a level of output that is consistent with full employment of the nation's supply of labor (except for seasonal and a small amount of frictional unemployment). This level is called *potential* or *full employment GNP* (Chart 2-1). The major objectives of fiscal policy are to stabilize the economy at full employment, maintain price stability, and promote economic growth and efficiency.

Stabilization Policy

The federal government exerts great influence on total spending, and hence on output, through its expenditure and tax policies. It alters total spending directly by varying its own spending, or indirectly by raising or lowering taxes. If expenditures are increased or taxes lowered, the spending of higher incomes by the recipients requires additional output, which generates additional income and spending, and the cycle repeats itself. The cumulative increase in GNP is, therefore, a multiple of the initial increase in government expenditures or reduction in taxes. Correspondingly, reductions in expenditures or increases in taxes reduce GNP by a multiple of the initial action.

Impact of Expenditure and Tax Changes

The process of income and output creation through fiscal policy may be illustrated by the following hypothetical examples. Assume that out of each dollar of GNP, 25 cents is taken in federal taxes and the remaining 75 cents goes to consumers and business. Assume also that consumers and business together spend 80 percent of any additional income they receive.

If the government increases its purchases by $10 billion, private income before tax will initially increase by the same amount. Tax revenues will be $2.5 billion higher, and private disposable personal income will rise by $7.5 billion, of which consumers and business will spend $6 billion. This additional spending will generate another increase in income, with $1.5 billion going to taxes and the remaining $4.5 billion to consumers and business. Of this latter amount, consumers and business will spend $3.6 billion, which will generate still another round of income and spending, and so on. The total increase in GNP (including the initial $10 billion of government purchases) will amount to $25 billion ($10 + $6 + $3.6 + . . .). This is a multiplier of 2.5 times the original increase in spending.

Consider what happens if, instead of increasing expenditures, the government reduces taxes by $10 billion. Consumers and business will again spend 80 percent of the higher after-tax incomes, or

$8 billion. This will generate the same amount of additional private income, of which consumers and business will receive $6 billion and spend $4.8 billion, and so on. The total increase in GNP is $20 billion ($8 + $4.8 + . . .), or two times the original tax cut. The difference between the multipliers in the two illustrations reflects the differences in first round effects of the expenditure and tax changes: output is raised by the entire amount of the expenditure increase on this round, but only by 80 percent of the tax reduction.

If expenditures and taxes are increased simultaneously by the same amount, the effects of these two actions will not cancel one another because, dollar for dollar, expenditures have a more potent effect on the economy than tax changes. For example, given the assumptions in the previous illustrations, if a tax increase of $10 billion were enacted together with a $10 billion increase in government spending, the former would reduce GNP by $20 billion while the latter would stimulate a $25 billion increase, leaving a net increase of $5 billion. In other words, an increase in expenditures that is fully financed by an increase in taxes will on balance increase the GNP. (This theorem assumes that spending from an increase or decrease in private disposable income will be the same regardless of the source of the income change, and that investment and other economic behavior will not be influenced by the government's action. The multipliers used are illustrative only; estimates of the multipliers vary greatly.)

The effect of changes in government expenditures and taxes on the size of the government's deficit depends on the increase in GNP generated by the fiscal stimulus and on tax rates. In the previous examples, federal taxes were assumed to account for about 25 percent of an increment to GNP. Thus, the increase in GNP would raise tax receipts by $6.25 billion if expenditures were increased by $10 billion (.25 × $25), causing an increase in deficit (or reduction in surplus) of $3.75 billion. If taxes were reduced by $10 billion, the increase in GNP would raise tax receipts $5 billion (.25 × $20), causing a $5 billion increase in deficit. If expenditures and taxes were raised simultaneously by $10 billion, the increase in GNP would raise tax receipts by $1.25 billion (.25 × $5) and *reduce* the deficit (or increase the surplus) by that amount.

Monetary policy also plays an important role in stabilization policy. Suppose the federal government increases expenditures or reduces taxes. As GNP increases, individuals and business firms will need additional cash to conduct their business affairs. If the money supply fails to increase, the higher demand for cash will drive up interest rates. The higher interest rates will tend to reduce residential construction, business investment, and state-local construction, thus offsetting the effect of the initial increase in spending. Fiscal policy thus requires assistance from monetary policy to be fully effective, but the precise combination of monetary and fiscal measures necessary to obtain any desired response is not known.

Built-in Stabilizers

In addition to discretionary changes in taxes and expenditures (that is, deliberate government actions to vary taxes or the rate of expenditures), the fiscal system itself contributes to stabilization by generating automatic tax and expenditure adjustments that cushion the effect of changes in GNP. These *built-in stabilizers* moderate the fall in private income and spending when GNP declines and restrain private income and spending when GNP rises. They are automatic in the sense that they respond to changes in GNP without any action on the part of the government.

The two major groups of built-in fiscal stabilizers are: (1) taxes, in particular the federal individual income tax; and (2) transfers, such as unemployment compensation and other welfare payments.

The federal individual income tax is the leading tax stabilizer. When incomes fall, many individuals who were formerly taxable drop below the taxable level; others are pushed down into lower tax brackets. Conversely, when incomes rise, formerly nontaxed individuals become taxable and others are pushed into higher tax brackets. In recent years, federal individual income tax receipts have automatically increased or decreased about 10 percent more than the percentage increase or decrease in GNP. Since consumption depends on disposable personal income, these automatic changes in the individual income tax tend to keep consumption more stable than it would otherwise be.

Variations in the corporation income tax are proportionately larger than variations in the individual income tax, because profits fluctuate widely over a business cycle. These variations in tax liabilities affect expenditures through their influence on corporate dividends and investment. The effect on dividends is relatively small because corporate managers try to keep dividends in line with long-term earnings. Fluctuations in investment are probably reduced to some extent, but the precise effect is unknown.

On the expenditure side, the major built-in stabilizer is unemployment compensation. Insured workers who become unemployed are entitled to benefits up to twenty-six weeks in most states. These benefits help to maintain consumption as output and employment fall, even though the recipients are not participating in production. As incomes go up and employment increases, unemployment compensation declines. Other transfer payments (old-age insurance, public assistance, and the like) also tend to vary inversely with changes in GNP.

It is possible to calculate the effect of built-in stabilizers on the federal surplus, as distinct from the discretionary actions of the government. On the basis of these calculations, it is clear that the built-in stabilizers have made a major contribution to the stability of the economy since the end of World War II. In each of the four postwar recessions they have automatically pushed the federal budget strongly toward deficit as economic activity declined, then reversed that deficit as soon as recovery began. They have accounted for changes in surplus ranging from 43 percent of the fall in GNP during the 1948-49 contraction to 400 percent during the 1960-61 contraction (when GNP declined by only $1.4 billion while the built-in stabilizers cut federal receipts by $5.6 billion). In recoveries, the automatic reductions in the deficits were between 25 percent and 33 percent of the rise in GNP (Table 2-1).

Expenditure vs. Tax Adjustments

Expenditure changes are not necessarily preferable to tax changes for stabilization purposes, even though they have somewhat larger multiplier effects. In the first place, government expenditures should be determined on the basis of long-run national need and not on the basis of short-run cyclical considerations. The controlling principle is that government outlays should not exceed the point where the benefit of an additional dollar of expenditures to the nation's citizens is the same in public and private use. It is hardly likely that this point would shift sharply in one direction or the

TABLE 2-1. Effects of Built-in Stabilizers on the Federal Surplus, Postwar Recessions and Recoveries[a]

Recession and Recovery	Effect on Surplus (Billions of dollars)		Ratio to Change in GNP	
	Peak to Trough[b]	Trough to Terminal Quarter of Recovery	Peak to Trough[b]	Trough to Terminal Quarter of Recovery[c]
1948–50	−3.7	6.1	0.43	0.30
1953–55	−6.6	10.4	0.93	0.31
1957–59	−8.7	17.4	0.75	0.33
1960–62	−5.6	13.4	4.00	0.25

Source: First three recessions and recoveries are from Wilfred Lewis, Jr., *Federal Fiscal Policy in the Postwar Recessions* (Brookings Institution, 1962), p. 30 (using revised GNP estimates as denominators). 1960–62 are supplementary estimates by Lewis prepared on a consistent basis.

[a] National income and product account basis. Figures are seasonally adjusted annual rates, adjusted to eliminate the effects of discretionary actions, such as changes in tax rates and temporary extensions of unemployment benefit duration.

[b] Peaks and troughs of GNP.

[c] Change, trough to terminal quarter for first three recoveries; for 1960–62, first six quarters of recovery only 1961-I to 1962-II).

other during such short periods as a business contraction. Second, considerations of economic efficiency argue against large short-run variations in expenditures. For example, it would be wasteful to slow down construction of a road or hydroelectric facility, once construction has begun, in the interest of reducing aggregate spending. Third, there may be a long time lag between a decision to undertake an expenditure and its effect on output and employment. When recessions are relatively brief—as they have been since the end of World War II—the impact of a decision to make an expenditure change often is not felt until recovery is under way. By contrast, the effect of a tax change on disposable income is immediate and continues as long as the legislation is in force.

Among the various taxes, the individual income tax is best suited for stabilization purposes. Under the withholding system for wages and salaries, changes in tax rates can be made effective in a matter of days and terminated quickly. For most workers, the effect of a tax change on take-home pay is indistinguishable from the effect of a change in his gross weekly wage. Corporation income tax changes are not likely to have significant effects on investment if they are known, or expected, to be of short duration. Consumption tax changes may have a perverse effect in the short run: the expectation of a reduction may delay spending and the expectation of an increase may accelerate spending. Nevertheless, once they become effective, consumption tax changes are at least as powerful as income tax changes in stimulating or restraining consumer demand.

Some economists believe that consumption depends on income that is expected to be received regularly, and is not much affected by temporary or transitory changes in income. On this hypothesis, temporary tax changes would have relatively little impact on consumption. However, this is a minority view. Most economists believe that a temporary income tax change would have a strong effect on consumption, although they agree that it would be less powerful than a permanent tax change.

Countercyclical tax changes are often assumed to be most effective if they are confined to the lower income classes. This view presupposes that poor people spend proportionately more out of any additional dollars they may receive than the rich. There is no evidence, however, to confirm or deny this assumption. For policy purposes, it is probably satisfactory to assume that this incremental consumption rate is fairly high throughout most of the income distribution. This would suggest that, if the distribution of the tax burden is considered equitable by the large majority of taxpayers, tax rates can be moved up and down uniformly for countercyclical purposes by a simple formula such as an equal percentage change for all taxpayers.

Tax rate changes are sometimes criticized on the ground that they are too small to exert a significant economic effect. With 50 million taxpayers, a $10 billion individual income tax cut is equivalent to an increase in take-home pay of only $4 a week, a negligible amount in comparison with the total GNP of more than $700 billion. The comparison is erroneous, however, because it compares weekly and annual income flows. A $10 billion tax cut is about 1.5 percent of the GNP, whether expressed on a weekly, monthly, or annual basis. Since tax changes have a multiplier effect, a tax cut of this magnitude would provide a substantial stimulus to the economy, since the deviation from full employment GNP which tax cuts would be intended to narrow is usually less than 5 percent.

Tax adjustments can be used to restrain as well as to stimulate demand, and are therefore important policy instruments for counteracting inflation. It may be impractical, if not impossible, to cut back government expenditures when inflation threatens. Over 60 percent of federal expenditures are for defense, foreign aid, education, and research and development, which should not be altered for short-run reasons. Much of the remainder of the federal budget provides assistance to low income persons who are particularly hard-pressed during an inflation. Moreover, the inflationary pressures may have been due to an increase in government spending for defense or war purposes. In these circumstances, tax increases must be used to withdraw excess purchasing power from the income stream.

The time required for the legislative process to be completed is the major obstacle to prompt use of tax changes for countercyclical purposes. Congressional consideration of major tax legislation may take as long as eighteen months. Proposals have been made to give the President authority to make temporary changes in individual income tax rates, or to speed up congressional procedures for action on presidential recommendations. However, Congress has not seriously considered such plans (see Chapter 3).

Policies To Promote Economic Growth

Fiscal policies are useful in promoting long-run economic growth as well as short-run stability. Growth may be disappointing for two reasons: either the resources of the economy are not employed up to their full potential, or the rate of growth of potential output at full employment is too low. The policies required under these two circumstances differ, although they are often confused.

Achieving Full Employment

An economy operating at less than full employment is one in which potential GNP is larger than actual spending by consumers, business, and government. The remedy for this deficiency is to increase private or public spending through fiscal and monetary stimulation.

On the fiscal side, the degree of stimulation is popularly regarded as a function of the *current* budget surplus or deficit (that is, the budget is interpreted to be restrictive or deflationary when it is running a surplus, and expansionary or inflationary when it is in deficit). However, actual surpluses or deficits are poor guides for

CHART 2-2. Effect of Level of Activity on Federal Surplus or Deficit

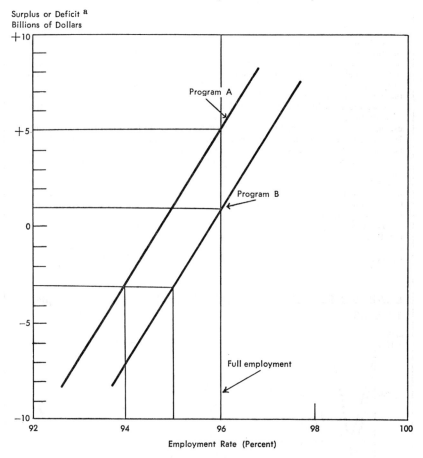

Surplus or Deficit [a]
Billions of Dollars

Program A

Program B

Full employment

Employment Rate (Percent)

Source: Adapted from *Economic Report of the President,* January 1962, page 79.
[a] National income accounts basis.

evaluating the economic effects of the budget because they reflect prevailing levels of income and employment as well as the government's fiscal policy. The policy can be understood only by separating the effect of automatic and discretionary changes in expenditure programs and tax rates.

Chart 2-2 illustrates how this separation is made. Each line in the chart shows the surplus or deficit that would be realized at var-

The Three Budgets

The official budget statement of the federal government is the *administrative budget*, which is an instrument of management and control of federal activities financed with federally owned funds. The *cash budget* includes cash flows to and from the public resulting from all federal fiscal activity, including the trust funds. This budget provides a comprehensive picture of the financial impact of federal programs, but it does not measure their contribution to the current income and output of the nation. For this purpose, economists make use of the statement of receipts and expenditures in the official national income accounts, often called the *national income accounts budget*.

Like the cash budget, the national income accounts budget includes the activities of trust funds and excludes purely intragovernmental transactions (for example, interest on federal bonds owned by federal agencies) which do not affect the general public. However, there are significant differences in timing and coverage. The national income accounts budget includes receipts and expenditures when they have their impact on private incomes, which is not necessarily when the federal government receives cash or pays it out. This adjustment involves putting receipts (except personal taxes) on an accrual basis and counting expenditures when goods are delivered rather than when payment is made. The adjustment for coverage excludes purely financial transactions because these represent an exchange of assets or claims and not a direct addition to income or production.

There are substantial differences in the amounts of surpluses or deficits among the three accounts, and even in their movements (Chart 2-3). From 1962 to 1965, the national income accounts budget showed the smallest deficit (or largest surplus), the administrative budget the largest deficit (or smallest surplus), and the cash budget was between the two.

CHART 2-3. Federal Deficits and Surpluses, Three Budget Concepts, 1948–65

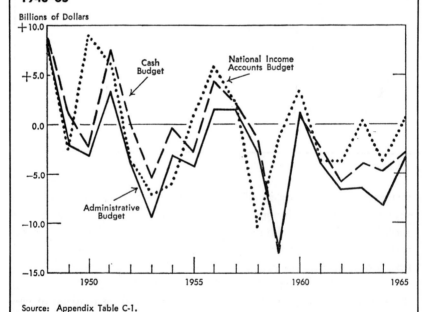

Source: Appendix Table C-1.

18

ious levels of employment under two different budget programs, A and B. For simplicity, it is assumed that the tax system is the same, but that expenditures are $4 billion higher under Program B (the surplus is, therefore, $4 billion lower or the deficit $4 billion higher). The lines slope upward, indicating that as employment and income increase the deficits become smaller or the surpluses larger. The effect of the built-in stabilizers is given by the slope of each line: the greater the slope, the larger the impact of the built-in stabilizers on the surplus or deficit. As drawn in Chart 2-2, both programs show the same built-in stability features, because the tax systems are identical. However, an actual deficit of $3 billion is realized when employment is at 94 percent of the labor force under Program A and 95 percent under Program B. Clearly, Program B is more expansionary than Program A.

The economic effects of the two programs may be compared by examining the surplus or deficit at any given level of employment. By convention, the comparison is made at full employment which is assumed to be at 96 percent of the labor force. Defined in this way, the "full employment surplus" is $5 billion under Program A and $1 billion under Program B. The difference of $4 billion reflects the assumed difference in expenditures. In practice, the differences will be due to differences in taxes as well as expenditures.

There are three types of budget statements in current use—the administrative budget, the cash budget, and the national income accounts budget. The full employment surplus is usually computed on a national income accounts basis, but it can be adjusted to the other definitions (see page 18).

The budget program that is appropriate at a given time depends upon the strength of private demand for consumption and investment goods. When private demand is high a large full employment surplus is called for; when private demand is weak, a small full employment surplus, or even a full employment deficit, is required. Efforts to achieve a larger surplus or a lower deficit than is consistent with full employment would depress employment and incomes. If the budget called for too small a full employment surplus, total demand would be too high and prices would rise.

Another characteristic of the full employment surplus is its tendency to increase with the passage of time and the growth of the economy. With the growth of the labor force, the stock of capital, and productivity, potential federal receipts also rise. At current tax rates and assuming full employment, federal receipts increase about $7 billion per year. Thus the full employment surplus will creep up by about $7 billion each year, or about 1 percent of GNP in 1966, unless the government takes steps to prevent it. In other words, Program B in Chart 2-2 could become as restrictive as Program A in less than one year.

This upward creep in the full employment surplus is called the *fiscal drag*. It acts as an automatic retarding influence on the economy. If private demand increases at a sufficiently fast rate to offset it, fiscal drag would help prevent prices from rising. But increases in private demand are rarely timed to do this. Under ordinary circumstances, therefore, to prevent a drop in total demand, the federal government must increase expenditures and/or reduce taxes to provide a fiscal stimulus averaging $7 billion per year.

According to current estimates, the federal budget would have been in surplus in every quarter between mid-1955 and the end of 1965, had full employment been maintained (Chart 2-4). However, the actual budget showed a deficit during most of the period, reflecting the disappointing performance of the economy. It was only after the full employment surplus was sharply reduced in 1964 to stimulate the economy that employment began to move toward 96 percent of the labor force, which is regarded by most people as the minimum acceptable level. This record illustrates the principle that planning for a budget surplus, without regard to the strength of private demand, may produce unsatisfactory rates of employment and output, and create budget deficits besides.

Although the full employment surplus is a useful measure, it must be used with considerable care. The restrictiveness of a given amount of surplus, say $10 billion, is much greater in a $500 billion economy than in a $750 billion economy. Furthermore, differences in the level and composition of expenditures and taxes have an important bearing on the significance of the full employment surplus. For example, an increase in the full employment surplus resulting from a reduction in government expenditures on goods and services would be more restrictive than a tax increase of the same amount. For these reasons, the meaning of changes in the full employment surplus is likely to be unambiguous only during relatively short periods when changes in expenditures and taxes

CHART 2-4. Full Employment Surplus, National Income Accounts Basis, 1955–65

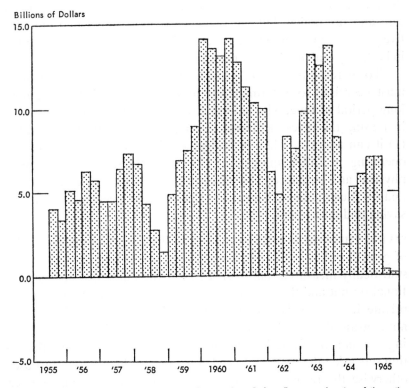

Billions of Dollars

Source: Unpublished data from Nancy H. Teeters, Bureau of the Budget. For an explanation of the estimates, see her "Estimates of the Full-Employment Surplus, 1955-1964," *Review of Economics and Statistics,* Vol. 47, No. 3 (August 1965), pp. 309-21.

are likely to be relatively small. Analysis of the fiscal impact of the budget over long periods requires more detailed information than the full employment surplus provides by itself.

Raising the Growth Rate

Once excess unemployment has been eliminated, the rate of economic growth will depend on the ability of the economy to raise potential output at a faster rate. The factors affecting potential output are the size of the labor force, the average workweek and workyear, and productivity (output per man-hour). Productivity depends on the size of the capital stock, the quality of human resources, the attitudes and skills of management, the efficiency of resource use, and the amount of technological progress. Most of these factors are influenced to some extent by government expenditure and tax policy, but the influence is most direct and quantitatively most important with respect to the rate of national investment in both physical and human resources.

To increase the rate of growth, the rate of national investment must be raised to a permanently higher level and held there for a long period of time. The federal government can contribute toward increasing the investment rate through fiscal policy in three ways: (1) it can adopt a policy of budget surpluses when the economy is operating at full employment; (2) it can increase investment in physical and human capital directly through its own expenditures; and (3) it can adopt tax measures that provide incentives for private saving and investment.

SAVING THROUGH BUDGET SURPLUSES. The key to an understanding of growth policy is the relation between saving and investment. As statistically measured, national saving is the difference between national output and the amounts spent by consumers and government; private investment is also that part of the national product that is not consumed or used for government purposes. Thus, national saving is equal to private investment. In effect, through saving the nation sets aside the resources needed for private investment purposes; otherwise the resources would be used to produce goods and services for consumers and government.

When the federal government runs a budget surplus, it adds its own saving to that generated by the private economy. When the budget is in deficit, national saving is reduced. Since more saving and investment are needed to raise the growth rate, the federal government stimulates a higher growth rate by running budget surpluses at full employment. Moreover, the larger the surplus at full employment the larger the potential contribution to growth.

This growth strategy can be implemented only if there is sufficient investment demand in the private economy to use up the saving generated in the federal budget. If private demand for investment is too low, the federal surplus generates unemployment rather than more growth. In other words, the full employment surplus must be just large enough to offset the deficiency in private saving. If there is more than enough private saving for the existing investment demand, the budget should be in deficit even at full employment.

An important ingredient of any strategy to increase the rate of private investment is monetary policy. Easy money provides ready access to credit and lowers the cost of borrowing for investment purposes by reducing interest rates. Tight money restrains the growth of credit and raises interest rates. Therefore, the best policy to promote private investment would combine a budget surplus with easy money. In implementing such a policy, of course, it is important to avoid taxes that impair investment incentives.

In practice, the extent of monetary ease that a nation can afford is limited by balance of payments considerations. If interest rates are driven down too far, private capital will leave the country to take advantage of higher interest rates abroad. In extreme cases, the outflow of funds may require devaluation of the nation's currency to restore international equilibrium. When interest rates must be kept up for balance of payments reasons, fiscal policy must be easier (that is, the surplus must be lower or the deficit higher) to prevent a drop in demand and employment. The reduction in the full employment surplus in 1962 and 1964 (see Chart 2-4) occurred when the domestic economy was operating at less than full potential and there was a serious balance of payments problem.

INCREASING INVESTMENT DIRECTLY. It is not generally realized that investment is undertaken by government as well as by private firms. Outlays for education, training of manpower, health, research and development, roads, and other public facilities are essential elements of national investment. Such outlays are not substitutable for private investment, or vice versa. Education and research expenditures are perhaps the most important components of national investment, yet most of these expenditures are paid for by government (primarily state and local in the case of education, and primarily federal in the case of research). There is no basis for prejudging how total investment should be distributed between the public and private sectors, and it is important to avoid doctrinaire positions about one or the other. Both types of investment contribute to the nation's economic growth.

Public investment is financed directly by government through the tax system. If private demand is strong, the appropriate policy for growth would be to raise enough taxes to pay for needed government investment as well as to leave an additional margin of saving for private investment.

INCREASING SAVING AND INVESTMENT INCENTIVES. Given the aggregate level of taxation, the tax structure can be an important independent factor in determining the growth potential of the economy. The tax structure may encourage consumption or saving, help to raise or lower private investment in general or in particular industries, stimulate or restrain the outflow of investment funds to foreign countries, and subsidize or discourage particular expenditures by individuals and business firms. Most tax systems, including that of the United States, have numerous features specifically intended to promote saving and investment. For example, the federal income taxes provide liberal depreciation allowances, a 7 percent investment credit, full offsets for business losses against other income over a period of nine years, averaging of individual income for tax purposes over a period of five years, and preferential treatment of capital gains. These and other provisions will be discussed in later chapters.

Automatic Budget Rules

It is now widely understood that an annually balanced budget policy would accentuate business fluctuations. But many people continue to believe that it is unwise to rely exclusively on discretion to guide budget decisions. Discretionary policy depends heavily on forecasting techniques that are still subject to error. There is also a fear that removal of a budgetary restraint will lead to excessive federal expenditures. To avoid these pitfalls, attempts have been made to formulate rules that would reduce the element of judgment in budget decisions without impairing economic growth and stability.

The best known plan is the *stabilizing budget policy* of the Committee for Economic Development (CED), a nonprofit organization of influential businessmen and educators. Under this policy, tax rates would be set to balance the budget or yield a small surplus at full employment. Tax rates would remain unchanged until there was a major change in the level of expenditures. Reliance would be placed on the built-in stabilizers to moderate fluctuations in private demand.

The CED plan would operate successfully only if full employment could be achieved with a balance or small surplus in the federal budget. Moreover, the CED plan does not provide a systematic method of removing the fiscal drag that accompanies economic growth. With federal receipts currently rising by about 1 percent of the GNP each year, it would be hazardous to keep tax rates and expenditure levels unchanged for long periods.

A plan that is intended to help solve the fiscal drag problem would provide for individual income tax rates to be reduced each year by a given amount, say 1 percentage point (which is equivalent to about $2.5 billion per year at 1966 income levels), with the remainder of the fiscal drag of approximately $7 billion to be used for increasing federal expenditures. Presumably, the plan would begin with a surplus or deficit consistent with full employment. The difficulty with this approach is that it would freeze the allocation of increased federal receipts between tax reduction and increased expenditures ($2.5 billion for the former, $4.5 billion for the latter). Periods during which it would have been desirable to cut tax rates by a fixed amount or a fixed percentage each year have been rare in the nation's history.

A third version of an automatic budget policy is to build into the budget a formula that would trigger upward or downward changes in tax rates when certain predetermined economic indices are reached. For example, legislation might provide for a 1 percentage point reduction in income tax rates for every increase of 0.5 percent in unemployment above 4.5 percent of the labor force, or an increase of 1 percentage point for every rise of 2 points in a general price index, such as the consumer or wholesale price index. While this type of formula flexibility would add to the effectiveness of the built-in stabilizers if the changes were correctly timed, no one index or set of indices can be used with confidence to signal an economic movement justifying tax action.

It is evident that budget policy cannot be conducted on the basis of a rigid set of rules. Nevertheless, the search for budget rules has greatly improved public understanding of the elements of fiscal policy. Great emphasis is placed on the automatic stabilizers for their cushioning effect on private disposable incomes and spending. Recognition of the capacity of the federal tax system to generate rising revenues has alerted policy makers to the need for positive action to remove the retarding effect of fiscal drag. However, there is less widespread understanding that the major objective of budget policy should be to balance the economy at full employment without inflation, regardless of whether this will yield a surplus or deficit in any given year or period of years.

The "Debt Burden"

Effective use of fiscal policy to promote the full employment and growth objectives is hindered by public concern over the growth of the national debt. There is widespread fear that a long succession of annual deficits and a resulting rise in the national debt will impose dangerously heavy burdens on later generations. There is also concern about the economic burden of interest payments.

Growth of the national debt can impose a burden on future generations if it interferes with private capital formation. In this respect, there is a difference between debt created under conditions of excessive unemployment and debt created under conditions of full employment. In the first case, the debt cannot be a burden on future generations; in the second case, it may or may not be a burden.

In a situation of substantial unemployment, increased public debt finances deficits which are used by government to purchase goods and services directly or to provide transfer payments. Since there are unemployed resources, the goods and services acquired by government or by the recipients of transfer payments do not replace goods and services that might otherwise have been produced. If accompanied by the appropriate monetary policy, the new debt can be absorbed without impeding the flow of funds into private capital formation. In fact, private investment will rise as a result of the stimulus that arises from a higher level of economic activity. The community is better off when the expenditures are made; and later generations will also benefit to the extent that the expenditures increase private and public investment in human or physical capital yielding future services.

The situation is more complicated if the economy is at full employment. In this setting an increase in the government deficit cannot increase total output. This means either that prices will rise or

CHART 2-5. Relation Between Net Federal Debt and Interest on Net Debt to the Gross National Product, 1942–65[a]

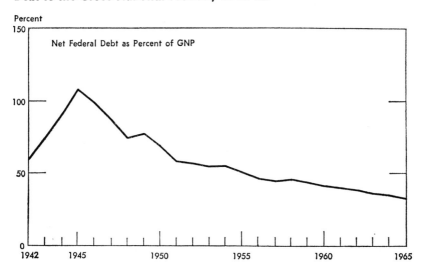

Net Federal Debt as Percent of GNP

Net Interest on Federal Debt as Percent of GNP

Sources: Net federal debt: *Economic Report of the President,* January 1966, p. 274. Net interest, 1946-65: Interest payments to the public shown in *Budget of the United States Government,* various years, less Federal Reserve bank earnings on U. S. Government securities by fiscal years (supplied by Board of Governors of the Federal Reserve System); 1942-45: Estimated from data in *Federal Reserve Bulletins.* Gross national product: *Survey of Current Business* (August 1965; February 1966).

a Net federal debt is debt held outside U. S. Government investment accounts and Federal Reserve banks. Interest on net federal debt is total interest payments to the public less interest earned by Federal Reserve banks.

that offsetting monetary restraint will be required. If inflation is to be avoided, the necessary credit restraint will reduce private investment. Later generations will be worse off to the extent that the rate of growth of productive capacity is reduced.

Since the federal government usually runs surpluses when the economy is at full employment (see Chart 2-4), there is little likelihood that the federal debt added in peacetime will be burdensome in an economic sense. Deficits incurred to restore or maintain full employment raise output and employment, and actually increase the resources available to current and later generations.

The existence of the national debt does require interest to be paid to holders of the debt, and tax rates are therefore higher than they would be without the debt. The transfer of interest from general taxpayers to bondholders is a burden on the economy only if the taxes levied to pay interest on the debt reduce economic efficiency. This burden, if any, is small in the United States economy because net interest payments represent a relatively small proportion of federal cash expenditures (7 percent in 1965). Moreover, the ratio of net federal debt to the gross national product has been declining since the end of World War II (Chart 2-5), and interest payments on the net debt, which fell markedly in the early postwar years, have amounted to only slightly more than 1 percent of GNP since the early 1950's. The growth of the economy over this period has kept the burden of the debt in relation to total production from rising, even though the interest rates at which debt can be issued have shown a rising trend over the entire period.

Summary

The strength of the economy depends heavily on the fiscal policies pursued by the federal government. These policies involve the use of tax and expenditure changes to promote full employment, economic growth, and price stability. The fiscal system itself generates automatic tax and expenditure changes which help dampen fluctuations in private disposable income and spending. Although they are extremely important, these built-in stabilizers can only moderate downward and upward movements in business activity. To halt and reverse such movements, the built-in stabilizers must be

supplemented by discretionary changes in government expenditures
or tax rates.

There is no basis for making *a priori* judgments regarding the
relative merits of tax and expenditure changes. At any given level
of government expenditures, the level of economic activity depends
on the *ratio* of taxes to expenditures. When private demand is low
and the economy is operating below capacity, taxes are too high
relative to expenditures. In these circumstances, the ratio should be
reduced—by cutting taxes, by raising expenditures, or by doing
both. Conversely, when demand is too high, taxes should be raised or
expenditures reduced, or both. The appropriate action at any particular time depends upon the relative need for private and public
expenditures.

The first step toward a policy to promote economic growth is to
maintain full employment of resources. It is impossible to predict
whether this will require surpluses or deficits in the federal budget.
If private demand is weak, full employment may not be possible
without federal deficits. If private demand is strong, surpluses will
be needed to prevent prices from rising. On the basis of the past record, there is little reason to expect that the U.S. economy will need
the stimulus of sustained deficits to remain at full employment.

After full employment has been reached, the growth rate can be
increased only by raising the rate of growth of potential output.
This will require more saving and more investment. The best strategy for increasing saving and investment is to combine a large budget surplus with an easy money policy. The surplus increases national saving, while easy money increases private investment by
making credit more readily available and by reducing interest rates.
Saving and investment incentives may also be improved through
higher depreciation allowances, investment credits, and other structural tax provisions.

CHAPTER 3

The Tax Legislative Process

THE PROCESS OF DECISION MAKING in tax policy is one of the most interesting, puzzling, and controversial features of the federal legislative process. It can be speedy and effective, or slow and ponderous. A small army of people participates, but only a few key figures are familiar to the public. The process has been criticized by many, but attempts to alter it even in minor respects have been unavailing.

Basic to an understanding of how the process works is the stipulation in Article I, Section 8, of the Constitution that "Congress shall have power to lay and collect taxes." Congress has always guarded its taxing power jealously. Presidents can recommend changes, but only Congress has the power to translate these recommendations into law. Practically every major presidential tax proposal is thoroughly revised by Congress, and not a few are rejected outright.

A tax law is always a compromise among the views of powerful individuals and groups. The President, the Secretary of the Treasury, and members of the two congressional tax committees—the House Committee on Ways and Means and the Senate Committee on Finance—are subject to great pressures from the numerous political, economic, and social groups affected by the bill or attempting to have it changed to their advantage. Substantial delays in enactment of tax legislation occur when the participants have difficulty finding a formula to reconcile major opposing interests.

The tax legislative machinery is backed by competent staffs of experts in both the legislative and executive branches of the federal government. Taxation is one of three major policy areas deemed important enough to warrant a joint congressional committee (atomic energy and economic policy are the other two). Established in 1926, the Joint Committee on Internal Revenue Taxation consists of five ranking members each from the Ways and Means Committee and from the Finance Committee, with three from the majority party and two from the minority party. Its official functions are to review large refunds proposed by the Commissioner of Internal Revenue and to make studies for the two tax committees. The Joint Committee itself does not participate in the legislative process. In practice, however, its major function is to provide a technical staff of about fifteen lawyers and economists to prepare tax legislation for the committees. Additional help is provided by the committees themselves and by the legislative counsels of the House and Senate, who do the actual drafting. Treasury experts are also available for assistance during the legislative process. Through long and intimate association, the committees have learned to rely on the various staffs for background information needed to help formulate a consensus and to assist in translating committee decisions into legislative language.

The present tax structure is an outgrowth of legislation dating back to the beginning of the republic. The laws were first assembled and codified in the *Internal Revenue Code of 1939*, which was completely revised and superseded by the *Internal Revenue Code of 1954*. Changes in the tax laws have since been enacted as amendments to the 1954 Code.

The Code is a technical and complex legal document. Many of its sections reflect years of study and analysis by government and nongovernment tax experts. Few people have mastered its technicalities and nuances. Nevertheless, it is the vehicle through which the federal government now collects nearly $150 billion of internal revenues annually. It is also the basis upon which each year 100 million tax returns are filed, 40 million refunds are paid, 2 million deficiency notices are served to taxpayers, and almost 1,000 people are convicted of tax crimes.

Between 1948 and 1965, Congress enacted ten major tax bills (involving revenues of $1 billion or more) and dozens of lesser bills. Each bill required months of preparation before the President made his recommendation, and from one to eighteen months before it was passed by the Congress. The two tax committees listened to hundreds of witnesses presenting thousands of pages of testimony. The final bills ranged in size from a few pages to 984 pages in 1954, when the Code was recodified. Five of the major bills increased taxes on balance, and the other five reduced them; the amounts involved ranged from a net increase of $5.7 billion in 1951 to a net reduction of $11.4 billion in 1964 (Table 3-1).

TABLE 3-1. Legislative History of Major Federal Tax Bills Enacted, and Revenue Gain or Loss, 1948–65

Title of Act	Date of President's Message	Date of House Passage	Date of Senate Passage	Date of Enactment	Time Between Initiation and Enactment (Months)	Full-Year Revenue Gain (+) or Loss (−) (Billions of dollars)
Revenue Act of 1948	a	2/2/48	3/22/48	4/2/48[b]	3[c]	−5.0
Revenue Act of 1950	1/23/50	6/29/50	9/1/50	9/23/50	8	+4.6
Excess Profits Act of 1950	d	12/5/50	12/20/50	1/3/51	3	+3.3
Revenue Act of 1951	2/2/51	6/22/51	9/28/51	10/20/51	8	+5.7
Internal Revenue Code of 1954	1/21/54[e]	3/18/54	7/2/54	8/16/54	7	+1.4
Excise Tax Reduction Act of 1954	a	3/10/54	3/25/54	3/31/54	2[c]	−1.0
Federal Aid Highway Act of 1956	2/22/55	4/27/56	5/29/56	6/29/56	16	+2.5
Revenue Act of 1962	4/20/61[f]	3/29/62	9/6/62	10/16/62	18	−0.2[g]
Revenue Act of 1964	1/24/63	9/25/63	2/10/64	2/26/64	13	−11.4
Excise Tax Reduction Act of 1965	5/17/65[f]	6/2/65	6/15/65	6/21/65	1	−4.7

Sources: *Congressional Record, Congressional Quarterly, Annual Reports of the Secretary of the Treasury.*
a Not recommended by the President.
b Passed by Congress over President's veto.
c Time elapsed from date of first consideration by House Ways and Means Committee.
d Revenue Act of 1950 directed tax committees to report excess profits tax to both houses retroactive to July 1 or October 1, 1950. No special message by President.
e Recommended by President in his Budget Message.
f Recommended initially in the Budget Message transmitted in January of the year indicated.
g Net after offsetting revenue increases of about $800 million.

The tax system cannot be understood without an appreciation of the personalities, pressures, forces, and conflicts involved in making the many difficult decisions that shape a tax bill. This chapter describes the manner in which Congress considers and enacts tax legislation, and also describes some of the key people in the process. It will be concerned only with tax legislation; tax administration and enforcement, which are extremely important in the overall tax process from the standpoint of the individual taxpayer, fall outside the scope of this volume.

Executive Preparation of a Tax Bill

The Treasury Department has primary responsibility for the vast amount of work that goes into preparation of the President's tax recommendations. The work is supervised by an assistant secretary for tax policy (or occasionally by an undersecretary). He has at his disposal two staffs: an Office of Tax Analysis consisting of about thirty-five economists and statisticians who provide the economic analysis of tax problems, revenue estimates of the effects of tax changes, and revenue projections for the budget; and an Office of the Tax Legislative Counsel consisting of about twenty tax attorneys and an adviser on accounting, who are responsible for legal and accounting analyses of tax problems, drafting of tax legislation, and review and approval of tax regulations. The assistant secretary calls on the technical, legal, and statistical facilities of the Internal Revenue Service for assistance as needed. He may also seek advice or assistance from consultants in academic, business, and professional fields, or in other government agencies.

It is difficult to pinpoint how and when the decision is made to study a particular tax or set of taxes. The impetus often comes from outside groups and experts after considerable public discussion, agitation, and pressure. Occasionally, the congressional committees request assurances that certain matters will be taken up in the next tax bill. Or the President, after formal or informal consultation with his advisers, may signal a new departure in tax policy in a speech or news conference. For example, the first official word that President Kennedy was considering a large tax reduction came in a news conference on June 7, 1962.

Studies of possible tax legislation are constantly in progress at the Treasury. Intensive work on a particular measure may begin after a decision by the President on advice from responsible officials in his administration. The Council of Economic Advisers and the Bureau of the Budget are equal partners in decisions on fiscal policy, and participate in decisions on major features of the tax bill. Decisions on technical tax questions in proposed legislation are usually made within the Treasury (subject, of course, to the approval of the President).

Materials prepared within the Treasury on the various aspects of the tax program include economic, legal, and accounting memoranda discussing each problem from almost every angle. The analysis reviews the history of the problem, evaluates its impact on particular groups and industries and on the economy as a whole, and presents the equity, economic, revenue, and administrative arguments for and against alternative solutions. Lawyers, accountants, economists, and statisticians participate in this evaluation. Task forces, committees, or informal working groups consisting of representatives of the Treasury and other federal agencies may be organized to consider alternative solutions. Most of the work is done within the executive branch, but the staff of the Joint Committee on Internal Revenue Taxation and outside experts may be consulted. Discussions are also held by senior staff members of the Treasury with industry and labor representatives, officials of business corporations, professional groups, the academic community, and other knowledgeable individuals.

Work on a major tax bill begins months before the administration's recommendations are transmitted to the Congress; in some cases, the lead time may be as much as a year or longer. The information amassed during these months of research and analysis is funneled through the assistant secretary. He may initiate new studies, suggest other approaches, and ask for still more information. He will also consult the various experts individually or in groups to narrow the range of alternatives. The Secretary of the Treasury keeps in touch with the work at all stages and makes the final decision on the program that is submitted to the President, often after consulting other government officials and members of the White House staff.

In a typical year, the main features of the tax bill are completed by mid-December. At this time, the President reviews the proposal and approves or modifies it. Final revenue figures are estimated by the Treasury on the basis of an economic projection prepared by the Council of Economic Advisers in consultation with other federal agencies. Drafts of sections to be included in the budget message and the economic report are prepared, and a start is made on the materials to be submitted for congressional consideration.

The President will sometimes mention the broad outlines of his tax program in the State of the Union message. Further elaboration is given in the budget message which must be transmitted fifteen days after Congress convenes, and the broad economic justification is presented in the economic report which is due on or before January 20. When the program covers a broad field or is particularly complicated, or when the President wishes to emphasize the importance of his recommendations, he will transmit a special tax message to Congress, usually at the end of January or in February, but sometimes as late as early spring.

Disclosure of a major tax program signals the beginning of public debate. Representatives of business, farm, labor, and other groups begin to make pronouncements about the wisdom of the program. National organizations like the Committee for Economic Development, the U.S. Chamber of Commerce, the National Association of Manufacturers, the AFL-CIO, the major international labor unions, trade associations, and citizens committees scrutinize the program carefully from the standpoint of their own interests and what they regard as the public interest. Newspapers, periodicals, radio, and television discuss major aspects of the program.

By the time the House Ways and Means Committee opens public hearings on the bill (usually in February or March), the lines of support and opposition are drawn. At this point Congress takes over.

The Bill in Congress

Article I, Section 7, of the Constitution states that "All bills for raising revenue shall originate in the House of Representatives." Accordingly, a tax bill begins its legislative history in the House and is transmitted to the Senate after the House has completed action. Otherwise, the Senate is an equal partner in the tax legislative process and frequently makes extensive and fundamental changes in the House version.

The Ways and Means Committee

The tax legislative process begins in the Committee on Ways and Means of the House of Representatives. It consists of twenty-five members, most of them relatively senior, apportioned between majority and minority parties in approximate proportion to their representation in the House. The committee has responsibility for revenue, debt, customs, trade, and social security legislation. It also selects the membership of other committees—a role which makes it the most powerful committee in the House.

The committee begins its study by scheduling public hearings for persons who request an opportunity to testify. The Ways and Means Committee room, which seats more than a thousand people, is usually filled to capacity for the first witness, the Secretary of the Treasury. His testimony typically begins with a long, carefully prepared document which gives the full rationale for the administration's position. For example, Secretary Dillon's presentation on the 1964 bill in January 1963 lasted two days and totalled 527 closely printed pages including a main oral statement of 29 pages and 498 pages of supplementary tables, legal and technical explanations, and memoranda of analysis.

The Secretary ordinarily reads his statement without interruption. The chairman opens the interrogation and then turns the questioning over to each member of the committee, alternating between majority and minority party members in order of seniority. Committee members may take this opportunity to make a public record for the positions they expect to take. Sympathetic members ask questions to buttress the administration's position or to help prepare the way for suitable compromises on difficult issues; those who are opposed attempt to trap the Secretary into making untenable, erroneous, and inconsistent statements so as to discredit the tax proposals. Key committee members have a detailed knowledge of the tax law and the intricacies of the new tax bill. The Secretary, in turn, is usually well briefed and handles most of the questions himself, turning to an associate for assistance only in connection with technical matters. Occasionally, he will handle a question by promising a written reply to be included in the printed record.

After the Secretary's testimony, the committee may hear witnesses from other executive agencies. For example, in 1963, the Secretaries of Commerce and Labor and the Director of the Bureau of the Budget appeared before the committee. Testimony is then heard from bankers, businessmen, lawyers, economists, and others representing the interests of private groups (and sometimes of individual clients). Aside from the administration's witnesses, the broader "public interest" is seldom represented. On rare occasions unaffiliated individuals and representatives of public-spirited organizations take the trouble to testify. In a few instances, the committee has invited professional economists to appear as experts, but this is not general practice.

Meanwhile, the committee members are besieged in private by large numbers of people seeking changes in the bill. Through these contacts, the committee evaluates the strength of the forces aligned for and against the bill.

The hearings continue until all interested parties have testified. The length of the hearings depends on the importance of the bill, the controversy it has aroused, and the positions of the committee chairman and ranking members. If there is considerable opposition, the hearings may continue for months. For example, no hearings were held by the Ways and Means Committee on the Excise Tax Reduction Act of 1965, while the hearings on the controversial Revenue Act of 1964 lasted almost eight weeks.

After concluding the hearings, the committee goes into executive session. These sessions are conducted in an informal, seminar-type atmosphere. Members of the committee discuss the bill freely, calling on the staffs of the Joint Internal Revenue Committee and the Treasury for information, advice, and assistance as needed. Each proposal is carefully explained by Treasury officials and staff members, and the relevant information and opinions assembled during the hearings are summarized. Votes are taken only after members are satisfied that they have all the information needed to make up their minds.

Several people play a major role in the process of negotiation and compromise that takes place in executive sessions. The most important figure is the chairman of the Ways and Means Committee, who is not only presiding officer but also chief moderator. The ranking spokesman for the minority also exercises substantial influence, particularly if he can persuade a few members of the majority to side with him. The chief of staff of the Joint Internal Revenue Committee supervises the large secretariat which assists the Ways and Means Committee in its deliberations. He attends all sessions, joins in negotiations on the bill, and helps shape the compromise proposed by the chairman and other committee members. The assistant secretary of the Treasury acts as chief negotiator for the administration (under instructions from the President and the Secretary of the Treasury). The Secretary often participates in the executive sessions when key issues are discussed.

As tentative decisions are reached, they are translated into legislative language. Preparation of the legislative draft is the responsibility of the legislative counsel of the House of Representatives, but the staffs of the Joint Internal Revenue Committee and the Treasury are regularly called on for assistance. The drafting process is usually slow and time-consuming in the attempt to make the intent of the committee explicit and the provisions of the bill as unambiguous as possible. Considering the pressure under which the draftsmen operate and the complexity of the material, remarkably few errors are made in the process which is generally completed for quick final action by the committee shortly after the last tentative decision has been made.

At this time, work begins on the committee's report under the direction of the chief of staff of the Joint Internal Revenue Committee. The report, frequently several hundred pages in length, contains a detailed statement of the committee's rationale for recommending the bill, estimates of its effect on revenues, and a section-by-section analysis of its provisions. It also contains the minority views of committee members who disapprove the bill. As the only written record of the reasons for the committee's actions, the report serves to inform members of the House and provides a basis for later interpretation of the legislation by the Internal Revenue Service and the courts.

When the report is completed, the Ways and Means Committee approves it and instructs the chairman to send the bill to the House.

House Approval

According to the rules of the House of Representatives, revenue legislation is "privileged" business which obtains priority consideration on the floor. In practice, however, the approval of the Rules Committee is always sought before the bill is placed on the calendar for floor action. This is done so that the tax bill can be debated under a "closed rule," which requires the House to accept or reject the entire bill except for amendments approved by the Ways and Means Committee.

Because it is conducted under a closed rule, debate on the tax bill in the House is brief, usually lasting only two or three days. The Ways and Means Committee chairman acts as floor manager and chief proponent. Other members of the majority are assigned to defend particular aspects of the bill. The opposition, usually led by the ranking minority member of the committee, attacks the bill with vigor and often predicts great harm to the nation if it is enacted.

At the end of the debate, the opposition presents a motion to recommit the bill to the Ways and Means Committee with instructions to report it back with one or more specified amendments. This motion, which provides the test vote on the most controversial aspects of the bill, enables the opposition to obtain a vote on a modified version without having to reject the bill altogether. Then there is a final vote on the bill itself. Only on rare occasions has a major tax bill reported by the Ways and Means Committee been rejected by the House.

The Senate Finance Committee

After House passage, the bill is sent to the Senate, where it is immediately referred to the Committee on Finance. This committee of seventeen senior and influential senators has jurisdiction over tax, trade, and social security legislation, veterans' affairs, and other financial matters. Its organization and operations are similar to those of the Ways and Means Committee.

The Finance Committee begins by holding public hearings and the Secretary of the Treasury is again the first witness. His appearance here is no less an ordeal than his appearance before the Ways and Means Committee. He may largely repeat his arguments, although focussing his testimony on the House version of the bill. He may ask the committee to modify or reject certain provisions which are unacceptable to the administration; or he may accept the House modifications with only a slight demurrer. The Secretary is followed by much the same parade of witnesses that appeared before the Ways and Means Committee, in many instances repeating their earlier statements.

In executive session, most of the cast of characters that assisted on the House side now appear on the Senate side. The Finance Committee usually starts with the first section of the bill and considers amendments proposed by the members in order. On rare occasions the committee approves a substantially unamended version of the bill, but typically the bill is changed in significant respects before it is reported to the Senate. For example, the Senate Finance Committee report on the 1964 tax bill listed twenty-five major amendments to the House bill and estimated that the tax reduction would be $600 million higher ($11.7 billion instead of $11.1 billion).

When the Finance Committee has agreed on a bill, the staff prepares the committee report, which covers the same ground as the Ways and Means Committee report (often in identical language) and explains the reasons for the Finance Committee amendments.

The Senate Debate

Unlike the House, there is no limit on debate or amendments in the Senate. Many amendments are offered on the floor. Some of them are intended to change the entire character of the bill, and some are completely unrelated. Administration officers are usually very active at this stage. The President's aides and Senate leaders of his party work together to defeat amendments that are unacceptable to the administration or to restore provisions deleted by the Finance Committee.

Senate discussion of a tax bill is longer and more colorful than in the House. Individual senators take the occasion not only to make a record but also to attempt to persuade their colleagues. The debate usually concerns features of the bill that directly affect the pocketbooks of particular groups and individuals, and is often highly technical. The debates on some of the postwar tax bills (for example, on the 1951, 1962, and 1964 Acts) rank among the most informed discussions held on the Senate floor.

Most of the amendments proposed on the floor are opposed by the administration or the Finance Committee and are rejected; but the Senate has been known to act against the wishes of both the administration and the committee majority. On the other hand, the Senate floor is the only place in the entire legislative process where the administration may successfully exercise pressure against the wishes of the powerful committee chairman and ranking committee members. Such pressure, of course, is used sparingly and only when needed on major issues.

After the bill has been debated and amended to the satisfaction of the Senate, it is brought to a vote. If it fails to pass, the legislation is abandoned. If the Senate passes the House bill without amendments, it is sent directly to the President. If the Senate amends the bill—and this is the rule rather than the exception— further congressional action is necessary. The House generally adopts a motion to disagree with the Senate amendments, thus calling for appointment of a conference committee to adjust the differences between the two versions.

The Bill in Conference

The Committee of the Conference is appointed by the Speaker of the House and the President of the Senate. Both usually appoint three from the majority and two from the minority. On occasion, there is a difference in the number of conferees from the two chambers, but this has no bearing on the final decision reached by the committee, since each chamber votes as a unit with a majority controlling each group. The members of the committee are normally the senior members of the two tax committees, unless they elect not to serve.

Conferences may last from a day or two to a week or more, depending on the number of amendments, differences between the versions, and the complexity of the bill under consideration. Joint Committee and Treasury staff members are often called upon to explain the issues, evaluate the feasibility of suggested compromises, and provide revenue estimates. The bill remains in conference until all differences between the House and Senate versions have been reconciled. High officials of the administration, including the Secretary of the Treasury and the President, follow the deliberations of the committee carefully and may intervene (directly or through subordinates) with individual conferees to obtain support for the administration's position.

The conference report merely lists the amendments accepted by each house and is highly technical. Floor statements explaining how the two bills were reconciled provide the essential information necessary for interpreting the legislation.

After approval of the conference report by both houses, the bill is sent to the White House.

Presidential Action

As in the case of all legislation, the President has ten days to consider the bill. During this period, the various government departments analyze the bill and submit their views in the form of written memoranda to the Bureau of the Budget. The major issues are then summarized by the Bureau, and the President makes his final decision, often after hours of consultation and soul-searching with key officials and White House staff members.

By the time the bill reaches the President's desk, administration forces in Congress have tried every legislative device to modify it to meet his requirements. For this reason, the President rarely vetoes a tax bill, even though very few of them satisfy him in every detail. In the past twenty-five years, only two important bills—the Revenue Act of 1943 and the Revenue Act of 1948—have been vetoed, the former by President Roosevelt and the latter by President Truman on three occasions in 1947 and 1948. In both cases, the Congress passed the bill over the President's veto by the necessary two-thirds majority. (The 1943 veto led to the temporary resignation of Senator Alben Barkley from his position as majority leader.) Since 1948, the President has signed every major tax bill that has passed both houses.

The President usually issues a statement when he has acted on the bill. If he has approved it, the statement is brief and usually expresses pleasure on its enactment. Occasionally he takes exception to some of its provisions, even though he has signed it. If he has vetoed the bill, he issues a longer statement or message explaining why it is unacceptable.

A tax bill may provide that the rates take effect within a few days after its final approval. For example, the lower withholding rates provided by the 1964 Act became effective seven days after the President signed it. The excise tax reductions of 1965 were put into effect within three days. Some tax bills have been retroactive, reducing or increasing tax liabilities from the beginning of the calendar year, fiscal year, or quarter in which the bill was finally approved. Others have taken effect at the end of the year.

After the President has signed the bill, the Treasury issues regulations to explain its interpretation of the new law and the Internal Revenue Service prepares to administer it by issuing new tax forms, advice to taxpayers, revised instructions to withholding agents, and so on. The issuance of regulations may itself be a lengthy process, sometimes requiring over a year when the legislation is particularly complex. Long before these tasks have been completed, a new tax bill may be under way and the same harassed officials who are responsible for implementing the old law begin the new tax legislative cycle.

Improving the Process

The tax legislative process has been examined by numerous congressional committees, political scientists, students of taxation, citizen and professional committees, and other groups. Opinion is generally critical: the process is said to be unnecessarily influenced by special interest groups who do not speak in the national interest; it does not provide Congress with an opportunity to make decisions on the government's overall fiscal policy or to weigh the needs for public services against tax costs; and its slowness restricts the possibilities of using tax action for countercyclical purposes. Each of these criticisms has some validity, but practical solutions are difficult to devise.

Representation of the Public Interest

Individuals who appear before the two tax committees hardly represent a cross section of opinion on tax matters. The committees generally permit anyone to testify and, except for administration officials, rarely invite expert testimony. The result is that, day after day, the committees are subject to a drumfire of complaints against the tax system, arguments why special tax advantages should not be eliminated, and reasons why additional preferences are needed.

In such an atmosphere, the Secretary of the Treasury assumes the role of defender of the national interest. He spends much of his time fighting off new tax advantages, and is only moderately successful in eliminating old ones. Whether taxes are to be raised or lowered, most of the witnesses find good reasons for favoring the groups or individuals they represent. The Secretary takes a broader national view and attempts to strike a balance among competing claims. Occasionally, he is supported by some of the national citizens' organizations, but such testimony—although more frequent in recent years—is still the exception rather than the rule.

Fortunately, the committee members are not neophytes in the legislative process. Most of them have the capacity to detect a self-serving witness. Furthermore, they have an excellent opportunity to check the merits of the public testimony in executive session with the staffs of the Joint Internal Revenue Committee and the Treasury. When the hearings are particularly long and involved, the staffs prepare confidential summaries of the pros and cons of the various positions. Through such methods, individual committee members familiarize themselves with the major issues and evaluate the mass of information hurled at them.

It would be helpful, nevertheless, to give the public, congressmen, and committee members easier access to impartial analysis and expert opinion on tax matters. Two things can be done to improve consideration of tax legislation in committee without altering the present balance of power.

First, the Joint Internal Revenue Committee or the two separate committees might organize special subcommittees to provide background materials *before* a tax issue is put on the legislative calendar. Subcommittees are used sporadically now, and are generally confined to highly technical subjects. It should be possible to divide the entire field of taxation among several subcommittees that would be responsible for continually reviewing the subjects assigned to them and for soliciting new ideas. These reports might follow the pattern set by the Ways and Means Committee's own famous 1959 *Tax Revision Compendium,* a three-volume collection of articles by leading tax experts which has greatly influenced all tax legislation since its publication.

Second, the method of scheduling the open hearings held by the tax committees could be revamped. Most witnesses now simply read prepared statements and depart without any interrogation by committee members. To help balance the testimony, the committee chairmen might be given the authority (which would, in practice, be exercised by the committee counsel) to invite testimony from selected experts when it becomes evident that some points of view will not be represented. More regular use could also be made of panels of experts which have been invited on occasion in recent years. To speed the hearings, the chairmen should limit the number of witnesses representing one point of view. This would not preclude the filing of statements by others for publication in the official record of the hearings.

Consideration of Overall Fiscal Policies

Legislative control over the fiscal policies of the federal government is now divided between the appropriations committees and the tax committees. The result is that Congress cannot make decisions about the size of the budget in relation to total taxes collected. Nor can it decide whether economic conditions warrant a surplus or a deficit, or how large the surplus or deficit should be.

Some have argued that this fractionation of the expenditure-tax process encourages higher expenditures, since no one committee must face up to the need for balancing benefits against costs. In fact, however, the process has probably been too restrictive in recent years. Congress has been slow to accept the principle that a major objective of fiscal policy should be to promote full employment, although a good deal of progress has been made since the enactment of the Revenue Act of 1964 (see Chapter 2). The appropriations committees, which act through a large number of subcommittees working on individual agency appropriations, view their roles primarily as watchdogs over the efficiency of government operations, rather than as general policy makers; and the tax committees are conservative about changing the level of taxes either upward or downward. The disappointing performance of the economy in the late 1950's is now widely acknowledged to have been in large part the result of overly restrictive fiscal (and monetary) policies.

Fiscal policy planning and guidance by the President are undertaken primarily through his annual budget messages and economic reports. These are reviewed and considered by the Joint Economic Committee, which was created by the Employment Act of 1946. Its hearings, which are usually brief but structured to bring out opposing views, and its report on the President's economic report, have improved public and congressional understanding of economic policy problems. However, the Joint Economic Committee does not have authority to propose or initiate legislation.

Suggestions are made from time to time for the creation of a Joint Committee on the Budget to give Congress a greater role in fiscal policy planning. This was tried in 1947 and 1948, but the results were disappointing. The committee did not have enough information to make judgments regarding overall fiscal policy, and its recommendations were not binding on the appropriations and tax committees. As a result, the committee resolutions were political in nature and served little purpose. The effort was abandoned after both houses ignored the resolutions.

Since the appropriations and tax committees cannot be expected to give up any of their authority, hope for improving consideration of overall fiscal policy must lie in better liaison with the Joint Economic Committee. After twenty years of effective operation, this committee now commands considerable respect from members of Congress and the public. To make its influence felt more directly on actual legislation, the chairman and the two ranking members of the Joint Economic Committee might be made voting members of the appropriations and tax committees. Closer cooperation between the staffs of the Joint Internal Revenue Committee and the Joint Economic Committee would be desirable, perhaps through special task forces to consider problems of national interest and through participation of key staff members in the executive sessions of other committees operating in the economic field.

Accelerating Countercyclical Tax Action

The most serious drawback of the tax legislative process is that it cannot be used to provide a prompt stimulus or restraint to the economy when needed. The President does not have a practical method of obtaining immediate congressional consideration of a countercyclical tax proposal, since tradition dictates that all tax changes must be carefully considered by the Ways and Means Committee and the Finance Committee. To combat a recession, exclusive reliance has been placed on expenditure changes, which have two shortcomings. They create inefficiencies in the conduct of government programs that should not be turned on and off for short-run economic reasons. They also tend to have a delayed impact on the economy because of the long lead time generally required to put them into effect.

Many tax experts and national citizens' organizations have recommended that the President be authorized to make temporary increases or reductions in tax rates. This approach would emphasize changes which are neutral in their impact on the existing tax structure, as opposed to changes which would alter the distribution of the tax burden. More fundamental reforms would be reserved for long-run revisions of the tax structure which necessarily involve lengthy and searching debate.

In general, the proposals would permit the President to make a uniform change in individual income tax rates up to some maximum percent or maximum number of percentage points for a period of six months, with the authority to renew the change for additional six-month periods as conditions require. The change would take effect thirty or sixty days after submission to Congress, unless rejected by a joint resolution. President Kennedy made such a recommendation (limited to changes in a downward direction) in 1962 and 1963, and President Johnson renewed it in 1964, but the tax committees have shown no interest in this approach and have not even brought it up for discussion.

President Johnson modified the proposal in his *1965 Economic Report* to allay suspicion that he sought to preempt congressional authority over tax rates. He suggested that Congress merely alter its procedures to permit rapid action on temporary income tax cuts proposed by the President to combat recession (tax increases were not mentioned). Because of congressional sensitivity, the President did not fill in the details, preferring to have Congress make the decision.

After Congress acted swiftly on excise tax legislation in 1965,

President Johnson modified his position still further. His *1966 Economic Report* simply stressed the need for background studies to establish guidelines for temporary tax changes. Administration spokesmen now believe that such studies could achieve general agreement on the kinds of short-range, temporary changes which should be made if needed. Nevertheless, granting of discretionary authority to the President, with Congress retaining a veto, would greatly improve the speed and flexibility of the tax legislative process.

Summary

The tax legislative process begins in the Treasury and other federal agencies where tax problems are analyzed and solutions are proposed for the President's consideration. The President transmits his recommendations to the Congress, where they are carefully reviewed by the two powerful tax committees, revised to compromise the conflicts of major opposing interests, and sent in turn to the House and Senate floors for approval. Differences between the two bills are settled by a Conference Committee; the revised version is returned to both houses for approval; and the bill becomes law when the President signs it or when Congress passes it over his veto.

The tax legislative process is unique in several respects. The work concerns a highly complex set of laws, yet all the decisions are made (as they should be) through the political process. Key roles are played by the President, the Secretary of the Treasury and his assistant secretary for tax policy, the chairmen of the two tax committees, and the chief of staff of the Joint Internal Revenue Committee. Behind the scenes, competent staffs in both the executive and legislative branches help move the tax bill through its various stages. For all these people, a tax bill is a grueling experience, demanding physical stamina as well as political acumen.

Reform of the tax process is needed: (1) to better represent the public interest in the open hearings conducted by the Ways and Means Committee and the Finance Committee; (2) to increase attention to overall fiscal policies by the appropriations and tax committees and both houses of Congress; and (3) to accelerate congressional action on temporary tax changes to combat recession or inflation. Suggestions for implementing these objectives are frequently made, but Congress has not given them serious consideration.

Despite all its faults, the achievements of the tax legislative process have been impressive on balance. While numerous questionable provisions have crept into tax laws, erosion of the tax base has been halted in recent years, and some steps have been made to reverse it. Moreover, the overall distribution of federal taxes continues to be substantially progressive despite the strong forces arrayed against progression and equitable taxation. Imperfect as it is, the tax legislative process has produced a tax system that contributes to the nation's welfare.

CHAPTER 4

The Individual Income Tax

ANY SURVEY OF TAX SOURCES should begin with the nation's fairest and most productive source of revenue, the individual income tax. All advanced industrial countries levy a direct tax on individual incomes, but nowhere is this tax as important as in the United States. In recent years, about 40 percent of federal cash receipts has been collected from this source.

The individual income tax is uniquely suited for raising revenue in a democratic country where the distribution of income, and therefore of ability to pay, is unequal. Theoreticians may disagree about the meaningfulness of the term "ability to pay," but the close association between a man's income and taxpaying ability is commonly accepted. There is also general acceptance of the idea of progression in income taxation.

The individual income tax has still another attractive feature. Income alone does not differentiate a man's ability to pay—his family responsibilities are also important. A single person may be able to get along on an income of $3,000 a year, but a married man with two children would have great difficulty making ends meet. The individual income tax takes such differences into account through the personal exemptions and deductions, which are subtracted before arriving at the income subject to tax.

The revenue potential of the individual income tax has been recognized only recently. For almost thirty years after its adoption in 1913, the tax applied mainly to a small group of high income people. Exemptions were high by current standards and few incomes were large enough to be subject to the starting rate, let alone the higher graduated rates. In the national effort to raise needed revenue during World War II, exemptions were drastically reduced. They were increased in 1946 and 1948, but have remained low by prewar standards. Tax rates were also raised in wartime, and have remained much higher than in earlier years. At the same time, personal incomes have continued to increase with the growth of the economy (and with the inflation that occurred during and after World War II and the Korean War). The combination of lower exemptions, higher rates, and higher incomes increased the yield of the individual income tax manyfold. In 1939, tax liabilities were about $1 billion; in 1966, they are in excess of $50 billion.

This tremendous expansion could not have been possible without ready compliance with income tax laws and effective administration. In many countries where compliance is poor and administration is weak, there is great reluctance to rely heavily on the income tax. In this country, the record of compliance is good—although it can still be improved—and practical methods have been developed for administering a mass income tax (at a cost of only about 1/2 of 1 percent of tax collected). In the late 1930's many people—even high-placed officials of the Internal Revenue Service—doubted that an income tax covering almost everyone could be administered effectively. Although some problems remain, in an advanced country the administrative feasibility of an individual income tax of almost universal coverage is no longer questioned.

There are good economic reasons for using the income tax as a major source of revenue. The automatic flexibility of the income tax promotes economic stability and the progressive rates help prevent excessive concentration of economic power and control. Some believe that the income tax is also needed to moderate the growth of private savings of high income people, which is likely to hold down private demand for goods and services. Others believe that a high income tax impairs work and investment incentives and, therefore, reduces the nation's economic growth. These are difficult questions which will be discussed later. Nonetheless, it is correct to say that the modern individual income tax, if carefully designed and well administered, is a powerful and essential economic instrument for a modern industrial economy.

Structure of the Federal Income Tax

The basic structure of the federal income tax is simple. The taxpayer adds up all his taxable sources of income, subtracts certain allowable deductions and exemptions for himself, his wife, children, and other dependents, and then applies the tax rates to the difference. But this procedure has many pitfalls for the taxpayer, and difficult questions of tax policy arise at almost every stage. Consequently, it is important to understand the main features of the income tax structure.

Adjusted Gross Income and Taxable Income

The two major concepts of income that appear on the tax return are: adjusted gross income and taxable income.

ADJUSTED GROSS INCOME is the closest approach in tax law to what an economist might call "total income." But it departs from an economic definition of income in some important respects. It represents the total income from all taxable sources, less certain expenses incurred in earning that income. In general, only *money* income is treated as taxable, but many items are excluded. Such exclusions include one-half of realized capital gains on assets held six months or more, interest on state and local government bonds, all transfer payments (for example, social security benefits and unemployment compensation), fringe benefits received by employees from their employers (the most important of these are contributions to pension plans), and income on savings through life insurance. The emphasis on money income automatically excludes unrealized capital gains and such imputed income as the rental value of owner-occupied homes.

Adjusted gross income is used on the tax return in two ways. First, it is the income concept built into the simplified tax table, which is used for determining tax on more than 25 million returns. Second, it provides the basis for placing limits on some of the personal deductions which are subtracted in computing taxable income.

TAXABLE INCOME is computed by making two sets of deductions from adjusted gross income. The first are personal expenditures which are allowed as deductions by law—charitable contributions, interest paid, state-local income, general sales, property and gasoline taxes, medical and dental expenses above 3 percent of adjusted gross income, and casualty and theft losses above $100 for each loss. In lieu of these deductions, the taxpayer may use the *standard deduction* of 10 percent of adjusted gross income (with a minimum of $200 plus $100 for each exemption, and a maximum of $1,000 for single persons and married persons filing joint returns and $500 for married couples filing separate returns).

When the present standard deduction was first adopted in 1944, it was used by over 80 percent of the persons filing returns. As incomes have risen and deductible expenditures have increased, the percentage using the standard deduction has declined. In 1963, the standard deduction was still being used on 35.8 million returns, or 56 percent of the 63.9 million filed (Appendix Table C-6). But the amount of the standard deduction was small compared to the itemized deductions, which have increased with the growth of home ownership, state-local taxes, and use of consumer credit, as well as the normal increase in expenditures that occurs as incomes rise. Total deductions reported on all 1963 returns amounted to $59.2 billion; of this amount, $46.1 billion were itemized deductions and $13.1 billion were standard deductions.

The second set of deductions provides an allowance for personal exemptions. The present exemptions for the taxpayer, his wife, and dependents are on a per capita basis at the rate of $600 per person. The law also gives an additional $600 exemption each to taxpayers and their wives if they are over 65 years of age, and still another $600 exemption to the blind.

Chart 4-1 traces the changes in the tax base (that is, taxable income) since the beginning of World War II. In 1939, only $7.2 billion or about 10 percent of personal income was subject to tax; by 1964, it had risen to $229.9 billion or 46 percent of personal income. This spectacular increase was caused by the two factors men-

CHART 4-1. Ratio of Taxable Individual Income to Personal Income, 1939–64

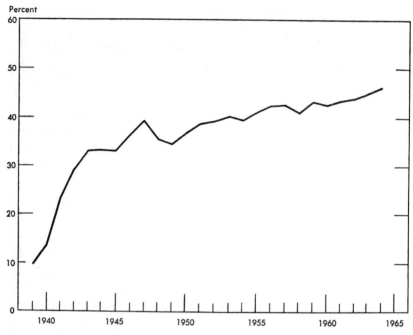

Source: Appendix Table B-5.

tioned earlier—the substantial reductions in exemptions, and the upward shifts in incomes. The rise has been interrupted only when nontaxable military pay was very large (1944 and 1945), when exemptions were increased (1948), and when nontaxable transfer payments increased during recession years (1949, 1954, 1958, and 1960).

Between 1948 and 1963, when the definition of the tax base remained virtually unchanged, 52.6 percent of the increase in personal income went into the tax base, 14.2 percent represented differences in definition between personal income and adjusted gross income, 3.9 percent was either not reported on tax returns or was received by persons who were not taxable, 14.4 percent was accounted for by exemptions, and another 14.9 percent by deductions (Table 4-1). Stated somewhat differently, about $5.25 billion out of every $10 billion increase in personal income went into the tax base.

TABLE 4-1. Comparison of Increases in Personal Income and the Federal Individual Income Tax Base, 1948–63

Derivation of the Tax Base	Increase, 1948–63 (Billions of dollars)	Percentage Distribution
Personal income..	254.5	100.0
Conceptual differences between adjusted gross income and personal income[a]..	36.1	14.2
Adjusted gross income not reported on tax returns and reported by individuals who were not taxable....................	10.0	3.9
Personal exemptions on taxable returns......................	36.6	14.4
Personal deductions on taxable returns......................	38.0	14.9
Taxable income (tax base).................................	133.9[b]	52.6

Source: Appendix Tables B-2 and B-4. Figures are rounded and will not necessarily add to totals.
[a] For details, see Appendix Table B-1.
[b] Does not include $500 million of taxable income on nontaxable returns.

Tax Rates

The tax rates are graduated by the bracket system (Table 4-2). Other methods of graduation have been used elsewhere, but this seems to be the most practical. Under this system, the income scale is divided into segments, or brackets, and rates are applied only to the income in each bracket. Rates increase by no more than 4 percentage points from one bracket to the next, in order to avoid large and abrupt increases in tax rates as incomes rise.

For single persons basic tax rates range from 14 percent on the first $500 of taxable income to 70 percent on the amount of taxable income above $100,000. For married couples filing joint returns, the tax rates are applied to half the taxable income of the couple and the result is multiplied by two. As Table 4-2 shows, this income splitting feature doubles the width of the brackets for married couples. Single persons who are heads of households use a special rate schedule that provides half the advantage of income splitting.

Although the rates are graduated up to $100,000 of taxable income, most of the tax base is concentrated in the lowest rate brackets. Based on the 1963 distribution, 59 percent of taxable income is now subject to the 14, 15, 16, and 17 percent rates in the first four brackets, and only 1.5 percent is taxed at rates of 50 percent or more (Appendix Table B-6).

TABLE 4-2. Federal Individual Income Tax Rates, 1966

Taxable Income		Tax Rates (Percentages)
Single Persons (Dollars)	Married Couples (Dollars)	
0– 500	0– 1,000	14
500– 1,000	1,000– 2,000	15
1,000– 1,500	2,000– 3,000	16
1,500– 2,000	3,000– 4,000	17
2,000– 4,000	4,000– 8,000	19
4,000– 6,000	8,000– 12,000	22
6,000– 8,000	12,000– 16,000	25
8,000– 10,000	16,000– 20,000	28
10,000– 12,000	20,000– 24,000	32
12,000– 14,000	24,000– 28,000	36
14,000– 16,000	28,000– 32,000	39
16,000– 18,000	32,000– 36,000	42
18,000– 20,000	36,000– 40,000	45
20,000– 22,000	40,000– 44,000	48
22,000– 26,000	44,000– 52,000	50
26,000– 32,000	52,000– 64,000	53
32,000– 38,000	64,000– 76,000	55
38,000– 44,000	76,000– 88,000	58
44,000– 50,000	88,000–100,000	60
50,000– 60,000	100,000–120,000	62
60,000– 70,000	120,000–140,000	64
70,000– 80,000	140,000–160,000	66
80,000– 90,000	160,000–180,000	68
90,000–100,000	180,000–200,000	69
Over 100,000	Over 200,000	70

Source: Internal Revenue Code.

Methods of Tax Payment

Between 1913 and 1942, federal income taxes were paid in quarterly installments during the year following receipt of income. When the coverage of the income tax was extended to the majority of income recipients during World War II, it was realized that the old system could not operate successfully. Low income people tend to use their income as it becomes available. Their future incomes are uncertain and it is difficult to budget taxes which do not coincide with the receipt of income. If income stops because of unemployment or sickness, an income tax debt accrued in the prior year may become a serious burden. Even high income taxpayers find it easier to meet tax payments currently than a year later, particularly when incomes fluctuate. Synchronization of tax payments and receipt of income is also desirable from an economic standpoint to maximize the stabilizing effect of the income tax.

The current payment system, introduced in 1943, is based on the principle that taxes become due as incomes are earned, rather than the following year when the tax return is filed. In practice, the system has been fully current for most wage and salary earners because their taxes are withheld by their employers. Persons who receive other types of income estimate their tax and pay it in quarterly installments during the current year.

WITHHOLDING. Withholding for income tax purposes applies to wages and salaries received by all employees, except farm workers and domestic servants, at rates ranging from 14 percent to 30 percent. The amounts withheld by the employer are remitted to the government quarterly if they total less than $100 per month. Employers withholding between $100 and $4,000 are required to deposit the tax withheld in an authorized bank within fifteen days after the end of each month. Employers withholding $4,000 or more per month are required to make deposits of the amounts withheld twice each month.

The withholding system is the backbone of the individual income tax. In recent years, it has collected about four-fifths of total individual income tax liabilities each year. In 1963, the latest year for which data are available, the total tax liability amounted to $49.2 billion. Withholding brought in $40.2 billion; payments of estimated tax, $9.7 billion; and final payments on April 15 of the following year, $6.3 billion. These payments exceeded the total tax due by $6.9 billion, which was, of course, refunded to the taxpayers (Appendix Table C-7).

DECLARATION OF ESTIMATED TAX. Since withholding applies only to wages and salaries and the rate cuts off at 30 percent rather than 70 percent, millions of taxpayers do not have their taxes fully withheld; and no tax is withheld at all from nonwage sources. The declaration system was devised to take up the slack.

A declaration is required for all persons with estimated tax payments of $40 or more and who have relatively large incomes ($200 of nonwage income or a gross wage income of more than $10,000 if they are married and filing joint returns or are heads of households, and of more than $5,000 if they are married and filing separate returns or are single). These requirements were set so that persons whose income is not subject to withholding—farmers, businessmen, and recipients of property income—will pay their tax currently, and so that wage and salary earners in the higher brackets will pay that part of their tax which is not withheld on a current basis. Farmers and fishermen may file their declarations on January 15 of the following year, or omit them entirely if they file their final returns by February 15.

Taxpayers who do not pay as much as 80 percent of their final tax through withholding and declaration (66⅔ percent in the case of farmers and fishermen) must pay a charge of 6 percent per year for the amount falling short of 80 percent. However, no penalty is applied to any installment if the tax paid by that date is based on (a) the previous year's tax; (b) the previous year's income with current rates and exemptions; or (c) 90 percent of the tax on the actual income received before the installment date.

As a result of these liberal provisions, the sums collected through declarations of estimated tax have been relatively small. Whereas taxes withheld increased from $9.6 billion to $40.2 billion between 1944 and 1963, declaration payments increased from $5.5 billion to only $9.7 billion during the same period (Appendix Table C-7).

The Final Tax Reconciliation

The reconciliation between an individual's final tax liability and his prepayments is made on the final tax return which is filed not later than April 15. If the taxpayer owes more tax, he sends a check for the balance due to the Internal Revenue Service along with his return; if too much tax has been withheld, the excess is refunded.

Few returns have identical prepayments and final liabilities. In 1963, only 3.3 million out of a total 63.9 million returns showed prepayments exactly equal to final liabilities (including taxpayers who file but are not subject to any tax). Of the remaining 60.6 million, 41.4 million received a refund check (or chose to credit the overpayment against the estimated tax for the following year or to invest the overpayment in federal savings bonds) and 19.3 million had a balance of tax due (Appendix Table C-8).

Refunds greatly outnumber balances of tax for several reasons: (1) Withholding is based on the assumption that the employee works regularly (part-time or full-time) so that his withholding exemptions are accurately divided up among his payroll periods; but employment is often irregular because of seasonality, changes of jobs, illness, and the like. (2) Employees may claim fewer exemptions than they are entitled to for withholding purposes. (3) The withholding tables allow only for the standard deduction, whereas many employees—particularly those who own homes—have large deductions which they itemize when filing their returns. To moderate overwithholding on this score, the Tax Adjustment Act of 1966 permitted those who have large itemized deductions to claim additional exemptions for withholding purposes.

When the current payment system was adopted, great concern was expressed that overwithholding might be resented by taxpayers. Since the end of World War II, the number of refunds has never fallen below 30 million in any one year and reached 41 million in 1963 (Appendix Table C-8). Nevertheless, there have been few complaints. Apparently, people prefer to receive a check from the government than to pay a tax bill, particularly since most of the refunds are mailed within two months after the tax return is filed.

Possible Modification of the Current Payment System

Proposals have been made to expand the withholding system to include incomes other than wages and salaries. On several occasions Congress has rejected plans for withholding on interest and dividends at a flat rate. A withholding system without exemptions was considered too burdensome on the aged and other nontaxable persons; and corporations, banks, and other financial institutions paying interest and dividends argued that it would be too costly to administer a plan involving exemption certificates. In 1962, Congress compromised the issue by requiring payers of interest and dividends to send an information return (with a copy to the government) to all recipients receiving more than $10 of interest or dividends per year. Interest and dividend reporting has greatly improved, but interest underreporting is still large. The present method will be evaluated after a few more years of experience.

Economic Effects

Three issues are of particular importance in appraising the economic effects of the individual income tax: its role as a stabilizer of consumption expenditures; its effect on saving; and its impact on work and investment incentives.

Role as Stabilizer

Stability of tax yield was once regarded as a major criterion of a good tax. Today, there is general agreement that properly timed changes in tax yields can help increase employment during recessions and restrain prices during expansionary periods. The progressive individual income tax has the virtue that its yield automatically rises and falls more than in proportion to changes in personal income. Moreover, the current tax payment system has greatly accelerated the reaction of income tax revenues to income changes. An important by-product of current payment is that changes in tax rates have an almost immediate effect on the disposable income of most taxpayers. These features have made the personal income tax extremely useful for promoting economic stabilization and growth.

The automatic response of the individual income tax—its *built-in flexibility*—can be explained by the following example. Suppose a taxpayer with a wife and two children earns $5,000 per year when he is employed and uses the standard deduction. His taxable income is $2,000 ($5,000 less $600 for the minimum standard deduction and $2,400 for the personal exemptions) and his tax under present rates is $290. The following table shows the effect on his taxable income and tax if his income drops to $4,000:

Adjusted gross income	$5,000	$4,000
Deduct: Exemptions	2,400	2,400
Deduct: Minimum standard deduction	600	600
Equals: Taxable income	2,000	1,000
Tax	290	140
Disposable income	4,710	3,860

Whereas adjusted gross income declined by only 20 percent, taxable income declined 50 percent (from $2,000 to $1,000), and the tax declined 52 percent.

Such examples are multiplied millions of times during a recession, while the opposite occurs during boom periods. Those with lower or higher incomes find that their tax is reduced or increased proportionately more than their income. As a result, disposable income is more stable than it would be in the absence of the tax. (In the above example, disposable income declined only $850 while income before tax declined $1,000.) Since disposable income is the major determinant of consumption, expenditures by consumers are also more stable than they would be in the absence of the tax.

Individual income tax changes may also be used to restrain or stimulate the economy. The Revenue Act of 1964 reduced taxes by $11.4 billion, of which the individual income tax reduction amounted to $9.2 billion. The tax cut was designed to raise the level of expenditures by consumers and businessmen and thus to stimulate a higher rate of economic growth. Consumer expenditures had already increased in anticipation of the tax cut when it went into effect for withholding purposes early in March 1964; in the succeeding year, they rose $28 billion. While the increase in consumption cannot wholly be attributed to the tax cut, it was undoubtedly the most important factor. Most people are now persuaded that income tax changes can have a powerful effect in helping to regulate the rate of growth of private demand.

The full potential of the income tax as an instrument of economic policy has not yet been realized. Countercyclical changes in tax rates seem to be rare in most countries, partly because there are long delays in recognizing significant changes in economic conditions and partly because the legislative process is too slow. However, as indicated in Chapter 3, it should be possible to devise congressional procedures for varying tax rates quickly in response to changes in the level of economic activity.

Effect on Saving and Consumption

The individual income tax applies to the entire income of an individual whether it is spent or saved. Some have argued that the income tax is unfair to those who save because it applies both to the income which gives rise to the saving and to the income produced by the saving process. But almost all economists now agree that, on equity grounds, this double taxation argument does not have much merit. At any particular point in time, an individual has the option to make a new decision to spend or save from the income that is left to him after tax. If he decides to save the income, he does not necessarily incur a new tax. It is only if the saving is actually invested in an income producing asset that new income is generated and this new income is, of course, subject to additional tax.

The individual income tax is often contrasted with a general consumption or expenditure tax, which is an alternative method of taxing individuals in accordance with "ability to pay." In the case of the income tax, the measure of ability to pay is income; in the case of the expenditure tax, the measure is consumption. The tax on consumption may also be levied at progressive rates (but the rates must be greater than 100 percent to equal the impact of the progressive income tax in the higher brackets).

Consumption taxes can be avoided simply by reducing one's consumption. This means that an expenditure tax is more advantageous to saving than an equal-yield income tax which is distributed in the same proportions by income classes. In practice, where the income tax is paid by the large mass of people, much of the tax yield comes from income classes where there is little room in family budgets for increasing saving in response to tax incentives. As a consequence, the differential effect on total consumption and saving between an income tax and an equal-yield expenditure tax is likely to be small in this country.

Economics alone does not provide a basis for deciding whether the income tax is more or less "equitable" than an expenditure tax. The income tax reduces the gain made when an individual saves rather than consumes part of his income, while an expenditure tax makes future consumption relatively as attractive as present consumption. Under the income tax, the interest reward for saving and investing is reduced by the tax; under the expenditure tax, the net reward is always equal to the market rate of interest regardless of the tax rate.

While this subject has not been widely discussed in the United States, the continued heavy reliance on the income tax suggests that it is probably more acceptable on equity grounds than an expenditure tax might be. An expenditure tax was recommended by the Treasury during World War II, but it was rejected by the Congress primarily because of its novelty and complexity.

Graduated expenditure taxes are often proposed as a method of avoiding or correcting the defects of the income tax base, particularly in the top brackets where the preferential treatment of capital gains, tax-exempt interest, depletion allowances (see Chapter 5), and other favorable provisions permit the accumulation of large fortunes with little or no payment of income tax. An expenditure tax would reach such incomes when they are spent without resort to regressive taxation. Despite this advantage, the expenditure tax has not been widely used. It is more difficult to administer and also raises more serious problems of compliance for the taxpayer. Although it is difficult to imagine wholesale replacement of the income tax by an expenditure tax, it might be a useful supplement if and when it becomes necessary to discourage consumption.

Work and Investment Incentives

The individual income tax affects economic incentives in two different directions. On the one hand, it reduces the monetary rewards of greater effort and risk-taking and thus tends to discourage these activities. On the other hand, it may provide a greater incentive to obtain more income because it cuts down on the income left over for spending. There is no basis for deciding which effect is more important on an *a priori* basis.

Taxation is only one of many factors affecting work and investment incentives. This makes it extremely difficult to interpret the available statistical evidence or the results of direct interviews with taxpayers. The evidence suggests that income taxation does not reduce the amount of labor supplied by workers and managers. Work habits are not easily changed and there is little scope in a modern industrial society for most people to vary hours of work or the intensity of their efforts in response to changes in tax rates. Nearly all people who are asked about income taxation grumble about it, but relatively few state that they work fewer hours or exert less than their best efforts to avoid being taxed.

As for risk-taking, the problem is much more complicated. In the first place, the tax rates on capital gains are much lower than those on ordinary incomes. Numerous studies have demonstrated that the opportunity to earn income in the form of capital gains stimulates investment and risk-taking. Second, taxpayers may offset business losses against ordinary income not only for the current year but also for three prior years and five succeeding years; capital losses may be offset against capital gains and $1,000 of ordinary income per year for an indefinite period. Such offsets greatly diminish the consequences of loss by the investor. Third, much of the nation's investment is undertaken by large corporations. These firms are generally permitted to retain earnings after payment of the 48 percent corporation tax rate, which is more moderate than the rates applying to investors in the top personal income tax brackets. Finally, the law provides incentives for investment through generous depreciation allowances and an investment credit of 7 percent. In any case, experience suggests that the major stimulus to investment comes from a healthy and prosperous economy.

The discussion in the next section will indicate that much can be done to improve the structure of the income tax. But there is little basis for the assertions made from time to time that the income tax has had an adverse effect on the economy.

Structural Problems

The personal income tax is determined by the definition of income, allowable deductions, personal exemptions, and tax rates. These elements can be combined in various ways to produce a given amount of revenue. In recent years, there has been increasing recognition that the definition of taxable income under the United States tax law is deficient. Many of the exclusions and deductions are not essential for effective personal income taxation, and have cut into the income tax base unnecessarily. This process of "erosion" has been halted in recent years, but only limited progress has been made to reverse it.

Erosion of the income tax base makes higher tax rates necessary. It puts a premium on earning and disposing of incomes in forms that receive preferential treatment, thus often distorting the allocation of resources. Erosion also violates the principle that taxpayers with equal incomes should pay the same tax. These departures from horizontal equity, which often seem arbitrary, contribute to taxpayer dissatisfaction and create pressures for the enactment of additional special benefits—pressures that legislators find difficult to resist.

Chart 4-2 shows the practical effect of erosion. If the total income reported by taxpayers were subject to the nominal tax rates without any exemptions, deductions, or other special provisions, effective tax rates would begin at 14 percent and rise to almost 70 percent in the very highest brackets. But nobody pays these rates on his entire income. After allowing for all special provisions, the *maximum average effective rate* for any income class is less than 30 percent and the tax becomes slightly regressive above $200,000 of income. Exemptions are most important in the lowest classes, and deductions in the top classes. But, oddly enough, the combined effect of the two sets of provisions is about the same in all classes above the $2,000 income level. The capital gains provisions are most important at the top, while income splitting gives the largest benefits to persons with incomes between $20,000 and $100,000. The effective rates shown in Chart 4-2 are average values and there are wide variations in taxes paid at all income levels.

A personal income tax conforming strictly to the principle of horizontal equity is easily described, but difficult to implement. This tax would include in the tax base all income from whatever source derived, permit deductions for expenses of earning income, and also make an allowance for the taxpayer and his dependents through the personal exemptions. The term "income" is ordinarily defined by economists as consumption plus (or minus) the net increase (or decrease) in the value of an individual's assets during the taxable period, modified to exclude gifts and inheritances which are subject to separate taxes and, for practical reasons, to include capital gains only when realized or when transferred to others through gifts and bequests. In the discussion which follows, this comprehensive definition of income will be used as a basis for evaluating the major features of the income tax and the more important proposals for reform.

Personal Exemptions

The history of personal exemptions under the federal individual income tax in the United States since 1913 is summarized in Chart

CHART 4-2. Influence of Various Provisions on Effective Rates of Federal Individual Income Tax, 1964 Act[a]

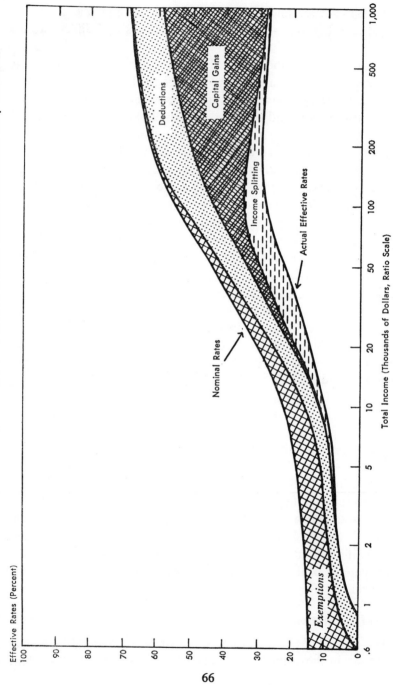

Effective Rates (Percent)

Total Income (Thousands of Dollars, Ratio Scale)

Deductions

Capital Gains

Income Splitting

Actual Effective Rates

Nominal Rates

Exemptions

Source: Special file of about 100,000 Federal Tax Returns for 1962. Chart reprinted from Joseph A. Pechman, "Individual Income Tax Provisions of the Revenue Act of 1964," *Journal of Finance*, Vol. 20 (May 1965), p. 265 (Brookings Reprint No. 96). Data are given in Appendix Table C-10.
[a] Based on 1962 incomes, with rates applicable beginning Jan. 1, 1965.

4-3. In both current and constant dollars, exemptions for single persons and families show an unmistakable downward trend. The 1965 exemption of $600 for single persons was worth $264 in 1939 prices, while the $1,200 exemption of a married couple with no children was worth $528, and the $2,400 exemption of a married couple with two children was worth $1,057.

The basic justification for the personal exemption is that very low income people have no taxpaying capacity. Taxation below minimum levels of subsistence reduces health and efficiency, and results in lower economic vitality, less production, and possibly higher public expenditures for social welfare programs. The personal exemptions also serve as an administrative device to remove from the tax rolls people with very low incomes and to contribute to progression (at a declining rate as incomes rise). At the higher income levels, the personal exemption moderates the tax burden as the number of dependents increases, but the differences in tax for equal income individuals with different sizes of families are small.

Two questions need to be discussed in evaluating the system of personal exemptions. First, are the allowances for single persons and families of different size fair relative to one another? Second, is the general level of exemptions adequate? Recent calculations of the incidence of poverty, which are based on concepts of income adequacy, can be used to shed light on these questions.

RELATIVE EXEMPTIONS FOR DIFFERENT FAMILY SIZES. If a family of two must spend x dollars to achieve a certain scale of living, what proportion of x would a single person spend and how much more than x would families of three, four, five, or more people spend to maintain an equivalent standard? Clearly, the answer depends on the criteria used for measuring equivalence. One standard developed by federal agencies is the amount of income needed to maintain an adequate diet. Two cost estimates for this diet have been made: (1) a *low-cost* plan adapted to the food patterns of families in the lowest third of the income range; and (2) an *economy* plan (costing from 75 to 80 percent of the basic plan) for emergency use when funds are low.

The two standards yield approximately the same results (Table 4-3). In both cases, the needs of a household do not increase in proportion to the number of people in the household. The relative

CHART 4-3. History of Federal Individual Income Tax Exemptions in Current and 1939 Prices, 1913–65

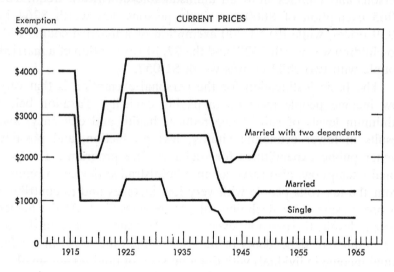

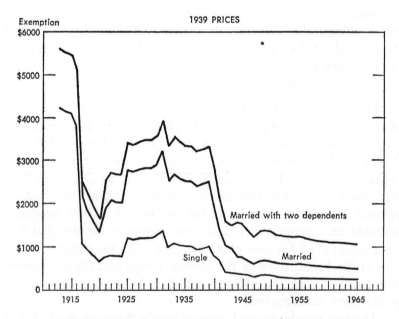

Source: Derived from data in Appendix Table A-1 and U. S. Department of Labor, Bureau of Labor Statistics, Consumer Price Index, all items, Series A.

Note: For 1941-45, exemptions shown are for surtax purposes only.

TABLE 4-3. Comparison of Federal Individual Income Tax Exemptions with Estimates of Incomes of Families of Different Size Corresponding to the Same Standard of Living

Two person family = 100

Size of Family	Exemptions[a]	Income Relatives Based on		
		Economy Level[b]	Low-Cost Level[c]	Average of Both
1	56	77	70	74
2	100	100	100	100
3	144	119	116	118
4	188	153	148	150
5	231	180	172	176
6	275	202	193	198

Source: Table 4-4.

[a] Allows for the minimum standard deduction; assumes taxpayer uses the simplified tax table to calculate tax.

[b] Relative amounts of income needed to provide nonfarm families with the food included in the Department of Agriculture's "economy" food plan for temporary or emergency use when funds are low.

[c] Relative amounts of income needed to provide nonfarm families with food included in the Department of Agriculture's "low-cost" food plan which is adapted to the food patterns of families in the lowest third of the income range.

incomes which would provide roughly equivalent standards of living appear to be in the ratio of 75:100:25 for single, married, and dependent persons, respectively, whereas the present exemptions (plus the minimum standard deduction) give a ratio of 55:100:45. On this basis, the present exemption is too liberal for dependents and too small for single persons.

THE LEVEL OF EXEMPTIONS. The adequacy of the *level* of exemptions may be judged by comparing the incomes needed by families of different size with the personal exemptions. This comparison is made in Table 4-4. The "gross" exemptions in this table exceed the statutory per capita exemptions by the amount of the minimum standard deduction ($200 plus $100 for each exemption, up to a maximum of $1,000).

According to Table 4-4, present exemptions do not cover the rock-bottom economy standard for single persons and married couples with no children, but are near adequacy for families of three, four, and five persons and more than adequate for families of six or more persons. On the low-cost standard, the exemptions are inadequate for families of all sizes.

It is clear from Table 4-4 that the minimum standard deduction

TABLE 4-4. Comparison of Federal Individual Income Tax Exemptions with Estimated Family Budgets, 1964

(In dollars)

Size of Family	Exemptions[a]	Estimated Cost of Budgets	Difference[b]
	Economy Level Budget[c]		
1	900	1,580	−680
2	1,600	2,050	−450
3	2,300	2,440	−140
4	3,000	3,130	−130
5	3,700	3,685	+ 15
6	4,400	4,140	+260
	Low-Cost Budget[c]		
1	900	1,920	−1,020
2	1,600	2,760	−1,160
3	2,300	3,210	− 910
4	3,000	4,075	−1,075
5	3,700	4,755	−1,055
6	4,400	5,340	− 940

Source: Mollie Orshansky, "Counting the Poor: Another Look at the Poverty Profile," *Social Security Bulletin*, Vol. 28, No. 1 (January 1965), pp. 3–29. See especially, Table E, p. 28.
[a] Allows for the minimum standard deduction; assumes taxpayer uses the simplified tax table to calculate tax.
[b] Minus signs denote taxable portion of budgets in excess of present gross exemptions.
[c] For an explanation of these budgets, see Table 4-3, footnotes b and c.

plays an important and useful role in correcting part of the inadequacy of the per capita exemption. The purpose of the minimum standard deduction is to augment the regular exemptions at the bottom of the income scale without incurring the heavy cost of raising the exemptions for all taxpayers. Thus, a single person is not required to pay tax until his income exceeds $900 as compared with the previous $667. A married couple with two children, formerly not taxed until their income reached at least $2,675, is now exempt up to $3,000. The exemption system would now be grossly inadequate without the minimum standard deduction.

VARIABLE EXEMPTIONS. Since costs are relatively higher for the principal income recipient in the family than for dependents, a return to the pre-World War II variable exemption system is often suggested. For example, one combination might be $800, $1,600, and $400 exemptions for single persons, married couples, and dependents, respectively. With the minimum standard deduction added, this would be equivalent to $1,100, $2,000, and $500.

Two considerations argue against abandoning the per capita

exemption system. First, the per capita system commends itself as both fair and simple to many people. Although the bare physical needs of children may be provided for at less cost than those of adults, the obligation of parents goes beyond mere physical maintenance and a per capita exemption recognizes this obligation. Others believe that tax policy should provide liberal protection for those with children as a matter of social policy. In Great Britain and Canada, where the dependent exemption is lower than the exemption for the taxpayer and his wife, this protection is given in the form of a family allowance which is paid as a direct subsidy to those with children.

Second, abandonment of the per capita exemption would complicate administration and compliance. The withholding tax tables and the simplified tax table would become more cumbersome and unwieldy. Employers would have to keep track of their employees' marital status as well as the number of exemptions. Thus, the simplicity of the present system argues against departing from the per capita exemption, while the budget figures argue for higher exemptions for taxpayers and their wives than for dependents.

COST OF EXEMPTION INCREASES. Policy makers hesitate to raise the per capita exemption because it would be so expensive. An increase from $600 to $700 would cost $3 billion; an increase to $800 would cost $5.5 billion. By contrast, a reduction of only one percentage point in all the tax rates would cost $2.5 billion. Thus, the revenue loss of an exemption increase might preclude reductions in the individual income tax rates or in other tax rates. Since general tax cuts are not usually designed to be of benefit primarily to one taxpayer group, an exemption increase would be politically practical only when there is enough leeway to cut taxes substantially.

An alternative is to increase the minimum standard deduction. This would help those who are in greatest need, without incurring heavy revenue losses. For example, a minimum standard deduction of $400 plus $200 for each exemption (up to a maximum of, say, $2,000) would raise the effective exemptions to $1,200 for single persons, $2,000 for married couples without children, and $3,600 for married couples with two children. The cost of this reform would be about $1.8 billion, and it would go far to correct the inadequacy of present exemptions.

The main problem created by this approach is that persons with

low incomes who have large legitimate deductions, and are therefore in a position to itemize, gain little or nothing from an increase
in the standard deduction.

TAX CREDITS IN LIEU OF EXEMPTIONS. Allowances for taxpayers
and dependents have always been given in the form of exemptions
under the federal income tax. An alternative method, now used in
several states, is to convert the allowance to a tax credit computed
by multiplying the value of the exemption by the first bracket rate.
Thus, with the present 14 percent first bracket rate, the $600 ex-
emption would be converted to a credit of $84. The credit would
increase the tax liabilities for single persons with taxable income of
more than $500 and married couples with taxable income of more
than $1,000. It would also narrow the tax differential among fami-
lies of different sizes at all income levels.

The tax credit limits the tax value of the exemption to the same
dollar amount for all taxpayers. Carried to the extreme, the logic of
the tax credit would lead to an exemption which vanished at some
point on the income scale. A vanishing exemption is often supported
on the ground that exemptions are not justified for individuals with
very large incomes, since expenditures for children are not a hardship at these levels. However, few people have seriously recommended the conversion of the exemption to a credit in recent years,
primarily because it is considered undesirable to adopt a measure
that would bear more heavily on those with family responsibilities
and with relatively modest means.

THE NEGATIVE INCOME TAX. Raising the exemptions or lowering
the bottom bracket tax rates would do little to alleviate the economic
hardship of low income families. In the first place, to the extent that
poor families pay any tax at all, the amount is small—even full
relief from income taxation will not help much. Second, families
with incomes below the present gross exemption levels cannot be
helped at all by income tax reduction.

The traditional method of helping poverty-stricken families has
been through public welfare and other direct transfer payments (for
example, old-age assistance, aid to families with dependent children, medical assistance for the aged, aid to the blind and disabled
persons, and general relief). Most of these programs reach specific
categories of poor persons; except for general relief, which is inade-

quate almost everywhere, they provide no assistance to families headed by able-bodied workers who, for reasons of background, training, or temperament, do not participate effectively in the modern industrial economy.

Considerable thought has been given in recent years to the relationship between the welfare system and the income tax system. The two grew up side by side in response to different pressures, but it has become increasingly recognized that one may be regarded as an extension of the other. Direct assistance to low income persons is an extension of progression into the lowest brackets, with negative rather than positive rates. Once this relationship has been understood, it is only a natural step to consider the adoption of a "negative income tax."

The negative income tax would involve the same computations of taxable income as are involved in the positive income tax. A taxpayer would add up all his income and subtract his exemptions and deductions. If the result is negative, he would be entitled to a payment from the government. The payment would be computed by applying a new set of tax rates to the negative taxable income. The rates on negative taxable incomes might begin with the first bracket rate of 14 percent and increase as the negative income increased. But there is no necessary relationship between the first bracket rates of the positive and negative parts of the income tax. The rates on negative incomes could begin with, say, 30 percent and go as high as 70, 80, or even 100 percent.

Such a system would provide assistance to families on the basis of the deficiency in income below accepted minimum standards, without inquiring into the reason for the deficiency. The various welfare programs conducted by government and private nonprofit agencies do not reach all of the poor. The negative income tax is regarded primarily as a method of supplementing these welfare programs rather than replacing them. A number of experts have pointed out, however, that—in principle at least—a comprehensive negative income tax could be used to replace the categorical welfare payments.

The negative income tax is a novel idea for welfare and tax experts, as well as for the American public. To make it workable, a number of important, and difficult, questions would need to be resolved. Should the definition of taxable income be modified to

CHART 4-4. Itemized Deductions as a Percentage of Adjusted Gross Income, Taxable and Nontaxable Federal Individual Returns, 1962

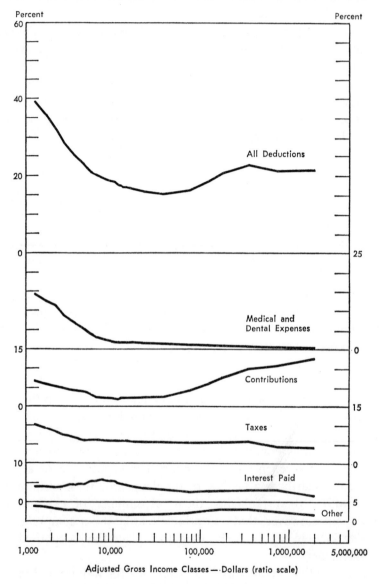

Adjusted Gross Income Classes — Dollars (ratio scale)

Source: Treasury Department, Internal Revenue Service, *Statistics of Income, 1962, Individual Income Tax Returns.*

74

avoid payments to persons who are not needy? Should the assets of the needy families as well as their income be taken into account? Should an offset against the negative income tax be made for existing welfare payments to avoid duplication? What criteria should be used to establish the negative income tax rate schedule? Should the negative income tax be applied at uniform rates throughout the country?

Personal Deductions

Personal deductions which were itemized on taxable returns in 1962 amounted to $38.7 billion. Of this amount, about $16 billion would have been deductible through the standard deduction in any event. The tax savings from the additional $22.7 billion of itemized deductions amounted to about $4.5 billion.

The relative importance of the itemized deductions at different income levels is shown in Chart 4-4. Because most people with incomes below $10,000 have the alternative of taking the 10 percent standard deduction, it is not surprising to find that, at these levels, those who itemize their deductions subtract much more than 10 percent on the average. As incomes go beyond $10,000 the deductions account for a smaller percentage, but they are still substantially in excess of 10 percent in the highest income classes. In 1962, they averaged 19 percent of adjusted gross income on taxable returns with itemized deductions. They were even more important for nontaxable returns, where they accounted for almost half of adjusted gross income (Appendix Table C-11).

The largest deductions at most income levels are interest and taxes, but medical deductions—which are subject to a 3 percent floor—are heaviest in the lowest income classes. Interest is most important between $3,000 and $25,000, undoubtedly because of the high incidence of mortgage-financed homeownership.

There is very little variation in the average ratio of standard *plus* itemized deductions in the various income groups, except at the very highest levels. In 1962, the standard and itemized deductions combined amounted to 14.3 percent of adjusted gross income on taxable returns below $5,000; 15.8 percent on those between $5,000 and $10,000; 14.0 percent between $10,000 and $25,000; 14.8 percent between $25,000 and $100,000; and 20.6 percent over $100,000. The large rise at the top is due to an increase in the ratio of contributions to income, reflecting the importance of philanthropy among the wealthy and the incentive for giftmaking provided by the tax deduction.

There is no recorded explanation of the justification for many of the personal deductions. Most of them have been allowed since the beginning of the income tax. Given the definition of "income" stated earlier, deductions would be allowed only for expenditures that are essential to earn income. An exception to this rule might be made for unusual personal expenditures that create hardships when incomes are low; but to avoid subsidizing personal consumption, the personal expense deductions should be kept to a minimum. The current tax law departs from these criteria to a substantial degree.

PURPOSES OF THE PERSONAL DEDUCTIONS. There are four major groups of itemized deductions under present law. The first is for large, unusual, and necessary personal expenditures. Deductions for extraordinary medical expenses are the best examples of this group. They are often involuntary, unpredictable, and may exhaust a large proportion of the taxpayer's total income in a particular year. When a serious illness strikes a family member, its ability to pay taxes is clearly lower than that of another equal income family whose members are healthy. For these reasons, taxpayers are permitted to deduct medical expenses in excess of 3 percent of their income, with generous maximum limitations. Other deductions for large, involuntary, and unpredictable costs are those for noninsured losses due to theft, fire, storms, accidents, or other casualties. Since 1964, these deductions are limited to amounts over $100 per casualty.

The second group of deductions in effect subsidizes particular groups of taxpayers. Thus, deductions for taxes paid on owner-occupied residences and for interest on home mortgages help the homeowner. Since the rental value of an owner-occupied house is not included in the owner's income, the deduction of expenses—including interest and taxes—connected with the home is not warranted. In addition to the direct benefit from the deductions and the exclusion from taxable income of the rental value of their homes, homeowners also derive an indirect benefit by being able to utilize other itemized deductions. Tenants with low and middle incomes rarely accumulate deductions aggregating more than the standard deduction. The result is that homeowners are the primary beneficiaries of the remaining deductions. Moreover, when a new deduction is added, the full benefit ordinarily goes to homeowners who already itemize. Other taxpayers must sacrifice the standard deduction before receiving some value from the new deduction.

Another deduction of the subsidy type is for contributions. Some question the incentive effect of this deduction. Others have argued that private philanthropy should not be encouraged at the expense of the federal treasury, since it involves the diversion of tax funds by individuals to organizations of their own choice. However, most people believe that the activities of these organizations are generally socially desirable.

The deduction for interest is justifiable where the interest is paid in connection with a loan used to produce taxable income. The interest payment is in effect a negative income which should be offset against the positive income produced by the asset purchased with the loan proceeds. Alternatively, an individual may prefer to borrow money and pay interest rather than sell an asset; in such cases, the interest deduction is also required to measure the individual's true net property income. However, a substantial proportion of the interest deducted on tax returns is for loans on homes and consumer durables or for other purposes that do not produce taxable income.

The third group of deductions is for income, property, gasoline, and sales taxes paid to state and local governments. A deduction for income taxes reduces the combined impact of federal, state, and local income taxes; it is also an effective way of moderating interstate tax differentials in the higher income brackets. For example, if an income were subject to the highest state rate of 14.6 percent and also to the 70 percent rate for federal tax purposes, the combined marginal rates would be 84.6 percent. By allowing taxpayers to deduct the state tax on their federal returns, the maximum combined rate is reduced to 74.4 percent. If the state also permits a deduction for federal taxes, the maximum combined rate is 71.5 percent.

At one time, federal excises and all the minor state and local taxes were allowed as deductions, but these were gradually eliminated. The deductions for general sales and property taxes survived because it was felt that some federal relief for these taxes was needed to encourage state and local governments to raise needed revenue, without coercing them to use a particular source. The deduction for gasoline taxes was retained for the same reasons, but here the rationale is strained.

The fourth group of deductions contains the only theoretically necessary deductions, namely, those that make allowances for expenses of earning income. These deductions are required to correct the deficiencies of the adjusted gross income concept. To avoid complicating the tax return, expenses incurred in earning nonbusiness incomes (that is, wages and salaries, interest, and dividends) are generally not allowed as deductions in arriving at adjusted gross income. This deficiency is corrected by permitting taxpayers to deduct some of these expenses in arriving at taxable income. Examples of these deductions are fees for investment counselors, rentals of safety deposit boxes used to store income producing securities, custodian fees, work clothing, and union dues. Moving expenses and nonreimbursed travel expenses of employees are deductible in arriving at adjusted gross income.

The deduction for child care, which was enacted in 1954 and liberalized in 1964, permits all employed single persons and married couples having incomes of less than $6,000 with both husband and wife employed to deduct up to $600 for the cost of the care of one child while they are at work, and $900 for two or more children. Congress justified this deduction on the ground that child care expenditures must be incurred by many taxpayers to earn a livelihood, and are comparable to ordinary business expenses.

POSSIBLE REVISIONS OF THE PERSONAL DEDUCTIONS. Revision of the personal deductions should begin with those that subsidize personal expenditures, which account for the major share of itemized deductions on taxable returns (Appendix Table C-11). They include the deductions for charitable contributions, interest on personal loans, and state and local taxes other than income and sales taxes.

Among these deductions, only charitable contributions seem to have such overwhelming social priority under present institutional arrangements as to warrant the use of tax incentives. However, the deduction for contributions probably has little effect on charitable giving by the lower and middle income classes, since the income tax advantage is relatively small at these levels. If an income tax deduction is deemed necessary to encourage large contributions, it might be better to give the deduction only when the contribution is larger than some average amount. For example, the deduction might be allowed for the amount of contributions in excess of, say, 2 or 3 percent of adjusted gross income, with the total deduction limited to the present 30 percent of adjusted gross income.

With respect to the medical expense deduction, recent surveys indicate that the 3 percent minimum is about equal to the median expenditure of families with incomes below $10,000. However, the median is only an arbitrary dividing line between "usual" and "extraordinary." The lower limit could be restored to 5 percent for all taxpayers without violating its basic rationale. This would still permit deductions for about 40 percent of all families.

The interest deduction presents a special difficulty because interest is paid on both business and personal debts, and it is often difficult to distinguish between the two. Clearly, the deduction should be allowed for interest on a loan made to the owner of a grocery store to carry inventories, while interest on a loan to purchase a consumer durable hardly merits a deduction. As already indicated, the inventory loan produces taxable income, while the consumer durable goods loan generates income in the form of services which do not enter into the tax base. However, owners of unincorporated enterprises often take out personal loans to finance their business activities and vice versa. The best plan would probably be to permit deductions (with carryover privileges) for interest paid up to the amount of property and business income reported by the taxpayers, on the ground that interest paid must be subtracted to obtain *net* income from these sources. This test would exclude about three-quarters of the interest now deducted.

Among the deductible taxes, gasoline taxes are least justified as a deduction. The federal deduction in effect places part of the burden of user charges levied for automobile use on the general taxpayer. This is unfair between automobile and nonautomobile users, and also among people with different incomes. The deduction of property taxes on owner-occupied houses discriminates against renters, and these might also be excluded in the interest of equity. This would leave deductions for state and local income and sales taxes, which can be justified as a method of encouraging the use of general taxes for state-local purposes.

It may be concluded that the itemized deductions are too generous and substantial revenues might be obtained by trimming them to the most essential items. But this is not all. If the itemized deductions were curtailed, it would be possible also to reduce the standard deduction. To an important degree, the standard deduction violates the rationale of the itemized deductions since it tends to reduce differentiation in tax liabilities. The existence of both standard and itemized deductions suggests that there is some ambivalence towards many of the personal deductions.

Under the circumstances, interest has been expressed of late in an alternative approach that would not involve repeal or modification of the questionable deductions. One possibility—first suggested by Senator Russell B. Long, chairman of the Senate Finance Committee—involves the use of an *optional* tax calculation based on gross income. The taxpayer would be entitled to use the present tax system, or he could elect to compute his tax on the basis of a comprehensive income concept at lower rates. (The comprehensive concept would include realized capital gains in full, tax-exempt interest, and other items of income now omitted from the tax base.) Except for the personal exemptions, no deductions for personal expenses would be allowed. The particular schedule of rates suggested would not exceed 50 percent.

A second possibility would be to increase the standard deduction so that fewer persons would be encouraged to itemize personal deductions. The proposals include such variants as increasing the rate of the standard deduction and raising or eliminating the $1,000 ceiling. If the ceiling is removed, it might also be possible to require inclusion of tax-exempt income in adjusted gross income for those persons who elect to use the more liberal standard deduction.

Still a third possibility would be to eliminate the standard deduction and to convert it to a floor on itemized deductions. Thus, taxpayers would be permitted to deduct only the amount of their itemized deductions exceeding, say, 10 percent of their adjusted gross income. Since the standard deduction would be eliminated, this would permit substantial reductions in the marginal rates.

The common feature among the three alternatives is a recognition that horizontal equity would be better served by limiting the advantage of the itemized deductions and other provisions that erode the income tax base. Senator Long's proposal would introduce a comprehensive income concept into the Code, but it would not eliminate any existing tax benefits. The idea of setting up two tax systems side by side is attractive only if it is assumed that the one based on the comprehensive income concept will eventually be broadened to include all taxpayers without impairing the degree of progression now in effect.

The main objection to an increase in the standard deduction is that it would involve a substantial loss in revenue. For example, if the standard deduction were increased to 15 percent and the ceiling were removed, revenues would be reduced by at least $2.5 billion per year. This revenue loss would be sufficient to finance an average reduction in tax liabilities of about 5 percent, or to scale down the top bracket rates to a maximum of 30 percent.

The proposal to convert the standard deduction to a floor for the itemized deductions is consistent with the objective of broadening the tax base and lowering tax rates. However, it is to some extent ambiguous about the role of itemized deductions. Its basic conception is that the itemized deductions are hard to justify, yet it permits deductions only for those who have large expenditures of the type now permitted as itemized deductions.

On balance, equity would be better served by using the revenue lost through unnecessary personal deductions for reductions of the tax rates. The Congress has been slow to act because it hesitates to alienate those who benefit from the deductions. However, some progress has been made—most recently in 1964, when deductions for numerous state-local taxes and casualty losses of less than $100 were eliminated. Further scrutiny of the deductions may be expected when Congress again becomes interested in reducing income tax rates through the base-broadening approach.

The Family

During most of the history of the income tax, differentiation for family responsibilities was made among taxpayers through the personal exemptions. More recently, there has been a trend toward different tax rates to provide additional differentiation, particularly in the middle and higher tax brackets. In the United States and West Germany this has been accomplished by adoption of the principle of "income splitting" between husband and wife. In France, income splitting is permitted among all family members. Other countries achieve a similar objective by providing separate rate schedules for families of different size.

The adoption of income splitting in the United States arose out of the historical accident that eight states had community property laws which treated income as if divided equally between husband and wife. By virtue of several Supreme Court decisions, married couples residing in these eight states had been splitting their incomes and filing separate federal returns. Shortly after World War II, a number of other states enacted community property laws for the express purpose of obtaining the same advantage for their residents, and other states were threatening to follow suit. In an effort to restore geographic tax equality and to prevent wholesale disruption of local property laws and procedures, the Congress universalized income splitting in 1948.

The effect of income splitting is to reduce progression for married couples. The tax rates nominally begin at 14, 15, 16, and 17 percent on the first four $500 segments of taxable incomes and rise to 70 percent on the portion of taxable incomes above $100,000. A married couple with taxable income of $2,000 splits this income

CHART 4-5. Ratio of Federal Tax Saving from Income Splitting for Married Couples to Tax of Single Persons at 1966 Rates

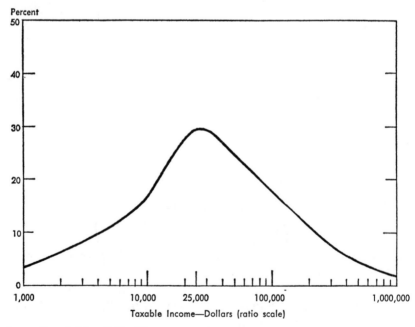

Source: Computed from Table 4-2.

and applies the first two rates to each half; without income splitting, the first four rates would apply to this income. Thus, whereas the nominal rate brackets cover taxable incomes up to $100,000, the actual rates for married couples extend to $200,000 (Table 4-2). The tax advantage rises from $5 for married couples with taxable income of $1,000 to $14,510 for couples with taxable incomes of $200,000 or more. In percentage terms, the tax advantage reaches a maximum of almost 30 percent at the $24,000 level (Chart 4-5).

The classic argument in favor of income splitting is that husbands and wives usually share their combined income equally. The largest portion of the family budget goes for consumption, and savings are ordinarily set aside for the children or for the enjoyment of all members of the family. Two conclusions follow from this view. First, married couples with the same combined income should pay the same tax irrespective of the legal division of income between them; second, the tax liabilities of married couples should be computed as if they were two single persons with their total income divided equally between them. The first conclusion is now firmly rooted in our tax law and seems to be almost universally accepted. It is the second conclusion on which opinions still differ.

The case for the sharing argument is most applicable to the economic circumstances of taxpayers in the lower income classes, where incomes are used almost entirely for the consumption of the family unit. At the top of the income scale, the major rationale of income taxation is to cut down on the economic power of the family unit, and the use made of income in these levels for family purposes is irrelevant for this purpose. Obviously, these objectives cannot be reconciled if income splitting is extended to all income brackets.

The practical effect of income splitting is to produce large differences in the tax burdens of single persons and married couples, differences which depend on the *rate of graduation* and not on the level of rates. Such differences are difficult to rationalize on any theoretical grounds. Moreover, it is difficult to justify treating single persons with families more harshly than married persons in similar circumstances. As a remedy, widows and widowers are permitted to continue to split their incomes for two years after the death of the spouse, and half the advantage of income splitting is given (through a separate rate schedule) to single persons who maintain a household for children or other dependents or who maintain a separate household for their parents. This is, of course, a makeshift arrangement which hardly deals with the problem satisfactorily. For example, a single taxpayer who supports an aunt in a different household receives no income splitting benefit; if he supports an aged mother he receives these benefits. There are growing pressures on the Congress to treat single persons more liberally—by liberalizing the head of household provision, increasing their exemptions, and other devices.

One of the major reasons for acceptance of the consequences of income splitting may well be the fact that personal exemptions do not provide enough differentiation among taxpayers in the middle and top brackets. Single persons, it is felt, should be taxed more heavily than married couples because they do not bear the costs and responsibilities of raising children. But income splitting for husband and wife clearly does not differentiate among taxpayers in this respect since the benefit is the same whether or not there are children.

The source of the difficulty in the income splitting approach is that differentiation of family size is made through the rate structure rather than through the personal exemptions. It would be possible to differentiate among taxpayer units by varying the personal exemptions with the size of income as well as the number of persons in the unit, with both a minimum and maximum. This procedure could be used to achieve almost any desired degree of differentiation among families, while avoiding most of the problems and anomalies produced by income splitting.

Despite the theoretical objections to income splitting, the provision seems to be fairly popular in the United States. Under these circumstances, Congress has not considered alternative methods of allowing for marital status and family size.

The Aged

A graduated tax on income after allowances for personal exemptions and extraordinary medical expenses automatically allows for special circumstances of the taxpayer. Beyond this, the federal income tax has been particularly solicitous of the special circumstances of the aged. Taxpayers over 65 years of age have an additional exemption of $600, pay no tax on their social security or railroad retirement pensions, and receive a tax credit on other retirement income (if their earnings are below $1,524). Until the end of 1966, they were also allowed to deduct all of their medical and dental expenses, instead of only the excess over 3 percent allowed other taxpayers. (The latter benefit was eliminated when the federal program of hospital and medical insurance for the aged was enacted.)

The exemptions for age and blindness, which amount to over $2 billion on taxable returns, were justified on the ground that these taxpayers have less ability to pay than other members of the community. The aged and the blind are in fact concentrated at the lower end of the income distribution. However, the personal exemptions and the graduated income tax rates were specifically designed to differentiate among the taxpaying abilities of individuals with different incomes. The aged and the blind would have a valid claim for an additional exemption if it could be shown that they are required to spend more out of a given income than other taxpayers. There are no data on the expenditures of the blind, but the available evidence indicates that a family headed by an individual over 65 years of age actually spends less than a family headed by a young person in the same income group. It has also been argued that the aged find it difficult to obtain employment and, therefore, have less resilience to financial reverses than other taxpayers. However, many other groups of taxpayers are handicapped in one way or another (for example, physical or mental disabilities and lack of opportunity to receive training), and it would be impractical to take account of all these individual differences under an income tax.

The omission of social security and railroad retirement benefits from the tax base dates from the 1930's, when incomes were so low that it did not matter whether these payments were subject to tax or not. As incomes grew and social security was extended to almost the entire population, it became clear that the tax exemption for these benefits is extremely generous. Contributions by employees do not account for more than 10 to 20 percent of their benefits at the present time, and will account for much less than 50 percent even when the systems mature. By contrast, up to 1954, recipients of pensions from other publicly administered retirement programs and from industrial pension plans were fully taxable on the portion of their benefits which exceeded their contributions. This discrimination was deeply resented by the recipients of taxable pensions. As a result, a credit against tax of 20 percent of the first $1,200 of retirement income (other than social security and railroad retirement benefits) was enacted in 1954. The maximum income subject to the credit was raised to $1,524 in 1962.

Aside from the fact that special relief of this sort is questionable, the objections to these provisions are that it gives more tax advantage to aged persons the higher their income and discriminates against those who continue to work. In principle, it would be fairer to remove the additional exemption for age and make all retirement income taxable (with an allowance, of course, for the portion contributed by the employee on which tax was paid). The additional revenue could be used to good advantage to raise social security benefits for all aged persons. However, these suggestions appear to be politically impractical at this time.

As a substitute, in 1963, President Kennedy proposed the replacement of the extra exemption for the aged and the retirement income credit by a credit of $300 against tax at all levels. To avoid double benefits the credit would have been offset by an amount equal to the taxpayer's bracket rate times one-half the social security and railroad retirement benefits (the portion presumed to be attributable to the employer's contribution). These changes would have reduced the taxes of persons over 65 by more than $300 million on balance.

These proposals were eliminated from the 1964 tax bill, despite the fact that the administration proposed a substantial net tax reduction in the interest of reform in this area. A number of interested groups complained that a few elderly persons would be subject to somewhat higher taxes even taking into account the rate reductions; and this was obviously intolerable in an atmosphere of tax reduction. Although the final bill reduced the retirement income credit from 20 to 15 percent (to keep it at the average rate applicable to the first $2,000 of taxable income), it retained all the special provisions for the aged and added three additional concessions: (1) capital gains attributable to the first $20,000 of sales price on the sale of a personal residence by an individual aged 65 years or over were given a one-time exemption from tax; (2) the limit on income subject to retirement credit on joint returns was raised 50 percent, from $1,524 to $2,286, where both husband and wife are over 65 (to allow for the 50 percent supplementary social security payment received by a husband on behalf of his wife); and (3) the cost of all medicine and drugs purchased by persons over 65 was made fully deductible (instead of the excess over 1 percent of income, applying to all taxpayers).

Earned Income

Personal exemptions for the taxpayer and his dependents and deductions for business and certain personal expenses are the only adjustments now made under the federal income tax in deriving the taxable income of an individual from his total income. One further adjustment was made in the United States in the years 1924-31 and 1934-43, and is still made in the United Kingdom and other countries. This is an allowance for incomes earned from work rather than through property ownership. The earned income allowance is justified by those who support it on the ground that earned incomes are not on a par with unearned incomes. It is also urged as a method of increasing work and management incentives.

THE EARNED INCOME ALLOWANCE. In the United States, the earned income allowance was granted in the form of a deduction that ranged from 10 percent to 25 percent of earned net income. In some years, the deduction was allowed for normal tax purposes only; in others, it was allowed for both normal tax and surtax. In all years, a certain minimum amount of income ($3,000 or $5,000) was presumed to be earned, whether it was earned or not, and the deduction was limited to a maximum ranging from $10,000 to $30,000. The tax value of the deduction was always small. It was never worth more than $496 for a family of two (in 1928-31); immediately before it was eliminated in 1944 as part of the wartime simplification program, the maximum value was $84. Two states—Maryland and Massachusetts—now tax investment income at higher rates than earned income.

The equity argument in favor of an earned income allowance is that one person with a given amount of earned income has less ability to pay than another with the same amount of unearned income. Several reasons are cited to support this view. First, recipients of

earned income do not have the benefit of an allowance for depreciation, and yet their productive capacities decline as they grow older
and are ultimately exhausted. Second, expenses of earning an income are not taken into account fully by the individual income tax
deductions. It was only recently (in 1964) that the law permitted a
deduction for nonreimbursed moving expenses in connection with a
new job. But such outlays as commuting expenses or carfares, the
additional cost of lunches and other meals away from home, office
clothing, laundry and dry cleaning, make the earned income recipients' costs higher than the costs of property income recipients.
Third, earning an income involves psychic costs and the sacrifice of
leisure, warranting special income tax relief.

While these arguments appear to have some merit, there are
good counterarguments. An earned income allowance is at best
only a rough method of correcting for the alleged inequities. To the
extent that there are inequities, they should be corrected directly
through adjustments either in the structure of the income tax or in
other government programs. For example, the depreciation argument is essentially a question involving old age insurance; if retirement benefits are inadequate, the best method of providing more
adequate benefits is to increase them. If there are special costs involved in earning incomes, income tax deductions should be liberalized. Finally, in regard to the view that earned income recipients
have greater psychic costs, it can be argued that accumulation of
capital which produces unearned incomes also involves costs and
sacrifices.

On balance, the case for an earned income allowance does not
seem overwhelming. Where it has been employed, the allowance
has been given to all people with incomes below a certain level and
denied to those with incomes above a certain level, whether income
is earned or not. This means that, in practice, there was little
differentiation between earned and unearned incomes. There is also
no basis for calculating the earned income element of the incomes
of self-employed persons (for example, farmers and professional
persons); in practice, this separation is made on the basis of an arbitrary formula. Moreover, a substantial earned income credit can be
very expensive. For example, if the rate on all earned incomes
were reduced by 10 percent below the ordinary rates, the annual

cost would be at least $5 billion. Further, an earned income credit is not simple, and it would complicate the tax return form.

DEDUCTION FOR SAVINGS OF SELF-EMPLOYED. Although the United States does not have an allowance for earned income, the law permits self-employed persons to deduct half of any savings set aside for a retirement plan up to 10 percent of their earned income or $2,500, whichever is less. This provision was adopted because it was felt that self-employed persons found it difficult to accumulate tax-free savings for purposes of retirement. By contrast, wage earners and salaried employees do not pay tax on the amounts contributed to qualified pension plans in their behalf by the employers. The savings deduction for the self-employed was intended as an analogous provision for them, since they cannot participate in such plans.

When originally proposed, the plan did not have an upper limit to the allowable deduction for these contributions, and also granted capital gains treatment for withdrawals from the retirement funds in which the savings were invested. As a result, it was regarded as a device to avoid taxes rather than to correct an inequity. In its present form, the tax benefits are limited and the amount of the deduction has been relatively small. In 1963, 29,000 individuals reported $19.5 million for this deduction.

ALLOWANCE FOR WORKING WIVES. Wholly apart from the treatment of earned income generally is the difficult question of taxing the incomes of working wives. A special exemption is given to working wives under the British income tax system. In the United States, except for an allowance of up to $15 against the normal tax in 1944 and 1945, a working wife credit or deduction has never been granted.

Working wife allowances are supported partly on incentive grounds and partly on equity grounds. The incentive argument is that, if the husband already earns income, the wife's earnings are taxable beginning at the first dollar. The higher the income of the husband, the higher is the marginal rate of tax on the additional income from the wife's employment. This high rate plus the additional costs of operating the household may deter some wives from seeking employment.

The equity argument is that the ability to pay taxes is not com-

mensurate with the actual earnings of the working wife. The services which a wife performs at home (for example, housework,
care of children) are ordinarily performed by domestic servants if
she obtains gainful employment; moreover, clothing, laundry bills,
and food are usually more expensive if the wife works and the family purchases are, in general, less efficient. It is not considered fair
that all of the additional earnings of the wife be subjected to tax
since they are partly absorbed in meeting such extra expenses.

A deduction for working wives which would be generous
enough to encourage many to enter the labor market would be fairly costly. For example, if a deduction were allowed for 25 percent
of the earned income of women with family responsibilities, revenues would probably be reduced by about $2 billion annually. Most
of this benefit would go to women who are already at work, so
that the major part of the revenue loss would have little incentive
effect. A relatively small deduction—say, 10 percent of earned income with a limit of perhaps $2,000—would cost about $500 million per year.

Capital Gains and Losses

An economic definition of income would include all capital
gains in taxable income as they accrued each year. This method is
impractical for three reasons: first, values of many types of property
cannot be estimated with sufficient accuracy to provide a basis for
taxation; second, most people would regard it as inequitable to pay
tax unless income had actually been realized; and third, taxation of
accruals might force liquidation of assets to pay the tax. Thus, capital gains are included in taxable income only when realized.

The United States has taxed the capital gains of individuals since
it first taxed income, but this has not been the practice in many
other countries. Realized capital gains were originally taxed as ordinary incomes, but they have been subject to preferentially low
rates since 1921. The provisions applying to such gains changed frequently during the 1920's and 1930's, but were stabilized beginning
in 1942. In general, capital gains on assets held for periods longer
than six months are subject to half the rates on ordinary income, up
to a maximum of 25 percent. Gains on the sale of owner-occupied
houses are exempt if they are applied to the purchase of a new

home within twelve months. For persons over 65, gains on the sale of a house are entirely exempt up to $20,000 of the sales price.

The treatment of capital gains is a compromise among conflicting objectives. From the standpoint of equity, it is well established that capital gains should be taken into account in determining personal tax liability. Moreover, preferential treatment of capital gains encourages the conversion of ordinary income into capital gains. Preferential legislation and business manipulation of this sort distort patterns of investment and discredit income taxation. The low capital gains rates are now provided for patent royalties, coal and iron ore royalties, income from livestock, income from the sale of unharvested crops, and real estate investments. The amount of ordinary income thus converted into capital gains is unknown, but a great deal of effort goes into this activity.

In addition to the overwhelming rate advantage, the law permits capital gains to escape income tax completely if transferred from one generation to another through bequests. In the case of gifts, the gain is taxed only if the assets are later sold by the recipient. The result is that increases in the value of securities and real estate held in wealthy families may never be subject to income tax. Suppose a stock is now selling for $100 per share. An investor who bought 100,000 shares at $50 per share has a capital gain of $5,000,000. If he sold the stock, he would pay a capital gains tax of 25 percent, or $1,250,000. If he bequeathed the stock to his children, no tax would ever be paid on the $5,000,000 gain.

On the other hand, bunching of capital gains in years of realization requires some moderation of the rates or some provision to average them over a period of years. Full taxation of capital gains is also criticized because it might have a substantial "locking-in" effect on investors and reduce the mobility of capital. It is also argued that preferential treatment of capital gains helps to stimulate a higher rate of economic growth by increasing the attractiveness of investment generally, and of risky investments in particular.

The "bunching problem" that would arise with full taxation of capital gains could easily be handled either by prorating capital gains over the length of time the asset was held or by adopting a general averaging system which would apply to other types of income as well as capital gains. However, unless the marginal rates were reduced drastically, the tax might still discourage the transfer of assets. Part of the difficulty is that adherence to the realization principle permits capital gains to be transferred tax free either by gift or at death. The solution to this problem is to treat capital gains as if constructively realized at gift or at death, with an averaging provision to allow for spreading of the gains over a period of years. (This method was proposed by President Kennedy in 1963, but was not approved by Congress.) Under such a system, the only advantage taxpayers would have from postponing the realization of capital gains would be the accumulation of interest on the tax postponed. Unless the assets were held for many years, this advantage would be small compared to the advantage of the tax exemption accorded to gains transferred at death; in any event the net advantage is small because the interest on the tax postponed would be subject to income tax when the assets are transferred. Under these circumstances, the incentive to hold on to gains indefinitely for tax considerations alone would be very greatly reduced.

In the quest to reconcile equity and economic objectives in the taxation of capital gains, tax experts differ as to the best approach. A sizeable number believes that realized capital gains and those transferred by gift or at death should be taxed in full, with a provision for averaging either over the period during which the asset was held or over an arbitrary but lengthy period. Some believe that present arrangements may be the best that can be devised, while others insist that the capital gains rates are still too high. Most experts agree that there is little justification for granting preferential treatment (if retained) to income that is not genuine capital gain.

The preferential rates apply to capital gains on assets which have been held for six months or longer. This "holding period" has been criticized as being both too long and too short. Investor groups urge that the holding period be reduced to three months and some even recommend that it be eliminated entirely, maintaining that the resulting additional security transactions would increase capital gains tax revenues. On the other hand, in an annual income tax, there is no logical equity reason for reducing the tax rate on incomes earned in less than a year. There has been disagreement on this point since the six-month holding period was enacted in 1942.

In principle, capital losses should be deductible in full against either capital gains or ordinary income. However, when gains and losses are recognized only upon realization, taxpayers can easily time their sales so as to take losses promptly when they occur and to postpone gains for as long a period as possible. There is no effective method of avoiding this type of asymmetry under our system of capital gains taxation. The stopgap used in the United States is to limit the deduction of losses. From 1942 through 1963, individuals were allowed to offset their capital losses against capital gains plus $1,000 of ordinary income in the year of realization and in the five subsequent years. In 1964, the loss offset up to $1,000 of ordinary income was extended to an indefinite period. The annual limit on the amount of the offset is perhaps most harmful to small investors, who are less likely than those in the higher brackets to have gains from which to subtract their losses. The only solution to this problem is a pragmatic one that is reasonably liberal for the small investor without opening the door to widespread abuse of the provision and large revenue losses.

State and Local Government Bond Interest

Interest received from state and local government bonds has been exempt from income tax ever since its enactment in 1913. The tax exemption has been criticized by Secretaries of the Treasury, tax experts, and others who believe that it is inequitable, reduces risk investment by high bracket taxpayers, and costs an excessive amount to the federal government. Interest rates on state-local bonds have increased as state-local debt has risen in recent years, and the relative advantage of the exemption to the top income classes has greatly increased. Proponents of the exemption argue that its elimination would make state-local borrowing costs prohibitive and that it would be unwise to impair the borrowing ability of these units of government in view of their mounting needs. Bills to remove the exemption have reached a vote in Congress six times, but each time they have been defeated.

By discriminating between income from municipals and from other securities, and by giving an advantage to investors in the high income brackets, the exemption violates the generally accepted principles that an income tax should apply equally to equal incomes and should be progressive. It also reduces investment in productive enterprises by diverting risk or venture capital from the private sector. It distorts the allocation of resources within the private sector, and between the public and private sectors when state and local governments issue tax-exempt securities to finance such "business" enterprises as public utilities and housing developments, or to subsidize the growth of local industry. (Even many who favor the exemption agree that the use of so-called industrial development bonds to build tax-exempt facilities for private firms should be halted.)

Further, the exemption is an inefficient type of subsidy. Empirical studies suggest that the saving in interest payments by state and local governments is less than half the revenue loss to the federal government. There are less costly ways to assist or subsidize capital outlays by state and local governments. There are also more equitable methods, since governmental units benefit more from the exemption to the extent that they issue more debt, rather than on the basis of need.

Interest costs of state and local governments would rise if the exemption were removed. Municipals are more difficult to market than corporates and other securities. Many issues are too small to appeal to large institutional buyers. Moreover, lack of information about the finances of small units of local government discourages some investors. Thus, if the municipals were fully taxable, they would have to bear higher interest rates than corporate bonds of comparable quality. This would probably discourage borrowing in some localities, and thus reduce capital expenditures for public purposes. If total outlays were to rise in some areas, state and local taxes would ultimately be increased to meet higher interest charges. Since local taxes tend to be regressive, a greater burden might fall on the lower income groups. It has also been argued that the heavier financial burden on state and local governments added to existing unmet needs for public facilities would intensify pressure for federal aid, bring greater federal participation in local affairs, and further reduce the fiscal independence of states and localities.

Because opponents of the exemption concede that some desirable investment in social capital might be curtailed if the localities had to pay higher interest charges, they have often coupled suggestions for abolishing the exemption with proposals to provide alternative federal subsidies. These have generally taken one of two forms: (1) subsidies tied to state and local borrowing (for example, the payment of a portion of the interest on state-local debt by the federal government) as a *quid pro quo* for giving up the exemption, or (2) subsidies tied to capital outlays rather than borrowing and thus not allocated strictly according to exemption benefits lost.

Proposals to remove the exemption have usually been limited to new issues only. This approach reflects the belief that taxing outstanding securities would be a breach of faith by the federal government, causing capital losses and the inequitable application of taxes to holders of existing securities.

Some lawyers have argued that taxing state-local bond interest is unconstitutional, whether the proposal is to apply the tax to new issues only or to existing as well as new issues. The majority opinion seems to be that there is no constitutional bar to taxing state-local bond interest if Congress wished to do so.

The major problem is political. If the tax exemption is replaced by a generous subsidy, many people fear an unhealthy increase in federal control over state and local fiscal affairs. Even the possibility of more federal control is often sufficient argument for some to oppose removal of the exemption. In this view, inefficiencies or tax inequities arising from the exemption are trivial compared to the dangers of more centralization of fiscal activity. Others argue that efficiency and tax equity are important enough to justify exploring the possibility of substituting for the tax exemption an alternative formula which would not involve greater federal control.

These differing views are irreconcilable, and it seems clear that modification of the exemption would not stand a chance of adoption unless an alternative method of compensation for state and local governments could be devised which would not involve any federal participation, let alone interference, in the purposes for which state-local borrowing is undertaken.

Income Averaging

The use of an annual accounting period combined with progressive income taxes results in a heavier tax burden on fluctuating incomes than on an equal amount of income distributed evenly over the years. For example, a single taxpayer who has a taxable income of $25,000 in each of two successive years pays a total tax of $17,060 in the two years. If he received $50,000 one year and nothing the next, his tax would be $22,590.

This type of discrimination is hard to defend on either equity or economic grounds. Taxpayers usually do not and cannot arrange their business and personal affairs to conform with the calendar. Annual income fluctuations are frequently beyond the control of the taxpayer, yet the individual is taxed as if twelve months were a suitable horizon for decision making. In addition, in the absence of averaging, there are great pressures for moderating the impact of the graduated rates on fluctuating incomes by lowering the rates applicable to them. As already indicated, reduced rates on capital gains have been justified on this basis although the rate reductions for such gains more than compensate for the lack of averaging.

There is general agreement on the need for averaging, but the roadblock has always been the administrative problem. Keeping an accurate account for a number of years is difficult for the government as well as for the taxpayer. It was felt, therefore, that it would be desirable to start modestly.

A start was made under the Revenue Act of 1964 which permits averaging income over a five-year period where the income in the current year exceeds the average of the four prior years by more than one-third, and this excess is more than $3,000. The provision is available to taxpayers who have been self-supporting for five years. The averaging technique is (a) to compute a tentative tax on one-fifth of the "averageable income," and (b) to multiply the tentative tax by five. The restriction of averaging to those who have an *increase* in income eliminated from the averaging system the millions of persons who have a sharp reduction in their income at retirement. It would be desirable to provide averaging for those who have reductions in income, if a suitable method of handling retired persons can be devised. The 1964 provision was nevertheless a step in the right direction. Doubtless, the scope of the system, as well as the method of averaging, will be revised as experience is gained with the present limited provision.

Summary

The individual income tax—the most important tax in the federal tax structure—is widely regarded as the fairest method of raising government revenues. Its yield expands or contracts more rapidly than personal income during a business cycle, thus imparting built-in flexibility to the revenue side of the federal budget. The tax is less burdensome on consumption and more burdensome on saving than an equal-yield consumption or expenditure tax. Its effect on work and investment incentives is unclear. There is no evidence to support the contention that the income tax significantly retards growth. The nation has grown at a satisfactory rate during most of the period since the income tax was enacted.

Numerous unsettled problems remain regarding some of the major features of the individual income tax. These include the treatment of the family, the aged, earned income, special deductions for personal expenditures, capital gains and losses, tax-exempt interest, and the appropriate length of the tax accounting period. Even in its present form, however, the individual income tax continues to be the best tax ever devised. Further improvement by broadening the tax base and lowering the tax rates would pay handsome dividends in still greater equity and better economic performance.

CHAPTER 5

The Corporation Income Tax

THE CORPORATION INCOME TAX was enacted in 1909, four years before the introduction of the individual income tax. To avoid a constitutional issue, Congress levied the tax as an excise on the privilege of doing business as a corporation. The law was challenged, but the Supreme Court upheld the authority of the federal government to impose such a tax and ruled that the privilege of doing corporate business could be measured by the corporation's profits.

Since 1909, the corporation income tax has been a mainstay of the federal tax system. It produced more revenue than the individual income tax in seventeen out of the twenty-eight years prior to 1941, when the latter was greatly expanded as a source of wartime revenue. In the postwar period, corporation income tax revenues have been second only to those of the individual income tax, accounting for 20 to 22 percent of federal cash receipts in recent years. Like the individual income tax, a tax on corporation profits is likely to be a major federal revenue source for a long time to come.

A special tax on the corporate form of doing business is considered appropriate because corporations enjoy special privileges and benefits.These include perpetual life, limited liability of shareholders, liquidity of ownership through marketability of shares, growth through retention of earnings, and possibilities of intercorporate

98

affiliations. Moreover, the modern corporation—particularly the large "public" corporation in which management and ownership are separated—generates income which nobody may claim for personal use. The growth of the corporate sector could not have taken place if the corporation had not been endowed with these valuable privileges. The Supreme Court's acceptance of the constitutionality of the corporation income tax was based on the view that the corporation owes its life, rights, and power to the government.

Whether or not this basic rationale is accepted, the corporation income tax is needed to safeguard the individual income tax. If corporate incomes were not subject to tax, individuals could avoid the individual income tax by accumulating income in corporations. Short of taxing shareholders on their share of corporate incomes whether or not they are distributed (a method which seems attractive in theory but is impractical for all but closely held corporations), the most practical way to protect the individual income tax is to impose a separate tax on corporate incomes. Of course, the existence of two separate taxes side by side creates other problems; these will be discussed at some length in this chapter.

Despite its prominence in the federal revenue system, the corporation income tax is the subject of considerable controversy. In the first place, there is probably less agreement about who really pays the corporation income tax than there is about any other tax. Some believe that the tax is borne by the corporations and, hence, by their stockholders. Others argue that the tax is passed on to consumers through higher prices. Still others suggest that the tax may be shifted back to the workers in lower wages. A substantial group believes that it is borne by all three groups—stockholders, consumers, and wage earners—in varying proportions. This uncertainty regarding the incidence of the tax makes strange bedfellows of individuals holding diametrically opposed views, and often puts them in inconsistent positions. Some staunch opponents of a sales tax vigorously support the corporation income tax even though they believe it is shifted to the consumer; while many who believe that the corporation tax is "just another cost" (and is, therefore, shifted) demand reduction of the corporation income tax and substitution of some form of consumption tax for all or part of it.

Second, the proper relation between the individual and corporation income taxes has never been settled. At various times, dividends have been allowed as a credit or deduction in computing the tax on individual income. Today, individuals are allowed a $100 exclusion for dividends which is intended to relieve the small shareholder from paying both individual and corporation income taxes on his dividends. The present situation is makeshift and satisfies few people.

A third set of issues has to do with the impact of the corporation tax on the corporate sector and on the economy in general. It has been argued that the tax curtails business investment and thus reduces the nation's growth rate. Since interest paid is deductible in computing taxable corporation profits while dividends paid are not, the tax is said to favor debt over equity financing. Some question the desirability of a tax that discourages the corporate form of business. Others believe, however, that alternative tax sources yielding the same revenue would be much more harmful to the economy.

Characteristics of the Tax

Since the corporation income tax is a tax on business, many of the refinements required in the computation of taxable income of individuals do not arise. For example, with the exception of the deduction for charitable contributions, the deductions allowed under the corporation income tax are confined to expenses incurred in doing business. State-local bond interest is exempt from the corporation income tax as well as the individual income tax, and the treatment of capital gains and losses is similar (though not identical). Corporations are also required to pay taxes as profits are earned.

The Tax Base

The corporation income tax is a complicated instrument because it must be applied to a wide variety of organizations doing business in the corporate form or in a form that closely resembles a corporation. The major features will be discussed in a later section of the chapter; but at this point, a number of the significant provisions may be noted.

1. As in the case of individuals, capital gains realized on assets held more than six months are taxed at a maximum rate of 25 percent. However, the treatment of losses is different. Whereas in-

dividuals may deduct up to $1,000 of net capital losses against ordinary income, corporations are allowed to offset capital losses only against capital gains. The remaining capital losses may be carried forward for five years to be offset against capital gains in future years.

2. Net operating losses may be carried back and offset against taxable income of the three preceding years. If the income in these years is not sufficient, the remaining losses may be carried forward for five years. In effect, this provides a nine-year period for offsetting losses against gains.

3. Generous provision is made for recovery of capital. In the case of plant and equipment, the original cost may be amortized over the useful life of the asset. Formerly, the law in effect limited the rate of amortization for most corporations to the straight-line method (that is, the cost was allocated evenly over the life of the asset). New methods adopted in 1954 permit a faster rate of depreciation in the early years. In addition to depreciation, an investment credit of 7 percent against tax liability was enacted in 1962 for purchases of new equipment (buildings are not entitled to the credit). For minerals and gas and oil, the law allows deductions for exploration, discovery, and depletion which often exceed the cost of the mine or oil or gas fields.

4. All current outlays for research and development may be deducted in full in the year they are made. Taxpayers may elect to capitalize such expenditures and, if regular depreciation cannot be used because the useful life cannot be determined, the expenditures may be written off over a period of five years.

The provisions for net operating losses, recovery of capital, and research and development expenses (items 2, 3, and 4 above) are also available to individuals and partnerships under the individual income tax.

5. Intercorporate dividends paid by one corporation to another are subject to tax at a relatively low rate. Corporations are allowed to deduct 85 percent of the dividends they receive from other domestic corporations. This means that intercorporate dividends are subject to an extra tax of 7.2 percent (the regular 48 percent rate multiplied by 15 percent). The tax on intercorporate dividends is waived, however, if the two corporations are members of a group of affiliated corporations claiming only one surtax exemption. These

provisions encourage the use of consolidated returns on the presumption that only in this way can the true net income of the affiliated group be determined.

6.   Corporations are subject to U.S. tax on foreign as well as domestic income. Income received from foreign branches is included in the corporation's tax return in the year it is earned. If the corporation operates through a subsidiary, foreign earnings are subject to tax when they are distributed to the U.S. parent corporation as dividends. However, credit against the domestic tax is allowed for foreign income taxes paid on earnings and dividends received from abroad. A reduction in the corporation income tax of 14 percentage points is granted to domestic trade corporations conducting 95 percent of their business outside the United States, but in the western hemisphere.

7.   Corporations with no more than ten shareholders may elect to be treated as partnerships for tax purposes. Such shareholders are subject to individual income tax on the entire earnings of the corporation, whether or not distributed, and may deduct any losses from other personal incomes. In 1963, 138,000 small corporations reporting profits of $1.2 billion and deficits of $438 million elected this treatment.

8.   Religious, scientific, and charitable organizations, trade associations, labor unions, and fraternal organizations are exempt from the corporation income tax, but the tax does apply to the "unrelated business income" of most of these organizations. Cooperatives are subject to special provisions designed to tax their earnings at least once under the individual or corporation income tax, but the revenue collected from them is small. Investment funds distributing at least 90 percent of their dividends and realized capital gains to their shareholders are not taxable. Mutual financial institutions, including saving and loan associations, mutual savings banks, and life insurance companies are taxed, but they are permitted to accumulate substantial tax-free reserves because of their fiduciary character.

Tax Rates

Since corporations do not have "ability to pay" in the same sense as individuals, the corporation income tax is levied at a flat rate on most corporate incomes. A lower rate is applied to the first

$25,000 as a concession to small business; the remainder is taxed at one rate. Today, the corporate tax consists of a 22 percent normal tax and a 26 percent surtax, with an exemption of $25,000 for the surtax only. Thus, the combined rates are 22 percent on the first $25,000 and 48 percent on the excess over $25,000. Roughly 88 percent of the corporate taxable income is subject to the 48 percent rate (Appendix Table B-9).

Tax Payment

The provision for current tax payment applied only to individuals when it was enacted during World War II. Corporations continued to pay their tax, as they did from the beginning: in four installments in the year following the tax year. This state of affairs continued until 1950 when payments were gradually shifted over a period of five years to two installments to be paid in the first six months of the year following the tax year.

Further acceleration of corporation tax payments was legislated in 1954. After another transition of five years, corporations were required to pay half of their estimated tax over $100,000 in September and December of the tax year, and the remaining liability in two installments in March and June of the following year.

The final steps to place corporations on a current payment basis were taken in 1964 and 1966. After an additional transition of four years (originally seven years under the 1964 legislation), corporations will pay their estimated tax (in excess of $100,000) in four installments in the current year. By 1967, large corporations and individuals filing declarations of estimated tax will be paying tax on the same time schedule (Appendix Table C-13).

Shifting and Incidence of the Tax

There is no more controversial issue in taxation than the question: *Who bears the corporation income tax?* On this question, economists and businessmen alike differ among themselves. The following quotations are representative of these divergent views:

> The initial or short-run incidence of the corporate income tax seems to be largely on corporations and their stockholders. . . . There seems to be little foundation for the belief that a large part of the corporate tax comes out of wages or is passed on to consumers in the same way

that a selective excise [tax] tends to be shifted to the buyers. (Richard Goode, *The Corporation Income Tax,* John Wiley, 1951, pp. 71-72.)

The corporation profit tax is almost entirely shifted, the government simply uses the corporation as a tax collector. (Kenneth E. Boulding, *The Organizational Revolution,* Harper and Brothers, 1953, p. 277.)

Corporate taxes are simply costs, and the method of their assessment does not change this fact. Costs must be paid by the public in prices, and corporate taxes are thus in effect concealed taxes. (E. M. Voorhees, chairman of the finance committee, U.S. Steel Corporation, reported in the *New York Times,* Oct. 10, 1943.)

The observation is frequently made that because in the long run the [corporate] tax tends to be included in the price of the product, it is to this extent borne by consumers. This observation misconstrues the nature of the tax. Fundamentally, it is a tax on a factor of production: corporate equity capital. (Arnold C. Harberger, "The Corporation Income Tax, An Empirical Appraisal," *Tax Revision Compendium,* House Ways and Means Committee, Vol. 7, 1959, p. 241.)

. . . an increase in the [corporate] tax is shifted fully through short-run adjustments to prevent a decline in the net rate of return [on corporate investment], and . . . these adjustments are maintained subsequently. (Marian Krzyzaniak and Richard A. Musgrave, *The Shifting of the Corporation Income Tax,* Johns Hopkins Press, 1963, p. 65.)

Unfortunately, economics has not yet provided a scientific basis for accepting or rejecting one side or the other. This section presents the logic of each view and summarizes the evidence.

The Shifting Mechanism

One reason for the sharply divergent views is that the opponents frequently do not refer to the same type of shifting. It is important to distinguish between short- and long-run shifting and the mechanisms through which they operate. The "short-run" is defined by economists as a period which is too short for firms to adjust their capital to changing demand and supply conditions. The "long-run" is a period in which capital can be adjusted.

SHORT-RUN SHIFTING. The classical view in economics is that the corporation income tax cannot be shifted in the short run. The argument is as follows: all business firms, whether they are competitive or monopolistic, seek to maximize net profits. This maximum occurs when output and prices are set at the point where the cost of producing an additional unit is exactly equal to the additional revenue obtained from the sale of that unit. In the short run, a corporation income tax should make no difference in this decision. The output and price which maximized the firm's profits before the tax will continue to maximize profits after the tax is imposed. (This follows from simple arithmetic. If a series of figures is reduced by the same percentage, the figure that was highest before will still be the highest after the percentage reduction is made.)

The argument against this view is that today's markets are neither characterized by perfect competition nor by monopoly; instead, they exhibit considerable imperfection and mutual interdependence or oligopoly. In such markets, business firms may set their prices at the level which covers their full costs *plus* a margin for profits. Alternatively, the firms are described as aiming at an after-tax target rate of return on invested capital. Under the cost-plus behavior, the firm treats the tax as an element of cost and raises its price to recover the tax. Similarly, if the firm's objective is the after-tax target rate of return, imposition of a tax or an increase in the tax rate—by reducing the rate of return on invested capital—will have to be accounted for in making output and price decisions. To preserve the target rate of return, the tax must be shifted forward to consumers or backward to the workers, or is partly shifted forward and partly backward.

It is also argued that the economists' models are irrelevant in most markets where one or a few large firms exercise a substantial degree of leadership. In such markets, efficient producers raise their prices to recover the tax and the tax merely forms an "umbrella" that permits less efficient or marginal producers to survive.

When business managers are asked about their pricing policies, they often assert that they shift the corporation income tax. However, there is little evidence to support this position. Economists have debated whether firms actually behave in this way, but have not reached a consensus.

Even if this behavior on the part of business firms is accepted, some doubts must be expressed about their ability fully to shift the corporation income tax in the short run. In the first place, the tax depends on the outcome of business operations during an entire year. The businessman can only guess the ratio of the tax to his gross receipts and it is hard to conceive of his setting a price which would recover the precise amount of tax he will eventually pay. (If this were possible, there would be some instances of firms shifting more than 100 percent of the tax, but few economists believe that overshifting does in fact occur.)

Second, the businessman knows that any attempt on his part to recover the corporation income tax through higher prices (or lower wages) may not be followed by other firms. Some firms make no profit and thus pay no tax; in other firms, the ratio of tax to gross receipts is different. In multi-product firms, the producer has very little basis for judging the ratio of tax to gross receipts for each product. All these possibilities increase the uncertainty of response by other firms and make the attempt to shift part or all of the corporation income tax hazardous.

LONG-RUN SHIFTING. Long-run shifting of the corporation income tax has always been regarded as a distinct possibility by economists. The mechanism is through the reduction of corporate equity investment. The tax may discourage the use of capital altogether, or encourage investment in debt-intensive industries (for example, real estate) and unincorporated enterprises. The result will be a smaller supply of corporate products, unless the reduction in equity investment is offset by an increase in borrowing.

From the standpoint of the corporation, the burden of the corporation income tax is quite different under long-run shifting than it would be if the tax were shifted in the short run. Short-run shifting means that net after-tax rates of return are maintained at the levels prevailing before the tax; the burden of the tax falls on consumers or wage earners. If the tax is shifted in the long run, net after-tax rates of return are depressed and the amount of corporate investment is reduced. After-tax rates of return will tend to be equalized with those in the noncorporate sector, but in the process, corporate capital and output have been permanently reduced. Thus, in long-run shifting, the burden of the tax falls on the owners of capital.

The Evidence

The evidence on shifting of the corporation income tax is inconclusive. The data on short-run shifting do not permit a clear de-

CHART 5-1. Percentage of Business Income Originating in the Corporate Sector, 1929–64

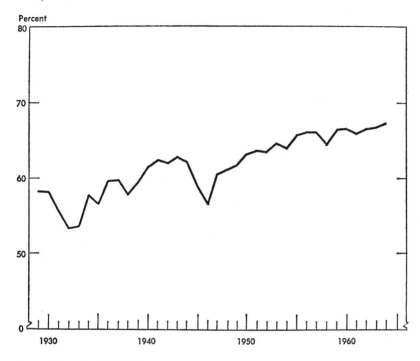

Source: Appendix Table C-14.

Note: Business income is national income originating in business enterprises.

termination of the factors affecting price decisions: different authors examining the same set of facts have come to diametrically opposite conclusions.

With respect to the long run, there is evidence, first, that unincorporated business has not grown at the expense of incorporated business. Corporations accounted for 58 percent of the national income originating in the business sector in 1929, 61 percent in 1948, and 67 percent in 1964 (Chart 5-1). Much of the increase comes from the relative decline of industries, particularly farming, in which corporations are not important; but, even in the rest of the economy, there is no indication of a shift away from the corporate form of organization. The advantages of doing business in the corporate form far outweigh whatever deterrent effects the corporation tax might have on corporate investment.

Beyond this, the data are conflicting. On the one hand, rates of return reported by corporations *after tax* now seem to be about the same as after-tax rates of return in the late 1920's when the corporation income tax was much lower. After-tax rates of return on equity capital in manufacturing were 7.8 percent in 1927-29, 8.7 percent in 1953-56, and 6.9 percent in 1957-61. On total capital (including debt), the returns were 7.8 percent, 7.8 percent, and 6.5 percent, respectively (Table 5-1). Before-tax rates of return have been 50 to 100 percent higher in the 1950's than in the late 1920's.

TABLE 5-1. Rates of Return and Debt-Capital Ratio, Manufacturing Corporations, Selected Years, 1927–61

(*In percentages*)

Item	1927–29	1936–39	1953–56	1957–61
Return on equity[a]				
Before tax	8.8	7.8	18.4	14.1
After tax	7.8	6.4	8.7	6.9
Return on total capital[ab]				
Before tax	8.7	7.3	15.6	12.2
After tax	7.8	6.2	7.8	6.5
Ratio of debt to total capital[c]	15.2	15.0	19.0	20.5
General corporation tax rate[d]	12.2	17.0	52.0	52.0

Source: Appendix Table C-15.
[a] Equity and debt capital are averages of book values for the beginning and end of the year.
[b] Profits plus interest paid as a percentage of total capital.
[c] End of year.
[d] Statutory rate of federal corporation income tax applicable to large corporations (average of annual figures).

On the other hand, the share of property income before tax (profits, interest, and capital consumption allowances) in corporate gross product changed little over the same period (Chart 5-2). Thus, corporations have been able to increase their before-tax profits enough to avoid a reduction in the after-tax return, without increasing their share of income in the corporate sector. These observations suggest that corporations have not increased rates of return before tax by marking up prices or by lowering wages, but by making more efficient use of their capital. However, what might have occurred in the absence of the tax is unknown, so that its long-run effect remains unclear.

CHART 5-2. Property Income Share in Corporate Gross Product Less Indirect Taxes, 1922–29 and 1948–65

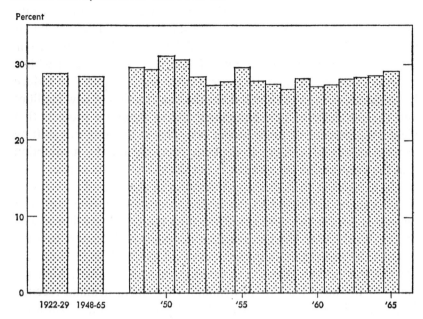

Sources: 1922–29: Worksheets of Office of Business Economics; 1948–64: Appendix Table C-14; 1965: *Survey of Current Business,* February 1966.

Note: Property income includes corporate profits before taxes, interest, and capital consumption allowances.

Economic Issues

The corporation income tax has been subject to a continuous barrage of criticism on economic grounds. The most critical issues have been its effect on: (1) investment and saving; (2) equity and debt finance; (3) resource allocation; (4) built-in flexibility of the tax system; and (5) the balance of payments. The charges and countercharges reflect different assumptions regarding who bears the tax, and the inherent difficulty of separating the effect of taxation from other factors.

Investment and Saving

The corporation income tax may affect investment in one of two ways: through investment incentives and through the availability of funds for investment.

INVESTMENT INCENTIVES. New investments will be undertaken by corporations if they promise to yield a satisfactory rate of return *after tax*. The higher the corporation tax, the higher the pre-tax rate of return must be to preserve the after-tax return. To be equally attractive, an investment which promised 10 percent in the absence of the tax must yield a pre-tax rate of return of 19.2 percent with a tax rate of 48 percent. If 10 percent after tax is required to induce investments, corporations will defer the construction of new facilities and the purchase of new equipment unless there are projects that yield 19.2 percent or more before tax. This is the long-run shifting process discussed earlier: it depends crucially on the assumption that the corporation income tax is not shifted in the short run.

Is it possible to detect any reduction in the rate of investment which can be attributed to the high corporation income tax? The answer is no, for two reasons. First, high tax rates were introduced during World War II when wartime demands and support by government helped maintain investment at a high level. In the immediate postwar period, the rate of investment was extremely high because of the huge backlog of demand. Investment demand receded in the late 1950's, but this is attributed primarily to the slowdown in the rate of economic growth.

Second, although the corporation tax rate has been kept at a high level in the last two decades, part of its adverse effect on investment has been cushioned by substantial increases in investment allowances. Whereas straight-line depreciation was the rule before World War II, regulations since 1954 have allowed more liberal depreciation methods. In addition, the 1962 Act introduced an investment credit for the first time. The effect of these changes may be illustrated by the following figures: in 1954, the corporation tax amounted to 32.8 percent of corporation profits before tax and before capital consumption allowances; it was reduced to 30.5 percent in 1959 and 27.8 percent in 1963 (Table 5-2). This five-point reduction in the effective rate occurred during a period when the general corporation income tax rate remained at 52 percent.

AVAILABILITY OF FUNDS. All other things being equal, the corporation income tax may be expected to reduce the amount of corporate funds available for investment, but other factors have been operating to maintain internal corporate funds at a high level. The rise

TABLE 5-2. Comparison of the General Corporation Income Tax Rate and Effective Rate of Federal Taxes on Corporation Profits Before Tax and Before Capital Consumption Allowances, 1946–65[a]

Year	General Corporation Tax Rate (Percentages)	Corporation Profits Before Tax and Capital Consumption Allowances[a] (Billions of dollars)	Federal Corporation Taxes	
			Amount (Billions of dollars)	Percentage of Profits Before Tax and Allowances
1946	38	28.9	8.6	29.8
1947	38	36.6	10.7	29.2
1948	38	41.4	11.8	28.5
1949	38	36.0	9.8	27.2
1950	42	50.4	17.0	33.7
1951	50.75	53.1	21.5[b]	40.5
1952	52	49.3	18.5[b]	37.5
1953	52	52.7	19.5[b]	37.0
1954	52	51.9	17.0	32.8
1955	52	64.4	20.6	32.0
1956	52	65.9	20.6	31.3
1957	52	66.1	20.2	30.6
1958	52	61.6	18.0	29.2
1959	52	73.8	22.5	30.5
1960	52	72.7	21.7	29.8
1961	52	74.2	21.8	29.4
1962	52	82.9	22.7	27.4
1963	52	88.0	24.5	27.8
1964	50	95.7	26.0	27.2
1965[p]	48	107.2	28.3	26.4

[p] Preliminary.
    Sources: 1946–64: *Survey of Current Business,* August 1965, p. 37, and September 1965, p. 52; 1965: *Survey of Current Business,* February 1966, p. 18.
  [a] Excludes corporation profits and capital consumption allowances originating in the rest of the world.
  [b] Includes excess profits tax liability.

in the corporation tax has been accompanied by a much larger rise in high-bracket individual income tax rates. Recent studies indicate that these high individual rates and the preferential rate on capital gains have stimulated a higher rate of corporation retentions (that is, lower dividend pay-out rates) than in earlier years. In addition, the generous depreciation allowances enacted in recent years have enabled corporations to set aside large amounts for investment purposes.

Since the end of World War II, dividends have averaged 25 percent of the cash flow of corporations, as compared with about

45 percent in the late 1920's (Appendix Table C-14). As a result of the lower dividend rates and higher depreciation allowances, gross corporate saving has more than kept pace with the growth of the economy. From 1929 to 1965 gross national product increased 556 percent, while gross corporate saving increased 639 percent. Thus, gross corporate saving rose from 7.3 percent of gross national product to 8.9 percent. During the large upswing in investment since 1960, internal sources of funds have equalled or exceeded plant and equipment expenditures of corporations in each year (Appendix Table C-16). There is no evidence in these figures that the supply of corporate funds has been impaired.

Equity and Debt Finance

Corporations are allowed to deduct from taxable income interest payments on borrowed capital, but there is no corresponding deduction for dividends which are paid out to stockholders in return for the use of their funds as equity capital. At the present 48 percent tax rate, a corporation must earn $1.93 before tax to be able to pay $1 in dividend, but it needs to earn only $1 to pay $1 of interest. This asymmetry makes the cost of equity more "expensive" to the corporation than an equal amount of borrowed capital.

Large corporations borrow long-term capital funds at interest rates ranging from 4 to 6 percent. With stocks selling at ten to twenty times net earnings, corporate earnings *after* tax on equity capital range between 5 and 10 percent. Under these conditions, the earnings rate before tax (at the rate of 1.93:1) must range between 9.6 and 19.3 percent to prevent equity financing from reducing the rate of return. It is in this sense that equity capital costs more than borrowed capital.

Financial experts discourage large amounts of debt financing on the part of corporations. Debt makes good business sense if there is a safe margin to pay fixed interest charges. However, business firms may be tightly squeezed when business falls off and the margin evaporates rapidly. At such times, defaults on interest and principal payments and bankruptcies begin to occur. Even though borrowed capital may increase returns to stockholders, corporations try to finance a major share of their capital requirements through equity capital (mainly retained earnings) to avoid these risks.

The available data suggest that these reasons for caution have tended to moderate the use of borrowed capital despite its lesser cost. The ratio of debt to total capital has increased only moderately since the 1920's when the corporation income tax rate was 75 percent lower than it is today. In 1927-29, the ratio was about 15 percent and it has been between 20 and 21 percent since 1957 (Table 5-1).

Resource Allocation

If the corporation income tax is not shifted in the short run, it becomes in effect a special tax on corporate capital. This does not necessarily mean that the tax permanently reduces rates of return on capital in the corporate sector. Capital may flow out of the taxed sector into the untaxed sectors and rates of return would tend to be equalized. In the process of shifting, the allocation of capital between corporate and noncorporate business is altered from the pattern that would have prevailed in the absence of the tax.

How much, if any, capital has left the corporate sector as a result of the corporation income tax is not known. It is possible that the corporate form of doing business is so advantageous for nontax reasons that, for the most part, capital remains in the corporate sector despite the tax. Moreover, the preferential treatment of capital gains under the individual income tax provides an offsetting incentive to invest in the securities of corporations that retain earnings for reinvestment in the business. These earnings show up as increased stock prices rather than as regular income. In any case, the data in Chart 5-1 indicate that the corporate sector has been getting larger, both relatively and absolutely, for several decades. The discouragement of investment in the corporate form induced by the tax system, if any, must have been relatively small.

Distortions may also take place if the tax is shifted in the short run, but the process is somewhat different. If prices increase in response to an increase in the tax, they rise in proportion to the use of corporate equity capital in the various industries. Consumers will purchase less of the goods and services produced in industries using a great deal of corporate capital, because prices of these products have risen most, and will purchase more of the goods and services produced in industries with less corporate capital. Within the corporate sector, profits will fall in the "capital intensive" industries as a result of the decline in sales and will rise in the "labor intensive" industries. In the end, not only will less capital be attracted to the corporate sector, but less will be attracted to the capital intensive industries in that sector and the economy will suffer a loss in efficiency as a result. The quantitative effect of this process is heavily dependent, of course, on the degree to which the noncorporate form of doing business can be substituted for the corporate form and output can be shifted from capital intensive to labor intensive industries. As in the nonshifting case, even a shifted corporate tax would tend to distort the composition of output, but in the aggregate this effect also is probably small.

Built-in Flexibility

Receipts from the corporation income tax are volatile over the business cycle because corporate profits rise and fall relatively more than other incomes. However, this characteristic does not necessarily qualify the tax as an effective built-in stabilizer. To qualify, a tax must automatically moderate the changes in consumer disposable income or reduce fluctuations in investment. When profits fall, dividends tend to be maintained, but this appears to be largely due to the dividend policy of corporations rather than the reduction in tax paid by corporations. Similarly, corporate investments are determined largely by current and prospective sales volume and rates of return, although the reduced tax liability may have an effect through its impact on cash flow. Thus, the corporation income tax is not regarded as one of the significant built-in stabilizers, despite the fact that it contributes heavily to the large swings in federal surpluses and deficits during business cycles.

The more important stabilizing feature of the corporate sector is the policy of cutting into saving when economic activity declines, rather than reducing dividends. A reduction in retained corporate earnings prevents a corresponding decline in disposable personal income, thus maintaining spending on the part of consumers. Quantitatively, corporate saving is second only to the federal tax structure as a built-in stabilizer. In three out of the four recessions since World War II, undistributed profits of corporations declined about as much as federal receipts (Table 5-3). Largely because of these two factors, disposable personal income declined much less than the gross national product in the first three recessions and actually rose in the 1960-61 recession.

TABLE 5-3. Comparison of Declines in Gross National Product, Federal Receipts, Federal Corporation Income Tax, and Undistributed Corporate Profits in Four Postwar Recessions

(*In billions of dollars*)

Prerecession Peak[a]	Recession Trough[a]	Gross National Product	Federal Receipts	Federal Corporation Tax	Undistributed Corporate Profits
IV 1948–	II 1949	8.7	3.6	2.2	4.3
II 1953–	II 1954	7.1	9.0	4.6	1.7
III 1957–	I 1958	11.6	6.3	4.2	5.7
II 1960–	IV 1960	1.4	2.5	2.7	3.4

Source: *Survey of Current Business*, August 1965, pp. 24, 27, 36.
[a] Gross national product peaks and troughs.

Balance of Payments

The corporation income tax has figured prominently in recent discussions of ways to improve the United States balance of payments. France, Germany, and several other countries have a general broad-based commodity tax, which is rebated on exports. Hence, firms in these countries can sell goods abroad at prices below those charged their domestic customers. Imports are subject to a compensating tax. American exporters, on the other hand, are not subject to a federal consumption tax; they receive no refund for taxes on exports and cannot cut their prices in foreign markets. It has been contended that the United States should, for competitive reasons, reduce the corporation income tax, enact a value added tax (see Chapter 6) as a substitute, and rebate the value added tax on exports.

A major question surrounding this issue relates to the effects of the two taxes on prices. If the corporation income tax is not shifted, substitution of a value added tax with a rebate for exports would accomplish little. The value added tax would raise prices on all goods and services, while the rebate would return export prices to their former level. Trade in commodities produced by United States firms would not change because their prices in international markets would remain unchanged. On the other hand, if the corporation tax is shifted, the switch to a value added tax would keep domestic prices the same as before, but export prices would decline by the amount of the rebate. Prices of United States goods in foreign markets would be lower and the trade balance would improve (if the demand for goods produced in the United States were price elastic; that is, if foreign consumers actually increased their total expenditures as prices were reduced).

To the extent that the corporation income tax is not shifted in the form of higher prices, it reduces the rate of return to investment in this country. Removal of the corporation income tax and substitution of a value added tax that would bear more or less equally on all factors of production would raise the net yield to capital. This would encourage investment in the United States and might in the long run provide balance of payments relief by attracting capital from abroad and discouraging the outflow of capital from the United States.

Since views on corporation tax shifting are divided, no consensus has been reached on these matters. Some improvement in the balance of payments may be expected, either on trade or capital account, but the improvement would probably be small. In 1961, the ratio of corporation taxes to the gross national product was less than 3 percentage points higher in the United States than in other major industrial countries (Appendix Table C-4). This spread has probably narrowed in the intervening years. Thus, even if the United States greatly reduced its corporation income tax, its export prices are not likely to decline very much relative to the export prices of its foreign competitors. Under the circumstances, the balance of payments effect cannot be regarded as a major consideration in deciding whether a shift should be made from the corporation income tax to an indirect tax.

Structural Problems

The structural problems under the corporation income tax are highly technical and therefore rarely understood by the average taxpayer. The major issues are: (1) allowances for capital consumption; (2) depletion and other allowances for the minerals industries; (3) multiple incorporations to secure multiple surtax exemptions; (4) financial institutions; (5) tax-exempt organizations; and (6) foreign income. (The first, second, and sixth issues also apply to individual income taxation, but they are treated here because their revenue and economic implications are much more important in the corporation income tax.) The purpose of this brief discussion is to show how these technical issues affect particular firms and industries, the economy as a whole, and the equity and yield of the corporation income tax.

Capital Consumption Allowances

The law has always permitted a "reasonable allowance for exhaustion, wear and tear" of capital as a deduction for depreciation. Such a deduction is necessary to avoid taxing capital rather than income. In addition, liberalized capital consumption allowances are proposed as devices to stimulate investment.

DEPRECIATION. The annual deduction for depreciation is determined by spreading the cost of the depreciable asset over its "service life." Prior to 1954, the law and regulations were relatively strict, requiring fairly exact estimates of the period of use. Asset costs were amortized primarily by the "straight-line" method which assumes a uniform amount of depreciation each year. The "declining-balance" method at 1.5 times the straight-line rate was also permitted but seldom used. In 1954, the law was amended to permit the use of the declining-balance method at twice the straight-line rate or the "sum-of-years-digits" method.

The differences among the three methods are illustrated for a $1,000 asset with a service life of ten years in Table 5-4. The straight-line method provides a uniform annual depreciation deduction of $100 per year. The declining-balance method permits the taxpayer to use a *rate* of depreciation, and to apply this rate to the undepreciated amount each year. In the first year, the double declining-balance method provides a 20 percent allowance, or $200, leaving $800 undepreciated. In the second year, the 20 percent is applied to $800, giving an allowance of $160, and so on. (The taxpayer is permitted to switch to straight-line depreciation at any time; as shown in the example, this is profitable beginning in the seventh year.) Under the sum-of-years-digits method, the fraction allowed as depreciation each year is computed by dividing the number of years still remaining by the sum of years in the useful life.

TABLE 5-4. Comparison of Three Methods of Depreciation for a Ten-Year, $1,000 Asset

(In dollars)

Year	Depreciation		
	Straight Line	Double Declining Balance	Sum-of-Years Digits
1	100	200	182
2	100	160	164
3	100	128	145
4	100	102	127
5	100	82	109
6	100	66	91
7	100	65.5	73
8	100	65.5	55
9	100	65.5	36
10	100	65.5	18
Total	1,000	1,000	1,000
Present Value at 6 percent:			
Depreciation allowances	736	787	800
Tax value of depreciation allowances[a]	353	378	384

[a] At a tax rate of 48 percent.

With a ten-year asset, the sum of the years is 55 ($10 + 9 + 8 \ldots + 2 + 1$), so that the depreciation allowance is 10/55 in the first year, 9/55 in the second year, and so on until it reaches 1/55 in the tenth year.

As Table 5-4 shows, the two accelerated depreciation methods concentrate a larger percentage of the deductions in the early years. Under straight-line depreciation, half the original cost of a ten-year asset is written off in the first five years, as compared with 67 percent under the double declining-balance method and 73 percent under the sum-of-years-digits method. A useful way of comparing the value of the three methods is shown in the last line of the table. At the current corporation income tax rate of 48 percent, the present value at the time of investment of the tax savings from the depreciation deductions (assuming a 6 percent interest rate) is $353 under straight-line depreciation, $378 under double declining-balance depreciation, and $384 under sum-of-years-digits depreciation.

There seems to be some resistance to changing depreciation methods, but the inertia is being gradually overcome as manage-

TABLE 5-5. Use of Methods of Depreciation on Corporation Income Tax Returns, 1954, 1955, 1957, and 1960

Year	Depreciation Method					
	Straight Line	Declining Balance	Sum-of-Years Digits	Units of Production[a]	Other	Straight Line Only[b]
Percentage of number of corporations[c]						
1954	97.4	7.6	4.8	0.2	1.0	86.4
1955	97.3	11.3	6.8	0.2	1.8	79.9
1957	96.9	14.6	6.6	n.a.	0.6	78.2
1960	94.3	23.9	5.9	n.a.	0.5	69.7
Percentage of amount of depreciation allowances claimed						
1954	89.2	4.7	2.3	1.5	2.3	—
1955	80.7	9.9	6.2	1.3	1.9	—
1957	70.2	15.5	11.1	n.a.	3.2	—
1960	58.2	24.2	14.8	n.a.	2.8	—

n.a. Not available.

Source: Norman Ture, *Use of Alternative Depreciation Methods Under the Internal Revenue Code of 1954* (National Bureau of Economic Research, mimeo). Figures are rounded and will not necessarily add to totals.

[a] Depreciation based on ratio of output in current year to total estimated output over the life of asset. Used mainly in extractive and lumber industries.

[b] This is a minimum estimate obtained by subtracting the sum of the frequencies for all other methods from 100 percent.

[c] Figures total to more than 100 percent because some corporations use severa methods.

ment becomes more aware of the tax advantages. The proportion of corporations using the accelerated methods increased from 12 percent in 1954 to 30 percent in 1960, while the proportion of the amount of depreciation computed under the accelerated methods increased from about 7 percent to 39 percent (Table 5-5).

SERVICE LIVES. Suggested useful lives were first published by the Internal Revenue Service in 1931. These were incorporated in *Bulletin F,* a small pamphlet listing about 5,000 separate items which was first published in 1942. *Bulletin F* remained substantially unchanged until 1962, when the Service issued a new set of depreciation rules entitled *IRS Revenue Procedure 62-21.* The new procedure assigned "guideline" lives to much broader classes of facilities, numbering about one hundred. These new guidelines reduced the write-off period in manufacturing industries by about 15 percent below those used earlier.

A second innovation made in the 1962 revenue procedure was

a set of rules governing the determination of depreciation allowances, which is called the "reserve ratio test." This test is intended to permit taxpayers to gear depreciation allowances to actual experience in replacing facilities. (The reserve ratio is the ratio of depreciation actually taken to the cost of the asset or group of assets in a depreciation account.) Taxpayers who replace assets more frequently than is implied by the guideline lives would find that their reserve ratios are lower than the ratio computed by the Internal Revenue Service. In such cases, they are allowed to shorten the service lives of their assets. On the other hand, taxpayers who use assets for longer periods than those implied by the guideline lives would be required to lengthen service lives.

To give taxpayers enough time to conform with the reserve ratio test, all firms were considered to have met the test for the first three years. They were also given a period of years equal to the guideline life to bring their reserve ratios down to the appropriate range or to show that it was moving toward that range. Nevertheless, it became clear that many taxpayers would not be able to meet the reserve ratio test within the three years, and the Treasury further extended the transition period in 1965 to prevent an increase in tax liabilities of $600-$800 million.

It is difficult to predict what the situation will be in another three to five years when the reserve ratio test begins to apply under the revised rules. Many taxpayers believe that the test is inequitable and unworkable; they urge that the guideline lives be permitted without requiring use of the reserve ratio test. If the test again turns out to be too onerous when the new transition rules expire, the whole question may have to be decided by legislation rather than through further amendment of the regulations.

INVESTMENT CREDIT. The introduction of the investment credit in 1962 was a major innovation in tax policy. Under this provision, business firms are permitted to deduct as a credit against their tax 7 percent of the amount of new investment with service lives of eight years or more (3 percent for utilities). One-third of the full credit is allowed for assets with service lives of four to six years, and two-thirds for those with service lives of six to eight years. Qualified investments include all tangible personal property and exclude all buildings except research and storage facilities. The credit is allowed in full for firms with tax liabilities up to $25,000 and up to one-quarter of the tax above $25,000.

The 1962 law required deduction of the credit from the cost of the asset before computing depreciation for tax purposes. However, this requirement complicated accounting for the credit, and it was eliminated in the 1964 Act. Thus, taxpayers now have the benefit of the full credit plus the liberalized depreciation allowances adopted in 1954, 1962, and 1965. At 1966 profit and investment levels, the revenue cost of the credit is about $2 billion.

The effect of the investment credit is similar to an increase in the depreciation allowances above 100 percent of the cost of the asset. For corporations subject to the 48 percent rate, the same results could have been achieved by allowing the taxpayer to deduct an additional 14.8 percent in the first year. However, the credit has two virtues. First, it is simpler to understand and does not interfere with depreciation accounting. Second, it provides the same credit for all taxpayers regardless of their marginal rate. (It will be recalled that individuals are subject to rates up to 70 percent; and, in addition, small corporations are subject only to the normal tax rate of 22 percent if they have incomes below $25,000.)

Even though the credit appears small, it provides a sizeable incentive for new investment (assuming that the corporation income tax is not shifted into higher prices). In effect, the credit reduces the cost of the asset and hence increases the rate of return. For example, for an investment yielding 10 percent after straight-line depreciation and after the 48 percent corporation income tax, the credit increases the rate of return to 11.5 percent for an asset with a ten-year life, 11.2 percent for a fifteen-year life, and 11.0 percent for a twenty-year life. To increase the rates of return by equivalent amounts would require rate reductions of 8.8, 7.3, and 6.3 percentage points, respectively.

COMBINED EFFECT OF INCREASED CAPITAL CONSUMPTION ALLOW-
ANCES. It has already been noted that the liberalization of capital consumption allowances beginning in 1954 reduced the effective rate of corporation income tax even though the tax rate remained constant through 1963 (Table 5-2). Another measure of the benefits provided by the various provisions is given in Chart 5-3, which shows their effects on after-tax rates of return for assets with ten-,

CHART 5-3. Effect of 7 Percent Investment Credit and Declining-Balance Depreciation on Rate of Return of Ten-, Fifteen-, and Twenty-Year Assets Yielding 10 Percent with Straight-Line Depreciation[a]

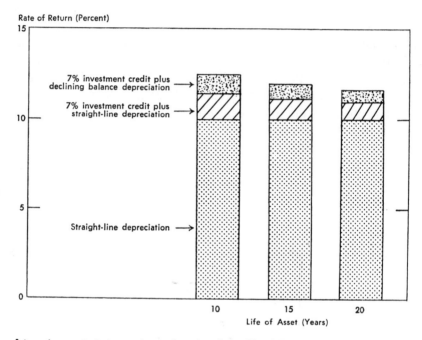

Rate of Return (Percent)

7% investment credit plus declining balance depreciation →

7% investment credit plus straight-line depreciation →

Straight-line depreciation →

Life of Asset (Years)

[a] Assuming constant stream of annual receipts during life of the asset.

fifteen-, and twenty-year service lives, assuming that the assets yield 10 percent on a straight-line depreciation basis.

The combined effect is dramatic in all three cases. The rate of return is increased to 12.5 percent for a ten-year asset, 12 percent for a fifteen-year asset, and 11.7 percent for a twenty-year asset. The investment credit accounts for about 60 percent of the increase in rates of return.

When first introduced, there was substantial resistance to liberalization of capital consumption allowances on equity grounds. But the attitude toward liberalization changed in the early 1960's when the government began using its fiscal powers aggressively to promote a rapid rate of economic growth. The widespread use of these methods in other countries also made them more acceptable in the United States. Today, except for the disagreement on the merits of the reserve ratio test, depreciation allowances no longer provoke much controversy in this country.

The investment credit encountered considerable resistance before it was finally enacted—even from businessmen who were to benefit from the new provision. While many still oppose the credit on equity grounds, few deny its effectiveness as a method of stimulating investment incentives. The credit was originally enacted as a permanent feature of the tax system, but the rate of the credit could be raised or lowered as a stabilization measure. Proposals to reduce or suspend the investment credit were strongly advocated to counteract the inflationary pressures that developed in early 1966.

Allowances for the Minerals Industries

Firms engaged in extracting oil and gas and other minerals from the ground are entitled to a "depletion" allowance for exhaustion of the mineral deposit in computing their taxable income, just as other firms are entitled to a depreciation allowance for wear and tear on the capital they use.

Although there is little distinction in theory between depletion and depreciation, there are substantial differences in practice. First, it is difficult to estimate the proportion of a mineral deposit used up. Second, the value of a mineral deposit may be substantially larger than the amount invested in discovering and developing it. Some argue that depletion allowances should be based on the higher "discovery value" of the deposit, rather than on the amount invested. Others argue that there is no reason to treat minerals differently from other investments and that only the original investment in producing the mine or oil field should be amortized.

Present allowances for the minerals industries are more generous than depreciation allowances. Allowances in excess of depletion based on costs were first granted for 1918 in the form of *discovery depletion* to stimulate exploration for war purposes and to reduce taxes of small-scale prospectors who often made discoveries after years of fruitless searching. (The 1918 Act was not actually passed until after the war was over.) Discovery value proved to be difficult to estimate and in 1926 Congress substituted *percentage depletion* for oil and gas properties. Under percentage depletion, taxpayers deduct 27.5 percent of receipts from the sale of oil and gas as a depletion allowance, irrespective of the amount invested. Beginning in

TABLE 5-6. Ratio of Annual Amounts of Depletion Claimed on Federal Corporation Tax Returns to Adjusted Basis Depletion, by Mineral Products, 1958–60

Mineral Product	1958	1959	1960
Oil and gas (27½ percent depletion)	12.5	10.6	11.0
Products allowed 23 percent depletion[a]	4.9	4.5	5.4
Products allowed 15 percent depletion[b]	50.0	29.4	90.9
Products allowed 10 percent depletion[c]	17.2	14.3	17.5
Products allowed 5 percent depletion[d]	6.8	7.6	8.1
All mineral products	13.0	11.0	11.9

Source: *The President's 1963 Tax Message*, Hearings before the House Committee on Ways and Means, 88 Cong. 1 sess. (1963), Part 1, p. 305.
[a] Sulfur, uranium, bauxite, lead, zinc, etc.
[b] Iron, copper, gold, silver, clay, calcium carbonate, limestone, phosphate rock, etc.
[c] Bituminous coal, lignite, anthracite, sodium chloride, etc.
[d] Sand, gravel, stone, clay, shale, etc.

1932, the same method was extended to other products taken from the ground, at percentages currently ranging from 23 percent for sulfur, uranium, and other rare metals to 5 percent for gravel, sand, clay used in the manufacture of brick and tile, and mollusk shells (including clam and oyster shells). The deduction for percentage depletion cannot reduce the net income from the property (computed without regard to the depletion allowance) by more than 50 percent.

In addition to depletion, an immediate write-off is permitted for certain capital costs incurred in exploration and development without limit in the case of oil and gas, and up to $400,000 in the case of other minerals. This treatment of expenses does not reduce percentage depletion, so that a double deduction is allowed for the same capital investment. Studies made over the years by the Treasury Department indicate that the annual depletion deductions for oil and gas average out to more than ten times the deduction computed on the basis of the original investment (after allowance for depreciation) and at even larger multiples for some other minerals (Table 5-6). The tax benefits of these special provisions are now in excess of $1.5 billion per year.

This special treatment is justified by its proponents on several grounds: there are unusual risks in oil and mineral exploration and development; national defense requires continuous exploration and development; the allowances are needed to finance new discoveries; and the present provisions serve as a strong impetus for taxpayers who discover new sources of oil and minerals to operate these properties rather than to sell them for the preferential capital gains rates.

On the other hand, the risks in these industries could be satisfactorily handled by the general deductibility of losses; the industries involved are no more strategic from a national defense standpoint than many other industries; and the large revenue cost of the benefits requires the imposition of higher tax rates to raise the same amount of revenue, thus penalizing other taxpayers. Moreover, the provisions lead to overinvestment in the favored industries and hence seriously distort the allocation of resources. The policy of allowing percentage depletion on foreign oil is particularly irrational since the major economic justification of the allowance has been the need for stimulating the domestic industry.

The allowances for oil and gas and other minerals have been the subject of acrimonious debate for many years. In 1950, President Truman recommended the reduction of percentage depletion to a maximum of 15 percent. However, Congress took no action and in later years extended percentage depletion to other minerals and also raised the percentage depletion rates. Bills are introduced frequently to curtail the allowances, but only minor changes have been made in recent years.

Multiple Surtax Exemptions

The $25,000 surtax exemption, which was intended to help small corporations, provides a strong monetary incentive for larger business firms to form multiple corporations. With a surtax rate of 26 percent, each additional corporation reduces the annual tax liability by $6,500 ($25,000 × .26). Thus, a firm with net profit of $1,000,000 pays a tax of $473,500 if it is a single corporation, but only $220,000 if it operates through forty corporations each having a $25,000 profit. Since incorporation is relatively inexpensive, many firms have taken the opportunity to spin off a large number of subsidiaries. In some instances, several hundred corporations are involved and the tax savings are large.

There are valid business reasons for incorporating different units of a business enterprise, but this hardly justifies treating each unit for tax purposes as if it were an independent small business. Moreover, present rules often provide an incentive for uneconomic corporate arrangements and discriminate against firms and industries in which multiple corporations are impractical. Chain stores, personal finance companies, movies, and other businesses involving separate outlets are particularly easy to break up into separate corporations. As a consequence, the reduced rate for the first $25,000 of profits has conferred unintended benefits to many medium-sized and large businesses.

The Treasury Department has attempted to prevent such abuse on a number of occasions, with limited success. In 1963, it proposed that corporations subject to 80 percent common ownership and control be limited to a single surtax exemption. Controlled corporations were to be defined as corporations which are 80 percent owned by the same corporate parent (parent-subsidiary type) or by five or fewer individuals or corporations (brother-sister type). The proposal was watered down under the Revenue Act of 1964. First, the definition of controlled corporations of the brother-sister type was restricted to corporations which are 80 percent owned by one person instead of five. Second, a controlled group of corporations was permitted to continue claiming separate surtax exemptions by paying an additional tax of 6 percent on the first $25,000 of corporate income. This removes only 23 percent (6/26) of the advantage of the surtax exemption and is therefore less effective in discouraging multiple corporations.

The 1964 Act also eliminated the 2 percent penalty tax previously paid by a group of affiliated corporations for the privilege of filing a consolidated return. Consolidated reporting of income results in a more meaningful and fair representation of taxable income than unconsolidated reporting. Consolidation also has the advantage of providing offsets for losses of one corporation against the gains of other members of the group and of eliminating the tax on intercompany dividends (15 percent of which are included in taxable income). The dividend tax could be eliminated entirely if the rules against multiple corporations were tightened to prevent abuses of the surtax exemption.

Financial Institutions

Financial institutions have always presented a difficult problem for income taxation because many of them are organized on a mutual basis. At one time, mutuals were completely exempt from tax on the theory that they belonged to their members and were not corporations in any ordinary sense. But with the growth in numbers and size of mutuals, it became increasingly evident that the mutual status was not sufficient reason for exempting them from taxation. Attempts have recently been made to tax financial institutions—whether they organize as mutuals or not—like other corporations, but many observers feel that they are still not paying their fair share of the tax burden. Since the problems depend on the type of business conducted, it is necessary to discuss separately: (a) the thrift institutions (savings banks and building and loan associations); (b) life insurance companies; (c) fire and casualty companies; and (d) commercial banks.

THRIFT INSTITUTIONS. Savings banks and building and loan associations were made subject to the corporation income tax by the Revenue Act of 1951, which required them to pay the regular corporation income tax rate on retained earnings over and above allocations to reserves. Payments of interest to depositors were allowed as a deductible expense, as in the case of the ordinary commercial bank. However, the law permitted thrift institutions to build a reserve for bad debts of up to 12 percent of their deposits, while the regulations permitted commercial banks to set aside a reserve of three times their annual loss experience over a twenty-year period (or less than 3 percent on the average). With steady growth in deposits, the amounts covered by the 12 percent ceiling increased steadily and the result was that savings banks and building and loan associations paid very little tax.

The ineffectiveness of the 1951 law was remedied by a 1962 amendment providing, in effect, that thrift institutions may add to their reserves for bad debts an amount equal to 60 percent of their taxable income. While this falls short of full taxation, the tax paid by savings and loan associations and mutual savings banks increased from $6.4 million in 1960 to $155 million in 1963.

LIFE INSURANCE COMPANIES. The problem in life insurance company taxation also concerns the method of computing appropriate reserves. The intention of the law is to exempt that part of their income deemed necessary to meet contractual obligations to policyholders. Methods of achieving this objective have been considered periodically by the Congress in the last forty-five years.

Initially, life insurance companies were taxed as ordinary corporations, but this method was abandoned because of the administrative difficulties of establishing deductions for additions to reserves. Beginning in 1921, a deduction of a specified percentage of legal reserves (4 percent from 1921 to 1931 and 3.75 percent from 1932 to 1941) was permitted. Because of this high allowance, insurance companies paid practically no tax during the 1930's and the law was again amended in 1942. This time, they were allowed a tax credit for the amount presumed to be needed to meet policy commitments. The credit was a flat percentage of net investment income, determined by the Secretary of the Treasury on the basis of a formula which yielded high reserve figures for the industry when interest rates declined during the war. As a result, the life insurance companies paid virtually no tax.

A new formula for taxing the industry was enacted as stopgap legislation in 1951. Life insurance companies were subjected to a tax of 6.5 percent on their net investment income in lieu of the regular corporation income tax. This rate was equivalent to the 52 percent tax on the assumption that the industry required 87.5 percent of its investment income for policy reserves.

The present method of taxing life insurance companies was enacted in 1959, effective with respect to 1958 incomes. The theory was that life insurance companies should be taxed not only on their net investment income but also on the "underwriting" profits resulting from the fact that the life expectancy tables upon which premiums are based usually understate actual life expectancies. To reach such profits, the 1959 law required companies to report premium as well as investment income and allowed deductions for benefit payments, insurance losses, and other ordinary business expenses. Additions to reserves were also allowed, but were to be computed on the basis of each company's needs and experience.

The 1959 law had a number of technical provisions which did not become fully applicable until 1961. Tax payments of life insurance companies rose from $294 million in 1957, the year before the 1959 law became effective, to $681 million in 1963. Most of this increase was due to the change in the method of taxation which, now correct in principle, is likely to be stable for the first time since the corporation income tax was enacted.

FIRE AND CASUALTY INSURANCE COMPANIES. Stock companies selling fire and casualty insurance have long been taxed on both their investment and underwriting profits (as life insurance companies have been taxed beginning in 1958). However, between 1942 and 1961, mutual fire and casualty insurance companies paid tax under special formulas which excluded underwriting profits. In 1962, underwriting profits were included in the formula for these companies, but they were allowed to set up a deferred income account which, in effect, permanently defers one-eighth of their underwriting gains from taxation and, in addition, defers taxation of another large portion of their underwriting gains for five years.

COMMERCIAL BANKS. Commercial banks are regarded as ordinary business corporations for tax purposes and are subject to tax on their profits, after allowing for payment of interest on their deposits. The peculiarity in their taxation is the treatment of capital losses. Long-term capital gains of commercial banks are taxed at a maximum rate of 25 percent, as are the gains of ordinary business corporations. However, capital losses of commercial banks are deductible in full not only against capital gains but also against ordinary income. This treatment has been justified on the ground that dealings in securities are part of normal business operations in commercial banking and losses should therefore be treated as ordinary losses. By this reasoning, capital gains should be regarded as ordinary income and subjected to the ordinary corporation income tax rate. Nevertheless, no effort has been made to correct this asymmetrical treatment.

Tax-Exempt Organizations

The federal tax law exempts a variety of nonprofit organizations, including religious, charitable, educational, and fraternal organizations. Favorable tax treatment for these organizations dates from a time when the federal government assumed little responsibility for relief and welfare activities and the value of the tax exemption was relatively small. Today, the federal government has substantial responsibilities for public assistance and welfare activities, while the revenue loss from tax-exempt organizations has become significant.

The tax status of these organizations might never have been altered had they remained small and not entered into activities that competed with private business. In recent years, numerous complaints have been made against tax-exempt organizations for unfair competition. As a result, some of their income has been made taxable under the corporation income tax, even though they are still designated as "exempt organizations" by the Internal Revenue Code. The special taxes apply to (a) unrelated business income, (b) rental income from "lease-back" arrangements, and (c) the income of cooperatives.

UNRELATED BUSINESS INCOME. The major change in the tax status of exempt organizations was made in 1950, when Congress decided to tax their "unrelated business income." Such income is defined as income from a business which is not substantially related to the exercise of charitable, educational, or other exempt purposes. Unrelated business income is subject to the regular corporation income tax rates, after an exemption of $1,000. Churches and affiliated organizations are not subject to this tax.

LEASE-BACK ARRANGEMENTS. Exempt organizations often purchased property from private business firms with borrowed funds and then leased the property back to the same firms. In some cases, the original owners were given lower rentals or were paid a higher price for the property than going market rates. Even where the transaction was at arms-length, the exempt organization was trading on its tax exemption to accumulate property. To solve these problems, the 1950 legislation redefined unrelated business income to include rental income from leased property owned by tax-exempt organizations to the extent that the ownership is financed by borrowed funds. This change permits tax-exempt organizations to use their funds for investment in real estate, but makes it more difficult to use their exemption as a means of acquiring property.

COOPERATIVES. Cooperative irrigation, telephone, and electric companies are exempt from income tax. Other nonfinancial cooperatives are taxable. However, all cooperatives are allowed to deduct from their income amounts paid as "patronage dividends" to their patrons on the ground that they represent readjustments in prices initially charged patrons.

Originally, patronage dividends were deductible even if distributed in noncash form ("written notices of allocation"). The deductibility of noncash patronage dividends enabled cooperatives to expand from earnings not taxed at the cooperative level. Furthermore, such dividends often were not taxable to patrons until redeemed at some future date because the written allocations had no fair market value.

The law was revised beginning with the income year 1963. Earnings of taxable cooperatives distributed as written notices of allocation cannot now be deducted by the cooperatives unless at least 20 percent of the face amount of the allocation is in cash. Deductibility of noncash allocations is limited further to those which: (1) the patron, at his option, can redeem in cash for the face amount within ninety days of the payment thereof; or (2) the patron has consented to include at face value in his income in accordance with the federal income tax laws. Thus, taxable cooperatives may, in effect, retain 80 percent of their earnings by the use of noncash patronage dividends. At the same time, noncash dividends currently are taxable to patrons to the extent that the dividends are related to transactions entered into for business purposes. Dividends on purchases for personal consumption are not required to be included in a patron's income.

Foreign Income

Before 1962, the income earned by foreign subsidiaries of United States corporations was subject to tax when it was "repatriated" through the payment of dividends to the parent corporation. To avoid double taxation, the parent was allowed a credit against the U.S. tax for any tax paid on these dividends to a foreign government. Income of foreign branches was (and still is) included in the taxable income of the parent, but credit was also allowed for any foreign tax paid on this income.

The deferment of tax on income of foreign subsidiaries was at one time considered to be a desirable feature of the tax system because it encouraged foreign investment by U.S. firms. Attitudes toward this policy changed in the 1950's and early 1960's as a result of two developments. First, the United States encountered a serious balance of payments problem, which was aggravated by private capital outflows. Second, some U.S. corporations were using the deferral privilege as a method of tax avoidance. This was done by establishing "tax haven" subsidiaries in a country with little or no tax on foreign income and using these subsidiaries as a base company for accumulating earnings from foreign operations.

To solve both problems, President Kennedy in 1961 recommended the elimination of deferral on earnings of U.S.-owned foreign subsidiaries, except for those in underdeveloped countries. The deferral provision had originally been designed to achieve *foreign neutrality* in the taxation of U.S. companies doing business abroad (that is, to permit their foreign income to be taxed at the rates applicable abroad). In view of the changed balance of payments circumstances, the government argued that it was time to give priority to *domestic neutrality* (that is, to eliminate the tax as a factor in the choice between domestic and foreign investment).

The business community launched a successful campaign to convince Congress that complete elimination of deferral was too extreme. Congress agreed, but was annoyed by the factual evidence that some foreign subsidiaries were able to avoid paying taxes in any country through the use of tax havens. In the end, the Revenue Act of 1962 contained new methods of dealing specifically with tax havens for business operations in developed countries, but left the basic deferral provisions unchanged. The technique was to single out certain tax avoidance transactions of tax haven corporations for inclusion in the taxable income of the parent corporation in the year in which income is earned.

With the improvement in the U.S. balance of payments, the likelihood of removing the deferral provision is remote. But it is still too early to say whether the 1962 amendments solved the problems of the tax havens. Some experts argue that the 1962 provisions are too weak; others believe they are complicated and unnecessary.

Integration of the Corporation and Individual Income Taxes

Taxation of corporate earnings under two taxes continues to be controversial. Some people regard double taxation as inequitable and urge its elimination or moderation on this ground alone. Others believe that taxation of corporations as a separate entity is justified. Whether something needs to be done about double taxation depends in part on an evaluation of the economic issues discussed earlier. With respect to the equity issue, few people realize that the problem is tricky.

TABLE 5-7. Additional Burden of the Corporation Income Tax on $100 of Corporation Income[a]

(In dollars)

Marginal Individual Income Tax Rate (Percentages) (1)	Corporate Income Before Tax (2)	Corporate Tax at 48 Percent (3)	Dividends Received by Stock-holders (4)	Stockholder's Individual Income Tax (5)	Total Tax Burden[b] (6)	Additional Burden of the Corporate Tax (7)
0	100	48	52	0	48.00	48.00
10	100	48	52	5.20	53.20	43.20
20	100	48	52	10.40	58.40	38.40
30	100	48	52	15.60	63.60	33.60
40	100	48	52	20.80	68.80	28.80
50	100	48	52	26.00	74.00	24.00
60	100	48	52	31.20	79.20	19.20
70	100	48	52	36.40	84.40	14.40

Column (3) =.48 ×Column (2)
Column (4) =Column (2) −Column (3)
Column (5) =Column (4) ×Column (1)
Column (6) =Column (3) +Column (5)
Column (7) =Column (6) −Column (1)
[a] Assumes corporation income after tax is devoted entirely to the payment of dividends.
[b] Does not take into account the effect of the exclusion of the first $100 of dividends from the individual income tax base.

The Additional Burden on Dividends

Assuming that all or a significant portion of the corporation tax rests on the stockholder, the effect of the corporation tax is to impose the heaviest burden on dividends received by persons in the lowest income classes. This can be seen by examining the illustrative calculations in Table 5-7, which show the total and additional tax burden (ignoring the effect of the present $100 exclusion) on stockholders who receive $52 of dividends under present tax rates. Given the present rate of 48 percent, the corporation income before tax from which $52 of dividends were paid must have amounted to $100. If this $100 had been subject to individual income tax rates only, the tax on these dividends would go from zero at the bottom of the income scale to a maximum of 70 percent at the top. With the corporation tax, the combined individual and corporation income tax increases from $48 for those subject to a zero rate to $84.40 for those subject to a 70 percent rate (Table 5-7, column 6).

However, the *additional* burden resulting from the corporation tax falls as income rises. For example, the taxpayer subject to a zero individual rate would have paid no tax on the $52 of dividends; the additional burden of the corporation income tax in this case is the full $48 tax. By contrast, a taxpayer subject to the 70 percent rate pays an individual income tax of $36.40 on the dividend and the total tax burden on the original $100 of corporate earnings is $84.40. But since he would have to pay $70 under the individual income tax in any case, the additional burden to him is only $14.40 (Table 5-7, column 7).

The test of an equitable method of moderating or eliminating the "double tax" on dividends is whether the method removes a uniform portion of the additional burden shown in Table 5-7. If the percentage removed is the same for all individual income tax rate brackets, the method deals evenly at all levels. Deviations from a constant percentage indicate the income classes favored or penalized by the method.

Methods of Integration

Four basic methods of integrating the corporation and individual income tax have been used at various times in different countries: (1) a dividend received credit for individuals; (2) a deduction for dividends paid by the corporation in computing the corporation income tax; (3) a method which considers all or a portion of the corporation income tax to be withholding on dividends at the source; and (4) an exclusion for all or a portion of the dividends received from the individual income tax base. A fifth method would be to treat all corporations like partnerships and tax their income to the stockholders whether or not it is distributed. Of these methods, only (2) and (3) and the partnership method would remove the same proportion of the additional burden of the corporation tax at all individual income levels. The analysis assumes that there is no shifting of the corporation income tax.

THE DIVIDEND RECEIVED CREDIT. Under this method, dividend recipients are allowed to deduct a percentage of their dividends as a credit against their individual income tax. Between 1954 and 1963, U.S. taxpayers were allowed a credit of 4 percent for dividends in excess of the $50 exclusion ($100 for joint returns).

Although the credit grants the same relief on a dollar of divi-

TABLE 5-8. Portion of the Additional Burden of the Corporation Income Tax Removed by the 4 Percent Dividend Received Credit

Marginal Individual Income Tax Rate (Percentages)	Additional Burden Resulting From Corporate Tax (Dollars)	Dividend Received Credit (Dollars)	Percentage of Additional Burden Removed by the Dividend Credit
(1)	(2)	(3)	(4)
0	48.00	0	0
10	43.20	2.08	4.8
20	38.40	2.08	5.4
30	33.60	2.08	6.2
40	28.80	2.08	7.2
50	24.00	2.08	8.7
60	19.20	2.08	10.8
70	14.40	2.08	14.4

Column (2) = Column (7) of Table 5-7.
Column (3) = 4 percent of $52.
Column (4) = Column (3) ÷ Column (2).

dends at all income levels, it removes an increasing proportion of the additional burden of the corporation tax as incomes rise. For those subject to a zero rate, the credit is worthless. For a taxpayer subject to a 10 percent rate, the 4 percent credit would remove 4.8 percent of the additional burden, while for a taxpayer subject to the maximum 70 percent rate, the credit would remove 14.4 percent (Table 5-8). This pattern of relief led to its repeal.

THE DIVIDEND PAID DEDUCTION. This is the simplest method of dealing with the double taxation problem; it was used in the United States in 1936 and 1937. Corporations deduct from their taxable income all or a portion of the dividends they pay out, and the corporation tax applies to the remainder. Table 5-9 shows the relief that would be granted under this method if a deduction of 12.5 percent were allowed to the corporation. As shown in column 6, the relief would be exactly 6.5 percent of the additional tax imposed by the corporation income tax at all income levels.

Aside from granting the same proportionate relief at all income levels, the dividend paid credit has the merit of treating dividends more like interest (if a full deduction were allowed, the treatment would be identical). This would reduce the discrimination against

TABLE 5-9. Portion of the Additional Burden of the Corporation Income Tax Removed by the Dividend Paid Deduction

(*Assuming a deduction by the corporation of 12.5 percent of dividends paid*)

Marginal Individual Income Tax Rate (Percentages)	Additional Burden Resulting From Corporate Tax (Dollars)	Tax Benefit of Dividend Paid Deduction (Dollars)			Percentage of Additional Burden Removed by Dividend Paid Deduction
		Reduced Corporate Tax (paid to stockholders as additional dividends)	Tax on Additional Dividends	Net Benefit	
(1)	(2)	(3)	(4)	(5)	(6)
0	48.00	3.12	0	3.12	6.5
10	43.20	3.12	0.31	2.81	6.5
20	38.40	3.12	0.62	2.50	6.5
30	33.60	3.12	0.94	2.18	6.5
40	28.80	3.12	1.25	1.87	6.5
50	24.00	3.12	1.56	1.56	6.5
60	19.20	3.12	1.87	1.25	6.5
70	14.40	3.12	2.18	0.94	6.5

Column (2) = Column (7) of Table 5-7.
Column (3) = Amount of additional dividends corporations could pay out with a 12.5 percent dividend paid deduction.
Column (4) = Column (1) × Column (3).
Column (5) = Column (3) − Column (4).
Column (6) = Column (5) ÷ Column (2).

equity financing by corporations. Nevertheless, the dividend paid credit is rarely proposed seriously because its use during the 1930's raised a storm of protest. Corporations complained that it reduced their ability to save and invest at a time when the market for corporate equities was almost dried up. The method is also criticized on the ground that it discourages internal financing by corporations and might reduce total saving and investment. On the other hand, some believe it unwise to permit corporations to avoid the capital markets for financing their investment programs. Forcing them "to stand the test of the market place" might exercise a desirable restraint on bigness, and also give the investor-owner more control over the disposition of his funds.

THE WITHHOLDING METHOD. Under this method, all or a portion of the individual income tax is regarded as having been paid at the source (through the corporation tax). For example, if 6 percent of

TABLE 5-10. Portion of the Additional Burden of the Corporation Income Tax Removed by Withholding Method

(Assuming 6 percent of dividends received regarded as withheld)

Marginal Individual Income Tax Rate (Percentages)	Additional Burden Resulting from Corporate Tax (Dollars)	Withholding Credit (Dollars)			Percentage of Additional Burden Removed by the Dividend Credit
		Amount Withheld at Source	Tax on Amount Withheld	Net Credit	
(1)	(2)	(3)	(4)	(5)	(6)
0	48.00	3.12	0	3.12	6.5
10	43.20	3.12	0.31	2.81	6.5
20	38.40	3.12	0.62	2.50	6.5
30	33.60	3.12	0.94	2.18	6.5
40	28.80	3.12	1.25	1.87	6.5
50	24.00	3.12	1.56	1.56	6.5
60	19.20	3.12	1.87	1.25	6.5
70	14.40	3.12	2.18	0.94	6.5

Column (2) = Column (7) of Table 5-7.
Column (3) = 6 percent of $52.
Column (4) = Column (1)×Column (3).
Column (5) = Column (3) − Column (4).
Column (6) = Column (5) ÷ Column (2).

the dividend received is regarded as having been withheld, a shareholder receiving a $52 dividend would include $3.12 (.06 × 52) in his income and then take the $3.12 as a credit against his tax. In this illustration, the portion of the additional burden of the corporation income tax removed is exactly 6.5 percent at all income levels (Table 5-10).

The withholding method achieves the same result as the dividend paid deduction for corporations, but is less likely to discourage corporate saving. This advantage frequently makes the withholding method more attractive, even though it is more difficult to understand and would also complicate the individual income tax return. The withholding method was a basic part of the British tax structure from 1803 until 1965, when a separate corporation income tax was enacted for the first time.

THE DIVIDEND EXCLUSION. This method, adopted in the United States in 1954, permits the individual income taxpayer to exclude all or a portion of his dividends from his taxable income.

In 1964, the exclusion was raised from $50 to $100 ($200 on joint returns). Like the dividend received credit, the exclusion grants an increasing amount of relief on a dollar of dividends as incomes rise. Accordingly, it cannot remove the same proportion of the additional tax burden at all levels of income.

THE PARTNERSHIP METHOD. The most radical solution to the double taxation problem is to regard the income of corporations as belonging to their stockholders in the year it is earned. The corporation income tax would be abolished and stockholders would pay individual income tax on their prorated share of the earnings of corporations in which they held stock. Tax would be payable by individuals on corporate earnings whether they were distributed or not.

This method would automatically apply the correct individual income tax rates to all corporate earnings, but it is impractical for the United States. Many stockholders would not have funds to pay tax on earnings which they did not receive. This would force them to liquidate security holdings, or apply pressure on corporations to distribute a much larger portion of their retained earnings. In either case, the result is considered to be bad public policy: in the former, because it would discourage stock ownership among people with modest means; in the latter, because it would greatly reduce corporate saving.

Treatment approximating this method is available under present law for closely held corporations with fewer than ten shareholders. These corporations operate substantially like partnerships and can arrange to distribute enough earnings to the partners to avoid forced liquidations. Moreover, the decision to be treated like a corporation for tax purposes is made only if it is advantageous to the shareholders. Most experts agree that it is not practical to extend the partnership method to large publicly held corporations with complex capital structures, frequent changes in ownership, and thousands or millions of stockholders.

The Value Added Tax as a Replacement for the Corporation Tax

Another method of dealing with double taxation that has been proposed with increasing frequency is to replace the corporation income tax with a value added tax. This tax is imposed at a flat rate on the "value added" by each firm (computed by subtracting from gross receipts the value of purchases from other firms). Assuming the same yield, a value added tax would reduce the tax burden of firms and industries relying heavily on capital and increase it on those relying heavily on labor. The value added tax has been supported recently by those who see in it a method of increasing the after-tax rate of return on U.S. capital, and thus helping the balance of payments by encouraging U.S. firms to keep more capital at home and by attracting capital from abroad.

The value added tax will be discussed in the next chapter. Here it should be noted that use of this tax in place of the corporation income tax would raise difficult equity issues. Repeal of the corporation income tax would probably increase stock prices and generate large capital gains. It would also stimulate additional retention of corporate earnings, and thus enable shareholders to avoid the individual income tax. Since a departure of this sort would change the complexion of the federal tax system, it should not be adopted without fundamental revisions (particularly in capital gains taxation) to prevent windfall gains to the minority of taxpayers who have large stockholdings.

Summary

The corporation income tax maintains second place in the federal tax system despite continued criticism. It produces a large amount of revenue that would be hard to replace with any other tax, and protects the equity and yield of the individual income tax. Without it, a substantial part of the individual income tax would be permanently lost from the tax base through retention of earnings by corporations.

The arguments that are made against the corporation income tax are largely economic. The tax may: reduce the saving capacity of corporations and their incentives to invest; encourage debt financing by discriminating against equity financing, thus exposing many corporations to unnecessary risks; protect marginal producers by keeping up the prices of more efficient producers; and distort the allocation of resources, both as between the corporate and noncorporate sectors and capital and labor intensive industries. However, there is no evidence in the available data that high corporation tax rates have impaired the growth of the corporate sector.

Numerous changes have been made in the structure of the corporation income tax since the end of World War II. Foremost among these have been the liberalization of depreciation and the addition of the investment credit to encourage investment. Revisions have also been made to prevent tax avoidance by tax-exempt organizations, mutual financial institutions, and cooperatives. Nevertheless, some difficult problems remain. The treatment of oil and gas and other minerals industries is still a major issue. Multiple incorporations continue to be profitable because of the saving of surtax on each additional corporation. There is also some question whether the tax treatment of foreign income has been permanently solved.

The most difficult issue concerns the so-called double taxation of dividends. Even if it were agreed that something needs to be done about double taxation, there is no easy solution. Among the various alternatives, the theoretically correct methods are the partnership method, deduction of dividends from the corporation tax base, and the withholding method. The partnership method is impractical; the dividend deduction would tend to discourage corporate saving; and the withholding method is difficult to understand.

CHAPTER 6

Consumption Taxes

CONSUMPTION TAXES are not very popular in the United States. It is true that general sales taxes are used by state and local governments (see Chapter 9), but even when they are taken into account, consumption taxes are less important here than anywhere else in the world (Chart 6-1). In fiscal year 1967, excise taxes and customs will account for only about 10 percent of federal cash receipts, and this proportion will decline somewhat as the excise tax reductions scheduled for later years take effect.

There is a bewildering variety of consumption taxes. An *expenditure* tax is levied on the total consumption expenditure of the individual; a *sales* tax is levied on the sales of goods and services; and a *value added* tax is levied on the difference between a firm's sales and purchases. Expenditure taxes can be proportional or progressive; sales and value added taxes are imposed at a uniform rate on all commodities or at several rates on various groups of commodities. Expenditure taxes are collected from the consumer, while sales and value added taxes are collected from the seller. Sales taxes are in widespread use throughout the world; the value added tax is used only in France, but seems to be gaining in popularity; the expenditure tax has been used—without much success—only in India and Ceylon.

CHART 6-1. Importance of Consumption Taxes and Customs in Selected Countries, 1961[a]

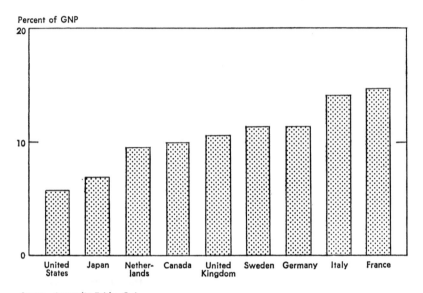

Source: Appendix Table C-4.

[a] Includes state and local taxes.

The sales tax can be a single or multistage tax. Canada levies its sales tax at the manufacturers level; Great Britain at the wholesale level; and United States state and local governments at the retail level. Italy levies a *turnover* tax, which derives its name from the fact that the tax is levied every time a commodity "turns over" from one firm to another. The value added tax is also a multistage tax, but it is figured on the *net* value added by each firm.

A common form of consumption tax is the *excise* tax on the sale of a particular commodity or group of commodities. Excise taxes are levied almost everywhere on alcoholic beverages and tobacco products, but they apply to many other products as well. They are also employed as "user charges" to collect part or all of the cost of government services enjoyed by specific groups of taxpayers. Gasoline taxes and taxes on automobiles and automotive products are used in this way to pay for highway construction and maintenance. Appendix Table A-5 summarizes the major excises used by the federal government since 1913.

Customs duties, which are levied on imports, are used in this country primarily to protect domestic industries against foreign competition. The policy of the United States Government is to reduce trade barriers in the interest of promoting world trade, but the size and pace of the reductions depend on international negotiations, which are complicated and time-consuming. The negotiations are concerned with the role of customs duties in the nation's foreign economic policy, rather than with their role as taxes to produce revenue. Customs duties will therefore not be discussed in this book.

The major issue regarding consumption taxes in this country is equity. Because the poor consume more of their income than the rich, the burden of a flat rate sales tax falls as incomes rise. The sales tax also bears more heavily on families who have larger expenditures relative to their incomes than others, such as families with a large number of children or families who are just beginning a household. Some excise taxes may be progressive, but they are usually levied on mass consumption items and tend to be regressive on balance.

Sales and excise taxes are also criticized on economic grounds. Consumption taxes are never levied at a uniform rate on all goods and services, so that they interfere with the freedom of consumer choice and misallocate the nation's resources (except, as will be noted below, when they are employed as user charges or to discourage consumption of items, such as narcotics, that lead to increased social costs). They rank low as automatic stabilizers, because they respond no more than in proportion to changes in income. Moreover, purchasers may be charged more than the amount of the tax through *pyramiding* when markups are applied to the same goods as they move through the channels of production and distribution. On the other hand, sales and excise taxes are often supported for their relative stability of yield, a characteristic which commends itself for financing state-local activities, but not federal.

As a result of the equity and economic shortcomings of sales and excise taxes, other forms of consumption taxation have been proposed as substitutes. Some economists have been partial to a graduated expenditure tax, but this tax is generally regarded as too difficult to administer. Value added taxation, on the other hand, is beginning to spread, particularly among countries that have relied heavily on turnover taxes and have come to recognize their economic deficiencies.

In this country, the allocation of consumption taxes as a source of revenue between the federal and state-local governments has been stabilized and is not a major issue. Federal consumption taxes are restricted to selective excises, while the state and local governments levy general sales taxes (and, in one case, a value added tax) as well as excises. In 1965, all but a few major federal excise taxes were eliminated. Substitution of a value added tax for part or all of the corporation income tax has been suggested, but Congress has not shown interest in such a trade. Forty-two states and many local governments levy retail sales taxes, and the trend is toward greater use of this tax at the state and local levels.

Issues in Excise Taxation

The imposition of heavy taxes on particular commodities substantially alters the results of the market mechanism. Such interference should be avoided, but there are circumstances under which excise taxes are useful and even necessary.

Economic Effects of Excise Taxes

The immediate effect of an excise tax is to raise the price of the taxed commodity. The consumer's response will be to consume less of the taxed commodity, and to purchase other commodities or to save more. The burden of the tax is thus borne in part by consumers and in part by producers (and distributors) of the taxed commodity. If demand is relatively inelastic (that is, if the consumer does not reduce his consumption very much as the price of the article increases), most of the burden is borne by the consumer. On the other hand, if supply is relatively inelastic (if the producer does not or cannot reduce his production as price declines), the burden is borne mainly by the producer.

In general, the objective of excise taxation is to place the burden of the tax on consumers; and most excise revenues are derived from taxes imposed on articles for which the demand is relatively inelastic. For example, taxes on alcohol, tobacco, and gasoline accounted for almost 60 percent of excise revenues in the year before the 1965 tax cuts went into effect, and will account for almost 85 percent when the cuts become fully effective in 1969 (Table 6-1).

TABLE 6-1. Federal Excise Tax Revenue Before and After the Enactment of the Excise Tax Reduction Act of 1965, by Major Source

(Dollar amounts in millions)

Major Source	Revenue Prior to the Enactment of the 1965 Act[a]		Revenue After the Enactment of the 1965 Act[b]	
	Amount	Percentage of Total	Amount	Percentage of Total
Liquor	3,855	25.2	3,855	36.4
Tobacco	2,240	14.7	2,222	21.0
Highway and auto taxes	6,163	40.4	4,213	39.8
Gasoline	2,800	18.3	2,800	26.4
Other	3,363	22.0	1,413	13.3
Retailers' excise taxes	550	3.6	—	—
Communications	1,075	7.0	—	—
All other	1,387	9.1	304	2.9
Total	15,270	100.0	10,594	100.0

Source: Treasury Department, Office of Tax Analysis (mimeograph). Figures are rounded and may not necessarily add to totals.

[a] Based on consumption levels in fiscal year 1966.

[b] Rates to be effective January 1, 1969. The Tax Adjustment Act of 1966 delayed tax reductions for automobiles and telephone service scheduled for 1966 and 1967, but did not affect the final rates for January 1, 1969, enacted under the 1965 Act.

Furthermore, supply is generally so highly elastic in the taxed industries that, even where demand is relatively elastic, very little of the burden of consumer taxes is borne by the producers.

BURDEN OF EXCISES. The effects of excise taxes on the allocation of economic resources depend on the sensitivity of consumption to a rise in price. If consumption is not much reduced by increased price, the consumer responds by cutting his consumption of other commodities as well as the taxed commodity. The effect is much like that of an income tax which reduces disposable income and causes the consumer to reduce consumption of a wide range of commodities. There is little incentive for labor and capital to move out of the taxed industry, and the allocation of resources elsewhere in the economy is not altered significantly.

When consumption is quite sensitive to price, however, production and employment in the industry producing the taxed commodity will decline. Demand for other products increases at the expense of the taxed industry, and over time the labor and capital will move to other industries (assuming full employment is maintained). In this case, the tax substantially alters the pattern of production and consumption in the private economy. It also may create hardship for the employees and owners of capital in the industries affected.

Thus, an excise tax imposes a burden on the economy because consumers are not as well off as they would have been if the same revenue had been raised by another tax that did not change patterns of consumption. The loss due to this distortion is called the *excess consumer burden* of the excise tax. The amount of the excess burden is the difference between (a) the value placed by consumers on the consumption they give up and (b) the yield of the tax. Excess burden is, in other words, the loss in economic efficiency caused by the imposition of the tax.

This analysis holds only in a world in which the allocation of resources before imposition of the commodity tax is optimum. In the real world there are substantial departures from the conditions necessary for this optimum for reasons other than taxes, and there is no *a priori* basis for making the judgment that a new excise tax necessarily involves a loss in consumer welfare. Consumers may value additional items of the newly taxed commodity less highly than other items which they consume in its place after the tax is imposed, particularly if the imposition of the new tax leads consumers to shift their consumption to commodities that are already heavily taxed.

Nevertheless, the case for selective excise taxes is weak. Conceivably there are excise taxes that would not reduce consumer welfare, but there is no basis for making such a selection. Excise taxes should be avoided unless there is a compelling reason for altering the allocation of resources, and for discriminating among individuals and families on the basis of their consumption preferences.

EXCISE TAXES IN WARTIME. One situation in which the government has a definite interest in changing the pattern of resource use is in wartime or in a similar national emergency. Numerous materials that are in short supply are needed for production in war industries. In extreme cases, as in the two World Wars, the government is forced to replace the market mechanism with direct rationing and to halt production of items that conflict with the war effort. During a more limited emergency, such as the Korean War, it may not be necessary to take such drastic steps. In such circumstances, excise taxes may be helpful both as a rationing device and as a selective method of reducing consumer demand. By increasing prices of the taxed commodities, the government can reduce demand and divert it to other commodities in more plentiful supply, or to saving.

Excises are among the first taxes to be raised in a national emergency. Criticism of such use usually develops on the legitimate ground that the taxes chosen are hard to justify on economic and equity grounds. Further, the rationale of discouraging consumption on a selective basis is quickly forgotten once excises are imposed, and the revenue objective becomes paramount. Even in wartime, use of excise taxes as a major revenue source should be avoided; first, because there are better ways to raise general revenues and, second, because the wartime taxes are apt to linger on—and do considerable damage—for many years. For example, the excises levied by the federal government on many electric, gas, and oil appliances in 1941 were not repealed until 1965.

USER CHARGES. Selective excise taxes may be used to good advantage as a method of obtaining payments from individuals who benefit from particular public services. When public programs lower the cost of a particular activity, that activity will be artificially stimulated and too many resources may be used in its performance. An excise tax, or other method of charging for the service, is needed to maintain economic efficiency.

Despite the sound theoretical justification for such "user charge" excise taxes, they are not employed nearly enough for this purpose at any level of government in the United States. Since 1956, when the Federal Highway Trust Fund was set up to pay for the interstate highway system, Presidents Eisenhower, Kennedy, and Johnson have recommended adoption of a wide range of special taxes as user charges, including payments for the use of federal air and inland waterway transportation facilities, recreation facilities, and numerous other federal services. Pollution of water and air by private individuals and businesses imposes heavy costs on society which should not be borne by the general taxpayer. Adoption of user charges to pay for such benefits and costs would ease the burden of other taxes, promote equity, and improve economic efficiency. But successive administrations have had little success in persuading Congress to accept this approach. User charges are strongly resisted by the groups that would be required to pay, and past experience suggests that their resistance is politically potent and difficult to overcome.

SUMPTUARY AND REGULATORY TAXES. Excises on commodities or services which are considered socially or morally undesirable are known as *sumptuary* taxes. The best examples are the excises on liquor and tobacco. The rationale for sumptuary taxes is that the use of some articles for consumption creates additional costs to society which are not costs the producers bear and are not reflected in the prices they charge. For example, mass consumption of liquor involves costs in the form of losses of working time, accidents, broken homes, and increased delinquency; and consumption of cigarettes has been shown to be associated with higher frequencies of a wide range of illnesses. An excise tax raises prices on such commodities to a level that more nearly reflects total social costs as well as private costs.

In some cases, the costs imposed by certain items are so great that society prohibits their consumption entirely. This is true, for example, of narcotics and gambling. The federal government prohibits the sale of narcotics except under very strict rules, while most states either outlaw or regulate gambling. Taxes are imposed on these items largely to aid in regulation and law enforcement.

In a democratic society, complete prohibition of the use of any one commodity or service requires virtually unanimous agreement that its consumption is harmful or immoral. Where such unanimity does not exist, the majority expresses its view by levying a heavy tax that will discourage consumption without eliminating it entirely. Those who place a high value on the consumption of such items are allowed to purchase them but at a differentially higher price. This explains why gambling is illegal in some states and is subject to regulation and to special taxes in others. Similarly, since opinion on the harmful effects of alcoholic beverages and cigarettes is not unanimous, purchases of these items are permitted but are heavily taxed by the federal and state governments and even by some local governments. The main effects of the taxes levied in the United

States are to tax smokers and drinkers heavily without curtailing their consumption very much and to introduce an element of regressivity into the system.

Another type of regulatory tax, introduced only recently in the United States, is the "interest equalization tax." This excise applies to purchases by United States residents of foreign securities issued in industrial countries (except for new Canadian bond issues), and to loans abroad with maturities of one year or more. The tax is levied on common stock at a rate of 15 percent and on foreign bonds and loans at rates that are equivalent to an interest rate increase of about one percentage point. The purpose of this discriminatory tax is to improve the United States balance of payments by discouraging the flow of capital abroad. The tax was applied to purchases after July 18, 1963, and is now scheduled to expire on July 31, 1967.

Equity Considerations

Excise taxes rank low in terms of equity on a number of grounds. First, consumers probably bear the major burden of the excise taxes which have been employed in the United States. How this burden is distributed depends on the proportion of income allocated to consumption of these items at the various income levels. For example, excise taxes on beer and cigarettes are highly regressive, while those on furs and some consumer durables are progressive. On balance, the post-World War II excise tax structure was regressive throughout the income scale (Table 6-2).

Second, excise taxes are unfair as among different people with the same income. Families whose preferences for the taxed commodities are high are taxed much more heavily than those who prefer other ways to consume their income. This violation of horizontal equity is not justified unless there are overriding social reasons for discouraging the use of particular goods or services. However, where there are special costs or benefits associated with the production or distribution of a particular commodity which are not borne or paid for by the individuals and firms creating the costs or receiving the benefits, imposition of a selective excise tax will improve horizontal equity.

Third, while most of the pre-1965 excise taxes were levied on goods and services used by consumers, some applied to items that were used primarily or exclusively by business (such as business and

TABLE 6-2. Effective Rates of Federal Excise Taxes and Customs, 1954, and of a Hypothetical Wisconsin General Retail Sales Tax, 1956

Money Income Class (Dollars)	Federal Excise Taxes and Customs, 1954[a] (Percentages)	Wisconsin Retail Sales Tax, 1956[b] (Percentages)	
		Including Food[c]	Excluding Food[d]
0– 1,000	} 7.3	4.9	4.8
1,000– 2,000		2.4	2.5
2,000– 3,000	4.8	2.0	2.1
3,000– 4,000	4.3	1.8	2.0
4,000– 5,000	4.1	1.7	1.9
5,000– 6,000	} 3.8	.1.7	1.8
6,000– 7,500		.1.6	1.8
7,500–10,000	3.5	1.4	1.7
10,000 and over	2.0	1.0	1.3
All classes	3.6	1.6	1.8

Sources: Federal excise taxes and customs: R. A. Musgrave, "The Incidence of the Tax Structure and Its Effects on Consumption," *Federal Tax Policy for Economic Growth and Stability*, Joint Committee on the Economic Report, 1956, p. 98. Retail sales tax estimates: Daniel C. Morgan, Jr., *Retail Sales Tax: An Appraisal of New Issues* (University of Wisconsin Press, 1964), p. 32.

[a] Effective rates are based on money income, including transfer payments and capital gains, plus retained corporate earnings and unshifted portion of the corporation profits tax attributed to individual stockholders.

[b] Effective rate on adjusted gross income; based on 1956 Wisconsin incomes and expenditures, assuming the tax is borne by Wisconsin residents.

[c] At a 2 percent rate.

[d] At a 3 percent rate.

store machines, lubricating oils, long distance telephone, and trucks). Taxes levied on such items enter into business costs and are generally reflected in higher prices for consumer goods. Since low income persons spend a larger proportion of their income than those in the higher income classes, taxes that enter into business costs are by nature regressive. Furthermore, they often create unfair competitive situations by discriminating against firms that use the taxed commodity or service and distort the choice of production methods. The classic example of a bad excise tax is the one on freight since it discriminates against firms that are distant from the market. The freight tax was eliminated in 1958.

The Excise Tax Reduction Act of 1965 eliminated most federal excises, except for a few regulatory taxes and highway taxes that recover the costs of services or facilities directly benefiting individuals and business firms. The Act reduced the tax on passenger cars in stages from 10 percent to 1 percent on January 1, 1969, and also reduced the 10 percent telephone tax in stages until it is completely eliminated on January 1, 1969. The scheduled reductions were suspended by the Tax Adjustment Act of 1966 until April 1, 1968, but the 1 percent automobile tax and the repeal of the telephone tax will be effective as originally scheduled on January 1, 1969.

A General Consumption Tax?

The major drawback of selective excise taxes is that they are not neutral, that is, they discriminate among different consumption items. A broad-based tax is a much more appropriate method of taxing consumption. The three broad-based taxes mentioned most often are the general sales tax, the value added tax, and the expenditure tax.

The General Sales Tax

Sales taxation has been used extensively throughout the world, and there is almost no limit to the variations in the structure of these taxes. On the whole, experience suggests that a single-stage tax is preferable to a multistage or turnover tax, and that the scope of the tax should be as broad as possible. Among single-stage taxes, the retail sales tax is to be preferred on economic and equity grounds, but it is somewhat more costly to administer than either a manufacturers' or wholesalers' tax.

SINGLE-STAGE VERSUS MULTISTAGE TAXES. The advantage of the multistage tax is that any particular revenue goal can be realized at the lowest possible rate. This makes the turnover tax politically attractive, but highly objectionable on other grounds. A turnover tax levied at a uniform rate will result in widely varying total rates of tax on different goods, depending on the complexity of the production and distribution channels. This means that the total tax burden will differ among commodities, much as it does under a selective excise tax system. Moreover, the multistage tax provides a strong incentive for firms to merge with their suppliers and contributes to greater concentration in industry and trade.

Even the uniform rate turns out to be a will-o'-the-wisp whenever the turnover tax is tried. The discriminatory effects of the uniform rate soon become very serious and the government finds it difficult to resist pressures to moderate the tax load where it is demonstrably out of line. Once introduced, modifications of the uniform rate proliferate and the tax becomes a maze of complications and irrational distinctions. Thus, a tax that was originally intended to be relatively simple turns out to be an administrative monstrosity and highly inequitable.

WHOLESALERS' AND MANUFACTURERS' SALES TAXES. Administrative complications are reduced if the tax is levied at the wholesale or manufacturing level. The number of firms is smaller, their average size is larger, and their records are more adequate. These advantages are offset, however, by the difficulty of identifying taxable transactions and of determining the price on which the tax is charged.

The most troublesome feature of the wholesalers' tax involves the determination of wholesale values when manufacturers sell directly to retailers. This problem is usually handled by raising the manufacturers' prices to allow for the normal wholesalers' markup. The adjustment goes the other way in the case of the manufacturers' tax: the price charged by a manufacturer to a retailer must be lowered to eliminate the value of the wholesale services.

Both taxes are subject to the criticism that the rate tends to be pyramided as goods move to the retail level. Thus, a 10 percent manufacturers' tax may become a 20 percent tax at the retail level, after the wholesaler and retailer have applied their customary markups. There is less pyramiding under a wholesalers' tax, but the problem is by no means avoided. In time, competition will tend to wipe out the effect of pyramiding, but the adjustment process may be slow.

On balance, there is little to choose between the wholesalers' and manufacturers' tax. The wholesalers' tax is more practical when the wholesale and retail stages are fairly distinct; on the other hand, complications arise if there is a substantial degree of integration between manufacturers and retailers. The manufacturers' tax is more practical when there is either a high degree of integration in most consumer lines or none at all; the mixed situation raises the most difficulties.

RETAIL SALES TAX. A retail sales tax is intended to apply uniformly to most goods and services purchased by individual consumers, and is basically much less complicated than a wholesalers' or manufacturers' tax. However, retail sales taxes are rarely completely general, although they are usually imposed on a broad base. It is difficult to reach many consumer services, although it is possible to include such services as admissions, repairs, laundry, and dry cleaning. The retail sales tax does not apply to housing—the largest service in most consumer budgets—but housing is subject to the property tax. Many state sales taxes in the United States exempt food and other commodities that are regarded as necessities.

Although the retail sales tax often falls short of complete generality, it has much to commend it over the taxes levied at earlier stages of the production or distribution process. Its most important advantage is that there is little or no pyramiding. For goods purchased by consumers, wholesale and retail markups are not inflated by the tax since it applies only to the final price. An attempt is sometimes made to exempt investment goods purchased by business firms from the retail sales tax, but taxes on business purchases often run as high as a fifth of sales tax receipts. Such taxes enter into business costs and are probably pyramided, but the extent of pyramiding must be only a small fraction of that which occurs under a manufacturers' or wholesalers' sales tax.

The broader base of the retail sales tax permits the use of lower rates than other single-stage taxes to yield a given amount of revenue. The difference in rates is not small, since prices may be 50 or 100 percent higher at the retail level. Thus, a retail tax of 5 percent may be the equivalent of a manufacturers' tax of 7.5 or 10 percent.

On administrative grounds, the retail sales tax has both advantages and disadvantages. It is more difficult to deal with the large number of small retailers than with the less numerous and more sophisticated manufacturers or wholesalers. On the other hand, the problems of defining a transaction and of determining the base of the tax are more easily handled at the retail level, although even at this level the problems are not insignificant. The state governments have had retail sales taxes for many years, and most of them have learned that the tax is not easy to administer and enforce.

The introduction of a retail sales tax by the federal government would involve duplication of existing state and local taxes. The state and local governments would interpret this as an unwarranted interference with their freedom of action in regard to rates and coverage of their own taxes. At the minimum, some effort would have to be made to coordinate the definition of the tax bases and perhaps also to administer collection of the taxes on a cooperative or joint basis.

The strongest objection to a retail tax, which also applies to wholesale and manufacturing taxes, is its regressivity. It has been estimated that a 2 percent sales tax in Wisconsin on all tangible commodities, including food, but excluding all services except gas, electricity, admissions, and communications, would amount to 4.9 percent of income for families below the $1,000 level and only 1.0 percent for those above $10,000 (Table 6-2). These figures, based on income and consumption in a one-year period, probably overstate the regressivity of the sales tax, since persons temporarily in the lower income classes do not reduce their consumption by the entire reduction in their income and those temporarily in higher classes do not raise their consumption by the entire increase in their income. Some economists have suggested that the burden of the sales tax should be measured against income over a longer time period. On this basis, a retail sales tax might be proportional, but it is unlikely that it would turn out to be progressive in any significant degree, regardless of the time period used.

Many units of government have exempted food and other items of consumption from the sales tax to alleviate its burden on the poor. Such exemptions moderate, but do not eliminate, its regressivity (Table 6-2). As an alternative, experts have long suggested refunding the estimated tax paid by individuals with low incomes. This suggestion was disregarded until 1963 when Indiana introduced a retail sales tax and adopted a small tax credit against the income tax as a relief measure for the sales tax paid by low income recipients. Since then, Colorado, Hawaii, and Massachusetts have adopted the same device and other states are considering it.

The Value Added Tax

The value added tax, first proposed in 1918 by a German industrial executive, was discussed sporadically for another three decades before it was actually put to use. A modified version was adopted in 1953 by the state of Michigan; in the following year, the central government of France imposed such a tax. Other countries are now considering it as a substitute for other forms of consumption taxes. Some have advocated the addition of a value added tax to the federal tax system to provide a revenue source that could be raised or lowered in the interest of stabilization policy.

FORMS OF VALUE ADDED TAXATION. Conceptually, the value added tax is a general tax on the national income. For any given firm, value added is the difference between receipts from sales and the amounts paid for materials, supplies, and services purchased from other firms. The total of the value added by all firms in the economy is equal to total wages, salaries, interest, rents, and profits and is therefore the same as the national income.

In practice, there are two types of value added taxes that differ only in the way outlays for investment purposes are treated. The first type permits business firms to subtract purchases of capital goods in computing the tax base. Total value added is thus equal to total retail sales of final consumer goods. In the second type, purchases of capital goods are not deducted; instead, firms are permitted to deduct an allowance for depreciation over the useful life of the asset. Thus, only the second type is equivalent to a tax on the national income; the first, which is proposed most often, is a general consumption tax.

There are two methods of computing the allowance to be made for purchases from other firms. Under the "tax credit" method, the tax rate is applied to the total sales of the firm and the tax paid on goods purchased is then deducted. Where this method is used, the tax on all goods shipped must be shown separately on each invoice. Under the second, so-called "calculation" method, purchases are subtracted from sales and the tax rate is then applied to the net figure. Both approaches amount to the same thing, but some administrators believe that the tax credit method is easier to control, because it automatically provides an accounting of the tax to be remitted on exports (the standard practice to avoid putting domestic firms at a competitive disadvantage in foreign markets), and solves some of the problems raised by the inclusion or exclusion of various items such as charitable contributions that are troublesome under the calculation method.

ECONOMIC EFFECTS OF THE VALUE ADDED TAX. The value added tax reduces or eliminates the pyramiding that would occur under the turnover tax or manufacturers' and wholesalers' sales taxes. Since a firm receives credit for the tax paid by its suppliers, it is not likely to apply a markup to its purchases in computing the price to be charged. For example, suppose a retailer who pays $52.50 for an item (including $2.50 tax) wishes to apply a markup of 100 percent. Under the tax credit method, he will charge his customer $105 ($100 plus $5 tax) and take a credit of $2.50 in computing the amount to be paid to the government, leaving a net tax of $2.50. If the calculation method is used, the retailer deducts from the $100 the $50 paid to his supplier and then applies a tax rate of 5 percent to the remainder to obtain the same $2.50 net tax. The customer pays the same total price of $105, which consists of the $100 price net of tax, the $2.50 tax paid by the supplier, and the $2.50 tax paid by the retailer.

The base of the consumption-type value added tax is equivalent to that of a retail sales tax with the same rate, and confined to consumption goods. On the other hand, the income-type value added tax is equivalent to a proportional income tax. Whether the patterns of burden distribution of the income-type and consumption-type value added taxes are equivalent is in dispute, reflecting a difference of opinion regarding the impact of a proportional income tax and a general tax on consumption. The income-type value added tax is paid on capital goods at the time the purchase is made and the tax is presumably recovered as it is depreciated. Under the consumption-type value added tax, purchases of capital goods are free of tax. Thus, at any given time, the income-type value added tax imposes an extra tax on net investment. Some argue that prepayment of the tax under the income-type of tax reduces the return on capital; others believe that it is reflected in higher prices for final consumption goods and has no effect on the rate of return. The difference is not likely to be significant, however.

THE VALUE ADDED TAX VERSUS THE RETAIL SALES TAX. The consumption-type value added tax and the retail sales tax are similar on both economic and equity grounds. Both taxes are, for all practical purposes, taxes on general consumption. The retail sales tax involves fewer administrative problems because determination of tax liability is less complicated and the number of taxpayers is smaller. But in practice retail sales taxes always omit many items of consumption, while a value added tax could probably be levied on a more general basis.

The Expenditure Tax

The expenditure tax has long been discussed in the economic literature, but was not seriously considered until the U.S. Treasury Department recommended it during World War II. It was also advocated by the minority of the British Royal Commission on the Taxation of Profits and Income in 1955. Although neither recommendation was accepted, the tax has since come to be regarded as a respectable possibility.

Unlike the consumption taxes already discussed, the expenditure tax is levied on the individual consumer rather than on the seller of goods and services. In practice, there is little difference in the method of administration between the expenditure tax and the individual income tax. The individual taxpayer submits a form at the end of the year estimating the amount of his expenditures. Deductions for selected expenditures may be allowed, as well as personal exemptions. The rates may be proportional or graduated; usually, however, the expenditure tax is suggested in its graduated form.

Expenditure taxation is intended either to replace or to supplement the income tax. It is supported strongly by those who believe that the income tax has an adverse effect on investment and saving incentives (see Chapter 4). It is also supported as a useful supplement to income taxation when capital gains and other incomes are either not taxed or are taxed at a preferential rate. While capital gains are not reached by the expenditure tax as such, the tax does apply to consumption financed out of capital gains.

Some believe that the income tax is inequitable because it taxes income when it is saved and then again when the savings earn additional income. It is now generally agreed that this double taxation argument is sterile. Both the expenditure tax and the income tax may be progressive and redistributional in effect. If one considers income the better measure of ability to pay, the expenditure tax is inferior. If expenditures are considered the better measure, the income tax is inferior.

The expenditure tax is not more widespread primarily because of difficulties of compliance and administration. It is impractical to ask taxpayers to estimate their expenditures directly, since almost no one keeps adequate expenditure records. Thus, expenditures must be estimated by subtracting saving from income received during the year. This requires the taxpayer to provide balance sheet information (to estimate saving) as well as an income statement. Some proponents of the expenditure tax have pointed out that the requirement to supply balance sheet information should be regarded as a major advantage and not as a disadvantage of the expenditure tax, since the information would be helpful in administering the income tax. However, it is generally agreed that the administrative and compliance problems of an expenditure tax are formidable and that it would be very difficult for most countries to enforce such a tax with the present state of administrative know-how.

Consumption vs. Income Taxes

Until recently, the major argument for adoption of a general consumption tax by the federal government was the arbitrariness of the excise tax system. Except for sumptuary and benefit taxes, the excises which were in effect between 1945 and 1965 could hardly be defended on rational grounds. If revenues from consumption taxes were permanently needed, it would have been better to replace the miscellaneous excises by a general low rate tax on consumer goods.

This argument was eliminated by enactment of the Excise Tax Reduction Act of 1965. For all practical purposes, it can be said that the federal government has reduced consumption taxation to a minimum. The appeal of a general consumption tax must now rest on the substantive ground that it would be better national policy to replace part of the income tax by a general consumption tax.

Heavier reliance on a general consumption tax by the federal government is opposed for several reasons:

First, the shift from income taxes to a consumption tax would impair the built-in flexibility of the tax system. The automatic reductions in income tax revenues during the four postwar recessions were of major importance in moderating the declines of disposable income, and made a major contribution to the brevity and mildness of the recessions. Although the United States has avoided a recession for more than five years, the business cycle has not been eliminated. Maintenance of built-in flexibility is good insurance against the possibility of a serious business contraction in the future.

Second, the use of a general consumption tax would involve federal entrance into a field that is now the most important source of state revenue, and is also becoming important at the local level. Federal use of this tax source would almost surely restrict its use by the state and local governments, which would impair their fiscal capacities at a time when they face large financial responsibilities.

Third, because of the opposition of the state and local governments, any general consumption tax enacted by the federal government would probably be a tax at the manufacturers' or wholesalers' levels. As has been seen, such taxes tend to be pyramided through conventional markups and thus to burden the consumer by more than the amount of revenue collected. Moreover, experience in other countries has shown that there are numerous difficulties in defining the tax base to avoid serious inequities.

Fourth, taking federal, state, and local taxes together, the tax load on low income recipients is already heavy. The increases in state-local taxes in the years immediately ahead will be obtained largely from sources that are most burdensome on these low income groups. Additional consumption taxes at the federal level would make the combined structure at the lower part of the income scale even more regressive. Such a policy would be particularly inappropriate at a time when the federal government has just begun a major effort to moderate the impact of poverty in the United States.

On the other hand, several arguments are advanced supporting greater use of consumption taxes by the federal government:

First, even though income taxes were reduced in 1964, the income tax rates are still too high, particularly for individuals with high incomes. These high rates may reduce incentives and the willingness and capacity to save.

Second, built-in flexibility does not require that all elements of the federal tax system be highly sensitive to changes in income. Furthermore, large automatic growth of tax receipts has the undesirable by-product of promoting higher federal expenditures. If these tax receipts were not so easily obtained, federal expenditures might be much lower.

Third, the federal government need not impair the fiscal capacities of the state and local governments in order to build up its own consumption tax revenue. Use of a value added tax would avoid duplication of state-local revenue sources by the federal government. Since practically all business enterprises already file income tax returns, the administrative and compliance problems of a value added tax should not be insurmountable.

Fourth, adoption of a general consumption tax in lieu of part of the corporation income tax would improve the United States balance of payments position. This substitution would either improve the trade surplus, if the corporation income tax is shifted in the form of higher prices, or the capital account, if the tax is borne by the owners of capital (see Chapter 5). Even a modest improvement in the nation's balance of payments would be a contribution, since the problem has not been easy to solve.

While there are a number of important peripheral considerations, the major issue in the income tax versus consumption tax controversy concerns the degree of progression. Proponents of a general consumption tax rarely recommend a graduated expenditure tax as an alternative to income taxation. Their concern is to reduce progression, and they propose a flat rate sales or value added tax as a method of accomplishing this objective. On the other hand, those who oppose a general consumption tax either defend the present degree of progression or believe it is inadequate. Most of them would support a graduated expenditure tax if a new consumption tax were necessary, but would oppose adoption of a sales or value added tax.

Summary

The federal government has relied exclusively on selective excises for consumption tax revenues. These taxes were increased during every major war, and were subsequently de-emphasized as the need for revenue declined. The cycle lasted somewhat longer during and after World War II, but the last vestige of the wartime excises was eliminated by the 1965 Excise Tax Reduction Act. Under this law, which will become fully effective January 1, 1969, the only excise taxes remaining in the federal revenue system will be the sumptuary taxes on alcohol and tobacco, the benefit taxes for highways, airways, and some recreational activities, and certain regulatory taxes.

Sumptuary taxes help to offset the additional cost imposed on society by the consumption of certain commodities; taxes imposed on those who benefit from particular government services are needed to prevent excessive use of such services; and regulatory taxes are used primarily to assist law enforcement rather than to raise revenues. Otherwise, excise taxes are bad taxes: they discriminate arbitrarily against the consumption of the taxed commodities and distort the allocation of resources in the economy.

If consumption taxes are needed for revenue purposes, economic and equity considerations suggest that a general consumption tax would be more appropriate than a series of selective excise taxes. A general tax does not discriminate against particular forms of consumption and therefore produces less distortion in the economy.

Among general consumption taxes, manufacturers' and wholesalers' sales taxes are probably easiest to administer, but they are pyramided through the markup of prices as goods go through production and distribution channels. Retail sales taxes and the value added tax involve much less pyramiding, if any. All these taxes are either regressive or, at best, proportional. Progression can be achieved by the adoption of a credit for sales taxes paid against the individual income tax, or by taxation of consumption through a graduated expenditure tax. The expenditure tax has a number of attractive features, but it is generally regarded as too difficult to administer.

Consumption taxes are more burdensome on the low income classes than income taxes, and have less built-in flexibility. Adoption of a general consumption tax by the federal government would also interfere with a revenue source that has become a mainstay of state and some local tax systems. Consumption taxes are vigorously supported, however, by those who believe that the federal tax system is too progressive and that income taxation has impaired economic incentives. More recently, some have been supporting the adoption of a value added tax as a replacement for part of the corporation income tax to help improve the United States balance of payments.

CHAPTER 7

Payroll Taxes

TAXES ON PAYROLLS, first introduced into the federal revenue system by the Social Security Act of 1935, have grown markedly during the last three decades. They already rank third in order of importance, accounting for about 17 percent of federal cash receipts in fiscal years 1964 and 1965 (Chart 7-1). Payroll taxes will continue to increase in the 1970's and 1980's as scheduled rate increases go into effect.

Unlike income, excise, estate, and gift taxes, payroll taxes do not contribute to the general revenues of the federal government. Instead, they are "earmarked"—through trust funds—to finance the nation's social insurance programs.

Most countries levy special taxes on payrolls (or income) to finance social insurance. When the United States passed its Social Security Act, twenty-eight countries had well-developed national retirement systems. The depression of the 1930's demonstrated that the state and local governments and private industry did not have the capacity to develop and finance a stable and adequate retirement program for the general population.

The 1935 Act established two social insurance programs: a federal system of old-age insurance (now OASDHI and commonly called "social security") and a federal-state system of unemployment insurance. The first is financed by equal payroll taxes col-

162

CHART 7-1. Payroll Taxes as a Percentage of Gross National Product, Federal Cash Receipts, and Individual Income Tax Receipts, Fiscal Years 1948–65

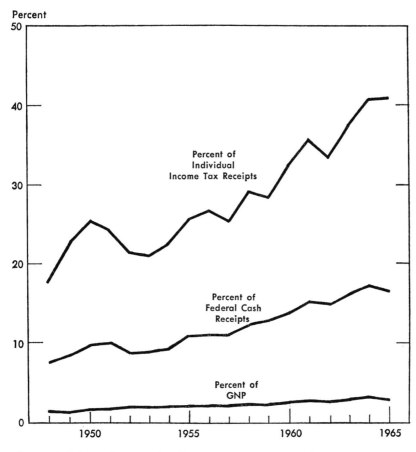

Sources: GNP from *Budget of the United States Government, 1967*, p. 432; all other data from Appendix Table C-3.

lected from employees and employers; the second is financed mainly by payroll taxes on employers (a few states tax both employers and employees). The major characteristics of these programs are summarized in Table 7-1.

The original programs have undergone considerable change in coverage, benefits, and tax rates. Old-age insurance was supplemented by survivors insurance in 1939, disability insurance in 1957, and hospital and medical insurance for persons 65 and over in 1966. The tax rate, initially 1 percent each on employers and

TABLE 7-1. Major Characteristics of the Social Insurance Programs as of July 1, 1966

Program	Contribution Rates		Maximum Earnings Subject to Tax	Eligibility Requirements for Benefits	Benefits
	Employee	Employer			
Old-age, survivors, and disability insurance	3.85%[a]	3.85%[a]	$6,600 per yr.	OASI: 1½ to 10 years of coverage after 1950; aged 62 and over for men and women workers and wives; age 60 for widows[b]	Individual: Maximum $168 per month[c] Individual: Minimum $44 per month Family: Maximum $368 per month[c] Family: Minimum $66 per month
				Disability: Insured status for OASI and recent employment; 6 months' waiting period following total disability	Same as OASI
Hospital	0.35%[d]	0.35%[d]	$6,600 per yr.	Over 65 years of age[e]	60 days (with $40 deductible) plus 30 days at $10 per day; also post-hospital services[f]
Medical (voluntary)	$3 per month premium[g]	—	—	Over 65 years of age	$50 deductible and 20% co-insurance[h]
Unemployment compensation	—	3.1%[i]	$3,000 per yr.	Typically one year of covered employment	Typically 50% of weekly wage up to 26 weeks
Railroad retirement	7.95%[j]	7.95%[j]	$550 per mo.	10 years of coverage, age 65 and over[k]	Individual: Maximum $367.80 per month[l] Individual: Minimum $50.00 per month Family: Maximum $404.80 per month[l] Family: Minimum $72.60 per month
Railroad unemployment compensation	—	4%[m]	$400 per mo.	Compensation of at least $750 in base year[n]	Typically 60% of daily pay for last employment in base year up to 130 days[n]

[a] Increases to 4.85 percent in 1973 and after.
[b] Permanently reduced benefits payable for retirement between ages 62 and 65, or between 60 and 62 for widows.
[c] Generally not payable for many years to come. Maximum payable to a retired worker at age 65 in 1966 is $135.90; to a family, $309.20.
[d] Increases to 0.8 percent in 1987 and after.
[e] No work requirements before 1968; shorter work requirements than under OASI between 1969 and 1974; and after 1974, same as OASI.
[f] Post-hospital services include care in a nursing home (cost of first 20 days and excess over $5 for next 80) under a registered professional nurse, or care in a private home (for 100 visits) if only intermittent nursing is needed.
[g] Rate before 1968. Beginning January 1, 1968, the Secretary of Health, Education, and Welfare will determine premiums necessary to collect one-half the projected expense of the program.
[h] Includes most physician and related services.
[i] Rates are reduced on basis of experience rating in most states.
[j] Increases to 10.15 percent in 1987 and after.
[k] Reduced benefits payable at age 60 with 30 years of service. Survivors and disability insurance also available to railroad employees.
[l] Not generally payable for some time. Maximum payable in 1966 to retired worker at age 65, $217.30; to a family, $340.20.
[m] Statutory rates vary from ½ to 4 percent depending on balance in trust fund.
[n] Base year is calendar year preceding the beginning of the benefit year which runs from July 1 to the following June 30.

164

employees for wages and salaries up to $3,000 annually, is now (1966) 4.2 percent on each and is scheduled to rise to 5.65 percent by 1987. Effective January 1, 1966, the top limit on earnings subject to tax was raised to $6,600. Self-employed persons with net earnings in excess of $400 per year were added to the social security system in 1951, with a tax rate 1.5 times the rate applying to employees. For hospital insurance, the rate for the self-employed is the same as that for employees.

The federal unemployment insurance tax rate started at 1 percent of payrolls of employers of eight or more persons; it is now a maximum of 3.1 percent for employers of four or more persons on wages and salaries up to $3,000 (lower rates are permitted in most states, depending on the stability of the employer's past record of employment). Railroad workers, who are covered for both retirement and unemployment under separate systems, are subject to higher rates.

The employee share of payroll taxes is withheld at the source by employers, but these taxes differ from the pattern established by the individual income tax in other respects. In the first place, they are levied at a flat rate on gross wages and salaries up to a maximum amount each year, with no exemptions or deductions. Second, the employee—even though liable for half the OASDHI tax—does not file a return. The reporting of earnings, which provide the basis for the calculation of benefits, is handled entirely by the employer. Taxes by the self-employed are paid when the individual files his final income tax return.

The federal old-age, survivors, disability, and health insurance programs now cover approximately 90 percent of all persons in paid jobs; 84 percent of the population age 65 and over are drawing benefits or are eligible for benefits. The hospital insurance program covered about 19 million people age 65 or over as of July 1, 1966. In 1965, unemployment insurance covered an average of about 50 million persons, or more than four-fifths of the total number of wage and salary earners.

Although social insurance is financed by taxes, there is a resemblance between these taxes and insurance premiums. The contributory element was emphasized in the original Social Security Act, in the belief that the individual is primarily responsible for his own security and that of his family. For this reason both the OASDHI and the unemployment insurance programs are administered through special trust funds, and pay benefits geared to a person's earning record as well as the number of his dependents (though relatively few state unemployment insurance programs take account of dependents).

Increases in benefits and expansion of the social security programs have been financed by higher payroll taxes. These taxes are regressive, and the recent increases have raised the tax burden on low income wage earners substantially. With federal revenue from these taxes already exceeding $20 billion, increasing attention is being paid to alternative methods of financing further improvements in the programs.

Features of Payroll Taxes

For the most part, payroll taxes have been regarded as contributions and have not been subject to the same scrutiny as have other taxes in the tax system. Nonetheless, they have a significant effect on the distribution of tax burdens and may also have a substantial impact on the economy. From the standpoint of tax analysis the important features are their regressivity; built-in flexibility; effect on prices, employment, and wages; and effect on personal and public saving.

Regressivity

The OASDHI taxes seem to be progressive with respect to income up to about $4,000 of money income, proportional between $4,000 and $7,500, and regressive thereafter (Table 7-2). This pattern of tax incidence reflects the changing importance of covered earnings as incomes rise. In the lower part of the income scale, the ratio of covered earnings to total income increases; covered earnings then become a fairly constant percentage of income; and, finally, the ratio begins to fall because the payroll taxes apply only up to $6,600, and because property income which is not subject to tax becomes increasingly important as incomes rise above this point.

On the basis of 1960-61 data, the current OASDHI taxes are more progressive than an equal-yield proportional tax on consumption up to about $7,500 of income, and at least as regressive above this point. The income tax is, of course, much more progressive

TABLE 7-2. Effective Rates of OASDHI Taxes and of Alternative Methods of Raising the Same Revenue,[a] **by 1960–61 Family Money Income Classes, with 1966 Tax Rates**

(In percentages)

1960–61 Family Money Income Class[b] (Dollars)	OASDHI Effective Rates		Effective Tax Rates Assuming OASDHI Revenue Raised by	
	Assuming Backward Shifting of Employer Tax[c]	Assuming Forward Shifting of Employer Tax[d]	1961 Income Tax[e]	Hypothetical Proportional Consumption Tax[f]
1,000– 2,000	1.6	4.3	0.8	7.3
2,000– 3,000	3.3	4.9	1.4	6.4
3,000– 4,000	4.3	5.2	2.3	6.2
4,000– 5,000	5.7	5.7	3.4	5.7
5,000– 6,000	5.9	5.7	4.0	5.4
6,000– 7,500	6.0	5.6	4.6	5.2
7,500–10,000	5.5	5.2	5.1	4.8
10,000–15,000	4.9	4.7	5.8	4.4
15,000 and over	3.1	3.2	8.3	3.2
All classes	4.9	4.9	4.9	4.9

Source: Special tabulation by the Treasury Department of 1961 Bureau of Labor Statistics Consumer Expenditure Survey, adjusted to reflect 1966 OASDHI tax rates and taxable maximum.

[a] Includes OASDHI revenue from employee, employer, and self-employment taxes.

[b] Income class below $1,000 not shown because income is after subtraction of net losses and percentages in this class are therefore distorted.

[c] Employer and employee taxes are distributed in proportion to taxable wages and salaries by income class.

[d] Employer tax is distributed in proportion to consumption by income class; employee tax is distributed in proportion to taxable wages and salaries.

[e] Assumes that OASDHI revenue is raised by an income tax with the same characteristics as the 1961 federal income tax. Computed by distributing OASDHI revenue in proportion to income tax reported in each income class

[f] Assumes that OASDHI revenue is raised by a proportional tax on consumption. Computed by distributing OASDHI revenue in proportion to consumption reported in each income class.

throughout the income scale than the payroll taxes. These conclusions are the same whether the employer and employee OASDHI taxes are assumed to be borne entirely by the wage earners or whether it is assumed that only the employee tax is borne by wage earners and the employer tax is shifted to the consumer (compare the last two columns of Table 7-2 with the first two).

The increases in payroll taxes made in the Social Security Act of 1965 will have a significant impact on the tax payments of the lowest income groups. When fully effective in 1987, the employee contribution for social security, disability, and hospital care will reach 5.65 percent of wages up to $6,600, or a maximum of

TABLE 7-3. Maximum Taxes on Employees and the Self-Employed Under the OASDI and Hospital Insurance Programs, 1966 and Later Years

(In dollars)

Year	Combined Tax on Employees			Combined Tax on Self-Employed		
	OASDI	Hospital Insurance	OASDI and Hospital Insurance	OASDI	Hospital Insurance	OASDI and Hospital Insurance
1966	254.10	23.10	277.20	382.80	23.10	405.90
1967–68	257.40	33.00	290.40	389.40	33.00	422.40
1969–72	290.40	33.00	323.40	435.60	33.00	468.60
1973–75	320.10	36.30	356.40	462.00	36.30	498.30
1976–79	320.10	39.60	359.70	462.00	39.60	501.60
1980–86	320.10	46.20	366.30	462.00	46.20	508.20
1987 and after	320.10	52.80	372.90	462.00	52.80	514.80

Source: Appendix Table A-6.

$372.90 (Table 7-3). This will exceed present (1966) income tax liabilities for single persons with incomes of less than $3,250, married persons with incomes of $4,150, and married persons with two children and incomes of $5,518. In 1966, the federal payroll tax will be the highest tax paid by at least 25 percent of the nation's income recipients, and $350 million will be paid by persons officially classified as living below poverty levels.

Built-in Flexibility

Payroll taxes are much less sensitive to fluctuations in national income and employment than the federal individual income tax. Since payroll taxes are regressive through a substantial portion of the income scale, their yield (assuming constant tax rates) fluctuates proportionately less than personal income over a business cycle. Automatic increases in tax rates, which are enacted many years ahead, have occasionally aggravated this effect. OASDI tax increases went into effect when the country was in the midst of the 1953-54 recession, and only a few months before the onset of recessions in 1957 and 1961. However, benefits have generally been raised along with or shortly after tax increases, thus offsetting their deflationary impact.

Pressures for increasing payroll tax rates at inappropriate times in the business cycle have also been experienced in state unemployment insurance programs. When the trust funds are threatened by lack of reserves, the states are forced to raise tax rates regardless of the level of economic activity. Moreover, almost all states have adopted the "experience rating" system which reduces tax rates for firms with stable employment. As a result, state unemployment taxes may fluctuate *inversely* with national income and employment levels.

By contrast, the expenditure side of the social insurance trust accounts has been extremely effective in promoting economic stability. Unemployment insurance benefits increase automatically as demand slackens and unemployment increases; they decline automatically as employment picks up. This automatic effect has been supplemented during the last two recessions by temporary federal programs to pay thirteen additional weeks of benefits to workers who have exhausted their benefits under the regular state programs. In addition, older workers have an opportunity to fall back on old-age insurance when they cannot find employment during slack periods.

On balance, despite the regressivity of the taxes and the inappropriate timing of tax rate increases, the social insurance system has contributed notably to the nation's economic stability during the postwar period.

Effect on Prices, Employment, and Wages

It is popularly assumed that the employee share of the payroll taxes is borne by wage earners, and that the employer share is shifted forward to the consumer in the form of higher prices. But this is a substantial simplification of a complicated situation.

The employee OASDHI tax is a proportional tax on wages and salaries up to $6,600. Although a few categories of workers are excluded, the tax may be regarded as virtually universal. Since the tax is paid in every occupation and industry, employees have no incentive to move elsewhere in order to avoid it. Thus, like the personal income tax, the employee payroll tax is not shifted and is probably borne by those who pay it.

It is more difficult to analyze the impact of payroll taxes paid by employers. In the short run, producers will treat the payroll tax as any other production cost and will attempt to recover the additional cost through higher prices. At higher prices they will not sell as much as they did at the pre-tax price level, and output and employment will tend to decline. This effect can be offset if the government maintains real demand at the old level (through a combination of monetary and tax policies), but relative prices and output will be altered in any event. If money demand does not expand sufficiently, output and employment will fall.

In the long run, the impact of the payroll tax depends on the reaction of wage earners to a reduced wage. Business firms aim to use just the right amount of labor and capital to produce at lowest cost. A payroll tax will not make labor any more productive, so employers will have no reason to pay higher total compensation after the imposition of the tax unless some wage earners react to their reduced earnings by withdrawing from the labor force (that is, unless the supply of labor is less than completely inelastic with respect to wages). If some wage earners do withdraw, employers will have to bid up wages to attract additional employees or to keep those that remain; wages will rise as a result of the tax (though not necessarily by the exact amount of the tax) and less labor will be employed.

However, it is generally agreed that the supply of labor is inelastic with respect to wages: lower wages will not induce wage earners to withdraw from the labor force. In these circumstances, the same number of workers will be seeking the same number of jobs, wages will remain unchanged, and the workers will bear the full burden of the tax. Since the employee share of the payroll tax is not shifted, the entire payroll tax—employer and employee contributions—is borne by wage earners in the long run.

It is also possible that workers will bear the tax even if the supply of labor is not completely inelastic with respect to wages. Employees may be willing to accept a lower wage after the tax is imposed if they regard the benefits to be financed by the tax as an adequate *quid pro quo*. If this were the prevailing attitude, the tax would be similar to a user charge, the supply of labor would not be altered, earnings would fall by the amount of the tax, and the full burden would be borne by the wage earners.

The conclusion that the burden of payroll taxes—whether imposed on employers or employees or both—falls on the wage earner must be qualified in one respect. The economic model upon which the analysis is based assumes rational behavior in labor markets, and takes no account of the possible effect on wages of collective bargaining decisions between large firms and labor unions. Labor unions will resist any cut in the wages of their members and may succeed in inducing management to raise gross wages by an amount sufficient to offset the effect of the payroll tax. In such circumstances, part or all of the employer and employee taxes may be transferred to the consumer. Critics of this view argue that, if such market power existed, labor and management could have exercised it to raise prices and wages before the tax was imposed. Nevertheless, one cannot dismiss the possibility that the adoption of a new payroll tax, or an increase in the old one, may be the occasion when labor and management choose to exercise this power.

Personal and Public Saving

National social insurance provides protection against loss of income due to retirement, death, unemployment, permanent disability, and illness. Before the enactment of these governmental programs, individual savings were the only protection against these hazards. It is sometimes suggested that social insurance encourages individuals to set aside a smaller amount of personal saving on the ground that a major reason for saving has now been satisfied. On the other hand, the availability of social insurance may well provide an incentive for individuals to save more: with major hazards already covered, other savings goals may appear to be within reach.

The available evidence suggests that, over the long run, individuals covered by government and industrial pension plans tend to save more than those who are not covered. But nothing is known about the effect on saving of unemployment and disability insurance. At any given time, those who are contributing to social insurance have higher incomes than those who are receiving benefits, so that there is a current redistribution of income from high to low savers. There is no basis for judging how these opposing tendencies have affected total personal saving on balance. While personal saving rose from 5.0 to 5.4 percent of disposable income between 1929 and 1965, many other factors have had a significant influence on the saving ratio.

The effect of the social insurance system on *government* saving is also unclear. As of June 30, 1965, the trust funds had accumulated assets of $34 billion. Had these balances not been accumulated, other taxes might have been raised to yield approximately the same revenue, expenditures might have been reduced, or additional debt might have been issued to the public. An increase in other taxes or expenditure reduction would not have changed the *cash consolidated* surplus or deficit; on the other hand, if other taxes and expenditures had been unchanged, and more debt had been issued to the public, the cash surplus would have been reduced or the deficit increased. Since the federal administrative budget excludes trust fund saving, and the cash budget has not had a great influence on congressional policy until recent years, federal saving has probably been larger (or dis-saving smaller) as a result of the existence of the trust funds. This may well have been a factor in the retardation of economic growth during the late 1950's. With increased emphasis by federal policymakers on the cash budget and the expected decline in the relative importance of trust accounts in the future, they will probably have a smaller impact on fiscal policies and, hence, on national saving, in future years.

Financing Social Security

In view of the multiple objectives of the social security (OASDHI) program, it is not surprising to find disagreement regarding financing methods. Some advocate recourse to the general revenues to finance future increases in benefits; others prefer continued use of payroll taxes; still others prefer a combination of the two.

The Contributory System

Financing of social security through contributory—and often regressive—taxes is well established in most countries. Receipts are earmarked to make workers feel that they are receiving benefits as a matter of right rather than as a government donation. The earmarked taxes emphasize the statutory nature of the benefit and may discourage benefit reductions when the budget is tight. Moreover, increases in benefits are believed to be easier to obtain if they are financed by the contributions of future beneficiaries rather than from taxes in general.

Those who oppose financing social security through the contributory system point out that benefits are not tied very closely to the tax payments. There are both minima and maxima to the level of benefits. Congress has been lenient in extending eligibility to persons with minimum periods of covered employment. Under the circumstances, the tax payments can hardly be said to approximate contributions even in a loose sense of the word. Regressivity of the taxes adds to dissatisfaction with the contributory system.

In practice, the financing of OASDHI in the United States is a compromise between these conflicting points of view. Although the taxes are regressive, the social security system does give the largest benefits relative to contributions to the poorest workers. The existence of balances in the reserve fund gives assurance to the millions of covered workers that their rights to benefits are protected. It would be possible to administer the present OASDHI system without the reserve fund device; nevertheless, every impartial commission that has ever examined this question has arrived at the conclusion that the reserve fund should be continued. However, the appropriate size of the reserve remains an issue.

A significant departure from the precedent of relying entirely on payroll taxes to finance social security benefits occurred in 1965, when the Congress added medical and hospital insurance to the OASDI system. Hospital care for the insured aged was funded by payroll tax contributions from employers and employees; the general fund will pay for those not insured. Medical insurance was made available to aged persons who voluntarily agree to pay $3 per month; an equal amount will be transferred to a new trust fund by appropriation from the general fund. In future years the premium rate for medical insurance will depend on actual experience, but the general fund will continue to match the individual's premium.

Another departure from payroll tax financing was made in 1966, when all individuals reaching the age of 72 before 1968 were granted a pension of $35 per month ($52.50 where a husband and wife both qualify). The pension is reduced by an amount equal to the benefits of any other federal, state, or local retirement program for which the individual is qualified. The cost of this extension of coverage is paid out of the general fund.

Proposals for Reform

Suggestions for changing the method of financing social security fall into three categories, which are not mutually exclusive.

REDUCE REGRESSIVITY. The simplest method to reduce regressivity would be to raise the amount of earnings subject to tax and eventually remove the limit entirely. The taxes would then become proportional taxes on payrolls, which would still be regressive with respect to total income but much less than under present law. Increases in the earnings base have financed higher benefits in recent years, and will doubtless continue to be used in the future.

INTEGRATE THE PAYROLL AND INCOME TAXES. A more straightforward method of removing regressivity is to incorporate the employee contribution into the individual income tax, either directly or through a credit for payroll tax payments against the individual income tax. Financing through the income tax could be made the occasion for eliminating social security contributions by income recipients below the exemption or poverty levels, but this final step is not essential for payroll-income tax integration. In the case of the credit, cash refunds could be paid to those whose payroll taxes exceeded the income tax due.

With coverage now available to more than 90 percent of the workers (in the case of OASDHI), the income tax population for any given generation of workers is not very different from the payroll tax population. The differences that do exist between the two taxes—the exemptions, personal deductions, and broader income concept—argue in favor of use of the income tax rather than the payroll tax. The psychological advantage of having a special earmarked tax to finance the social security programs can be duplicated by the credit device, or by allocating some percentage of the income tax receipts or a given number of percentage points of the income tax rates to the reserve funds.

The decision to integrate the employee tax with the individual income tax does not necessarily require a change in the employer tax, although the two would undoubtedly be considered together. One method might be to replace the employer tax by the necessary number of percentage points of the individual and corporation income taxes. For example, the OASDHI tax paid by employers on 1966 payrolls is equivalent to a 4 percentage-point increase in all individual and corporation income tax rates.

USE THE GENERAL FUND. As already indicated, precedent exists for using general fund receipts to finance social insurance. With the combined employer-employee OASDHI tax scheduled to exceed 10 percent by 1973, use of the general fund should be considered as an alternative to rate increases when additional funds are required to finance benefits. Since the general fund relies primarily on progressive taxes, this would automatically improve the equity of the overall tax system.

Financing Unemployment Insurance

Two major financial features of the unemployment insurance system have been subject to criticism in recent years: (1) the variation of tax rates by firms in accordance with their employment experience; and (2) the inadequacy of trust funds in states suffering heavy and prolonged unemployment.

The experience rating principle was adopted to induce employers to stabilize their employment, and also to avoid the criticism that firms with stable employment would be subsidizing those with irregular employment records. Although experience rating has survived for three decades, it has been subjected to almost continuous criticism. The major argument has been that individual firms have little control over unemployment, particularly of the cyclical variety. Moreover, the payroll tax savings are negligible in comparison with the costs of retaining workers when they are not producing, so that little employment stabilization can be expected. It has also been suggested that, since contribution rates vary among firms, only those employers paying the lowest rates are able to shift the tax to consumers or wage earners. This may well account for the resistance of employers to increases in coverage and benefits. Despite these objections, there is considerable hesitancy to abandon experience rating, partly because it provides an incentive for individual employers to prevent abuse of the system by their employees, and partly because there is strong objection to the redistribution of tax burdens among firms.

The uneven concentration of unemployment in particular industries and regions has had a very uneven effect on the state trust funds. The extension by the federal government of coverage for workers who exhausted their benefit rights in the 1958 and 1961 recessions was made in response to the need of many states for assistance. The 1958 legislation advanced funds to states that elected to participate, while the 1961 legislation financed the extension through a temporary increase in the federal unemployment compensation tax.

Since 1961, Presidents Kennedy and Johnson have recommended that Congress enact permanent legislation to finance extension of benefits automatically when unemployment becomes serious. The proposals contemplate federal assistance through increases in the federal portions of the unemployment compensation payroll tax or through contributions from the general fund. Benefits have not kept pace with the rise in wages; their liberalization will require either an increase in the earnings base from the $3,000 level enacted in 1939 or general fund contributions. Use of the general fund would be particularly appropriate to pay for further extensions of unemployment insurance benefits during periods of high unemployment.

In addition, the federal government now finances retraining or readjustment allowances under the Manpower Development and Training Act of 1962, the Trade Expansion Act of 1962, and the Economic Development Act of 1965. The multiplicity of programs points to the need for a thorough review and realignment of methods used to ease the financial strain on unemployed workers seeking employment or undergoing training. Viewed in this perspective, use of the general fund for at least partial financing of benefits is both logical and equitable.

Summary

Payroll taxes paved the way for enactment of a comprehensive social insurance system which protects workers against income losses due to retirement, unemployment, and disability. The 1965 legislation also provided protection for retired workers against the high cost of hospitalization and medical care. Many still believe that the psychological advantage of financing social insurance through earmarked payroll taxes outweighs the economic and equity drawbacks. These taxes lack the built-in flexibility of the individual income tax and are regressive throughout a substantial portion of the income scale (although benefits are proportionately greater for low-paid workers). In the long run, both the employer and employee payroll taxes are probably paid by the workers.

Although the trust fund device was introduced simultaneously with the payroll taxes, the two are separable issues. Funds for the trust funds could be raised from other earmarked tax sources or from the general fund. On the other hand, payroll taxes could be continued as the basic method of obtaining employee and employer contributions without a trust fund. In the past, the accumulation of reserves has probably been deflationary, but there is no reason why federal fiscal policies should disregard the effect of the trust funds on stability and growth. Increasing use of the consolidated cash budget should help in this respect.

Given the present importance of the payroll taxes and the increases in tax rates already scheduled, the effects of these taxes on the distribution of income can no longer be disregarded. Removal of the ceilings on the payroll tax bases, integration of the payroll and income taxes, or use of the general fund for financing increased social security benefits would improve the equity of these taxes.

CHAPTER 8

Estate and Gift Taxes

TAXES ON PROPERTY left by an individual to his heirs are among the oldest forms of taxation. In societies in which property is privately owned, the state protects the rights of the individual in his property and supervises its transfer from one generation to the next. Consequently, the state has always regarded property transfers as appropriate objects of taxation.

Transfer taxation can take several forms, depending on when the transfers are made and how the tax base is figured. The federal government imposes an *estate* tax on the privilege of transferring property at death, while most of the states impose *inheritance* taxes on the privilege of receiving property from the dead. Both taxes are usually graduated, the former on the basis of the size of the entire estate and the latter on the basis of the size of individual shares in the estate. Usually, the inheritance tax is also graduated on the basis of the relationship of the heir to the decedent, the rate being lowest for the closest relative.

Taxes at death could be avoided simply by transferring property by gift *inter vivos* (during life). Accordingly, the federal estate tax is associated with a *gift* tax, which is imposed on the donor. (However, only twelve out of the forty-nine states with death taxes levy a gift tax.)

Receipts from bequests and gifts, like income from work or investments, are a source of ability to pay. In theory, therefore, gifts and bequests should be taxable as income when received. However, property transfers are taxed separately, partly because death taxes antedate the income taxes and partly because it would be unfair to tax transfers at the full graduated income tax rates in the year of receipt. The impact of income tax rate graduation could be moderated by averaging, but this approach to transfer taxation has never been seriously considered in this country. (It is interesting to note, however, that the Income Tax Act of 1894, which was held unconstitutional, included in the definition of income "money and the value of all personal property acquired by gift or inheritance.")

Opinions about death taxes vary greatly in a society relying heavily on private incentives for economic growth. Some believe that these taxes hurt economic incentives, reduce saving, and undermine the economic system. On the other hand, there is general agreement that death taxes have less adverse effects on incentives than income taxes of equal yield. Income taxes reduce the return from effort and risk-taking as income is earned, whereas death taxes are paid only after a lifetime of work and accumulation and are likely to be given much less weight in decisions to work, save, and invest.

It is interesting that death taxes have been supported by people in all income classes. One of the strongest supporters was Andrew Carnegie, who had doubts about the institution of inheritance and felt that wealthy persons are morally obligated to use their fortunes for social purposes. In his *Gospel of Wealth,* Carnegie wrote that "the parent who leaves his son enormous wealth generally deadens the energies of the son, and tempts him to lead a less useful and less worthy life than he otherwise would." He applauded the growing acceptance of estate taxes and said: "Of all forms of taxation this seems the wisest." According to Carnegie, a wealthy man should live unostentatiously, ". . . provide moderately for the legitimate wants of those dependent on him, and, after doing so, to consider all surplus revenues which come to him simply as trust funds . . . to administer in a manner . . . best calculated to produce the most beneficial results for the community."

Despite the appeal of estate and gift taxes on social, moral, and economic grounds, taxes on property transfers have never provided significant revenues in this country. The federal government used an estate tax briefly for emergency purposes from 1862 to 1870, and 1898 to 1902; the present tax was enacted in 1916. The gift tax was first levied for two years in 1924 and 1925, and then enacted permanently in 1932. During and after World War II, income and excise tax rates were increased substantially; but the estate and gift tax rates and exemptions have remained unchanged since 1942, and structural changes made in the postwar period have greatly reduced their importance in the federal revenue system. Estate and gift taxes accounted for 4.4 percent of cash receipts in fiscal year 1941, 2 percent in 1948, and 1.2 percent in 1953. They have risen to a fraction above 2 percent in recent years as a result of the large rise in the value of corporate stock and other property.

One can only guess why the estate and gift taxes have not been more successful. A possible explanation is that equalization of the distribution of wealth by taxation is not yet accepted in the United States. In some countries, economic classes tend to be fairly stable with little crossing-over by succeeding generations. In the American economy, membership in economic classes is fluid. The average family in the United States still aspires to improved economic and social status, and the estate and gift taxes are erroneously regarded as especially burdensome to the family which is beginning to prosper through hard work and saving.

Moreover, property transfer taxes are not considered equitable taxes by many people. A surprising number resent even the relatively low taxes now imposed on small estates. This attitude may be due to the fact that the base of the property transfer taxes is in certain respects broader than what the public considers to be "wealth" properly subject to tax. The family home, the family car, Series E bonds, savings bank deposits, and similar property are not regarded as appropriate objects of taxation. The public is not aware that the major part of the estate tax base consists of stocks, bonds, and real estate, and that most people are not subject to estate taxes.

Characteristics of the Two Taxes

The calculation of the estate and gift taxes follows the pattern established by the income taxes. The total amount of property transferred is reported, deductions and exemptions are subtracted, and the graduated rates are applied to the remainder. But there are many complications.

The Estate Tax

The *gross estate* consists of all property owned by a decedent at the time of death, including stocks, bonds, real estate, mortgages, and any other property which technically belonged to him. (The property is valued either on the date of death, or one year later, at the option of the estate's executor.) The gross estate also includes gifts made in contemplation of death, the value of any trusts created during life that could be revoked by the decedent at any time, and insurance owned by the decedent. Deductions are allowed for funeral expenses and expenses of settling the estate, debts, legal fees, charitable bequests, and for a bequest to a surviving spouse up to one-half the estate (the marital deduction). A specific exemption of $60,000 is also subtracted to obtain the taxable estate. Estate tax rates begin at 3 percent on the first $5,000 of the taxable estate and rise to 77 percent on the amount of the taxable estate in excess of $10,000,000 (Appendix Table A-8).

As an example of the method of calculation assume that a married individual owning $1,000,000 of securities bequeathed half his wealth to his wife and half to his children. Assume also that the expenses of settling the estate amounted to $25,000, and that the decedent had $75,000 of debts at time of death. If this decedent had been single or had not left anything to his spouse, the net estate before the exemption would be $900,000 and the taxable estate after the exemption would be $840,000. However, the marital deduction reduces the net estate to $450,000 and the taxable estate to $390,000.

The estate tax rates would produce a tax of $110,500 on a taxable estate of $390,000. However, credit is allowed for any death taxes paid to the state of residence up to 80 percent of the 1926 federal tax. This amounts to $8,400. Thus, the net tax payable to the federal government would in this case be $102,100 ($110,500 —$8,400).

The Gift Tax

The gift tax is calculated in much the same way, except that the exemptions are more complicated and the tax is computed on the

basis of total accumulated gifts after 1932. The tax due in any particular year is the additional tax resulting from the gifts made in
that year. The marital deduction is also available for gifts made to a
spouse. In addition, for married persons, a gift can be treated as if
half is given by the husband and half by the wife. The gift tax rates
are three-quarters of the estate tax rates.

Suppose a married man with an estate of $1,000,000 decides to
distribute it to his two children systematically over a period of ten
years. The law gives both him and his wife a lifetime tax exemption
of $30,000 each, and an annual exclusion for each child of $3,000.
The total lifetime exemption for the couple is $60,000 and the an-
nual exclusions amount to $6,000 per year for each child, or an-
other $120,000. Thus, the taxable gifts amount to $820,000, and
the amount of gift tax paid is $175,350:

	Husband	Wife	Total
Total gifts	$500,000	$500,000	$1,000,000
Deduct:			
Lifetime exemption	30,000	30,000	60,000
Annual exclusions			
($3,000 per child per year)	60,000	60,000	120,000
Total taxable gifts	410,000	410,000	820,000
Total tax	87,675	87,675	175,350

By contrast, if the same amounts had been subject to the higher
estate tax rates, each spouse would have paid an estate tax of
$126,500, or a total of $253,000. Disposition of the estate through
gifts would save $77,650, or almost 31 percent.

The Tax Base

Estate and gift taxes are levied only on a small proportion of
privately owned property in the United States. About 3 percent of
the estates of adult decedents and less than one-fourth of the wealth
owned by the decedents in any one year are subject to estate or gift
taxes. The relatively small size of the tax base is explained in part
by the generous exemptions which exclude a large proportion of the
wealth transfers, and also by defects in the taxes that permit substantial amounts of property to be transferred free of tax.

The total number of taxable estate tax returns filed in 1963 was

55,207. The value of the gross estates reported on these returns was $14.7 billion (Appendix Table C-18). Exemptions and deductions reduced this amount by about 50 percent, leaving an estate tax base of $7.1 billion. The estate tax amounted to $1.8 billion, or 26 percent of the taxable estates.

Two-thirds of the taxable returns reported gross estates of less than $200,000, but only 10 percent of the total tax liability. Returns with gross estates of $1,000,000 or more, on the other hand, accounted for 49 percent of the total tax and only 3 percent of taxable returns. The tax liability (before state tax credit) ranged from 5 percent of gross estates in gross estate classes below $250,000 to 36 percent above $20,000,000.

Gifts reported for the year 1963 amounted to $2.6 billion, of which $1.4 billion were reported on 20,598 taxable returns. Taxable gifts totaled $790 million and gift tax paid amounted to $183 million, or 13 percent of the total gifts on taxable returns and 23 percent of the taxable gifts (Appendix Table C-19).

Structural Problems

Structural defects greatly impair the effectiveness of the present estate and gift taxes. These defects have unequal impact, depending on how and when dispositions of property are made. Such disparities are hard to justify, because many people—for reasons of early death or for personal or business reasons—cannot avail themselves of the opportunity to minimize the taxes on their estates. Rate increases or exemption reductions would aggravate these inequalities. Because property can be transferred in many different ways, it is difficult to devise one solution that will be equitable in all cases. The major problems are: (1) the treatment of transfers of husband and wife; (2) separate taxation of gifts and estates; (3) the use of trusts to escape taxation for one or more generations; (4) charitable foundations; and (5) tax payments by small businesses.

Transfers of Husbands and Wives

Transfers by married couples present a difficult problem because it is hard to decide whether they should be taxed as if their property is separate property or part of one estate. Since the estate and gift taxes are excises on transfers of property, the concept of legal ownership plays an important part in determining the amount of tax to be paid. The distinction between community and noncommunity property is crucial in this respect.

COMMUNITY AND NONCOMMUNITY PROPERTY. Under the community property system, which prevails in eight states, all property acquired during marriage by a husband and wife (except for property acquired by gift or inheritance) belongs equally to each spouse. The community property states vary as to whether the income from property owned before marriage or acquired during marriage by gift or inheritance belongs to both spouses equally or to the original owner or recipient alone. In noncommunity property states, each spouse retains ownership of all property acquired or accumulated out of his separate earnings or inheritance even after marriage.

Prior to 1942, federal estate and gift taxes recognized the community property system: only half of the community property transferred between spouses was taxable under the estate tax, and gifts to third parties were treated as if half was made by each spouse. In noncommunity property states the entire amount of property accumulated by a spouse was taxable to him.

To equalize estate and gift taxes between residents of community and noncommunity property states, the Revenue Act of 1942 provided that transfers of community property were taxable to the spouse who earned it. In effect, the 1942 law treated community property as if it were noncommunity property.

The Revenue Act of 1948 attempted to achieve equalization by moving in the opposite direction. In the spirit of income splitting for income tax purposes, transfers of community property were made taxable under the pre-1942 rules, while in the case of noncommunity property a deduction was allowed for the amount of the property transferred to the surviving spouse, up to half the estate. In the case of a gift of noncommunity property by one spouse to another, only half the gift was made taxable. Gifts to third persons were to be treated as though half was made by each spouse. These rules are still in effect today.

The marital deduction greatly increased the amount of property which married persons might transfer free of tax. Half of all interspousal transfers was eliminated from the bases of the estate and gift taxes. As a result, the estate tax exemption for married persons was in effect doubled from $60,000 to $120,000, provided the decedent transferred at least $60,000 to the surviving spouse. Gift splitting also in effect doubled the annual exclusion of $3,000 to $6,000 and the lifetime gift tax exemption of $30,000 to $60,000.

Transfers between spouses are, of course, subject to tax at the death of the recipient or when the recipient makes gifts, but the total tax on the couple was nevertheless substantially reduced by the marital deduction. For example, an estate of $10 million left by a married person was subject to a tax of over $6 million under the 1942 law. Under the 1948 law, assuming half the estate is left to the surviving spouse, the tax was reduced to $2.43 million. Even if the $5 million received by the spouse is later taxed in full under the estate tax, the subsequent tax is $2.43 million and the total tax on the original $10 million is $4.86 million, a tax decrease of $1.14 million, or 20 percent below the liability under the 1942 law (Table 8-1).

TABLE 8-1. Estate Taxes Paid by a Married Couple, by Net Estate Levels[a]

Net Estate Before Exemption (Dollars)	Tax on Husband (Assuming he leaves no bequest to wife) (Dollars) (1)	Tax on Husband (Assuming he leaves half of estate to wife)		Tax on Husband and Wife (Assuming bequest from husband is taxed in full at wife's death)	
		Amount (Dollars) (2)	Percentage of Column (1) (3)	Amount (Dollars) (4)	Percentage of Column (1) (5)
100,000	4,800	0	0	0	0
120,000	9,500	0	0	0	0
150,000	17,900	1,050	5.9	2,100	11.7
200,000	32,700	4,800	14.7	9,600	29.4
500,000	126,500	47,700	37.7	95,400	75.4
750,000	212,200	86,500	40.8	173,000	81.5
1,000,000	303,500	126,500	41.7	253,000	83.4
2,000,000	726,200	303,500	41.8	607,000	83.6
5,000,000	2,430,400	968,800	39.9	1,937,600	79.7
10,000,000	6,042,600	2,430,400	40.2	4,860,800	80.4
20,000,000	13,742,000	6,042,600	44.0	12,085,200	87.9

Note: Effective rates are *before* the credit for state death taxes.
[a] Assumes husband dies first.

These large tax differences might be tolerable—despite the large reduction in estate and gift tax revenues—if the 1948 amendments had accomplished their objective of equalizing the tax in community and noncommunity property situations. In fact, they did so in some, but not in others. Suppose a married man who accumulated a $1,000,000 estate through his own efforts bequeathed all the property to his wife and he dies first. Under the 1948 amendments, only half the estate would be taxable whether he lived in a community property state or in a noncommunity property state. (In the noncommunity property state he is allowed a marital deduction of 50 percent; in the community property state, his wife automatically owns half his estate, and he is taxable only on his half.) However, if the wife predeceases him and leaves her property to the children, she is taxable on half of the property accumulated by the husband in a community property state and he is later taxable on the second half when he dies. In the noncommunity property state, the husband is taxable on the entire estate when he dies, and because the rates are graduated, he pays more than the couple in the community property state. On the other hand, a couple in a community property state would pay a higher tax if the wife dies first and leaves her share of the community property to the husband.

INTERSPOUSAL EXEMPTIONS. If it is assumed that Congress will not restore the 1942 law, the problem can be solved by extending the marital deduction to include all transfers between husband and wife. This would permit transfers of noncommunity property between husband and wife to be made tax free. A man who gave as much as half his estate to his wife would be taxable only on his half whether he dies first or last, as in community property states.

Complete exemption for transfers between husband and wife suggests that the husband and wife are a single unit. It would follow that their combined estates should be cumulated for estate tax purposes. The initial installment on the combined tax would be collected on the death of one spouse, and the remainder (figured on the basis of the cumulated estates) would be collected on the death of the second spouse. The attractive feature of this proposal is that it would equalize the taxes paid by married couples in all states regardless of the order in which they disposed of the estate, without weakening the estate tax base.

However, estate cumulation may produce inequitable results where the wealth of the husband or wife was separately inherited or accumulated. For example, a woman married to a wealthy man for a relatively short period might be taxed at the maximum estate tax rates even though the amount of property she owned was small. This objection could be met by cumulating only as much of the property transferred by the wife (during life or at death) as was originally acquired from the husband. Tracing difficulties could be avoided by cumulating only transfers of the wife up to the dollar amount of property received from the husband. However, such a compromise would fail to take into account any increase in the value of the property taking place after the interspousal transfer.

A second approach would be to provide a 100 percent exemption for all interspousal transfers without cumulating the estates of the husband and wife. The advantage of this approach is that owners of noncommunity property could arrange their affairs in the same way as owners of community property. The disadvantage is that it would substantially reduce the yield of the estate tax. While it is conceivable that the revenue loss could be offset by rate adjustments, it is hardly likely that the adjustment, if any, would be precise and the benefits would go mainly to very wealthy individuals.

Still a third approach would be to give married couples the privilege of making an irrevocable election between (a) exemption of interspousal transfers and cumulation of transfers to third parties, or (b) waiver of the marital deduction and elimination of the automatic splitting of community property combined with noncumulation of transfers to third parties. The major difficulty with this approach is that many complexities would arise out of the instability of the family unit. Divorce, as well as remarriage after the death of one spouse, might provide avenues of escape from the cumulation of transfers which would otherwise be required. Moreover, it is probably unwise as a matter of policy to permit taxpayers to make such a decision irrevocably, since later changes in circumstances might create inequities and considerable dissatisfaction.

Separate Taxation of Estates and Gifts

A wealthy individual is well advised to transfer a substantial part of his property by gift during his lifetime rather than by

CHART 8-1. Estate or Gift Taxes for Alternative Property Transfers During Life and at Death

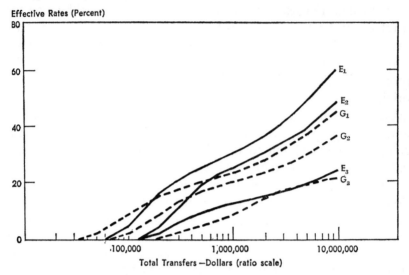

Effective Rates (Percent)

Total Transfers —Dollars (ratio scale)

Note: Effective rates are *before* credit for state taxes.
E_1—bequest not eligible for marital deduction.
E_2—bequest by husband with full marital deduction; wife's half subject in full to estate tax rates.
E_3—bequest with full marital deduction; no tax on wife's estate.
G_1—gift in one year, one donee, no marital deduction.
G_2—gift in one year, one donee, full marital deduction.
G_3—equal gifts in ten-year period, two donees, full marital deduction.

bequest, for four reasons. First, the estate is split between the estate and gift tax brackets, thus moderating the full impact of estate tax graduation. Second, the gift tax rates are 25 percent lower than the estate tax rates. Third, the lifetime exemption of $30,000 and the annual per donee exclusion of $3,000 under the gift tax permit additional tax-free transfers over and above the $60,000 estate tax exemption. Fourth, the amount paid as gift tax does not enter into the gift tax base, whereas the estate tax is computed on the basis of the decedent's entire property including that part used to pay the tax.

Chart 8-1 illustrates the estate and gift taxes paid on various combinations of bequests and gifts made by one individual to his wife and children. To minimize tax liability, he would have to take into account the large tax differences shown in the chart, as well as any tax that might be due on the death of his wife. Although there are many uncertainties, it is clear that a carefully drawn plan of wealth distribution during the life of a wealthy person can pay handsome dividends in lower tax burdens.

USE OF GIFTS. Information on the distributions of wealth during life and at death has been collected by the Treasury Department on the basis of the estate and matched gift tax returns of the wealthiest decedents for whom estate tax returns were filed in 1945, 1951, 1957, and 1959. Gifts made before 1932 were available on the 1945 and 1951 estate tax returns. Thus, it was possible to build up an aggregate figure for the property distributed by each decedent during life and at death for the two earlier years, and a total excluding gifts prior to 1932 for the two later years.

The figures (Table 8-2) show clearly that wealthy individuals prefer to retain the bulk of their property until death and fail to use gifts to maximum tax-saving advantage. The small proportion of gifts is accounted for by a number of reasons. First, there is a natural reluctance on the part of most people to contemplate death. Uncertainty regarding time of death encourages delay in making estate plans even by individuals with considerable wealth. Second, many wish to maintain control over their businesses. Disposal of stock or real estate frequently means loss of control over substantial enter-

TABLE 8-2. Frequency of Gifts and Percentage of Wealth Transferred by Gift During Life Among Millionaire Decedents, 1945, 1951, 1957, and 1959

Total Wealth Transferred During Life and at Death (Millions of Dollars)	Percentage of Decedents with Gifts During Life				Percentage of Wealth Transferred by Gift			
	1945	1951	1957	1959	1945	1951	1957	1959
1 – 1.25	77	74	52	56	14	12	5	5
1.25– 1.5	76	65	57	58	17	7	6	8
1.5 – 1.75	83	74	55	67	21	12	7	8
1.75– 2.0	89	70	67	71	28	10	6	8
2.0 – 3.0	84	88	65	68	20	14	6	8
3.0 – 5.0	88	84	69	84	20	14	7	11
5.0 –10.0	100	95	75	84	20	18	10	11
10.0 and over	91	100	92	100	38	25	15	17
Total	83	77	60	66	24	16	9	10

Source: Special tabulations by the Treasury Department.
Note: Includes only returns with total transfers before tax during life and at death of $1,000,000 or more. Data for 1945 and 1951 include gifts prior to 1932; those for 1957 and 1959 exclude such gifts.

prises. Third, donors may wish to delay transfers of property until their children have had an opportunity to make their own careers. Fourth, many people—even those who are wealthy—do not know the law, and often do not take the advice of their tax lawyers on such personal matters.

Whatever the reason, the present use of gifts has resulted in much less erosion of the tax base than might have been possible. The major criticism of the law is that it discriminates against those people who do not dispose of a substantial portion of their wealth during their lives for business or personal reasons.

INTEGRATION OF ESTATE AND GIFT TAXES. The remedy for the inequalities resulting from separate taxation of gifts and estates is to integrate them into one tax. Bequests would be added to gifts during life to determine the total wealth for transfer tax purposes. Tax would be paid on gifts on a cumulated basis (as under present law), and bequests would be regarded as the final transfer or "gift." As a substitute for separate exemptions, an integrated system would have a single exemption which would be used by the taxpayer first against his lifetime gifts and then against the estate for the remainder, if any. Since there are now separate exemptions of $60,000 and $30,000 for the estate and gift taxes, respectively, the exemption under an integrated system would presumably be between $60,000 and $90,000. The exclusion for lifetime gifts could be retained at the present $3,000 per donee per year.

Integration is opposed by those who believe that gifts should be encouraged through the incentive of lower tax rates. It is argued, in fact, that the lower gift tax rates tend to reduce the concentration of wealth by encouraging transfers in small amounts to a relatively large number of donees.

However, integration would not entirely remove the incentive to distribute property by gift if the gift tax is excluded from the integrated transfer tax base. Since a decedent's estate includes the amounts paid out in estate tax, full equalization of transfer taxes during life and at death would require the inclusion of the gift tax in the final integrated tax base.

An integrated system would eliminate the need for special estate tax provisions dealing with gifts in contemplation of death. Under a separate estate tax, gifts made just before death to escape the estate tax are usually included in the estate tax base. But it is almost impossible to determine objectively whether a gift was in fact made in contemplation of death. The federal law now presumes that gifts made within three years before death are in contemplation of death, but this presumption is rebuttable with evidence that the decedent did not expect to die. The British remove uncertainty by including all gifts made within two years of death in the estate tax base, and an increasingly smaller percentage of gifts between two and five years. Such provisions would be unnecessary under an integrated estate and gift tax.

Generation-Skipping Through Trusts

The most intractable problem in estate and gift taxation results from the existence of the *trust,* a legal institution used to administer funds on behalf of individuals or organizations. Suppose A wants his wife to have the income from his estate as long as she lives. He may place his property in a trust, the income of which would go to her for life; the trust might be dissolved at her death and the property distributed to the children. The trust is administered by a *trustee*—usually an old friend or associate, the family lawyer, or a bank—who is the legal owner. He is required by law to manage the trust strictly in accordance with the terms of the trust instrument.

Legal terms are used as shorthand in trust language for the various beneficiaries of a trust. In the above example, A's wife, who is entitled to receive the income of the trust, is the *life tenant.* Any number of life tenants may be designated, and they need not be confined to members of the same generation. The creator of the trust may designate his wife and children as joint or successive life tenants and prescribe the proportions in which the income should be distributed among them. When the trust is terminated, the trust property is legally transferred to the *remainderman* who then owns the property outright. More often than not, children are the remaindermen of family trusts; but grandchildren, or other relatives, and unrelated individuals may also be remaindermen. In some cases, the trust is created with the wife and children as life tenants and the remainder is distributed, after the last one dies, to one or more charities. In all but a few states, the trust cannot last longer than the last survivor among the persons living when it was created (*lives in being*) plus twenty-one years.

The trust has a profound influence on the taxation of property transfers. Trust property is not subject to estate tax when one life tenant is succeeded by another, or when the trust property is received by the remainderman. An estate or gift tax is paid when the trust is created, but tax is not paid again until the remainderman transfers the property. Given these characteristics, the trust is frequently used by wealthy individuals to avoid estate and gift taxes for at least one generation, and sometimes more. In extreme cases, trusts may be set up to last for the lives of the children and grandchildren, with the remainder to go to the great grandchildren, thereby skipping two estate and gift tax generations.

USE OF TRUSTS. The trust device is used frequently by wealthy individuals to transfer property to later generations. The data from the 1945, 1951, 1957, and 1959 studies indicate the following patterns:

1.   Since World War II, more than three out of five millionaires have transferred at least some of their property in trust. Transfers in trust accounted for at least one-third of noncharitable transfers by millionaires in this period (Table 8-3). The data also indicate that trusts are used primarily by wealthy people. Individuals with smaller estates give much more of their property outright.

2.   There is little difference between the eventual disposition of property transferred outright and in trust. Outright transfers are received in the first instance largely by the wife and children; these properties are in turn transferred to grandchildren and great grandchildren. In the case of trust transfers, wives, children, and grandchildren frequently receive only life interests so that the grandchildren and great grandchildren receive the property undiminished by estate or gift taxes. As Table 8-4 indicates, about half the trust property of wealthy decedents escapes estate and gift taxes until the death of the grandchildren or great grandchildren. Only a very small proportion of the property transferred outright will escape tax for a similar period.

ALTERNATIVE SOLUTIONS. There are legitimate reasons for trusts and it would be unwise to abolish them altogether. On the other hand, some economists have pointed out that it is also unwise to

TABLE 8-3. Frequency of Noncharitable Transfers in Trust and Percentage of Wealth Transferred in Trust by Millionaire Decedents, 1945, 1951, 1957, and 1959

Total Wealth Transferred During Life and at Death (Millions of dollars)	Percentage of Decedents with Noncharitable Transfers in Trust				Percentage of Noncharitable Transfers Made in Trust			
	1945	1951	1957	1959	1945	1951	1957	1959
1 - 1.25	75	72	57	56	44	39	28	26
1.25- 1.5	75	78	53	61	48	44	25	29
1.5 - 1.75	80	77	53	62	38	44	24	30
1.75- 2.0	71	80	63	69	37	49	37	31
2.0 - 3.0	89	69	61	64	55	39	34	34
3.0 - 5.0	84	87	63	70	42	51	32	35
5.0 -10.0	87	74	77	67	44	44	43	30
10.0 and over	91	100	73	92	58	59	33	30
Total	80	76	59	63	47	46	32	31

Source: Special tabulations by the Treasury Department.
Note: Includes only returns with total transfers before tax during life and at death of $1,000,000 or more. Data for 1945 and 1951 include gifts prior to 1932; those for 1957 and 1959 exclude such gifts.

encourage excessive use of the trust device because trust property is managed more conservatively than property owned outright, thus reducing the supply of capital available for risky investments. Moreover, since trust transfers go to the same people as outright transfers, there does not seem to be a good equity reason for imposing lower taxes on trust transfers. Equity suggests that the two types of transfers should be treated equally.

Several methods have been devised to remove or reduce the tax advantage of trust transfers. The most direct method would be to treat life estates as if property generating their income were owned by the income beneficiaries, a procedure now employed in Great Britain. Under this method, the capital from which the life estate is supported would be included in the life tenant's gross estate and the tax would be apportioned between the trust property and the life tenant's own property.

Although this method is consistent with the principles underlying the present estate tax, several objections have been raised against its use. First, while a life tenant enjoys the income from a trust, he does not possess the other attributes of ownership. Second, inclusion of trust property in an estate of a life tenant would

TABLE 8-4. Timing of Next Estate Taxes on Outright and Trust Transfers of Millionaire Decedents, 1945, 1951, 1957, and 1959

Person at Whose Death the Next Estate Tax Falls Due	Outright Transfers		Trust Transfers[a]	
	Amount (Millions of dollars)	Percentage of Total	Amount (Millions of dollars)	Percentage of Total
	1945			
Spouse	77	24		
Children	154	48		
Grandchildren	9	3		
Great grandchildren	b	b		
Other	80	25		
Total	320	100		
	1951			
Spouse	164	41	2	1
Children	137	34	95	28
Grandchildren	11	3	124	37
Great grandchildren	b	b	20	6
Other	89	22	96	28
Total	400	100	337	100
	1957			
Spouse	405	39	2	c
Children	362	35	90	18
Grandchildren	56	5	209	43
Great grandchildren	b	b	24	5
Other	212	21	162	33
Total	1,034	100	487	100
	1959			
Spouse	468	42	4	1
Children	366	33	91	18
Grandchildren	68	6	208	42
Great grandchildren	b	b	37	7
Other	214	19	160	32
Total	1,117	100	500	100

Source: Special tabulations by the Treasury Department. Figures are rounded and will not necessarily add to totals.

[a] Data not available for 1945.

[b] Outright transfers to great grandchildren were not tabulated separately, but the amount is negligible and is included in transfers to "others."

[c] Less than 0.5 percent.

increase the tax rate applying to the property he owns outright. Third, the method assumes that the alternative to a trust transfer is necessarily an outright transfer of the property to the life tenant. In the absence of life estates, owners of wealth might divide it between those who are now designated as life tenants and remaindermen. A more moderate tax would be appropriate under such circumstances. Finally, the tax on the trust property may be avoided in a number of ways. For example, the trustee might be given full discretion over the disposition of the trust and the life tenant would have no legal share on which a tax could be imposed. Lawyers generally believe that it would be difficult to prevent such practices.

An alternative to the British approach would be to impose a separate tax upon the entire value of the property in which a decedent has a life interest. This method would not eliminate the full advantage of transferring property in trust, since it would still be advantageous to fragment the estate tax base by a combination of trust and outright transfers.

A third possibility would be to impose a separate tax upon the remainderman when the trust dissolves. This method is more practical than the others, but it would be a substantial departure from the estate tax principle of taxing wealth at the point of transfer rather than at the point of receipt. Furthermore, it would permit the skipping of death taxes over the lives of the life tenants.

In brief, the trust presents a troublesome problem for which there is no easy solution. If a departure is to be made from the present liberal treatment, it is likely to be a compromise among conflicting objectives.

Charitable Foundations

Unlike the deductions for income taxes, charitable bequests and gifts are deductible without limit from the estate or gift tax bases. (Contributions are deductible up to 30 percent of income in the case of the individual income tax and up to 5 percent in the case of the corporation income tax.) The charitable deduction has stimulated only a minority of individuals to allocate substantial portions of their estates to charity. Among millionaires with 1957 and 1959 estate tax returns, slightly over half the decedents reported no contributions above the annual exclusion during life or at death, and only about 15 percent of the total transfers by this group was given to charitable organizations. Nevertheless, the total amounts deducted are significant; they rose from $254 million on 1945 estate and gift tax returns to $1.2 billion on 1961 returns.

Concern has been expressed about the charitable deduction in recent years as a result of the large growth of private foundations, some of which have been suspected of abusing the tax exemption privilege. Owners of closely held corporations may avoid the impact of the estate tax by dividing the stock into voting stock, which is retained in the family, and nonvoting stock, which is transferred to a foundation. In this way, the family continues to control the assets without being subject to the full estate and gift tax rates when control passes from one generation to the next. In many cases, the economic power of the family grows rapidly as the enterprise continues to expand; the estate tax does not encroach on the property because the property belongs to the foundation and has been permanently removed from the estate tax base. This type of transfer amounts to giving up the income from the property rather than the property itself, yet the transfer is treated as if control of the property has also been relinquished by the donor.

Private foundations were not even required to file statements regarding their financial operations until 1950 when the tax law was amended to require public information returns on their assets, earnings, and expenditures. These reports have not completely eliminated shady dealings on the part of a minority of donors and foundation officials. Recent investigations by a subcommittee of the House Banking and Currency Committee have revealed abuses ranging from excessive salaries for foundation officials to use of loans from foundation funds for personal investment purposes.

The large majority of foundations operate in the public interest. However, there is an increasing consensus that their affairs should be subject to stricter public controls. The suggestions include prohibitions against loans to contributors, officers, and directors; tight rules to require the use of foundation funds for charitable purposes only and to prevent unnecessary accumulation of income and assets; limitations on the proportions of stock held in one firm to prevent control by foundations; and methods to broaden the foundation's management so as to avoid indefinite control by the family.

Some have even suggested that foundations be required to dispose of their assets in a specified number of years (say, twenty-five), but such extreme proposals may not be necessary if the abuses are curbed. Legislation to clarify the status of foundations is already on the agenda of the congressional tax committees.

Small Business and the Estate Tax

A perennial problem in estate taxation is how it affects small business. Small businessmen have always felt that the estate tax is especially burdensome. Often, there is little more than the business in their estates. Heavy taxation or a rule requiring payment of taxes immediately after the death of the owner-manager may necessitate liquidation of the enterprise and loss of the business by the family.

As the previous discussion has indicated, a little advance estate planning would be sufficient to prevent or mitigate most of these problems. Nevertheless, payment difficulties may arise even in carefully planned situations, and the law contains two provisions to help in these situations:

First, tax payments on estates in which a small business plays a large role may be made in installments over a period of ten years (with interest of 4 percent—an attractive rate for small enterprises). This option, which is exercised by the executor, is available if the value of the business is more than 35 percent of the gross estate or more than half of the taxable estate. Installment payments are limited to the portion of the entire estate tax accounted for by the business.

The option to pay estate tax in installments is rarely exercised because the executor is personally liable for all future payments even if the estate loses its value. This can easily be corrected by limiting the executor's liability to the value of the estate on the installment date.

Second, liberal provision has been made for redemption of stock in closely held corporations to pay the estate tax and other costs of the estate. Such stock redemptions are, of course, indistinguishable from ordinary distributions of profits by private corporations, which are subject to tax. Since 1951, however, they have not been subject to the individual income tax.

Alternatives to the Estate Tax

Extensive reforms would be required to make the estate and gift taxes more equitable. Some have argued that it would be better to abandon the present transfer tax structure and start afresh. The alternatives most often recommended are based on the inheritance or accessions tax principle.

Although widely used by the states, the inheritance tax is rarely considered for use at the federal level. Its most serious deficiency in its unmodified form is that each receipt of a gift or inheritance is taxed separately. Thus, two individuals would pay the same tax on equal inheritances received in the same year. However, if one receives his inheritance in a lump sum and the other receives it from several decedents, they would pay different taxes.

This deficiency is remedied by the modern modification of the inheritance tax principle—the *accessions tax*. This is a progressive cumulative tax on the total lifetime acquisitions of an individual through inheritances and gifts. The tax in any one year is computed by subtracting the tax paid on earlier acquisitions from the tax on total acquisitions received. There would be small annual exclusions and a lifetime exemption. Although tax rates could be varied on the basis of the relationship of donor and donee, there is little support for such differentiation under an accessions tax.

The accessions tax has appeal for those who advocate a more equal distribution of wealth than the present estate tax provides. It is also more equitable than the estate tax since it is graduated on the basis of the total wealth received by any one individual. It is probably true that the accessions tax would encourage individuals to distribute their property among a larger number of heirs, but the result would not necessarily be a more equal distribution of wealth, since property is ordinarily kept in the immediate family. Moreover, in practice, only the wealthiest persons could afford to divert property from wife and children to more distant relatives to benefit from the tax savings offered by an accessions tax. Thus, to the extent that the accessions tax did encourage a more equal distribution of estates, it might do so by shifting some of the burden of the wealthiest estates to the smaller estates.

The accessions tax has some practical advantages. For one thing, it would equalize the taxes on transfers during life and at death, thus overcoming one major fault of the existing tax system. Second, it would eliminate the problem of handling gifts in contemplation of death. Some of the proponents of the accessions tax also claim that it would facilitate the inclusion of property settled in trust in the tax base. For example, receipt of trust property by remaindermen would automatically be subject to accessions tax, while it is not subject to estate tax. On the other hand, the estate tax collected when the trust is created would not automatically be recovered by the accessions tax. To include such transfers in the accessions tax base, the benefits received by the life tenant would have to be valued—a problem which has not been solved satisfactorily even after years of experience with the estate tax.

The most difficult problem in accessions taxation is the opportunity it creates for avoidance of the tax through discretionary trusts. With a discretionary trust, a family fortune could be tied up forever, with the accessions tax being levied only on those amounts that are actually distributed to the beneficiaries.

A practical argument against the accessions tax is that it would probably not raise as much revenue as the estate and gift taxes. To obtain a given yield, accessions tax rates would need to be much higher and exemptions much lower than under the present transfer taxes. Given the long experience with the current estate tax rates and exemptions, the drastic revisions necessary to preserve the revenue yield would be difficult to obtain. It follows that, unless the pattern of property distribution is altered radically, the accessions tax would be a less effective wealth equalizer than the estate tax.

Summary

In theory, estate and gift taxes are among the better taxes devised by man; in practice, their yield is disappointing and they make little change in the distribution of wealth. Tax rates are high, but there are ways to escape them. The major avenues are the marital deduction, distribution of estates by gifts during lifetime, settlement of property in trust for one or more generations, and use of the tax-free charitable foundation to maintain control without paying tax on the bulk of the estate. These problems can be solved, but the solutions are technical and some would regard them as unnecessarily harsh and inconsistent with the principles of property law.

Although tax theorists almost unanimously agree that estate and gift taxation should play a larger role in the revenue system, they have not been successful in convincing Congress. The public does not appear to accept the desirability of a vigorous estate and gift taxation system. The major obstacles to the improvement of these taxes are public apathy and the difficulty of understanding their major features and how they apply in individual circumstances. The merits of property transfer taxes will have to be more widely understood and accepted before they can become effective revenue sources.

CHAPTER 9

State and Local Taxes

THE STATE-LOCAL SEGMENT of the national revenue system is its most dynamic element. State and local expenditures have grown rapidly in recent years, and will continue to grow in the foreseeable future. These governments spent more than $69 billion in fiscal year 1964, almost 60 percent of federal cash expenditures and more than twice as much as federal nondefense expenditures (Chart 9-1). Whereas the federal government reduced tax rates by about 15 percent between 1962 and 1965, state and local tax rates increased steadily and sharply.

The growth in expenditures and taxes reflects persistently increasing demand for state and local services. State and local governments had a large backlog of unmet needs at the end of World War II; and population growth added to their problems. The age groups requiring the costliest government services and contributing least to the tax base increased the fastest: between 1954 and 1964, when the total population increased 18 percent, public school enrollment rose 36 percent and the number of persons over 65 rose 27 percent. The mobility of the people accentuated the problems of population growth. Entire new communities had to be developed with schools, roads, sewers, police and fire protection, and other public services. Since the Korean War ended in 1953, employment

CHART 9-1. Federal and State-Local Expenditures, Fiscal Years 1948–64

Billions of Dollars
(Ratio scale)

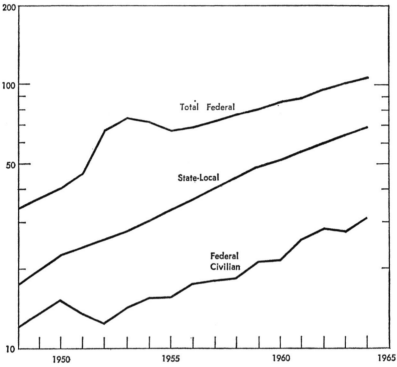

Sources: Department of Commerce, Bureau of the Census, *Census of Governments: 1962, Historical Statistics on Governmental Finances and Employment,* Vol. VI, No. 4, pp. 35–6, 38–9; *Governmental Finances in 1963,* pp. 18, 20; *Governmental Finances in 1963–64,* pp. 18–19.

Note: The figure for federal civilian expenditure comprises total general expenditures excluding expenditures for national defense and international relations, interest on the general debt, and grants to state and local governments. It excludes expenditures on insurance trust funds. The figure for state-local expenditures excludes expenditures by public utilities, liquor stores, and insurance trust funds.

by state and local governments has increased at a faster rate than employment in private industry or in the federal government.

The major characteristics of the state-local tax system are its regressivity and sluggish response to income growth. The states rely heavily on consumption taxes and local governments on property taxes—both regressive revenue sources. Fear of driving out commerce and industry and discouraging the entry of new business restrains the use of most taxes; this is particularly true of the income tax which is the most equitable and most responsive to growth. At constant tax rates, state and local taxes are barely rising in proportion to the gross national product, while the rate of growth of expenditures is at least 20 percent faster than the GNP growth rate.

In these circumstances, the federal government has filled a major part of the gap. Federal grants-in-aid to state and local governments have risen from $3 billion in 1954 to $10 billion in 1964 and will reach almost $15 billion in 1967. Most of these grants help finance needed expenditures for education, health, welfare, and roads.

The pressure for larger revenues has generated a great deal of fiscal activity throughout the country. Tax systems are being examined by official and unofficial commissions, legislative committees, and experts in order to increase revenues, achieve greater equity, improve administration, and reduce the cost of compliance by taxpayers. Many states have adopted new taxes, increased rates on old taxes, introduced withholding for income tax payments, and reformed their tax administrative machinery. Under pressure from the states, local governments have improved property tax administration. Some large cities in a few states have adopted municipal income and sales taxes. But much remains to be done to satisfy state and local financial needs.

The State-Local Tax Structure

In the ten years ending June 30, 1964, annual state and local expenditures for general purposes (all activities other than public utilities, liquor stores, and insurance trust funds) rose from $30.7 billion to $69.3 billion, an increase of $38.6 billion. In the same period, state and local revenues rose from $29 billion to $68.4 billion, an increase of $39.4 billion. Only 18 percent of the revenue increase came from federal grants; 82 percent came from state and local sources. Although the rise in receipts slightly exceeded the rise in expenditures for the entire period, expenditures were larger than receipts every year and state-local debt rose from $38.9 billion to $92.2 billion (Appendix Tables C-20, C-21, and C-22).

The state and local governments relied on all their major sources to produce the additional revenue: 35 percent came from property taxes, 26 percent from consumption taxes, 11 percent

CHART 9-2. Sources of Growth of State-Local Revenue, 1954–64

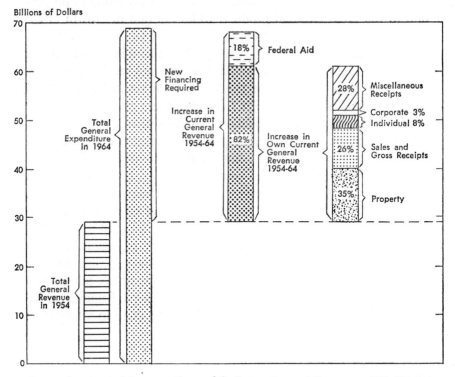

from income taxes, and the remaining 28 percent from user charges and other miscellaneous taxes (Chart 9-2).

While state and local tax sources are often lumped together, the two levels of government have very different tax systems. The state governments rely heavily on consumption and income taxes; local governments are largely dependent on the property tax.

State Taxes

State tax structures have changed dramatically since the turn of the century. In 1902, almost half of state revenue came from property taxes and the rest from selective excise taxes. Today, the general sales tax is the largest single source of state revenue, with automotive and income taxes next. Most states have relinquished the general property tax to their local governments; only Nebraska, Wyoming, and Arizona raise more than 10 percent of their revenues from this tax.

SALES AND EXCISE TAXES. State legislatures have been irresistibly attracted to the productivity and stability of revenues from consumption taxes. Selective excise taxes on gasoline, cigarettes, and liquor are now in extensive use throughout the country. These taxes have been increasingly supplemented by the retail sales tax in the last thirty years.

The retail sales tax emerged as a major source of state revenue in the 1930's. The tax is now in use in forty-two states, at rates ranging from 2 to 5 percent. To moderate its regressivity, twelve states exempt food, and an additional seventeen exempt medicine. A recent development, which is likely to spread, is a credit against state personal income tax for sales tax presumed to have been paid by the poor. For example, Indiana provides a $6 tax credit (equivalent to its 2 percent tax on $300 of purchases) against the personal income tax for the taxpayer and each of his dependents. Colorado, Hawaii, and Massachusetts have followed suit. (Wisconsin provides a similar income tax credit to the aged for property tax payments in excess of 5 percent of their income.) Cash refunds are paid to individuals and families who do not pay enough income tax to recover the entire credit.

INCOME TAXES. State individual and corporation income taxes in their modern form began in Wisconsin in 1911. (Hawaii adopted both taxes in 1901, but this experience apparently had no influence on the states.) General individual income taxes are now in force in thirty-three states and the corporation income tax in thirty-seven states. State tax rates are much lower than the federal rates, and personal exemptions are generally higher. Tax brackets are narrower and graduation is steeper but terminates at a much lower level, usually between $5,000 and $15,000. The maximum rates are levied in Alaska, where the top rate is 14.6 percent for the individual income tax and 9.4 percent for the corporate income tax. However, these overstate the *net* additional impact of the state income taxes because they are deductible from taxable income in computing federal taxes. In addition, many states permit the deduction of the federal taxes in computing taxable income for state tax purposes. After allowing for deductions, the maximum net rates for Alaska, which remain the highest in the nation, are 4.4 percent for the individual income tax and 4.9 percent for the corporation income tax (Appendix Table C-24).

State income taxes are generally patterned after the federal taxes, and in recent years there has been a movement toward uniformity with federal definitions. All but two of the personal income tax states have an optional standard deduction. Almost half modify the adjusted gross income concept by (1) subtracting interest on federal securities and (2) adding state income taxes and interest on out-of-state state-local bonds. Withholding for individual income tax purposes was introduced by Oregon in 1948, and twenty-eight states now withhold on wages and salaries. Twenty-one complement this by requiring declarations of estimated tax for incomes on which tax is not withheld.

DEATH AND GIFT TAXES. Death taxes were levied by states long before the federal government enacted an estate tax in 1916. Pennsylvania taxed inheritances as early as 1825, and Wisconsin set the modern pattern by adopting a progressive inheritance tax in 1903. Only Nevada does not tax bequests. The gift tax is levied in twelve states. For the United States as a whole, estate and gift taxes amount to less than 3 percent of total state tax collections.

Local Taxes

Municipal and county governments are limited in the tax sources they are able to use. They have always relied heavily on the property tax and, despite persistent efforts to diversify their sources of funds, the majority of local governments assign nonproperty taxes a relatively unimportant place in their finances.

PROPERTY TAX. The property tax provides two-thirds of the revenue from all local sources (seven-eighths of the tax revenue). This dependence reflects the reluctance of many state governments to give localities authority to levy other taxes. It also reflects local fears of inducing migration or purchases in neighboring communities: taxation of real property may have significant effects on land use, but not on its location.

Although critics have long predicted the demise of the property tax, it has performed creditably in the postwar period. State and local property tax collections rose from $6.1 billion in 1948 to $21.2 billion in 1964, an annual rate of growth of 8.1 percent during a period when the gross national product (in current dollars) grew at a rate of 5.7 percent. Average effective property tax rates are below 3 percent in all states; in 1962, the median state effective rate was 1.1 percent, and only eight states had average rates in excess of 2 percent.

NONPROPERTY TAXES. Some large cities in a limited number of states have successfully diversified their revenue sources. Sales taxes are the most productive nonproperty taxes, with taxes on earnings or income next. Local general sales taxes are now used in thirteen states by over 2,000 local governments, mainly in Illinois, California, Mississippi, and Utah. Local income taxes are levied in eight states, but are widespread only in Pennsylvania and Ohio.

NONTAX REVENUES. Nontax revenues are most important at the local level. In 1964, they accounted for 22 percent of local revenues from their own sources and for only 14 percent of comparable state revenues. Such nontax revenues include charges for water, electric power and gas, special assessments, licenses, fees, and user charges for transportation, medical care, and housing. Payments for most government services that yield measurable benefits are substantially below marginal cost, primarily because it is feared that user charges will hurt low income families.

State-Local Fiscal Performance, Capacity, and Effort

The fiscal performance and tax capacity of the fifty states during fiscal year 1964 are summarized in Chart 9-3. *Performance* is measured by per capita revenue collected from state-local sources; *capacity* is measured by personal income per capita; and *revenue effort* is the ratio of performance to capacity, or the ratio of revenue collected to personal income.

When the states are arrayed by size of per capita personal income, the per capita revenue obtained from state-local sources increases from low to high income states. In 1964, the poorest ten states raised only $214 per capita, whereas the richest ten states raised $349 per capita. This pattern of performance cannot be attributed to lack of effort on the part of the poorest states. On the

CHART 9-3. Per Capita State-Local Revenue and Revenue Effort, by States, by Quintiles of State Personal Income Per Capita, 1964ᵃ

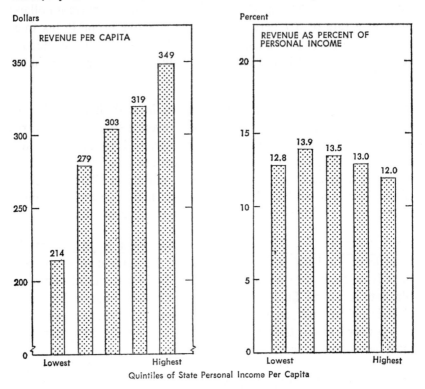

Quintiles of State Personal Income Per Capita

Source: Department of Commerce, Bureau of the Census, *Governmental Finances in 1963-64,* pp. 21, 23, 25.
ᵃ State-local revenue excludes federal grants.

contrary, the index of revenue effort tends to vary inversely with per capita income. Revenue effort increases from 12.8 percent to 13.9 percent from the lowest fifth to the second fifth of states, but then declines steadily to 12 percent in the highest fifth. If the ten poorest states made the same revenue effort as the richest states, they would have raised only $205 per capita instead of $214; and if the second ten made the same effort, they would have raised only $240 instead of $279. These figures indicate that the poorer states cannot provide adequate levels of public services even though they make a larger revenue effort than the richest states on the average.

Major Issues

The state and local tax systems are now in transition. Larger expenditures require higher taxes, which create equity and economic problems. Most of these problems are not new, but they have become acute as tax burdens have increased.

Income Taxes vs. Sales Taxes

The relative merits of an individual income tax versus a sales tax for state use continue to provoke emotional responses in many areas of the country. The debate is primarily over equity, but other considerations enter.

The major argument in favor of the income tax is its progressivity. Proponents of the income tax believe that state as well as federal taxes should be distributed according to ability to pay. Moreover, federal deductibility of state income taxes greatly moderates the impact of the top state rates on high income taxpayers (see discussion on deductibility below). The income tax is also much more responsive to economic growth than the sales tax.

Proponents of the sales tax believe that it is undesirable to pile a state income tax on top of the high federal rates. Even with deductibility, they fear that high income taxpayers will migrate to avoid the state income tax. Tax progressivity is not regarded as essential at all levels of government in these circumstances, provided the entire federal-state-local tax system is progressive on balance.

Both the income and sales taxes can be productive revenue sources for state governments, if they are levied on a broad base. A 1959 Wisconsin study estimated that a typical 2 percent sales tax not exempting food and medicine would yield more than the Wisconsin income tax which ranged from 1 to 7 percent and provided tax credits (in lieu of personal exemptions) of $7 for single persons and $14 for married couples. Most states levying both sales and income taxes derive more from the sales tax. While it is possible to devise an income tax equal to the yield of almost any sales tax, sales taxes of 3 to 5 percent are generally more productive than income taxes with rates graduated up to 10 percent. These are the ranges

TABLE 9-1. Combined Federal and State Tax Liabilities for a Married Couple with Two Dependents in an Income and Sales Tax State, 1965

(*In dollars*)

Adjusted Gross Income	Total Federal and State Taxes[a]		Difference (New York-Michigan)
	New York (Income Tax)	Michigan[b] (Sales Tax)	
3,000	0	95	− 95
4,000	140	235	− 95
5,000	281	396	−115
6,000	496	565	− 69
8,000	875	902	− 27
10,000	1,288	1,262	26
15,000	2,596	2,351	245
20,000	4,156	3,620	536
25,000	5,909	5,074	835

[a] After taking into account deductibility of the state income or sales tax in computing the federal income tax. All other deductions were assumed to be equal to the federal standard deduction.
[b] Sales tax as estimated by the Internal Revenue Service for purposes of federal deductibility (see instructions to 1965 Form 1040).

currently used in most states. The balance will, of course, swing toward the income tax as incomes increase.

Whether an income tax would drive wealthy residents to sales tax states is difficult to determine. For example, the 1965 Michigan sales tax and New York income tax yielded approximately the same dollar amounts per capita. Table 9-1 compares the combined federal-state tax burdens of individuals with different incomes in these two states, after taking into account the effect of the deductibility of state taxes in computing the federal income tax. A married New Yorker with two children paid $69 less tax if he had an adjusted gross income of $6,000, but $835 more tax if he had income of $25,000. Reactions to such a differential depend heavily on individual attitudes toward equity, the need for state revenues, and the benefits of improved public services. However, even if the differential does not affect location decisions, the opposition to state income taxes is often vocal and influential and may prevent use of income taxation as effectively as if the tax did in fact influence these decisions.

There is little to choose between income and sales taxes on administrative and compliance grounds. Costs of administration are somewhat lower for the income tax than for the sales tax. Compliance is more difficult for the taxpayer in the case of the income tax, while the sales tax imposes a burden on retailers. Some support the sales tax because its revenues come partly from tourists and other visitors who use the facilities of the state temporarily. On the other hand, income taxes can be, and generally are, imposed on employees who live outside the state and work within the state. These differences may be significant in a few places where interstate travel and commuting are important.

In recent years, the need for revenue has tended to soften attitudes on both sides of the controversy. At one time most states had either an income tax or a sales tax, but the number of states with both has been increasing. On September 1, 1966, twenty-seven states had both, fifteen had only a sales tax, six had only an income tax, and two (Nebraska and New Hampshire) had neither. In November 1966, Nebraska voters will be asked to approve the adoption of individual and corporation income taxes. Credits for sales taxes against state individual income taxes, adopted in four states, make it possible to eliminate the regressive feature of the sales tax. There are few remaining objections on equity grounds for states to avoid using either type of tax, or both.

Deductibility

The discussion of deductibility of state taxes in calculating the federal income tax base in Chapter 4 concluded that simultaneous use of the same tax base by two (or even three) levels of government is acceptable, provided the combined rates are not excessive. Federal deductions for income, sales, and property taxes are considered desirable to encourage state and local use of these taxes and to narrow interstate and intercommunity net tax differentials.

Most states with income taxes have borrowed the deductibility features of the federal law. While practices vary, state and local sales and excise taxes are deductible in arriving at taxable income in most states. In addition, twenty of the thirty-three individual income tax states permit deductions for the federal individual income tax and six permit deductions for the state individual income tax itself; thirteen of the thirty-seven corporation income tax states permit deductions for the federal corporation income tax and eight states allow a deduction for the state corporation income tax.

TABLE 9-2. Net Impact of State Income Taxes Under (a) Federal Deductibility and (b) Federal and State Deductibility, at Illustrative Marginal Rates

(In percentages)

Marginal Federal Tax Rate	Type of Deductibility	Marginal State Tax Rate				
		2	3	5	7	10
14	Federal only	1.72	2.58	4.30	6.02	8.60
	Federal and state	1.48	2.23	3.72	5.23	7.50
20	Federal only	1.60	2.40	4.00	5.60	8.00
	Federal and state	1.29	1.93	3.23	4.54	6.53
30	Federal only	1.40	2.10	3.50	4.90	7.00
	Federal and state	0.99	1.48	2.49	3.50	5.05
40	Federal only	1.20	1.80	3.00	4.20	6.00
	Federal and state	0.73	1.09	1.84	2.59	3.75
50	Federal only	1.00	1.50	2.50	3.50	5.00
	Federal and state	0.50	0.76	1.28	1.81	2.63
60	Federal only	0.80	1.20	2.00	2.80	4.00
	Federal and state	0.32	0.49	0.82	1.17	1.70
70	Federal only	0.60	0.90	1.50	2.10	3.00
	Federal and state	0.18	0.28	0.47	0.66	0.97

Deductibility of any tax from the base of another (or from its own base) has two effects: first, the burden of the deducted tax on the taxpayer is reduced by the marginal rate of the tax against which it is deductible; and second, the net yield of the tax with the deductible feature is reduced, requiring higher nominal rates to obtain any given amount of revenue. The net burdens of state taxes with federal and federal-state deductibility are illustrated in Table 9-2. For example:

1. A proportional 2 percent income tax is converted to a regressive tax by the deductibility feature of the federal income tax. Such a tax would impose a net burden of 1.72 percentage points for a taxpayer subject to the lowest federal rate of 14 percent, 1 point for a taxpayer subject to a 50 percent federal rate,

and only 0.6 point for a taxpayer subject to the top federal rate of 70 percent. If the state allowed its income tax to be deducted from its own income tax base, the regressivity would be further increased.

2. Federal deductibility of state income taxes already greatly reduces the burden of the top state income tax rates; as the following table shows, state deductibility accomplishes little more for the taxpayer at a substantial cost to the state. A 10 percent top state rate imposes a net additional burden of only 3 percentage points on a taxpayer subject to a federal rate of 70 percent. With state deductibility of the federal tax, the net additional burden of the same 10 percent state tax becomes 0.97 point. The 2.03 points net reduction in the taxpayer's burden costs the state 6.77 points, or more than three times the taxpayer's saving.

Level of Government	*Tax Collected (70 Percent Federal Rate, 10 Percent State Rate)*		
	Federal Deductibility Only	*Federal and State Deductibility*	*Difference*
Federal	63.00%	67.74%	+4.74%
State	10.00	3.23	−6.77
Total	73.00	70.97	−2.03

3. Federal deductibility reduces the progressivity of the state tax and, in the upper income classes, actually converts it to a regressive tax. Adding state deductibility aggravates matters. For example, if the state rates are paired with the federal rates along the diagonal in Table 9-2 the net impact of the state tax on an additional $1 of income is as follows:

Marginal Federal Rate	*Marginal State Rate*	*Net Impact of the State Tax*		
		Federal Deductibility Only	*Federal and State Deductibility*	*Difference*
14%	2%	1.72%	1.48%	−0.24%
20	3	2.40	1.93	−0.47
30	5	3.50	2.49	−1.01
40	7	4.20	2.59	−1.61
50	10	5.00	2.63	−2.37
60	10	4.00	1.70	−2.30
70	10	3.00	0.97	−2.03

With federal deductibility alone, the state tax adds 1.72 percentage points to the federal tax in the lowest federal bracket and rises to 5 points in the 50 percent bracket. With state deductibility added, the additional tax reaches a maximum of only 2.63 points.

Although the top income tax rates raise only a fraction of their nominal values in many states, they act as a psychological barrier to further use of the income tax for needed revenues. Deductions for state-local consumption taxes make even less sense. Since federal deductibility already protects taxpayers against excessive rates, removal of state deductibility would provide some additional state revenue and improve and simplify state income taxes.

Tax Coordination

Tax overlapping among different levels of government was at one time considered a major drawback of the national tax system, but attempts to divide revenue sources have had little success. The state and local governments failed to pick up the electrical energy tax which was repealed by Congress in 1951, although they had urged the federal government to relinquish this tax for their use. The same was true of reductions in the federal admissions tax during the 1950's. In 1958-59, the Joint Federal-State Action Committee (consisting of state governors appointed by the Governors' Conference and representatives of the federal government) could not reach agreement on a proposal to eliminate some federal grants in return for relinquishment of the local telephone tax by the federal government.

Such attempts fail because it is difficult to devise a plan that all states will regard as equitable; and because the state and local governments are likely to view the specific federal taxes relinquished with the same reservations that motivated Congress to give them up as revenue sources in the first place. Tax overlapping was moderated slightly by the 1965 federal excise tax reductions, but these cuts were made for other reasons. Experience to date suggests that the major cases of duplication—in income, estate and gift, and selective excise taxes—will persist.

The situation is by no means as serious as it appears, however. In recent years, new methods of administrative cooperation between federal and state governments have been developed. State income taxes resemble the federal taxes in major respects, and several states have simplified their tax returns. Most experts now accept some tax overlapping as inevitable, and even desirable, if the taxes used in common are good taxes. The approach now being taken is to relieve major taxpayer compliance problems and inequities resulting from tax overlapping, and to extend the area of intergovernmental administrative cooperation as much as possible.

ESTATE AND GIFT TAX COORDINATION. The adminstrative and compliance problems raised by overlapping estate and gift taxation are out of all proportion to their revenue yield. Most of the states use inheritance taxes, but they have a wide variety of exclusions, deductions, and exemptions. The federal credit for state death taxes (enacted in 1924 and enlarged in 1926) placed a floor under state taxes, but did not produce uniformity. The states left their own taxes unchanged, and later added "pickup" taxes to the maximum allowable credit. Today, thirty-five states have an inheritance tax plus a pickup tax, five have pickup taxes only, and nine states have estate taxes without pickup taxes.

The states have long felt that estate and gift taxes should be left to them, but would not have the credit arrangement repealed. They recognize that, without protection of the federal credit, interstate competition for wealthy taxpayers would quickly destroy most state death taxes. The credit ensures that any state can tax up to the credit without running the risk of losing its taxpayers to other states, but in its present form the credit provides no incentive to move toward uniform definitions of the tax base.

In 1961, the Advisory Commission on Intergovernmental Relations (ACIR)—a permanent commission created by act of Congress to make recommendations on intergovernmental relations—recommended substitution of a two bracket graduated credit for the present estate tax credit, which was originally computed as a flat percentage of the 1926 tax. The ACIR proposal would make available to the states a larger share of the tax on smaller estates, on two conditions: first, that they increase their death taxes by at least the increase in the amount of the credit; second, that they enact estate taxes. The first condition was considered necessary because existing state death taxes generally exceed the federal credit; without a revenue maintenance provision, the higher credit might result in net tax reduction rather than in larger state revenues. The second condition was intended to encourage the states to follow the pattern of the federal law, although it did not require uniformity in other respects.

The states have also asked for a federal credit for their gift taxes. The ACIR rejected a gift tax credit because it would force gift taxes on all the states, even though the revenue involved for the states is negligible and the states do not need gift taxes to safeguard their death taxes (the federal gift tax already serves this purpose). In any event, the increased federal estate tax credit could be made generous enough to compensate the states for not having gift taxes.

Action on the commission's recommendations for a higher estate tax credit has been deferred until estate and gift tax revision can be considered in its entirety. However, the recommendations have stimulated little interest in Congress or in the executive branch, partly because the degree of coordination they might achieve would not seem to justify the federal revenue loss. The federal government might be more receptive to the loss of revenue if the recommendations were modified to require greater uniformity.

STATE TAXATION AND INTERSTATE COMMERCE. For years the states have been reaching out to exact taxes from activities that cross state lines. Their claims were, on the whole, sustained by the Supreme Court. In 1959, however, when the Court upheld a corporation income tax on a firm whose activities consisted solely of the solicitation of sales within a state, interstate business interests promptly appealed for relief from the federal government. Congress responded by enacting stopgap legislation under its power to regulate interstate commerce. This halted further expansion of state income tax jurisdiction pending the outcome of a congressional study to determine what legislation, if any, was needed.

After four years of study, the Subcommittee on State Taxation of Interstate Commerce of the House Judiciary Committee recommended legislation affecting corporate income, sales, use, gross receipts, and capital stock taxes with particular reference to three issues: (1) the type of business activities within a state that should give rise to taxing jurisdiction; (2) rules to divide the income of multistate firms among the states; and (3) requirements for collection of use taxes by firms shipping into a state.

1. Because state laws are ordinarily couched in broad terms

and vary by type of tax, business firms are uncertain of their tax status if they have minimal activity in a particular state. The judicial process, limited as it is to case treatment, has not always produced solutions conducive to the free flow of commerce. States themselves have difficulty in achieving voluntary compliance from firms unless there is a physical presence in the state.

The subcommittee recommended restricting state taxing jurisdiction to firms that own or lease real property or maintain one or more employees within a state. This rule is proposed to promote certainty and improved voluntary compliance. It is consistent with the view that a taxpayer's obligations are to his "home" state, and it has the further advantage of being compatible with the subcommittee's recommended rule for division of multistate income for state corporation income tax purposes (see point 2 below).

The opposing view—which is supported by most state officials —is that the states' power to tax should extend to all business activities, including sales activities, within their borders. State officials contend that the use of the permanent establishment concept would discriminate in favor of the multistate operator enjoying tax immunity and against the local firm. Also involved is the attitude toward state "tax sovereignty." Spokesmen for the states contend that the states' power to tax gives them the right and obligation to balance a variety of considerations. According to this view, Congress should interfere with state taxation only on a clear showing that the taxes involved constitute a significant burden on interstate commerce.

2. The thirty-seven corporation income tax states have various formulas to compute the state allocation of profits of multistate firms. The majority gives some weight to property, payrolls, and sales, but the weights assigned differ. This diversity produces anomalous results: some interstate corporations are taxed lightly; others claim that they pay state taxes on an aggregate tax base that exceeds their net income. Reporting for state income tax allocation is time-consuming and costly, especially for small and medium-sized businesses with small accounting and legal staffs. Agreement is widespread that states should adopt uniform rules, but there is disagreement on who should prescribe and administer the rules and what factors should be used.

The subcommittee recommended national legislation to apportion all income on the basis of two factors—property and payrolls—

and to vest rule-making authority in the Secretary of the Treasury. The theory is that income should be apportioned according to the factors used in producing it, and sales should be taken into account only to the extent that they involve the use of company facilities or labor in a particular state.

The opposing view is that there is no realization of income without sales. Sales reflect the relative importance of each state as a market for the output of any particular company and should therefore be given recognition in the division of income rules. The opposition also holds that the elimination of the sales factor would create a competitive environment that discriminates against local firms.

Support for the two-factor formula reflects the interest of many small firms whose accounting and legal staffs are not prepared to cope with the current diversity in state apportionment formulas. The opposition to the formula mirrors the reluctance of the states to make the Treasury responsible for administrative interpretations traditionally within the purview of state tax officials.

The overall revenue consequences for the states of either approach are small: according to the subcommittee, the two- and three-factor formulas would change tax revenues by as much as 1 percent in only two states, and in a majority by less than one-half of 1 percent. Nonetheless, shifts in tax burden from "out of state" to "home state" firms in states with relatively high corporate income tax rates could be significant. This gives rise to concern about a state's competitive position for purposes of industrial location.

3.   All forty-two sales tax states levy "use" taxes on out of state purchases to supplement their sales taxes. This tax is imposed on the buyer for the privilege of using the commodity in the state. States cannot enforce such taxes by collecting them from the purchasers except for registered automobile owners and business purchasers who are registered vendors.

To eliminate tax avoidance in connection with out of state purchases, states began to require out of state sellers to collect the use tax for them. In 1941, the Supreme Court permitted Iowa to require a mail order house with retail stores in Iowa to collect a use tax on mail order sales sent to its out of state customers; and, in 1961, it upheld Florida's right to require use tax collections by a Georgia corporation with representatives in Florida, but no office or place of business there.

Although the volume of interstate as opposed to local sales is unquestionably small, sales across state lines constitute one of the most troublesome aspects of sales taxation. Interstate sellers object to the requirement that they collect use taxes. The tax base is not uniform from state to state and interstate sellers sometimes find compliance with use tax collection requirements more burdensome than compliance with state corporation income tax laws. Sales and use tax regulations are not only complicated, they are changed frequently. As more states place increasing reliance on these taxes and, as rates rise, state tax officials feel an increasing obligation to protect local firms from competition by enforcing the use tax on out of state sellers.

The problem could be solved if the states agreed to tax sales at the point where they originate (the "origin" principle). But the states could not tax on this basis without congressional authorization; moreover, they would be reluctant to enact a principle of taxation which would increase the costs of firms within their borders that ship across state lines. Thus, the "destination" principle is now the common rule. The subcommittee recommended a somewhat restricted state jurisdictional rule for the use tax. It also recommended an optional approach that would maintain the status quo or permit the states to join in a cooperative federal-state sales tax administration under a uniform sales and use tax law to collect use taxes on interstate shipments. To avoid such coercion, the only alternative is for the states to cooperate in the collection and mutual enforcement of each other's taxes.

Resolution of these issues involves a balancing of the values of state sovereignty in taxation against the advantages of, and constitutional requirement for, the free flow of commerce across state lines. With the increasing interdependence of all regions of the country, a higher degree of uniformity and certainty in state taxation of interstate activities is both desirable and inevitable, but the process of accommodation to the economic realities by the states is likely to be painful.

STATE TAXATION OF NONRESIDENTS. Rules regarding allocation of personal income for state income tax purposes vary greatly. The states assert their right to tax all the income of their residents, whether earned in the state or not. They also claim the right to tax income originating in the state and going to nonresidents. Most states have eliminated discrimination by allowing credits for income taxes paid by their residents to other states, provided the other states grant reciprocal credits. In addition to the resident credit, a number of states grant credits to nonresidents for income taxes they pay to their home states, provided those states reciprocate. The nonresident credit unnecessarily complicates state personal income taxes and has encouraged at least one state to impose a selective tax on its residents working out of state solely for the purpose of diverting its neighbor's tax dollars to its own treasury. However, the possibility of liability to two states on the same income is now small. Situations of multiple taxation do arise, nonetheless, when two states claim the same person as a resident, because their definitions of residence vary.

The problem is more acute where residents of a state without a personal income tax work in a state having such a tax. In these cases, the employees pay income tax to the state in which they are employed, but receive no credit in their home states, where their principal tax payments are in sales or property taxes. This problem would be solved, of course, if all states taxed personal incomes, as has been recommended by the ACIR. This group has also recommended the elimination of the nonresident credit and the adoption of a uniform definition of residence. Adoption of a uniform definition might be required as a condition for continuing the deductibility feature of the federal income tax, or for the enactment of a federal credit in lieu of, or as a supplement to, deductibility (see the discussion of federal assistance below).

COOPERATIVE TAX ADMINISTRATION. Formal federal-state cooperative tax administration dates back to 1926. The earliest form of cooperation involved examination of federal income tax returns by state tax officials; in 1950, a plan for coordinated federal-state use of income tax audits was developed. While the states benefitted from these arrangements, the federal government received little in return.

In 1957, a new series of "agreements on the coordination of tax administration" was launched to extend cooperation to other taxes and activities. These agreements, which had been negotiated with forty states and the District of Columbia by the end of 1965, provide for examination of federal tax returns by state officials and of state returns by federal officials, including the exchange of automatic data processing tapes and information disclosed by federal and state audits. In addition, special enabling legislation permitted the Internal Revenue Service to perform statistical services for state agencies on a reimbursable basis and to enroll state enforcement officers in its training programs. In 1952, federal agencies were authorized by Congress to withhold income taxes for state governments. Legislation to permit federal agencies to extend similar help to cities has so far failed to make headway although it has the support of the Treasury Department.

These evidences of federal-state cooperation suggest that there is a willingness of federal, state, and local tax officials to coordinate their activities in the interest of greater efficiency. The ACIR has recently recommended that Congress authorize the federal government to enter into agreements with the states for federal collection of state income taxes. Given the proper attitudes, there is no reason why most of the administrative and compliance benefits of unitary administration (including the same or similar tax returns for all units of government for any one tax, joint audits, and joint collection of taxes other than income taxes) could not be achieved by agreement between the federal and state governments rather than through federal coercion.

State-Local Fiscal Relations

Most public services enjoyed directly by a resident of the United States—education, health, water and sewage, welfare services, police and fire protection—are performed by local government. Yet local governments derive all their powers, including fiscal powers, from their parent state governments. Fortunately, the states are increasingly recognizing that local governments cannot be left to their own devices to finance an adequate level of public services.

PROPERTY TAX ADMINISTRATION. High on the agenda for local tax reform is improvement of property tax administration. A major criticism of this tax arises from the difficulty of assessing property values. Although two-thirds of the states require full valuation, se-

TABLE 9-3. Distribution of States by Ratios of Assessed Value to Sales Price of Real Property, 1956 and 1961

Assessed Value as Percentage of Sales Price[a]	Number of States	
	1956	1961
0– 9.9	2	3
10.0–19.9	16	15
20.0–29.9	16	13
30.0–39.9	4	6
40.0–49.9	7	10
50.0–59.9	2	2
60.0–69.9	1	1
	—	—
Total	48	50
Average assessment ratio	30%	29.5%

Source: James A. Maxwell, *Financing State and Local Governments* (Brookings Institution, 1965), p. 139 (citing the 1957 and 1962 Census of Governments).
[a] These are simple averages of assessment ratios of all properties included in the Census samples.

vere underassessment is the rule rather than the exception. In 1956 and 1961, for example, average assessment ratios exceeded 50 percent in only three states and were less than 20 percent in eighteen states (Table 9-3). Moreover, there is great variability in assessments of equal-value properties, creating irritating inequities among taxpayers and among different localities within the same state. Since local shares of state grants and debt and property tax rate limitations are often based on assessed valuations, underassessment impairs the ability of local governments to finance their needs.

Many state governments have taken the initiative to improve property tax administration; in some areas, progress has been encouraging. The reforms involve more state participation in the administration of the tax, greater reliance on professional personnel, and reorganization of local assessment districts into larger and more efficient units. Most states collect comparative statistics on assessment ratios, which reveal the diversity in assessment practices and permit state officials to locate the major areas of administrative weakness. The states are also beginning to take an active part in supervising local assessment practices, training assessment personnel, and providing technical assistance where needed. The ACIR has also recommended centralization of property assessment in one state agency, publication of the value of property which is exempt from local property taxes by state action, and elimination of unnecessary and inequitable property tax limitations.

With the growing sophistication of assessment techniques, it should be possible to reduce the major inequities in administration of this basic tax. Participation in the administrative process by state governments, with their superior financial and technical resources, should accelerate adoption of the latest techniques to the fiscal advantage of the local governments.

INCREASING LOCAL TAX CAPACITY. There are limits to the freedom that can be given to local governments in the taxing field. Unless restrained by the state governments, they might soon find themselves with a maze of complicated, burdensome, and inefficient taxes that would impair economic growth. However, several techniques permit local governments to take advantage of the revenue productivity and growth potential of the major nonproperty taxes— sales and personal income taxes—within limits set by the state governments for purposes of control. These include:

Tax supplements. Under this arrangement, the local rate is added to the state rate, the state collects the two taxes, and then remits the local shares. The tax supplement has advantages of simplicity, elimination of duplicate administrative costs, and ease of compliance for the taxpayer. It also retains the local governments' freedom of choice in selecting revenue sources. Local tax supplements on sales taxes are now used successfully in six states.

Tax sharing. Most state governments earmark one or more taxes for partial or complete distribution to the local governments. The state government decides the tax to be shared, the rate to be imposed, and the formula for allocating receipts. Taxes are frequently returned to the communities where they were collected, but other methods of distribution are also used. Tax sharing imposes statewide uniformity in tax rates and automatically eliminates intercommunity competition. Like the tax supplement, it eliminates duplicate tax administration and relieves local governments of unnecessary administrative costs. The device is widely used in the case of automotive taxes, but it may be applied to the entire gamut of state taxes, including income, sales, cigarette, and other excises and fees.

Tax credits. This is a little-used device to force local governments to employ a particular tax. The state levies a statewide tax, but gives a credit to the taxpayer for a specified portion of the tax (sometimes as much as 100 percent) paid to a local government. Credits for state taxes are given by the federal government under its estate and unemployment insurance taxes. California and Utah also use tax credits to divide the sales tax revenues between counties and cities by requiring counties to credit sales taxes levied by the cities within their jurisdictions. Florida credits municipal cigarette taxes and Virginia credits municipal taxes on bank shares against the corresponding state taxes. The tax credit is similar to the shared tax, except that local governments may exceed the credit if the state permits. On the other hand, the tax credit perpetuates duplicate tax administration although local governments often benefit from the spillover of experience under the state tax.

There is no *a priori* basis for judging which of these three devices is most appropriate in given circumstances, although each has advantages for particular objectives. In states where a specific tax is already in widespread use among its local governments, the tax supplement may be the best alternative. Tax sharing will be more acceptable where local taxes tend to be uniform or where the tax to be shared is not widely used at the local level. The tax credit provides the least coordination at the state-local level, but it may be the only alternative in states where the diverse interests of the local governments are difficult to reconcile.

STATE GRANTS-IN-AID. Grants are similar in many respects to shared taxes. However, instead of distributing funds on the basis of the local tax base, grants provide financial aid to local governments on the basis of some predetermined formula. The source of the revenue may be specified in the legislation, but the grants are often appropriated from general funds. Distribution formulas give weight to such factors as population, number of school children, income, property tax base, miles of paved streets, and so on. The grants are usually for specified purposes (such as schools, roads, and health services), but in some cases they are given on an unconditional basis for general local use.

State assistance to local governments is not a new phenomenon. It amounted to 6 percent of local general revenue in 1902 and rose to 23 percent in 1934; since World War II it has accounted for about 30 percent of local general revenue. In the last thirty years, state transfers to local governments have amounted to more than a third of all state expenditures (Chart 9-4).

Most state grant systems have grown without systematic planning. They are often complicated, inequitable, and may even defeat the purposes for which they were designed. Distribution formulas remain unchanged for decades, despite huge population shifts. Many of the nation's largest cities are denied appropriate shares of state grants by rural dominated state legislatures. However, the states have become more sensitive to the needs of their counties and cities, and this sensitivity is increasing as legislatures are reapportioned. Although there are entrenched interests to overcome, state grant systems are gradually being revamped to meet current requirements.

Federal Aid

State and local governments have received some federal financial assistance since early in the nineteenth century. The early grants, financed by the sale of federal lands, were used for road construction and, later, to establish and operate the land grant colleges. The amounts were relatively modest until the 1930's when the desperate financial condition of the states and localities led to the development of a great variety of grants to help finance their programs in education, health, welfare, transportation, housing, and other activities. Federal grants have risen from less than 1 percent of state-local revenue in 1902 to 10 percent in 1948, and 15 percent in 1964 (Chart 9-4).

CONDITIONAL GRANTS-IN-AID. Federal aid is now provided almost entirely through grants for specific government services. Such grants serve to stimulate increased state and local action in particular areas which serve the national interest. They may also be justified on the ground that the benefits of many public services "spill over" from the community in which they are performed to other communities. For example, an individual may receive his education in one state and migrate to another when he enters the labor force. In such circumstances, investment in education will be too low if financed entirely by state funds, because each state will be willing to pay only for benefits likely to accrue to its citizens.

CHART 9-4. Federal Aid to State-Local Governments, and State Aid to Local Governments, Selected Years, 1902–52, Annually, 1953–64

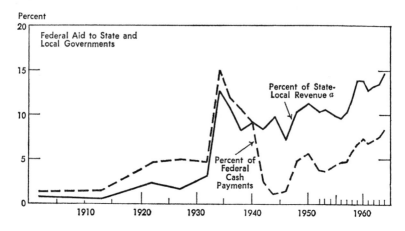

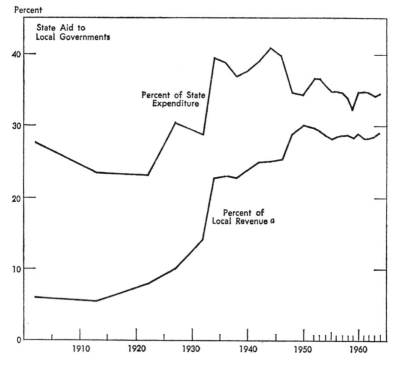

Sources: *Economic Report of the President,* January 1966; Department of Commerce, Bureau of the Census, *Historical Statistics of the United States, 1789-1945; Historical Statistics of the United States, Continuation to 1962; Census of Governments: 1962, Historical Statistics on Governmental Finances and Employment,* Vol. VI, No. 4; various issues of *Governmental Finances.*

a Including intergovernmental revenue.

Federal assistance is needed to raise the level of expenditures closer to optimum from the national standpoint.

Conditional grants permit the federal government to tailor its assistance to those activities with the largest spillover effects. It can set minimum standards and require matching funds to ensure state or local government support and participation. It can also allocate funds to states and communities where the need for a particular program is greatest or where fiscal capacity is least.

Conditional grants improve state-local services without transferring their operation to the federal government. However, the recent proliferation of grants makes them increasingly subject to criticism. It is charged that they are unnecessarily complex, involve excessive federal direction and interference with state-local prerogatives, divert large sums from other urgently needed state-local programs, and tend to be perpetuated long after their original objectives are met. On the other hand, the ability to control the use of funds and to require state-local financial participation is an appealing feature to Congress. On the basis of recent experience, it seems clear that conditional grants will remain the basic method of providing federal assistance to state and local governments.

GENERAL PURPOSE GRANTS. The federal government appropriated funds to the states for any state-local purpose in 1837, when federal surplus revenues were large enough—partly as a result of receipts from the sale of public lands—to retire the entire national debt and to accumulate a Treasury balance besides. The funds were distributed on the basis of the number of congressmen and senators from each state, which was very nearly the same as a per capita distribution. The federal surplus disappeared in 1838, a recession year, and the grants were terminated after three installments. Since then, all federal grants have been conditional.

General purpose grants are justified on two grounds. First, all states do not have equal capacity to pay for public services. Even though the poorer states make a larger relative revenue effort (Chart 9-3), they are unable to match the revenue-raising ability of the richest states. Furthermore, conditional grants do not have a substantial equalizing effect on balance (Chart 9-5). Second, federal use of the best tax sources leaves a substantial gap between state-local need and state-local fiscal capacity. Moreover, no state can

CHART 9-5. State-Local General Revenue from Own Sources and from Federal Grants, by States, by Quintiles of Personal Income Per Capita, 1964

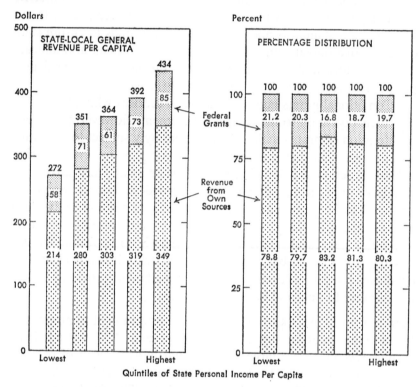

Quintiles of State Personal Income Per Capita

Sources: Department of Commerce, Bureau of the Census, *Census of Governments: 1962, Historical Statistics on Governmental Finances and Employment,* Vol. VI, No. 4, pp. 57, 107; *Governmental Finances in 1963-64,* p. 45.

push its rates much higher than the rates in neighboring states for fear of placing its citizens and business enterprises at a disadvantage. On this line of reasoning, all states need some federal assistance even for purely state-local activities, with the poorer states needing relatively more help because of their low fiscal capacity.

As federal revenues have increased in recent years, considerable support has developed for some method of using part of the growth in federal receipts for general purpose grants. Details of the proposals differ, but they have a number of features in common:

1. A certain percentage of a growing base—for example, total federal revenues, total income tax collections, or the individual

income tax base—would be automatically set aside in a special federal fund.

2. Disbursements from the fund would be made primarily on a per capita basis, a method which helps the poorer states relatively more than the richer states. More equalization could be provided by using a small part of the fund (perhaps up to 10 percent) only for the poorest states, or by weighting the per capita figures inversely to state tax capacity. Tax effort might also be given some weight in the formula to give the states an incentive to maintain or increase tax collections out of their own sources.

3. The funds would be turned over to the states, with the understanding that a major share would go to the local governments. The percentage could be stipulated in advance, or left to the state legislatures under procedures ensuring participation by local officials in the decision.

4. Various constraints on the use of the funds are visualized, but these would be much less detailed than those applying to conditional grants. They could be treated as "block grants" to be used in such general areas as health, education, and welfare; or they might be made available for any expenditures not otherwise prohibited by the legislation.

5. An audit of the actual use of the funds would be required, as well as certification by appropriate state and local officials that all applicable federal laws, such as the Civil Rights Act, have been complied with in the activities financed by the grant.

Reaction to such general purpose grants depends largely on attitudes toward the relations between the federal and state governments. They are opposed by those who wish to control the use of federal funds in great detail, who have little faith in the willingness or ability of state governments to use the funds wisely, and who believe that general purpose grants will weaken the role of conditional grants. They are supported by those who wish to strengthen the role of the state governments and to limit federal control over state-local spending, and who believe that conditional grants are already overworked in the federal system. Some oppose the expansion of federal assistance either in the form of conditional or general purpose grants, on the ground that separation of the expenditure and financing functions will lead to excessive and wasteful expenditures. However, in a tax system which restricts state and local governments to the least desirable and responsive tax sources, a general purpose federal grant makes sense as a supplement to conditional grants.

OTHER METHODS OF FEDERAL ASSISTANCE. Other alternatives for accomplishing the objectives of federal grants involve reduction of federal revenues. These include: (1) federal tax reduction or relinquishment of specific federal taxes; (2) sharing of federal tax collections with the states; and (3) credits for state and local taxes against federal taxes. These are the same methods used by state governments to provide assistance to the local governments. Such alternatives would help the state and local governments in varying degree, but they would not achieve the broad objectives sought through the grant device.

The response of the state and local governments to federal tax reduction or relinquishment is bound to be spotty because it depends on action by many separate executive and legislative bodies. State and local revenues would rise mainly through the indirect effect of the increased national income resulting from federal tax reduction, but this would be only a small fraction of the released federal revenues. To the extent that state and local tax rates increased, the richer states would benefit most.

As already indicated, tax sharing is a common arrangement at the state-local level, but not at the federal-state level. Now that the federal government has been left almost exclusively with income and estate and gift taxes, the tax sharing alternative would not be logical unless the states were willing to give up these taxes.

Tax credits would not automatically increase state-local revenues: state and local governments already imposing the taxes which can be credited would have to raise their rates. Since this could be done without raising the total taxes paid by their citizens they might be encouraged to do so, but there would be strong opposition from the groups that would prefer to enjoy the tax reduction provided by the credit. If the credit applied to income taxes, the seventeen states without individual income taxes would benefit only after they imposed such a tax. However, this might be regarded as federal coercion and, in some states, would face constitutional barriers. The earlier discussion of the estate tax credit indicated that the tax credit can be an effective coordinating device, but it would not redistribute resources to the neediest states. At best, the credit diverts federal revenues to the states where they originate.

Summary

Despite the sluggish response of their taxes to economic growth, the state and local governments have made a good record in the postwar period. But they will continue to be hard-pressed in the foreseeable future as their financial needs continue to grow at a faster rate than the national income.

Most of the additional revenue must be raised by the state and local governments themselves. At the state level, the trend is toward the use of moderate income and sales taxes. In some states, there are long-standing traditions against one or the other of these two major taxes, but historical precedents are breaking down. The recent adoption in four states of a credit against the income tax for sales taxes paid suggests that the objection to sales taxes on equity grounds can be dealt with effectively. The fact that the federal income tax permits deductions of state income taxes should make income taxation at the state level more acceptable. However, states that permit the deduction of federal income taxes from their own income tax bases should recognize that they lose much more revenue than their taxpayers save.

At the local level, there is need for immediate strengthening of property tax administration. This tax will continue to be the main revenue source of local governments; state governments should take a strong hand in promoting improvements in the professional quality of assessment personnel and assessment procedures. In addition, the states should seriously consider expanding their use of the tax sharing device. They also consider the feasibility of permitting local governments to supplement the overworked property tax with revenues from income or sales taxes. There are serious dangers in permitting local governments to levy such taxes, but unnecessary complications and inefficiencies can be avoided if local income and sales taxes are levied in the form of supplements to the corresponding state taxes.

Even if they make a substantial effort of their own, the state and local governments will be unable to meet their growing needs without substantial federal assistance. Part of this assistance will come from conditional grants, which will help finance activities in which the federal government has a strong interest. But the state and local governments will also need financial help for other state-local programs. As the nation faces up to the enormous tasks of improving education, providing welfare and health facilities, and reconstructing the blighted areas of its cities, a new program of supplementary federal grants for general purposes becomes an increasingly urgent need.

APPENDIXES

Historical Summary of Major Federal Taxes

THE FEDERAL TAX SYSTEM as we know it today is of relatively recent origin. From 1789 to 1909, the federal government relied almost exclusively on excise taxes and customs. An income tax was used for emergency purposes during the Civil War, and rudimentary death taxes were levied in 1797-1802, 1862-70, and 1898-1902. The corporation and individual income taxes—now the backbone of the federal revenue system—were enacted in 1909 and 1913, respectively. The modern estate tax was first levied in 1916 and the gift tax in 1924. Payroll taxation was first introduced by the Social Security Act of 1935.

The Individual Income Tax

The Civil War tax on individual incomes was in effect between 1862 and 1871. The tax contained a flat $600 exemption with no allowance for children, was graduated up to 10 percent (in 1865 and 1866), and was collected at the source on wages, salaries, interest, and dividends. Total revenues under this tax amounted to $376 million. At its peak in 1866, it accounted for almost 25 percent of internal revenue collections. The tax was allowed to lapse in 1872 when the urgent need for revenue disappeared.

For almost twenty years after the expiration of the Civil War tax, there was only isolated support for the reenactment of an income tax. As the country grew and prospered, great industries and fortunes were established, and inequalities in the distribution of income became more disturbing. The income tax was reenacted in 1894, when the country was in a mood for reform against the evils of monopolies and trusts. However, this tax was declared unconstitutional by the Supreme Court.

The high court decision declared that the portion of the personal income tax which fell on income from land was a "direct" tax, which was required by the Constitution to be apportioned among the states according to population. The decision was assailed by many groups, and agitation for a change in the Constitution continued until the ratification of the Sixteenth Amendment in 1913. This Amendment provided that "Congress shall have power to lay and collect tax on incomes, from whatever sources derived, without apportionment among the several States, and without regard to any census or enumeration."

The 1913 tax, which was enacted shortly after the Sixteenth Amendment was ratified, applied to wages, salaries, interest, dividends, rents, entrepreneurial incomes, and capital gains. It allowed deductions for personal interest and tax payments, as well as for business expenses. The tax exempted federal, state, and local government bond interest and salaries of state and local government employees; and also exempted dividends from the normal tax, but not from the surtax. Collection at source was applied to wages and salaries, interest, rents, and annuities in excess of $3,000. The tax contained a simple exemption system of $3,000 for single persons and $4,000 for married couples. Rates consisted of a 1 percent normal tax plus a surtax ranging from 1 percent to 6 percent.

The most significant changes made since the original 1913 Act have been: the allowance of a credit for dependents and a deduction for charitable contributions in 1917; elimination of collection at source in 1916 and its reenactment in 1943 for wages and salaries only; adoption of preferential rates on long-term capital gains in 1921; elimination of the exemption for salaries of state and local government employees and discontinuation of the sale of tax-exempt federal bonds in 1941; adoption of the standard deduction in 1944; enactment of the principle of "income splitting" for married couples in 1948; and introduction of an averaging system and a minimum standard deduction in 1964.

Rates and exemptions have changed frequently (Tables A-1 and A-2). Maximum marginal rates reached 77 percent during World War I, 94 percent during World War II, and 92 percent during the Korean War. They declined to 24 percent in the 1920's and rose to 79 percent in the 1930's; in the late 1950's and the early 1960's the maximum rate was 91 percent. At the present time, the maximum rate is 70 percent. Exemptions have shown a downward trend for the most part, reaching a low of $500 per taxpayer during World War II and then rising to the present $600 per capita in 1948.

The Corporation Income Tax

The corporation income tax rate began at 1 percent in 1909, reached 12 percent during World War I, 13.5 percent in the late 1920's, 40 percent during World War II, and 52 percent during the Korean War. The Revenue Act of 1964 reduced the rate to 50 percent for 1964 and 48 percent for later years (Table A-3).

Between 1909 and 1935, the tax was levied at a proportional rate on taxable income. A small exemption was allowed in computing taxable income for sporadic periods: $5,000 for 1909-13; $2,000 for 1918-27; and $3,000 for 1928-31. Graduation was introduced for the first time in 1936, with rates ranging from 8 percent on the first $2,000 of taxable income to 15 percent on income over $40,000.

Beginning in 1938, graduation was limited to corporations with incomes of $25,000 or less. Above this point, a flat rate applied to the entire taxable income of the corporation, on the theory that rate graduation in the corporation income tax cannot be defended on equity grounds as in the case of individuals. The limited graduation was intended as a concession to small business. This rationale produced a peculiar rate schedule which persisted until the end of 1953. For example, between 1942 and 1945, the rates began at 25 percent on the first $5,000 of taxable income and rose to 53 percent for taxable incomes between $25,000 and $50,000 (Table A-4). Beginning at $50,000, the rate was a flat 40 percent on total taxable income. The 53 percent rate—called the "notch" rate—was just enough to raise the corporate rate to 40 percent at $50,000 and thus avoided a discontinuity in effective rates at that point.

While it produced the desired result, the notch rate was regarded as a penalty on small business. After considerable agitation, the 1950 Act removed the notch rate and restored a simple two bracket system of graduation. This was accomplished by enacting a normal tax applying to all corporation profits and a surtax applying to profits in excess of $25,000. For the years 1952-63, the combined rates were 30 percent on the first $25,000 and 52 percent on the amount in excess of $25,000. In 1964, they were reduced to 22 percent and 50 percent, respectively; and, beginning in 1965, to 22 percent and 48 percent.

Dividends distributed by corporations were excluded from the individual *normal* tax before 1936 and were subject to the *surtax* (which was the progressive element of the individual income tax). In 1936, this exclusion was removed and a tax on undistributed profits was imposed at the corporate level. This tax was intended to force corporations to distribute most of their earnings as dividends. The tax was vigorously attacked as a deterrent to corporate growth, and was repealed after being in operation for only two years.

Between 1939 and 1954, the individual and corporation income taxes were levied without any attempt at integration of the two taxes as they applied to dividends. In 1954, individuals were allowed to exclude the first $50 of dividends from their taxable income ($100 for joint returns) and to subtract as a credit from the tax 4 percent of the dividends received in excess of the exclusion. After several years of debate, Congress reduced the credit to 2 percent in 1964, and eliminated it entirely beginning in 1965; at the same time, the exclusion was increased to $100 ($200 for joint returns).

The corporation income tax has been supplemented by an excess profits tax during World War I, World War II, and the Korean War. The method adopted was to tax at a very heavy rate (as high as 95 percent in World War II) the excess of a corporation's profits over a prewar base period or over a "normal" rate of return (specified in the statute) on invested capital. For example, the base period for the World War II excess profits tax was 1936-39. The excess profits tax creates difficult economic, equity, and administrative problems; taxation of even a portion of a corporation's net profits at rates close to 100 percent tends to be unfair. To relieve the most glaring inequities, the law provided alternative methods of computing excess profits and also permitted adjustments for hardship cases. But such provisions made a complicated law even more difficult to administer. The experience to date indicates that excess profits taxation is appropriate only for wartime use.

Excise Taxes

Immediately after the ratification of the Constitution, the new government introduced a fairly elaborate system of excise taxes, including taxes on carriages, liquor, snuff, sugar, and auction sales. Even at that time, these taxes were considered unfair and burdensome on the poor. The Whisky Rebellion of 1794 was a revolt by farmers against the federal tax which ran up to 30 cents per gallon. Except for the tax on salt, the early excises were abolished by the Jefferson administration in 1801, revived during the War of 1812, and then terminated again in 1817, not to reappear until the Civil War.

The Civil War excise tax system foreshadowed what was to happen during every major war thereafter. Liquor and tobacco taxes, which remained as permanent parts of the federal revenue system after the war, were supplemented by taxes on manufactured goods, gross receipts of transportation companies, advertising, licenses, legal documents, and financial transactions. During World War I, the list was again expanded, this time to include special occupational taxes and taxes on theater admissions, telephone calls, and retail sales of jewelry, toilet preparations, and luggage. Following the war, tobacco and stamp taxes remained as the major excise taxes. The liquor taxes remained in force throughout the prohibition era.

A break with peacetime precedent was made during the early 1930's, when Congress enacted a series of manufacturers' excise taxes on such items as automobiles, trucks, buses, appliances, and other consumer durables; also taxed were local and long distance telephone calls. These taxes were to be continued at varying rates and with varying degrees of comprehensiveness until 1965. The depression taxes were enacted after an attempt to introduce a general manufacturers' sales tax was defeated in the Congress. During World War II, the rates of most of the then existing excise taxes were increased and new excise taxes on retail sales of furs, jewelry, luggage, and toilet preparations, and on passenger and freight transportation were introduced.

Legislation to reduce the excise taxes had already been passed by the House when the Korean War began. These changes were quickly eliminated from the Revenue Act of 1950, which was enacted within two months after the beginning of hostilities. In the following year, the excise taxes on liquor, tobacco, gasoline, automobiles, consumer durables, and other products were increased and new taxes on wagering and diesel fuel were adopted.

A major innovation in excise taxation was introduced in 1956, when a number of excise taxes were earmarked for a specially created Highway Trust Fund to finance the construction of the 40,000-mile federal highway system. The earmarked taxes included the old manufacturers' taxes (with increased rates) on gasoline, diesel, and special motor fuels, trucks and tires, and new taxes on tread rubber and the use of heavy trucks and buses on the highways. Some of these taxes were increased in 1959 and again in 1962, when it became clear that the interstate system would be more expensive than was originally anticipated. The trust fund is now scheduled to be terminated in 1972; at that time, the 1956 rate increases and the new taxes enacted especially for the trust fund are to expire.

The Korean War excise tax structure was dismantled, beginning in 1954; the process took more than a decade. The original Korean War tax increases had been enacted for a period of three years, but most of them were extended each year as revenue requirements forced continued postponements of their repeal. The first significant break came in 1954, when all excise tax rates in excess of 10 percent were reduced to 10 percent, with the exception of the 20 percent cabaret tax. The freight tax was repealed in 1958; the cabaret tax was reduced to 10 percent in 1960; and in 1962, the railroad and bus passenger tax was eliminated, and the air transportation tax was reduced from 10 percent to 5 percent.

The present excise tax system was enacted in 1965, when Congress scaled down the Korean excises to all but a few major taxes levied for sumptuary and regulatory reasons and as user charges (Table A-5). The reduction, which amounted to almost $5 billion, was to be made in two $1.75 billion steps on July 1, 1965, and January 1, 1966, and in smaller steps on January 1 of the succeeding three years. In 1966, the reductions to be made on January 1, 1966, 1967, and 1968, were postponed until April 1, 1968. When the full reductions become effective on January 1, 1969, excises will be confined to three general categories: (1) alcohol and tobacco taxes; (2) highway user taxes, an air transportation tax of 5 percent, an automobile tax of 1 percent on manufacturers' prices, and a 10 percent tax on fishing equipment; and (3) regulatory taxes on narcotics, phosphorous matches, and wagering.

Payroll Taxes

The Social Security Act of 1935 imposed payroll taxes to finance the old-age insurance system and unemployment compensation benefits. Later, the OASI tax was used to finance disability and health insurance. Railroad employees are covered under a separate system of taxation which is similar to, but not identical with, the general social insurance system.

The OASI Tax

The 1935 Act established the principle that the retirement system would be financed by equal taxes on employers and employees. Under the original Act, the tax was 1 percent each for employer and employee on covered wages up to $3,000 per employee. The Act also provided a schedule of rate increases for subsequent years, reaching a maximum of 3 percent for 1949 and later years. However, the original increases were first deferred when the social security trust fund accumulated substantial reserves. Later, as benefits were raised, both the tax and earnings covered were increased repeatedly. Under the most recent amendments, beginning January 1, 1966, the payroll tax applies to the first $6,600 of earnings of employees with a maximum rate of tax of 5.65 percent each on employers and employees beginning in 1987 (Table A-6).

The original Act exempted agricultural and domestic labor, members of the professions, public employees, a few other classes of employees, and the self-employed. The coverage has been gradually expanded to include all employed persons, except for federal civilian employees (who are covered by their own retirement system), self-employed with self-employment income under $400 per year, and domestic and farm workers earning less than specified amounts from a single employer. The self-employed began to be covered in 1951 at a rate equal to one and one-half times the corresponding rate for employees rounded to the nearest 0.1 percent.

Unemployment Insurance Tax

The unemployment insurance tax was originally imposed in 1936 on employers of eight or more persons at a rate of 1 percent of payrolls, with automatic increases to 2 percent in 1937, and 3 percent in 1938 and later years. The coverage was expanded to employers of four or more in 1956, and the rate was increased to 3.1 percent in 1961. The rate was temporarily raised to 3.5 percent in 1962 and 3.35 in 1963, but was restored to 3.1 percent beginning in 1964. The tax was originally applicable to all wages, and has been limited to $3,000 of wages since 1939 (see Table A-7).

The federal government allows a credit against its tax for amounts contributed to state unemployment insurance programs, up to 2.7 percent of covered wages. The remainder of the federal tax is used to pay the administrative costs of the state programs.

State unemployment taxes are levied at the standard rate of 2.7 percent to use up the federal credit. In three states the tax is levied on employers and employees; in the others, it is levied only on employers. In almost all states, employers are taxed according to an experience rating which may result in a larger or smaller tax than the standard 2.7 percent. This device permits states to lower the tax rates on firms with stable employment and to increase it on those with unstable employment. However, the full 2.7 percent credit is allowed against the federal tax where the tax rate has been reduced by a good experience rating. As a result of these provisions, tax rates differ greatly from one state to another, as well as within a single state.

Railroad Taxes

The railroad payroll taxes have always been levied at higher rates than the taxes in other industries. The retirement tax for railroad employees dates back to 1937 when the rate was 2.75 percent each on employers and employees, and the maximum monthly wage subject to the tax was $300. Since 1937, the rates and wages subject to tax have been changed frequently. According to the present law, the tax on both employers and employees will reach 10.15 percent on earnings of up to $550 per month in 1987 (Table A-6).

The railroad unemployment insurance program is supported by a tax on wages of up to $400 per month per employee paid by the employers. Prior to 1948, the tax rate was 3 percent. It was reduced to 0.5-3 percent in 1948-59, depending on the financial condition of the trust fund, and raised to 1.5-3.75 percent on June 1, 1959, and 1.5-4 percent beginning in 1964 (Table A-7).

Estate and Gift Taxes

The 1916 estate tax was levied at rates ranging from 1 percent to 10 percent, with an exemption of $50,000. During World War I, the rates ranged from 2 percent to 25 percent. In 1926, the top rate was reduced to 20 percent, and the exemption was increased to $100,000.

One of the major developments during the 1920's was the enactment of a credit for state death taxes against the federal tax. Some of the states requested that the federal government vacate the death tax field entirely, but the credit was enacted instead. It was first limited to 25 percent of the federal tax in 1924 and was then raised to 80 percent in 1926. The same credit (based on the 1926 rates) exists today, even though the federal tax has been increased (Table A-8).

Substantial changes in rates and exemptions were made during the 1930's. The exemption was reduced to $50,000 in 1932, to $40,000 in 1935, and then raised to $60,000 in 1942 when a special $40,000 exclusion for life insurance (enacted in 1918) was repealed. The top rates were increased in several steps from 45 percent in 1932 to the present 77 percent in 1940 (Table A-9).

The gift tax was first levied for two years in 1924 and 1925, but was repealed on the ground that it was too complicated for the revenue it yielded. The tax was reenacted in 1932, when the estate tax rates were greatly increased, to limit avoidance of the estate and income taxes.

Gift tax rates have always been set at 75 percent of estate tax rates. A lifetime gift tax exemption of $50,000 was adopted in 1932 when the present gift tax was enacted. This exemption was reduced to $40,000 in 1935 and to $30,000 in 1942. In addition to the lifetime exemption taxpayers were allowed an annual exclusion of $5,000 for each donee under the 1932 Act. This exclusion was reduced to $4,000 in 1938 and to $3,000 in 1942. The lifetime gift tax exemption of $30,000 and the annual per donee exclusion of $3,000 are still in effect (Table A-10).

TABLE A-1. History of Federal Individual Income Tax Exemptions and First and Top Bracket Rates

Income Year	Personal Exemptions			Tax Rates			
				First Bracket		Top Bracket	
	Single Persons	Married Couples	Depen-dents	Rate (Percent-ages)	Amount of Income	Rate (Percent-ages)	Income Over
1913–15	$3,000	$4,000	—	1	$20,000	7	$ 500,000
1916	3,000	4,000	—	2	20,000	15	2,000,000
1917	1,000	2,000	$200	2	2,000	67	2,000,000
1918	1,000	2,000	200	6	4,000	77	1,000,000
1919–20	1,000	2,000	200	4	4,000	73	1,000,000
1921	1,000	2,500ᵃ	400	4	4,000	73	1,000,000
1922	1,000	2,500ᵃ	400	4	4,000	56	200,000
1923	1,000	2,500ᵃ	400	3	4,000	56	200,000
1924	1,000	2,500	400	$1\frac{1}{2}^b$	4,000	46	500,000
1925–28	1,500	3,500	400	$1\frac{1}{8}^b$	4,000	25	100,000
1929	1,500	3,500	400	$\frac{3}{8}^b$	4,000	24	100,000
1930–31	1,500	3,500	400	$1\frac{1}{8}^b$	4,000	25	100,000
1932–33	1,000	2,500	400	4	4,000	63	1,000,000
1934–35	1,000	2,500	400	4ᶜ	4,000	63	1,000,000
1936–39	1,000	2,500	400	4ᶜ	4,000	79	5,000,000
1940	800	2,000	400	4.4ᶜ	4,000	81.1	5,000,000
1941	750	1,500	400	10ᶜ	2,000	81	5,000,000
1942–43ᵈ	500	1,200	350	19ᶜ	2,000	88	200,000
1944–45ᵉ	500	1,000	500	23	2,000	94ᶠ	200,000
1946–47	500	1,000	500	19	2,000	86.45ᶠ	200,000
1948–49ᵍ	600	1,200	600	16.6	2,000	82.13ᶠ	200,000
1950ᵍ	600	1,200	600	17.4	2,000	91ᶠ	200,000
1951ᵍ	600	1,200	600	20.4	2,000	91ᶠ	200,000
1952–53ᵍ	600	1,200	600	22.2	2,000	92ᶠ	200,000
1954–63ᵍ	600	1,200	600	20	2,000	91ᶠ	200,000
1964ᵍ	600	1,200	600	16	500	77	200,000
1965 to dateᵍ	600	1,200	600	14	500	70	100,000

Source: *The Federal Tax System: Facts and Problems, 1964*, Joint Economic Committee, 88 Cong. 2 sess. (1964)ᶠ p. 233; based on data from U.S. Treasury Department, Office of Tax Analysis.

ᵃ If net income exceeds $5,000, married person's exemption is $2,000.

ᵇ After earned income credit equal to 25 percent of tax on earned income.

ᶜ Before earned income credit allowed as a deduction equal to 10 percent of earned net income.

ᵈ Exclusive of Victory tax.

ᵉ Exemptions shown are for surtax only. Normal tax exemption was $500 per tax return plus earned income of wife up to $500 on joint returns.

ᶠ Subject to maximum effective rate limitation: 90 percent for 1944–45, 85.5 percent for 1946–47, 77 percent for 1948–49, 87 percent for 1950, 87.2 percent for 1951, 88 percent for 1952–53 and 87 percent for 1954–63.

ᵍ Additional exemptions of $600 are allowed to taxpayers and their spouses on account of blindness and/or age over 65.

TABLE A-2. Federal Individual Income Tax Rate Schedules Under the Revenue Acts of 1944, 1945, 1948, 1950, 1951, and 1964

(In percentages)

Surtax Net Income	1944 Act — Calendar Years 1944–45	1945 Act — Calendar Years 1946–47	1948 Act — Calendar Years 1948–49	1950 Act — Calendar Year 1950	1951 Act — Calendar Year 1951	1951 Act — Calendar Years 1952–53	1951 Act — Calendar Years 1954–63	1964 Act — Calendar Year 1964	1964 Act — Calendar Year 1965 and Later Years
$0 to $500	23	19.00	16.60	17.40	20.4	22.2	20	16.0	14
$500 to $1,000								16.5	15
$1,000 to $1,500								17.5	16
$1,500 to $2,000								18.0	17
$2,000 to $4,000	25	20.90	19.36	20.02	22.4	24.6	22	20.0	19
$4,000 to $6,000	29	24.70	22.88	23.66	27.0	29.0	26	23.5	22
$6,000 to $8,000	33	28.50	26.40	27.30	30.0	34.0	30	27.0	25
$8,000 to $10,000	37	32.30	29.92	30.94	35.0	38.0	34	30.5	28
$10,000 to $12,000	41	36.10	33.44	34.58	39.0	42.0	38	34.0	32
$12,000 to $14,000	46	40.85	37.84	39.13	43.0	48.0	43	37.5	36
$14,000 to $16,000	50	44.65	41.36	42.77	48.0	53.0	47	41.0	39
$16,000 to $18,000	53	47.50	44.00	45.50	51.0	56.0	50	44.5	42
$18,000 to $20,000	56	50.35	46.64	48.23	54.0	59.0	53	47.5	45
$20,000 to $22,000	59	53.20	49.28	50.96	57.0	62.0	56	50.5	48
$22,000 to $26,000	62	56.05	51.92	53.69	60.0	66.0	59	53.5	50
$26,000 to $32,000	65	58.90	54.56	56.42	63.0	67.0	62	56.0	53
$32,000 to $38,000	68	61.75	57.20	59.15	66.0	68.0	65	58.5	55
$38,000 to $44,000	72	65.55	60.72	62.79	69.0	72.0	69	61.0	58
$44,000 to $50,000	75	68.40	63.36	65.52	73.0	75.0	72	63.5	60
$50,000 to $60,000	78	71.25	66.00	68.25	75.0	77.0	75	66.0	62
$60,000 to $70,000	81	74.10	68.64	70.98	78.0	80.0	78	68.5	64
$70,000 to $80,000	84	76.95	71.28	73.71	82.0	83.0	81	71.0	66
$80,000 to $90,000	87	79.80	73.92	76.44	84.0	85.0	84	73.5	68
$90,000 to $100,000	90	82.65	76.56	79.17	87.0	88.0	87	75.0	69
$100,000 to $136,719.10	92	84.55	78.32	80.99	89.0	90.0	89	76.5	70
$136,719.10 to $150,000	92	84.55	80.3225	82.503	89.0	90.0	89	76.5	70
$150,000 to $200,000	93	85.50	81.2250	83.43	90.0	91.0	90	76.5	70
$200,000 and over[a]	94	86.45	82.1275	84.357	91.0	92.0	91	77.0	70

Source: *The Federal Tax System*, p. 234 (see Table A-1).

[a] Subject to the following maximum rate limitations: Revenue Act of 1944, 90 percent; Revenue Act of 1945, 85.5 percent; Revenue Act of 1948, 77 percent; Revenue Act of 1950, 80 percent; Revenue Act of 1951, rates for 1951, 87.2 percent; rates for 1952–53, 88 percent; rates for 1954–63, 87 percent; Revenue Act of 1964, no limitation.

TABLE A-3. History of Federal Corporation Income Tax Rates

Year	Exemptions, brackets, or type of tax	Rate (Percentages)
1909–13	$5,000 exemption	1
1913–15	None after March 1, 1913	1
1916	None	2
1917	None	6
1918	$2,000 exemption	12
1919–21	$2,000 exemption	10
1922–24	$2,000 exemption	12½
1925	$2,000 exemption	13
1926–27	$2,000 exemption	13½
1928	$3,000 exemption	12
1929	$3,000 exemption	11
1930–31	$3,000 exemption	12
1932–35	None	13¾
1936–37	Graduated normal tax ranging from:	
	First $2,000	8
	Over $40,000	15
	Graduated surtax on undistributed profits ranging from	7–27
1938–39	First $25,000	12½–16
	Over $25,000	19[a]
1940	First $25,000	14.85–18.7
	$25,000 to $31,964.30	38.3
	$31,964.30 to $38,565.89	36.9
	Over $38,565.89	24
1941	First $25,000	21–25
	$25,000 to $38,461.54	44
	Over $38,461.54	31
1942–45	First $25,000	25–29
	$25,000 to $50,000	53
	Over $50,000	40
1946–49	First $25,000	21–25
	$25,000 to $50,000	53
	Over $50,000	38
1950	Normal tax .23 ⎫	42
	Surtax (over $25,000 surtax exemption) .19 ⎭	
1951	Normal tax .28¾ ⎫	50¾
	Surtax (over $25,000 surtax exemption) .22 ⎭	
1952–63	Normal tax .30 ⎫	52
	Surtax (over $25,000 surtax exemption) .22 ⎭	
1964	Normal tax .22 ⎫	50
	Surtax (over $25,000 surtax exemption) .28 ⎭	
1965 and later years	Normal tax .22 ⎫	48
	Surtax (over $25,000 surtax exemption) .26 ⎭	

Source: *The Federal Tax System*, p. 265 (see Table A-1).
[a] Less adjustments: 14.025 percent of dividends received and 2½ percent of dividends paid.

TABLE A-4. Marginal Rates of the Federal Corporation Income Tax Since 1942

(In percentages)

Taxable Income	1942–45	1946–49	1950	1951	1952–63	1964	1965 and later years
Under $5,000	25	21 ⎫					
$ 5,000 to $20,000	27	23 ⎬	23	28¾	30	22	22
$20,000 to $25,000	29	25 ⎭					
$25,000 to $50,000	53	53 ⎫	42	50¾	52	50	48
Over $50,000	40	38 ⎭					

Source: Table A-3.

245

TABLE A-5. Federal Excise Tax Rates on Selected Items as of December 31, Selected Years, 1913–69

(In dollars, except where percentages are indicated)

Tax	1913	1919	1928	1932	1944	1952	1954	1963	1969
Liquor taxes									
Distilled spirits (per proof or wine gallon)	1.10	2.20	1.10	1.10	9	10.50	10.50	10.50	10.50
Still wines (per wine gallon)									
Not over 14 percent	—	.16	.04	.04	.15	.17	.17	.17	.17
14 percent to 21 percent	—	.40	.10	.10	.60	.67	.67	.67	.67
21 percent to 24 percent	—	1	.25	.25	2	2.25	2.25	2.25	2.25
Beer (per barrel)	1	6	6	6	8	9	9	9	9
Tobacco taxes									
Cigars, large (per thousand)	3	4–15	2–13.50	2–13.50	2.50–20	2.50–20	2.50–20	2.50–20	2.50–20
Cigarettes (per thousand, 3 pounds or less)	1.25	3	3	3	3.50	4	4	4	4
Tobacco and snuff (per pound)	.08	.18	.18	.18	.18	.10	.10	.10	—
Documentary, etc., stamp taxes									
Conveyances (per $500, or fraction thereof, if value is over $100)	—	.50	—	.50	.55	.55	.55	.55	—
Bond and stock issues (per $100, respectively)	—	.05	.05	.10	.11	.11	.11	.11,.10	—
Playing cards (per package of not more than 54)	.02	.08	.10	.10	.13	.13	.13	.13	—
Manufacturers' excise taxes									
Lubricating oils (per gallon)	—	—	—	.04	.06	.06	.06	.06	.06
Matches, white, phosphorous (per hundred)	.02	.02	.02	.02	.02	.02	.02	.02	.02
Matches, in general (per thousand)	—	—	—	.02	.02	.02	.02	.02	—
Gasoline (per gallon)	—	—	—	.01	.015	.02	.02	.04	.04
Electrical energy (sale price)	—	—	—	3%	3⅓%	—	—	—	—
Tires (sale price 1919, per pound 1932 and after)	—	5%	—	.0225	.05	.05	.05	.10	.10
Inner tubes (sale price 1919, per pound 1932 and after)	—	5%	—	.04	.09	.09	.09	.10	.10

246

Item								
Tread rubber (per pound)	—	—	—	—	—	—	.05	.05
Trucks (sale price)	—	3%	2%	5%	5%	8%	10%	10%
Automobiles (sale price)	—	5%	3%	7%	10%	10%	10%	1%ª
Truck accessories (sale price)	—	5%	2%	5%	8%	8%	8%	8%
Automobile accessories (sale price)	—	5%	2%	5%	8%	8%	8%	8%
Radios and accessories (sale price)	—	—	5%	10%	10%	10%	10%	—
Refrigerators (mechanical, household, sale price)	—	—	5%	10%	10%	5%	5%	—
Firearms, shells, cartridges (sale price)	—	10%	10%	11%	11%	11%	11%	11%
Pistols and revolvers (sale price)	10%	10%	10%	11%	11%	10%	10%	10%
Sporting goods other than fishing equipment (sale price)	—	10%	10%	10%	15%	10%	10%	—
Fishing equipment (sale price)	—	10%	10%	10%	15%	10%	10%	10%
Musical instruments and phonographs (sale price)	—	5%	—	10%	10%	10%	10%	—
Records (sale price)	—	5%	5%	10%	10%	10%	10%	—
Electric, gas, and oil appliances (sale price)	—	—	—	10%	10%	5%	5%	—
Business and store machines (sale price)	—	—	—	10%	10%	10%	10%	—
Cameras and photographic apparatus (sale price)	—	10%	10%	25%	20%	10%	10%	—
Photographic film (sale price)	—	5%	—	15%	20%	10%	10%	—
Mixed flour (per barrel containing 99–196 pounds)	.04	.04	.04	—	—	—	—	—
Automatic slot vending and vending weighing machines (sale price, respectively)	—	5%, 10%	—	—	—	—	—	—
Candy (sale price)	—	5%	2%	—	—	—	—	—
Retailers' excise taxes								
Jewelry (sale price)	—	5%	10%ᵇ	20%	20%	10%	10%	—
Furs (sale price)	—	10%ᵇ	10%ᵇ	20%	20%	10%	10%	—
Toilet preparations (per 25¢ or fraction, 1919; sale price thereafter)	—	.01	10%ᵇ	20%	20%	10%	10%	—
Luggage (sale price)	—	10%	—	20%	20%	10%	10%	—

TABLE A-5. continued

Tax	1913	1919	1928	1932	1944	1952	1954	1963	1969
Miscellaneous excise taxes									
General telephone service (amount paid)......	—	—	—	—	15%	15%	10%	10%	°
Toll telephone service (amount paid; prior to 1944, per message)......	—	.05–.10	—	—	25%	25%	10%	10%	°
Cable and radio messages, domestic (amount paid; prior to 1944, per message)......	—	.10	—	.10–.20	25%	15%	10%	10%	—
Telegraph messages, domestic (amount paid; 1919 per message)......	—	.10	—	.10	25%	15%	10%	10%	—
Leased wires, or teletypewriter and wire mileage service (amount paid)......	—	10%	—	5%	25%	25%	10%	10%	°
Wire and equipment service (amount paid)...	—	—	—	—	8%	8%	8%	8%	—
Transportation of oil by pipe line (amount paid)	—	8%	—	4%	4½%	4½%	4½%	—	—
Bowling alleys, pool tables (per unit, per year)	—	10	—	—	20	20	20	20	—
Transportation of persons other than by air (amount paid)......	—	8%	—	—	15%	15%	10%	—	—
Transportation of persons, air (amount paid)..	—	—	—	—	15%	15%	10%	5%	5%
Transportation of property (amount paid)....	—	3%	—	—	3%	3%	3%	—	—
Use tax on highway vehicles weighing over 26,000 pounds (per 1,000 lbs. per year)..	—	—	—	—	—	—	—	3	3
Lease of safe deposit boxes (amount collected)	—	—	—	10%	20%	20%	10%	10%	—
Admissions (for every 10¢ or fraction, 1919–43; 5¢ or major fraction, 1944–63)......	—	.01	.01	.01	.01	.01	.01	.01	—
Leases of boxes or seats (amount for which similar accommodations are sold)........	—	10%	10%	10%	20%	20%	10%	10%	—
Cabarets, roof gardens, etc. (for every 10¢ [or fraction] of 20 percent of total charge, 1919–40; amount paid, 1941–63)........	—	.015	.015	.015	20%	20%	20%	10%	—
Wagers (amount of wager)......	—	—	—	—	—	10%	10%	10%	10%

248

Occupation of accepting wagers (per year)	—	—	—	—	—	50	50	50	50	50
Dues and initiation fees (amount paid)	—	10%	10%	10%	20%	20%	20%	20%	20%	—
Domestic oleomargarine (uncolored and colored, respectively, per pound)	.0025,.10	.0025,.10	.0025,.10	.0025,.10	.0025,.10	—	—	—	—	—
Butter (processed and adulterated, respectively, per pound)	.0025,.10	.0025,.10	.0025,.10	.0025,.10	.0025,.10	.0025,.10	.0025,.10	.0025,.10	.0025,.10	.0025,.10
Filled cheese (domestic and imported, respectively, per pound)	.01,.08	.01,.08	.01,.08	.01,.08	.01,.08	.01,.08	.01,.08	.01,.08	.01,.08	.01,.08
Use of boats (per foot, according to size, 1919, 1924; per boat, according to size or type, 1932; length, 1944)	—	1-4	—	10-200	5-200	—	—	—	—	—
Coin-operated devices (amusement and gambling, respectively, per unit, per year)	—	—	—	—	10,100	10,250	10,250	10,250	10,250	0,250
Narcotics										
Opium (per ounce)	.01	.01	.01	.01	.01	.01	.01	.01	.01	.01
Opium for smoking (per pound)	300	300	300	300	300	300	300	300	300	300
Importers of opium	24	24	24	24	24	24	24	24	24	24
Marihuana (per ounce)[d]	—	—	—	—	1	1	1	1	1	1
Marihuana, authorized users (per year)	—	—	—	—	24	24	24	24	24	24
Acquisition of securities of a foreign issuer ("interest equalization tax")[e]										
Stock	—	—	—	—	—	—	—	15	—	—
Bonds and loans of maturity 1 year or longer	—	—	—	—	—	—	—	2.75-1.5%[f]	—	—

Sources: 1913–63: Tax Foundation, *Federal Non-Income Taxes; an Examination of Selected Revenue Sources* (New York, 1965), pp. 23–26, supplemented by data for still wines and narcotics from U.S. Treasury Department, *Annual Report of the Secretary of the Treasury*, 1940, pp. 466–534; 1950, pp. 251–80; and 1962, pp. 370–402; 1969; Treasury Department, Office of Tax Analysis (mimeograph).

a Rates are 6 percent from January 1, 1966, through March 14, 1966; 7 percent from March 15, 1966, through March 31, 1968; and 2 percent from April 1, 1968, through December 31, 1968.

b Tax levied at manufacturers' level.

c Rates are 3 percent from January 1, 1966, through March 31, 1966; 10 percent from April 1, 1966, through March 31, 1968; 1 percent from April 1, 1968, through December 31, 1968.

d This tax applies to persons who have already paid the required taxes on importers, users, or producers of marihuana. A tax of $100 per ounce applies to other persons selling marihuana.

e Expires July 31, 1967.

f Applied to loans after February 10, 1965. Rates are equivalent to increase in interest rate of about one percentage point for all maturities.

TABLE A-6. History of Social Security and Railroad Retirement Tax Rates

Year	Maximum Taxable Wages (Dollars)	Tax Rate (Percentages)		
		Employer	Employee	Self-employed[a]
	Old-Age, Survivors, Disability, and Health Insurance			
1937–49	3,000 per year	1.0	1.0	[b]
1950	3,000 " "	1.5	1.5	[b]
1951–53	3,600 " "	1.5	1.5	2.25
1954	3,600 " "	2.0	2.0	3.0
1955–56	4,200 " "	2.0	2.0	3.0
1957–58	4,200 " "	2.25	2.25	3.375
1959	4,800 " "	2.5	2.5	3.75
1960–61	4,800 " "	3.0	3.0	4.5
1962	4,800 " "	3.125	3.125	4.7
1963–65	4,800 " "	3.625	3.625	5.4
1966	6,600 " "	4.20	4.20	6.15
1967–68	6,600 " "	4.40	4.40	6.40
1969–72	6,600 " "	4.90	4.90	7.10
1973–75	6,600 " "	5.40	5.40	7.55
1976–79	6,600 " "	5.45	5.45	7.60
1980–86	6,600 " "	5.55	5.55	7.70
1987 and after	6,600 " "	5.65	5.65	7.80
	Railroad Retirement Insurance			
1937–39	300 per month	2.75	2.75	
1940–42	300 " "	3.00	3.00	
1943–45	300 " "	3.25	3.25	
1946	300 " "	3.50	3.50	
1947–48	300 " "	5.75	5.75	
1949–51	300 " "	6.00	6.00	
1952–June 30, 1954	300 " "	6.25	6.25	
July 1, 1954–May 31, 1959	350 " "	6.25	6.25	
June 1, 1959–1961	400 " "	6.75	6.75	
1962–Oct. 31, 1963	400 " "	7.25	7.25	
Nov. 1, 1963–1964	450 " "	7.25	7.25	
1965–Aug. 31, 1965	450 " "	8.125	8.125	
Sept. 1, 1965–Dec. 31, 1965	450 " "	7.125	7.125	
1966	550 " "	7.95	7.95	
1967	550 " "	8.40	8.40	
1968	550 " "	8.65	8.65	
1969–72	550 " "	9.40	9.40	
1973–75	550 " "	9.90	9.90	
1976–79	550 " "	9.95	9.95	
1980–86	550 " "	10.05	10.05	
1987 and after	550 " "	10.15	10.15	

Sources: Robert J. Myers, *Old-Age, Survivors, Disability, and Health Insurance Provisions: Legislative History, 1935–65* (U.S. Department of Health, Education, and Welfare, Social Security Administration, July 1965); M. C. Hart, "Railroad Retirement Act as Amended in 1965," *Social Security Bulletin*, Vol. 29, No. 2 (February 1966), pp. 26–38.

[a] Does not apply to railroad retirement insurance.
[b] Not covered by the program until January 1, 1951

TABLE A-7. History of Unemployment Tax Rates

Year	Covered Wages (Dollars)	Actual Rates (Percentages)	Statutory Range of Rates[a] (Percentages)
	Federal Unemployment Insurance[b]		
1936	All Wages	1.0[c]	d
1937	" "	2.0[c]	d
1938	" "	3.0[c]	d
1939–60	3,000 per year	3.0[c]	d
1961	3,000 " "	3.1[c]	d
1962	3,000 " "	3.5[c]	d
1963	3,000 " "	3.35[c]	d
1964 and after	3,000 " "	3.1[c]	d
	Railroad Unemployment Insurance		
1939–47	300 per month	3.0	3.0
1948–June 30, 1954	300 " "	0.5	0.5–3.0
July 1, 1954–Dec. 31, 1955	350 " "	0.5	0.5–3.0
1956	350 " "	1.5	0.5–3.0
1957	350 " "	2.0	0.5–3.0
1958	350 " "	2.5	0.5–3.0
Jan. 1, 1959–May 31, 1959	350 " "	3.0	0.5–3.0
June 1, 1959–Dec. 31, 1961	400 " "	3.75	1.5–3.75
1962–1963	400 " "	4.0[e]	1.5–3.75
1964 and after	400 " "	4.0	1.5–4.0

Sources: Actual railroad unemployment insurance rates, 1948–62: *Federal Tax System*, p. 181 (see Table A-1). For all other data prior to 1963: *Annual Report of the Secretary of the Treasury*, 1940, pp. 522–3; 1950, pp. 270–1; and 1962, pp. 392–3. Federal unemployment insurance taxes 1963 and after: *Federal Tax System*, p. 177. Railroad unemployment insurance 1963 and after: Railroad Retirement Board, *Annual Report for the Fiscal Year Ended June 30, 1964*, p. 14.

[a] For railroad unemployment insurance the actual rate in any given year depends on the balance in the railroad unemployment compensation trust fund.

[b] Federal unemployment insurance applied to employers of 8 persons or more between 1936 and 1956, and to employers of 4 persons or more in 1956 and later years.

[c] For federal unemployment insurance a credit up to 90 percent of the tax is allowed for contributions paid into a state unemployment fund. Beginning in 1961 credits up to 90 percent are computed as if the tax rate were 3 percent.

[d] Employers are actually taxed by the states on the basis of an experience rating determined by past unemployment records. All employers are permitted to take the maximum credit allowed against the federal unemployment tax, even though they may, in fact, pay a lower rate because of a good experience rating. In 1964, the effective tax rate on covered wages ranged from 0.54 percent in Texas to 2.39 percent in Alaska.

[e] Consisting of the maximum rate of 3¾ percent under the schedule then in effect plus ¼ percent added by the Temporary Extended Railroad Unemployment Insurance Benefits Act of 1961.

TABLE A-8. Federal Estate Tax Rates and Rates of the State Tax Credit, 1942 to Date (1966)

Rates Before Credit for State Taxes		Rates for Computing State Tax Credit	
Taxable Estate (Dollars)	Rate (Percentages)	Taxable Estate (Dollars)	Rate (Percentages)
0– 5,000	3	0– 40,000	0
5,000– 10,000	7	40,000– 90,000	.8
10,000– 20,000	11	90,000– 140,000	1.6
20,000– 30,000	14	140,000– 240,000	2.4
30,000– 40,000	18	240,000– 440,000	3.2
40,000– 50,000	22	440,000– 640,000	4.0
50,000– 60,000	25	640,000– 840,000	4.8
60,000– 100,000	28	840,000– 1,040,000	5.6
100,000– 250,000	30	1,040,000– 1,540,000	6.4
250,000– 500,000	32	1,540,000– 2,040,000	7.2
500,000– 750,000	35	2,040,000– 2,540,000	8.0
750,000– 1,000,000	37	2,540,000– 3,040,000	8.8
1,000,000– 1,250,000	39	3,040,000– 3,540,000	9.6
1,250,000– 1,500,000	42	3,540,000– 4,040,000	10.4
1,500,000– 2,000,000	45	4,040,000– 5,040,000	11.2
2,000,000– 2,500,000	49	5,040,000– 6,040,000	12.0
2,500,000– 3,000,000	53	6,040,000– 7,040,000	12.8
3,000,000– 3,500,000	56	7,040,000– 8,040,000	13.6
3,500,000– 4,000,000	59	8,040,000– 9,040,000	14.4
4,000,000– 5,000,000	63	9,040,000–10,040,000	15.2
5,000,000– 6,000,000	67	10,040,000 and over	16.0
6,000,000– 7,000,000	70		
7,000,000– 8,000,000	73		
8,000,000–10,000,000	76		
10,000,000 and over	77		

Source: Internal Revenue Code.

TABLE A-9. History of Estate and Gift Tax Rates

Revenue Act	Date of Death	Tax Rates (Percentages)		Bracket Subject to:	
		Estates	Gifts	Minimum Rate (Thousands of dollars)	Maximum Rate (Thousands of dollars)
1916	Sept. 9, 1916, to Mar. 2, 1917	1.0–10.0	—	0–50	5,000 and over
1917[a]	Mar. 3, 1917 to Oct. 3, 1917	1.5–15.0	—	0–50	5,000 and over
1917[b]	Oct. 4, 1917, to Feb. 23, 1919	2.0–25.0	—	0–50	10,000 and over
1918	Feb. 24, 1919, to Feb. 25, 1926	1.0–25.0	1.0–25.0[c]	0–50	10,000 and over
1926	Feb. 26, 1926, to June 5, 1932	1.0–20.0	—	0–50	10,000 and over
1932	June 6, 1932, to May 10, 1934	1.0–45.0	.75–33.5	0–10	10,000 and over
1934	May 11, 1934, to July 29, 1935	1.0–60.0	.75–45.0	0–10	10,000 and over
1935	July 30, 1935, to June 24, 1940	2.0–70.0	1.55–52.5	0–10	50,000 and over
1940	June 25, 1940, to Sept. 19, 1941	2.2–77.0[d]	1.65–57.75[d]	0–10	50,000 and over
1941	Sept. 20, 1941, to date	3.0–77.0	2.25–57.75	0– 5	10,000 and over

Source: *The Federal Tax System*, p. 291 (see Table A-1).
[a] Act of March 3, 1917.
[b] Revenue Act of 1917.
[c] In effect June 2, 1924, to Dec. 31, 1925.
[d] Includes defense tax equal to 10 percent of tax liability

TABLE A-10. History of Estate and Gift Tax Exemptions and Exclusions

(In dollars)

Revenue Act	Estate Tax		Gift Tax	
	Specific Exemption[a]	Insurance Exclusion	Specific Exemption[b]	Annual Exclusion Per Donee
1916	50,000	—	c	c
1918	50,000	40,000	c	c
1924	50,000	40,000	50,000	500
1926	100,000	40,000	d	d
1932	50,000	40,000	50,000	5,000
1935	40,000	40,000	40,000	5,000
1938	40,000	40,000	40,000	4,000
1942	60,000	—	30,000	3,000

Source: *The Federal Tax System*, p. 291 (see Table A-1).

[a] Specific exemption granted to estates of nonresident citizens dying after May 11, 1934, on the same basis as resident decedents. No exemptions granted to estates of resident aliens until Oct. 21, 1942, when a $2,000 exemption was made available.

[b] Under the 1924 Act, exemption allowed each calendar year. Under the 1932 and later Acts, specific exemption allowed only once.

[c] No gift tax.

[d] Gift tax repealed.

Tax Bases of the Major Federal Taxes

THE CONCEPTS OF TAXABLE INCOME for both the individual and corporation income taxes as defined by the Internal Revenue Code differ substantially from the national income aggregates which are widely used for purposes of economic analysis. This appendix derives the tax bases of the two income taxes and compares them with the official estimates of personal income and corporate profits incorporated in the national income accounts. It also presents the latest distributions by rate brackets of the tax bases of the income and estate and gift taxes.

The Individual Income Tax

Among the various tax concepts, *adjusted gross income* most nearly resembles personal income. Total personal income exceeds the aggregate of adjusted gross incomes reported on tax returns by substantial amounts each year. However, a substantial portion of the disparity can be explained by differences in definition. The individual income tax base is derived below in two steps: (1) aggregate adjusted gross income of all persons in the United States is estimated from personal income; (2) personal exemptions and deductions are subtracted from adjusted gross income to obtain taxable income.

Relation Between Personal Income and Adjusted Gross Income

Table B-1 summarizes the conceptual differences between personal income and adjusted gross income for calendar year 1963, the latest year for which income tax statistics are available. The differences are:

(a) items of income that are included in personal income but not in adjusted gross income (for example, transfer payments, income in kind, tax-exempt interest), amounting to $84.2 billion; and (b) incomes that are included in adjusted gross income but not in personal income (primarily the social security taxes paid by employees and capital gains), amounting to $23.0 billion. When these differences are taken into account, the 1963 personal income of $464.8 billion corresponded to an adjusted gross income of $403.6 billion.

The relationship between personal income and adjusted gross income has been fairly stable in recent years. Since World War II, when a substantial portion of personal income was received by members of the armed forces in the form of nontaxable pay and allowances, the difference between personal income and adjusted gross income has been on the order of 11 to 13 percent of personal income (Table B-2). There has been a slight uptrend in the difference since the mid-1950's as a result of the rise in transfer payments.

If all income recipients were required to file returns and everybody reported his income accurately, the total adjusted gross income on tax returns would correspond closely to the amounts shown in Table B-2. Since neither of these conditions holds, adjusted gross incomes reported on tax returns are lower than the aggregate for all recipients. As Table B-3 indicates, this gap has been declining as a percentage of total adjusted gross income; by 1964 the figure was down to 8.2 percent. The decline was very sharp during World War II years, when exemptions and filing requirements were lowered drastically, but it has continued—although at a much slower rate and with some interruptions—throughout the 1950's and 1960's as the rise in incomes pushed more and more people above the filing requirement levels.

In 1963, the gross difference between personal income and adjusted gross income reported on tax returns was $96 billion (compare Tables B-2 and B-3). About 64 percent of this difference—or $61.2 billion—is explained by conceptual differences and only $34.8 billion did not appear on tax returns. But this $34.8 billion cannot be regarded as a measure of underreporting. Included in this figure is the income received by persons with incomes below $600 who are not required to file returns, the exact amount of which is unknown. Moreover, a large number of nontaxable individuals in such low paid occupations as domestic service and farming do not bother to file even though the law requires them to do so. Considering the large magnitudes involved, the portion of the gap between personal income and adjusted gross income that remains unexplained is relatively small. Even if as much as two-thirds of the $34.8

billion was due to underreporting, the degree of underreporting was less than 6 percent.

The Individual Income Tax Base

The steps in the derivation of the individual tax base for the years 1946 through 1963 are shown in Table B-4. In 1963, as previously indicated, adjusted gross incomes totalled $403.6 billion and, of this amount, $368.8 billion was reported on individual income tax returns. Nontaxable individuals reported $18.3 billion, while those who were taxable reported $350.4 billion. The personal exemptions of taxable individuals amounted to $87.4 billion and their deductions amounted to $54.4 billion. Subtracting these two items from adjusted gross income leaves a taxable income of $208.6 billion. To this must be added the small amount of taxable income—about $500 million—of individuals whose tax liabilities were wiped out by the dividend and retirement income credits. Thus, the tax base amounted to $209.1 billion in 1963.

Table B-5 compares the tax base with personal income since the beginning of World War II. From 9.9 percent of personal income in 1939, taxable income rose to 40.1 percent in 1953 and reached 46.4 percent in 1964.

Distribution of Taxable Individual Income

An estimated distribution of taxable income by rate brackets is shown in Table B-6 for calendar year 1963. Only a small proportion of taxable income is subject to the very high rates. Of the total taxable income of $209.1 billion, $122.7 billion, or 59 percent, was subject to the first bracket rate of 20 percent.

The Corporation Income Tax

Table B-7 gives a detailed reconciliation for calendar year 1962 among three concepts of corporate profits: (1) *profits before taxes* as defined in the national income accounts; (2) *compiled net profits* of all corporations as tabulated from federal corporate tax returns; and (3) *taxable income* of corporations.

Relation Between Profits Before Tax and Taxable Income

The major differences between the national income definition of profits before tax and compiled net profits are accounted for by differences in coverage and in definition of income. For example, profits before tax include the income of government financial institutions and adjustments of the profits of mutual financial intermediaries for national income purposes; on the other hand, they exclude dividends received from corporations and net capital gains, include estimated profits resulting from audit, and do not allow for the deductions for depletion, state corporation income taxes, and adjustment for bad debts. In 1962, the national income definition of corporate profits was $55.4 billion, while compiled net profits amounted to $50.8 billion. As shown in Table B-7, differences in coverage amounted to −$1 billion, while differences in definition of income amounted to −$3.5 billion.

To arrive at taxable income, the losses of deficit corporations must be added back to compiled net profits and the nontaxable components of compiled net profits must be eliminated. After these adjustments, corporate taxable income in 1962 was $51.7 billion, or $0.9 billion higher than compiled net profits.

A comparison of the three income concepts for the years 1958-63 is given in Table B-8. The official concept of profits before taxes has exceeded compiled net profits by $3 to $5 billion in recent years, while taxable income has been fairly close to compiled net profits.

Distribution of Taxable Corporate Income

Unlike the individual income tax, most of the corporation income tax base is concentrated in the top rate bracket. This reflects the great importance of large corporations in the corporate sector. For calendar year 1962, taxable corporate income amounted to $51.7 billion, of which $2.2 billion was subject to the alternative tax of 25 percent on long-term capital gains and $2.1 billion was mutual insurance company income subject to a special 1 percent tax, leaving $47.4 billion subject to the normal tax and surtax rates. Only $5.9 billion, or 12 percent, of the latter amount was subject to the 30 percent rate, and the remaining $41.6 billion, or 88 percent, was subject to the 52 percent rate (Table B-9).

Estate and Gift Taxes

In 1963, 55,207 taxable estate tax returns and 20,598 taxable gift tax returns were filed. The total amount of wealth subject to tax amounted to $7.9 billion—$7.1 billion under the estate tax, and $0.8 billion under the gift tax.

The decedents represented on the 1963 taxable estate tax returns were 3.3 percent of all adult decedents in that year (Table B-10). These returns showed gross estates of $14.7 billion; debts amounted to $0.6 billion, leaving *economic* estates of $14.1 billion. The $7.1 billion of taxable estates thus accounted for about half of the wealth left by decedents subject to estate tax (Table B-11). Most of the tax base was concentrated in the lower rate brackets: 40 percent was subject to rates below 30 percent; 53 percent was subject to rates between 30 percent and 50 percent; and the remaining 7 percent was subject to rates of 50 percent or more (Table B-12).

The total gifts of persons making taxable gifts in 1963 amounted to $1.4 billion. After allowing for deductions and exclusions, only $0.8 billion—or 56 percent—was taxable (Table B-13). About 80 percent of the gift tax base was subject to rates below 30 percent; 15 percent was subject to rates between 30 percent and 50 percent; and 5 percent was subject to rates of 50 percent or more (Table B-14).

TABLE B-1. Derivation of Adjusted Gross Income from Personal Income, 1963

(In billions of dollars)

Income and Adjustment Items		Amount
1. Personal income		464.8
2. Portion of personal income not included in adjusted gross income	84.2	
a. Transfer payments (except fees and military retirement pay)	34.6	
b. Other labor income (except pay of military reservists)	13.8	
c. Income in kind and imputed income	24.9	
d. Noncorporate nonfarm inventory valuation adjustment	a	
e. Value of change in farm inventories	0.8	
f. Nontaxable military pay and allowances	2.5	
g. Accrued interest on U.S. government bonds	0.7	
h. Tax-exempt interest	1.0	
i. Fiduciary income (other than capital gains) not distributed to individuals	1.5	
j. Property income of nonprofit organizations	3.0	
k. Excluded sick pay	0.9	
l. Excluded dividends	0.5	
3. Portion of adjusted gross income not included in personal income	23.0	
a. Contributions for social insurance by employees and the self-employed	11.8	
b. Net gains of individuals on the sale of capital assets	7.5	
c. Other income (except other income on Form 1040 A) reported on tax returns[b]	1.2	
d. Annuities and pensions reported on individual income tax returns	2.7	
e. Deductions for net operating loss carryover and depletion	−0.2	
4. Total adjustment for conceptual differences (2−3)		61.2
5. Estimated adjusted gross income (1−4)[c]		403.6

Source: Worksheets of U.S. Department of Commerce, Office of Business Economics.
[a] Less than $50 million.
[b] Includes net gains and losses on sale of property other than capita assets, net losses on capital assets, and ordinary gains from sales of depreciable property.
[c] Includes income of taxable and nontaxable individuals.

TABLE B-2. Comparison of Personal Income and Adjusted Gross Income, 1939–64

(Dollar amounts in billions)

Year	Personal Income	Adjusted Gross Income[a]	Difference Amount	Difference Percentage of Personal Income
1939	$ 72.8	$ 63.7	$ 9.1	12.5
1940	78.3	69.3	9.0	11.5
1941	96.0	84.8	11.2	11.7
1942	122.9	106.9	16.0	13.0
1943	151.3	128.8	22.5	14.9
1944	165.3	137.1	28.2	17.1
1945	171.1	139.6	31.5	18.4
1946	178.7	156.1	22.6	12.6
1947	191.3	171.4	19.9	10.4
1948	210.2	185.1	25.1	11.9
1949	207.2	182.6	24.6	11.9
1950	227.6	202.0	25.6	11.2
1951	255.6	228.9	26.7	10.4
1952	272.5	241.9	30.6	11.2
1953	288.2	256.5	31.7	11.0
1954	290.1	255.1	35.0	12.1
1955	310.9	275.7	35.2	11.3
1956	333.0	296.2	36.8	11.1
1957	351.1	309.2	41.9	11.9
1958	361.2	314.4	46.8	13.0
1959	383.5	337.2	46.3	12.1
1960	401.0	349.7	51.3	12.8
1961	416.8	362.5	54.3	13.0
1962	442.6	383.6	59.0	13.3
1963	464.8	403.6	61.2	13.2
1964	495.0	432.0	63.0	12.7

Sources: Personal income: *Survey of Current Business* (August 1965), p. 32. Adjusted gross income, 1939–53 and 1964: Author's estimates; 1954–63: Worksheets of Office of Business Economics.

[a] Includes incomes of individuals who were not required to file returns.

TABLE B-3. Comparison of Total Adjusted Gross Income and Adjusted Gross Income Reported on Tax Returns, 1939–64

(Dollar amounts in billions)

| Year | Adjusted Gross Income | | Difference | |
	Total U.S.	Reported on Tax Returns	Amount	Percentage of Total U.S.
1939	$ 63.7	$ 25.2	$38.5	60.4
1940	69.3	39.4	29.9	43.1
1941	84.8	62.5	22.3	26.3
1942	106.9	84.9	22.0	20.6
1943	128.8	105.7	23.1	17.9
1944	137.1	116.5	20.6	15.0
1945	139.6	120.0	19.6	14.0
1946	156.1	134.1	22.0	14.1
1947	171.4	149.7	21.7	12.7
1948	185.1	163.5	21.6	11.7
1949	182.6	160.6	22.0	12.0
1950	202.0	179.1	22.9	11.3
1951	228.9	202.3	26.6	11.6
1952	241.9	215.3	26.6	11.0
1953	256.5	228.7	27.8	10.8
1954	255.1	229.2	25.9	10.2
1955	275.7	248.5	27.2	9.9
1956	296.2	267.7	28.5	9.6
1957	309.2	280.3	28.9	9.3
1958	314.4	281.2	33.2	10.6
1959	337.2	305.1	32.1	9.5
1960	349.7	315.5	34.2	9.8
1961	362.5	329.9	32.6	9.0
1962	383.6	348.7	34.9	9.1
1963	403.6	368.8	34.8	8.6
1964	432.0	396.7	35.3	8.2

Sources: Adjusted gross income, total U.S.: Table B-2. Adjusted gross income reported on tax returns, 1939–43: Author's estimates; 1944–63: U.S. Treasury Department, Internal Revenue Service, Statistics of Income, Individua Income Tax Returns ;1964: Statistics of Income ,1964 ,Preliminary, Individual Income Tax Returns.

TABLE B-4. Derivation of the Individual Income Tax Base, 1946-63[a]

(In billions of dollars)

Year	Total Adjusted Gross Income	Deduct: Nonreported Adjusted Gross Income	Equals: Adjusted Gross Income Reported on Individual Returns	Deduct: Adjusted Gross Income Reported on Nontaxable Returns	Equals: Adjusted Gross Income Reported on Taxable Returns	Deduct: Exemptions on Taxable Returns	Deduct: Deductions on Taxable Returns	Equals: Taxable Income on Taxable Returns	Add: Taxable Income on Nontaxable Returns[b]	Equals: Total Taxable Income of Individuals
1946	156.1	22.0	134.1	16.0	118.1	39.6	13.2	65.3	—	65.3
1947	171.4	21.7	149.7	14.4	135.3	44.3	15.6	75.4	—	75.4
1948	185.1	21.6	163.5	21.5	142.1	50.9	16.5	74.7	—	74.7
1949	182.6	22.0	160.6	22.0	138.6	50.1	16.8	71.6	—	71.6
1950	202.0	22.9	179.1	20.6	158.5	55.2	19.0	84.3	—	84.3
1951	228.9	26.6	202.3	19.1	183.2	61.4	22.4	99.4	—	99.4
1952	241.9	26.6	215.3	18.7	196.6	64.5	24.6	107.5	—	107.5
1953	256.5	27.8	228.7	18.2	210.5	67.9	26.9	115.7	—	115.7
1954	255.1	25.9	229.2	19.6	209.7	67.0	27.5	115.2	.1	115.3
1955	275.7	27.2	248.5	18.9	229.6	71.2	30.5	127.9	.1	128.0
1956	296.2	28.5	267.7	18.2	249.6	74.6	33.5	141.4	.1	141.5
1957	309.2	28.9	280.3	18.2	262.2	76.8	36.2	149.2	.2	149.4
1958	314.4	33.2	281.2	19.0	262.2	75.8	37.2	149.2	.2	149.3
1959	337.2	32.1	305.1	17.3	287.8	79.7	41.7	166.4	.2	166.5
1960	349.7	34.2	315.5	18.3	297.2	81.2	44.5	171.5	.2	171.6
1961	362.5	32.6	329.9	18.6	311.3	82.5	47.1	181.6	.1	181.8
1962	383.6	34.9	348.7	18.1	330.6	85.1	50.6	195.0	.4	195.3
1963	403.6	34.8	368.8	18.3	350.4	87.4	54.4	208.6	.5	209.1

Sources: Total adjusted gross income from Table B-2; other data from *Statistics of Income, Individual Income Tax Returns.* Figures are rounded and will not necessarily add to totals.

[a] Excludes taxable income of fiduciaries.

[b] Taxable income of persons whose tax liability was completely offset by tax credits.

TABLE B-5. Comparison of Personal Income and Taxable Income, 1939–64

(Dollar amounts in billions)

Year	Personal Income	Taxable Income	
		Amount	Percentage of Personal Income
1939	$ 72.8	$ 7.2	9.9
1940	78.3	10.7	13.7
1941	96.0	22.7	23.6
1942	122.9	36.1	29.4
1943	151.3	50.1	33.1
1944	165.3	55.3	33.5
1945	171.1	57.1	33.4
1946	178.7	65.3	36.5
1947	191.3	75.4	39.4
1948	210.2	74.7	35.5
1949	207.2	71.6	34.6
1950	227.6	84.3	37.0
1951	255.6	99.4	38.9
1952	272.5	107.5	39.4
1953	288.2	115.7	40.1
1954	290.1	115.3	39.7
1955	310.9	128.0	41.2
1956	333.0	141.5	42.5
1957	351.1	149.4	42.6
1958	361.2	149.3	41.3
1959	383.5	166.5	43.4
1960	401.0	171.6	42.8
1961	416.8	181.8	43.6
1962	442.6	195.3	44.1
1963	464.8	209.1	45.0
1964	495.0ᵖ	229.9	46.4

ᵖ Preliminary.

Sources: Personal income: *Survey of Current Business* (August 1965). Taxable income, 1939–45: Author's estimates; 1946–63: Table B-4; 1964: *Statistics of Income, 1964, Preliminary, Individual Income Tax Returns.*

TABLE B-6. Distribution of Taxable Income and Individual Income Tax, by Rate Brackets, 1963

(Dollar amounts in millions)

Rate (Percentages)	Amounts		Percentage Distribution	
	Taxable Income	Tax	Taxable Income	Tax
20	$122,748	$24,550	58.70	49.96
21	1,348	283	0.64	0.58
22	45,385	9,985	21.70	20.32
24	541	130	0.26	0.26
26	15,020	3,905	7.18	7.95
30	6,550	1,965	3.13	4.00
32	74	24	0.04	0.05
34	3,738	1,271	1.79	2.59
36	52	19	0.02	0.04
38	2,504	952	1.20	1.94
39	39	15	0.02	0.03
42	30	13	0.01	0.03
43	1,797	773	0.86	1.57
47	1,310	616	0.63	1.25
49	15	8	0.01	0.02
50	952	476	0.46	0.97
52	24	12	0.01	0.02
53	712	337	0.34	0.77
54	18	10	0.01	0.02
56	553	309	0.26	0.63
58	19	11	0.01	0.02
59	785	463	0.38	0.94
62	717	445	0.34	0.91
65	414	269	0.20	0.55
66	9	6	a	0.01
68	10	7		0.01
69	261	180	0.12	0.37
71	7	5	a	0.01
72	177	127	0.08	0.26
74	4	3	a	0.01
75	192	144	0.09	0.29
76	3	2	a	a
78	121	95	0.06	0.19
80	2	2	a	a
81	82	66	0.04	0.13
83	7	6	a	0.01
84	59	50	0.03	0.10
87	175[b]	153	0.08	0.31
89	116	103	0.06	0.21
90	52	46	0.02	0.09
91	68	62	0.03	0.13
Subtotal	206,691	47,936	98.85	97.54
50[c]	2,415	1,207	1.15	2.46
Total	209,105	49,143	100.00	100.00

Source: *Statistics of Income, Individual Income Tax Returns, 1963*, p. 90. Figures are rounded and will not necessarily add to totals.

[a] Less than 0.005 percent.

[b] Includes $129 million of taxable income subject to maximum effective rate limitation of 87 percent

[c] Alternative capital gains tax rate.

TABLE B-7. Reconciliation of Corporation Profits Before Tax, Compiled Net Profits, and Taxable Income, 1962

(In billions of dollars)

Income and Adjustment Items	Amount
Profits before taxes, Office of Business Economics................................	55.4
Differences in coverage:	
Income of Federal Reserve Banks, Federal Home Loan Banks, and Federal Land Banks... −0.9	
Adjustment for mutual financial intermediaries.................... −1.3	
Corporate income from equities in foreign corporations and branches 3.8	
Total income received from equities in foreign corporations (including individuals), net of corresponding outflows.................... −2.6	
Subtotal... −1.0	−1.0
Differences in definition:	
Dividends received from domestic corporations.................. 3.6	
Net capital gains from sales of property....................... 3.5	
Costs of trading or issuing corporate securities.................. 0.3	
Income disclosed by audit................................. −4.3	
Depletion, drilling costs in excess of depreciation, and oil-well bonus payments.. −3.9	
State corporation income taxes.............................. −1.4	
Bad debt adjustment...................................... −1.3	
Subtotal...	−3.5
Equals: Compiled net profits, all corporations................................	50.8
Adjustments to compute taxable income:	
Losses of corporations with no net income...................... 6.6	
Wholly tax exempt interest................................. −1.2	
Dividends received deduction............................... −2.4	
Net operating loss deduction............................... −1.8	
Western Hemisphere deduction.............................. −0.2	
Taxable income of Subchapter S corporations.................... −1.1	
Regulated investment company income........................ −1.2	
Mutual insurance company income taxed at 1 percent............ 2.1	
Subtotal...	0.9
Equals: Taxable income...	51.7

Sources: *Survey of Current Business* (August 1965); Worksheets of the Office of Business Economics; and *Statistics of Income, Corporation Income Tax Returns, 1962*. Figures are rounded and will not necessarily add to totals.

TABLE B-8. Comparison of Corporation Profits Before Tax, Compiled Net Profits, and Taxable Income, 1939–63

(In billions of dollars)

Year	Profits Before Tax (National income definition)	Compiled Net Profits[a] (Reported on tax returns)	Taxable Income
1939	7.0	7.2	n.a.
1940	10.0	9.3	n.a.
1941	17.7	16.7	n.a.
1942	21.5	23.4	n.a.
1943	25.1	28.1	n.a.
1944	24.1	26.5	n.a.
1945	19.7	21.3	n.a.
1946	24.6	25.4	n.a.
1947	31.5	31.6	n.a.
1948	35.2	34.6	n.a.
1949	28.9	28.4	n.a.
1950	42.6	42.8	n.a.
1951	43.9	43.8	n.a.
1952	38.9	38.7	n.a.
1953	40.6	39.8	n.a.
1954	38.3	36.7	n.a.
1955	48.6	47.9	n.a.
1956	48.8	47.4	n.a.
1957	47.2	45.1	n.a.
1958	41.4	39.2	39.3
1959	52.1	47.7	47.6
1960	49.7	44.5	47.2
1961	50.3	47.0	47.9
1962	55.4	50.8	51.7
1963	58.6	55.6	54.3

n.a. Not available.
Sources: Profits before tax: *Survey of Current Business* (August 1965), p. 28. Compiled net profits and taxable income: *Statistics of Income, Corporation Income Tax Returns.*
[a] Includes corporations with and without net income.

TABLE B-9. Distribution of Corporation Taxable Income, by Rate Brackets, 1962

(Dollar amounts in millions)

Taxable Income Brackets	Tax Rate	Number of Corporations	Taxable Income	Tax
	Amount			
Normal tax and surtax				
Under $25,000.................	30%	487,011	$ 5,872	$ 1,761
$25,000 and over..............	52	111,027	41,558	21,610
Subtotal.....................	49[a]	598,038	47,430	23,371
Add: Long-term capital gains subject to alternative tax..................	25	—	2,157	539
Add: Mutual insurance company gross income subject to special tax.......	1	—	2,136	21
Totals before credits...........	46[a]	598,038	51,723	23,930
Less: Foreign tax credit.............	—	—	—	1,564
Less: Investment credit..............	—	—	—	834
Totals after credits.............	42[a]	598,038	51,723	21,533
Percentage Distribution				
Normal tax and surtax				
Under $25,000.................		81	12	8
$25,000 and over..............		19	88	92
Total........................		100	100	100

Source: *Statistics of Income, Corporation Income Tax Returns, 1962.* Figures are rounded and will not necessarily add to totals.

[a] Computed effective rate on taxable income.

TABLE B-10. Number of Taxable Estate Tax Returns Filed as a Percentage of Adult Deaths, Selected Years, 1939–63

Year	Adult Deaths[a]	Taxable Estate Tax Returns Filed	
		Number	Percentage of Adult Deaths
1939	1,204,080	12,720	1.06
1940	1,235,484	12,907	1.04
1941	1,215,627	13,336	1.10
1942	1,209,661	13,493	1.12
1943	1,275,400	12,726	1.00
1944	1,237,508	12,154	0.98
1945	1,238,360	13,869	1.12
1947	1,277,852	18,232	1.43
1948	1,284,535	19,742	1.54
1949	1,284,196	17,469	1.36
1950	1,303,171	17,411	1.34
1951	1,328,809	18,941	1.43
1954	1,331,498	24,997	1.88
1955	1,378,588	25,143	1.82
1957	1,475,320	32,131	2.18
1959	1,498,549	38,515	2.57
1961	1,548,061	45,439	2.94
1963	1,660,541	55,207	3.32

Sources: 1939–61: *The Federal Tax System*, p. 280 (see Table A-1). Adult deaths in 1963, U. S. Department of Health, Education, and Welfare, Public Health Service, *Vital Statistics of the United States 1963*, Vol. II, Part B, p. 7–77; taxable estate tax returns in 1963, *Statistics of Income, Fiduciary, Gift, and Estate Tax Returns, 1962.*
[a] Age 20 and over.

TABLE B-11. Number of Taxable Estate Tax Returns, Gross and Economic Estate, and Estate Tax Before and After Credits, Selected Years, 1939–63

(Dollar amounts in millions)

Year[a]	Number of Taxable Returns	Gross Estate on Taxable Returns	Economic Estate[b] on Taxable Returns	Taxable Estate[c]	Estate Tax Before Credits	Estate Tax After Credits
1939	12,720	$2,564	$2,390	$1,538	$330	$277
1940	12,907	2,448	2,295	1,479	296	250
1941	13,336	2,578	2,410	1,561	346	292
1942	13,493	2,550	2,373	1,525	354	308
1943	12,726	2,452	2,284	1,397	398	362
1944	12,154	2,720	2,551	1,509	452	405
1945	13,869	3,246	3,081	1,900	596	531
1947	18,233	3,993	3,804	2,319	694	622
1948	19,742	4,445	4,224	2,585	799	715
1949	17,469	4,272	4,059	2,107	635	567
1950	17,411	4,126	3,919	1,917	534	484
1951	18,941	4,656	n.a.	2,189	644	577
1954	24,997	6,288	6,007	2,969	869	779
1955	25,143	6,387	6,109	2,991	872	778
1957	32,131	8,904	n.a.	4,342	1,353	1,177
1959	38,515	9,996	9,540	4,651	1,346	1,186
1961	45,439	12,733	12,213	6,014	1,847	1,619
1963	55,207	14,714	14,059	7,071	2,088	1,841

n.a. Not available.
Sources: 1939–51: *Statistics of Income, Part I*; 1954–63: *Statistics of Income, Fiduciary, Gift, and Estate Tax Returns*. Data are for estate tax returns of citizens and resident aliens.
[a] Returns are classified by year in which they were filed.
[b] Economic estate is gross estate reduced by the amount of debt (including mortgages).
[c] Prior to 1953, "Taxable Estate" was labeled "Net Estate" in *Statistics of Income*.

TABLE B-12. Distribution of Taxable Estates, by Rate Brackets, 1963

Estate Tax Rate (Percentages)	Amount (Millions of dollars)		Percentage Distribution	
	Taxable Estate	Tax[a]	Taxable Estate	Tax
3	264	8	3.7	0.4
7	240	17	3.4	0.8
11	421	46	6.0	2.2
14	358	50	5.1	2.4
18	308	56	4.4	2.7
22	268	59	3.8	2.8
25	237	59	3.4	2.8
28	731	205	10.3	9.8
30	1,392	418	19.7	20.0
32	938	300	13.3	14.4
35	464	162	6.6	7.8
37	293	108	4.1	5.2
39	201	79	2.8	3.8
42	144	61	2.0	2.9
45	201	91	2.8	4.4
49	129	63	1.8	3.0
53	90	48	1.3	2.3
56	68	38	1.0	1.8
59	52	31	0.7	1.5
63	70	44	1.0	2.1
67	44	29	0.6	1.4
70	30	21	0.4	1.0
73	20	14	0.3	0.7
76	25	19	0.4	0.9
77	80	61	1.1	2.9
Total	7,071	2,088	100.0	100.0

Source: *Statistics of Income, Fiduciary, Gift, and Estate Tax Returns, 1962.* Figures are rounded and will not necessarily add to totals.
[a] Tax before credits.

TABLE B-13. Number of Taxable Gift Tax Returns, Total Gifts, Taxable Gifts, and Gift Tax, Selected Years, 1939–63

(Dollar amounts in millions)

Year[a]	Number of Taxable Returns	Total Gifts on Taxable Returns	Taxable Gifts (Current year)	Gift Tax
1939	3,929	$220	$132	$19
1940	4,930	347	226	34
1941	8,940	714	484	70
1942	4,380	222	121	25
1943	4,656	209	124	30
1944	4,979	276	148	38
1945	5,540	289	170	37
1946	6,808	426	265	62
1947	6,822	439	257	64
1948	6,559	391	209	45
1949	6,114	340	178	36
1950	8,366	596	338	78
1951	8,360	516	304	67
1953	8,464	489	258	56
1957	14,736	923	518	113
1959	15,793	928	478	105
1961	17,936	1,219	657	158
1963	20,598	1,402	790	183

Sources: 1939–53: *Statistics of Income, Part I;* 1957–63: *Statistics of Income, Fiduciary, Gift, and Estate Tax Returns.*

[a] Returns are classified by year in which they were filed.

TABLE B-14. Distribution of Taxable Gifts, by Rate Brackets, 1963

Rate (Percentages)	Amount (Thousands of dollars)		Percentage Distribution	
	Taxable Gifts	Tax	Taxable Gifts	Tax
$2\frac{1}{4}$	39,386	887	5.0	0.5
$5\frac{1}{4}$	31,671	1,664	4.0	0.9
$8\frac{1}{4}$	50,371	4,155	6.4	2.3
$10\frac{1}{2}$	38,513	4,044	4.9	2.2
$13\frac{1}{2}$	31,136	4,203	3.9	2.3
$16\frac{1}{2}$	26,129	4,311	3.3	2.4
$18\frac{3}{4}$	22,415	4,203	2.8	2.3
21	65,366	13,727	8.3	7.5
$22\frac{1}{2}$	122,698	27,607	15.5	15.1
24	91,880	22,051	11.6	12.0
$26\frac{1}{4}$	51,861	13,614	6.6	7.4
$27\frac{3}{4}$	33,964	9,425	4.3	5.1
$29\frac{1}{4}$	25,701	7,518	3.3	4.1
$31\frac{1}{2}$	22,590	7,116	2.9	3.9
$33\frac{3}{4}$	32,195	10,866	4.1	5.9
$36\frac{3}{4}$	19,780	7,269	2.5	4.0
$39\frac{3}{4}$	15,015	5,968	1.9	3.3
42	10,072	4,230	1.3	2.3
$44\frac{1}{4}$	6,641	2,939	0.8	1.6
$47\frac{1}{4}$	14,671	6,932	1.9	3.8
$50\frac{1}{4}$	11,510	5,784	1.5	3.2
$52\frac{1}{2}$	8,479	4,452	1.1	2.4
$54\frac{3}{4}$	4,703	2,575	0.6	1.4
57	2,939	1,675	0.4	0.9
$57\frac{3}{4}$	10,623	6,135	1.3	3.3
Total	790,311	183,351	100.0	100.0

Source: *Statistics of Income, Fiduciary, Gift, and Estate Tax Returns, 1962.* Figures are rounded and will not necessarily add to totals.

Statistical Tables

TABLE C-1. Federal Receipts, Expenditures, Surpluses, or Deficits Under Three Budget Concepts, Fiscal Years 1929–65

(In billions of dollars)

Fiscal Year	Administrative Budget			Consolidated Cash Budget			National Income Accounts Budget		
	Receipts	Expenditures	Surplus (+) or Deficit (−)	Receipts	Expenditures	Surplus (+) or Deficit (−)	Receipts	Expenditures	Surplus (+) or Deficit (−)
1929	3.9	3.1	+ 0.7	3.8	2.9	+ 0.8	3.8	2.6	+ 1.2
1930	4.1	3.3	+ 0.7	4.0	3.1	+ 0.9	3.0	2.8	+ 0.3
1931	3.1	3.6	− 0.5	3.2	4.1	− 1.0	2.0	4.2	− 2.1
1932	1.9	4.7	− 2.7	2.0	4.8	− 2.7	1.7	3.2	− 1.5
1933	2.0	4.6	− 2.6	2.1	4.7	− 2.6	2.7	4.0	− 1.3
1934	3.0	6.6	− 3.6	3.1	6.4	− 3.3	3.5	6.4	− 2.9
1935	3.7	6.5	− 2.8	3.8	6.3	− 2.4	4.0	6.5	− 2.6
1936	4.0	8.4	− 4.4	4.2	7.6	− 3.5	5.0	8.7	− 3.6
1937	5.0	7.7	− 2.8	5.6	8.4	− 2.8	7.0	7.4	− 0.4
1938	5.6	6.8	− 1.2	7.0	7.2	− 0.1	6.5	8.6	− 2.1
1939	5.0	8.8	− 3.9	6.6	9.4	− 2.9	6.7	8.9	− 2.2
1940	5.1	9.1	− 3.9	6.9	9.6	− 2.7	8.6	10.0	− 1.3
1941	7.1	13.3	− 6.2	9.2	14.0	− 4.8	15.4	20.5	− 5.1
1942	12.5	34.0	−21.5	15.1	34.5	−19.4	22.9	56.1	−33.1
1943	21.9	79.4	−57.4	25.1	78.9	−53.8	39.3	85.8	−46.6
1944	43.6	95.0	−51.4	47.8	94.0	−46.1	41.0	95.5	−54.5
1945	44.4	98.3	−53.9	50.2	95.2	−45.0	42.5	84.6	−42.1
1946	39.7	60.3	−20.7	43.5	61.7	−18.2	39.1	35.6	+ 3.5
1947	39.7	38.9	+ 0.8	43.5	36.9	+ 6.6	43.2	29.8	+13.4
1948	41.4	33.0	+ 8.4	45.4	36.5	+ 8.9	43.3	34.9	+ 8.4
1949	37.7	39.5	− 1.8	41.6	40.6	+ 1.0	38.9	41.3	− 2.4
1950	36.4	39.5	− 3.1	40.9	43.1	− 2.2	49.9	40.8	+ 9.1
1951	47.5	44.0	+ 3.5	53.4	45.8	+ 7.6	64.0	57.8	+ 6.2
1952	61.3	65.3	− 4.0	68.0	68.0	a	67.2	71.0	− 3.8
1953	64.7	74.1	− 9.4	71.5	76.8	− 5.3	70.0	77.0	− 7.0
1954	64.4	67.5	− 3.1	71.6	71.9	− 0.2	63.8	69.7	− 5.9
1955	60.2	64.4	− 4.2	67.8	70.5	− 2.7	72.1	68.1	+ 4.0
1956	67.8	66.2	+ 1.6	77.1	72.5	+ 4.5	77.6	71.9	+ 5.7
1957	70.6	69.0	+ 1.6	82.1	80.0	+ 2.1	81.6	79.6	+ 2.1
1958	68.6	71.4	− 2.8	81.9	83.5	− 1.6	78.7	88.9	−10.2
1959	67.9	80.3	−12.4	81.7	94.8	−13.1	89.7	91.0	− 1.2
1960	77.8	76.5	+ 1.2	95.1	94.3	+ 0.8	96.5	93.0	+ 3.5
1961	77.7	81.5	− 3.9	97.2	99.5	− 2.3	98.3	102.1	− 3.8
1962	81.4	87.8	− 6.4	101.9	107.7	− 5.8	106.4	110.3	− 3.8
1963	86.4	92.6	− 6.3	109.7	113.8	− 4.0	114.3	114.0	+ 0.3
1964	89.5	97.7	− 8.2	115.5	120.3	− 4.8	114.5	118.3	− 3.8
1965	93.1	96.5	− 3.4	119.7	122.4	− 2.7	124.1	123.3	+ 0.7

Sources: Administrative budget, 1929–65: *The Budget of the United States Government*, 1967, p. 430; consolidated cash budget, 1929–39: *The Federal Tax System*, p. 205 (see Table A-1); 1940–65: *The Budget of the United States Government*, 1967, p. 431; national income accounts budget, 1929–64: *Survey of Current Business* (August 1965), p. 36; 1965: *Survey of Current Business* (February 1966), p. 15. Figures are rounded and will not necessarily add to totals.
a Less than $50 million.

TABLE C-2. Relationship of Federal, State, and Local Government Receipts to Gross National Product, 1929–65

(National income accounts basis)

Year	Gross National Product (Billions of dollars)	Receipts of Federal, State, and Local Governments					
		Amount (Billions of dollars)			Percentage of Gross National Product		
		Total	Federal	State and Local[a]	Total	Federal	State and Local[a]
1929	103.1	11.3	3.8	7.5	11.0	3.7	7.3
1930	90.4	10.7	3.0	7.7	11.8	3.3	8.5
1931	75.8	9.4	2.0	7.4	12.4	2.6	9.8
1932	58.0	8.9	1.7	7.2	15.3	2.9	12.4
1933	55.6	9.4	2.7	6.7	16.9	4.9	12.1
1934	65.1	10.4	3.5	6.9	16.0	5.4	10.6
1935	72.2	11.4	4.0	7.4	15.8	5.5	10.2
1936	82.5	12.9	5.0	7.9	15.6	6.1	9.6
1937	90.4	15.3	7.0	8.3	16.9	7.7	9.2
1938	84.7	15.0	6.5	8.5	17.7	7.7	10.0
1939	90.5	15.4	6.7	8.7	17.0	7.4	9.6
1940	99.7	17.7	8.6	9.1	17.8	8.6	9.1
1941	124.5	25.0	15.4	9.6	20.1	12.4	7.7
1942	157.9	32.6	22.9	9.7	20.6	14.5	6.1
1943	191.6	49.2	39.3	9.9	25.7	20.5	5.2
1944	210.1	51.2	41.0	10.2	24.4	19.5	4.9
1945	212.0	53.2	42.5	10.7	25.1	20.0	5.0
1946	208.5	50.9	39.1	11.8	24.4	18.8	5.7
1947	231.3	56.8	43.2	13.6	24.6	18.7	5.9
1948	257.6	58.9	43.3	15.6	22.9	16.8	6.1
1949	256.5	56.0	38.9	17.1	21.8	15.2	6.7
1950	284.8	68.7	49.9	18.8	24.1	17.5	6.6
1951	328.4	84.8	64.0	20.8	25.8	19.5	6.3
1952	345.5	89.8	67.2	22.6	26.0	19.5	6.5
1953	364.6	94.3	70.0	24.3	25.9	19.2	6.7
1954	364.8	89.7	63.8	25.9	24.6	17.5	7.1
1955	398.0	100.4	72.1	28.3	25.2	18.1	7.1
1956	419.2	109.0	77.6	31.4	26.0	18.5	7.5
1957	441.1	115.5	81.6	33.9	26.2	18.5	7.7
1958	447.3	114.7	78.7	36.0	25.6	17.6	8.0
1959	483.6	128.9	89.7	39.2	26.7	18.5	8.1
1960	503.8	139.8	96.5	43.3	27.7	19.2	8.6
1961	520.1	144.7	98.3	46.4	27.8	18.9	8.9
1962	560.3	157.0	106.4	50.6	28.0	19.0	9.0
1963	589.2	168.3	114.3	54.0	28.6	19.4	9.2
1964	628.7	172.7	114.5	58.2	27.5	18.2	9.3
1965[p]	676.3	187.0	124.1	62.9	27.7	18.3	9.3

[p] Preliminary.

Sources: 1929–64: *Survey of Current Business* (August 1965), pp. 26, 36, 38; 1965: *Survey of Current Business* (February 1966), pp. 14–15. Figures are rounded and will not necessarily add to totals.

Note: The receipts in this table are on the national income and product account basis of the Department of Commerce and therefore differ from both "administrative" and "cash" receipts as defined in the budget message. In this table, receipts of trust funds and taxes other than corporation taxes are on a cash basis and receipts from corporation taxes are on an accrual basis.

[a] State and local receipts have been adjusted to exclude federal grants-in-aid.

TABLE C-3. Federal Receipts from the Public, by Source, 1934-65

Fiscal Year	Total	Taxes						Unemployment Insurance Deposits	Veteran Insurance Premiums	Other
		Individual	Corporation	Excises	Employment	Estate and Gift	Customs			
					Amount (millions of dollars)					
1934	3,126	410	393	1,691	—	110	299	—	66	157
1935	3,823	512	572	1,934	—	211	322	—	63	209
1936	4,154	666	746	1,693	—	376	371	19	64	219
1937	5,636	1,066	1,073	1,857	252	303	471	292	63	259
1938	7,040	1,287	1,328	1,864	714	413	342	748	63	281
1939	6,564	1,022	1,138	1,861	739	357	302	811	63	271
1940	6,879	959	1,123	1,973	836	357	331	860	60	380
1941	9,202	1,400	2,029	2,555	929	403	365	892	61	568
1942	15,104	3,205	4,727	3,393	1,191	421	369	1,096	102	600
1943	25,097	6,490	9,570	4,093	1,505	442	308	1,218	335	1,136
1944	47,818	19,701	14,737	4,761	1,747	507	417	1,349	836	3,763
1945	50,162	18,415	15,146	6,267	1,785	638	341	1,256	1,012	5,302
1946	43,537	16,157	11,833	6,999	1,707	659	424	1,010	903	3,835
1947	43,531	17,835	8,569	7,207	2,030	770	477	1,005	571	5,067
1948	45,357	19,305	9,678	7,356	2,388	890	403	1,007	434	3,895
1949	41,576	15,548	11,195	7,502	2,476	780	367	985	431	2,293
1950	40,940	15,745	10,448	7,549	2,881	698	407	1,098	440	1,673
1951	53,390	21,643	14,106	8,648	3,928	708	609	1,363	520	1,865
1952	68,013	27,913	21,225	8,851	4,563	818	533	1,439	473	2,197
1953	71,499	30,108	21,238	9,868	4,980	881	596	1,371	428	2,028
1954	71,627	29,542	21,101	9,945	5,423	934	542	1,246	426	2,469
1955	67,836	28,747	17,861	9,131	6,217	924	585	1,146	441	2,784
1956	77,087	32,188	20,880	9,929	7,228	1,161	682	1,330	441	3,249
1957	82,105	35,620	21,167	10,534	7,520	1,365	735	1,542	452	3,171
1958	81,892	34,724	20,074	10,638	8,565	1,393	782	1,501	485	3,730
1959	81,660	36,719	17,309	10,578	8,767	1,333	925	1,701	478	3,851
1960	95,078	40,715	21,494	11,676	11,067	1,606	1,105	2,167	482	4,766
1961	97,242	41,338	20,954	11,860	12,405	1,896	982	2,398	504	4,905
1962	101,865	45,571	20,523	12,534	12,561	2,016	1,142	2,729	501	4,288
1963	109,739	47,588	21,579	13,194	14,862	2,167	1,205	3,009	494	5,641
1964	115,530	48,697	23,493	13,731	16,832	2,394	1,252	3,042	494	5,596
1965	119,699	48,792	25,461	14,570	16,905	2,716	1,442	3,052	488	6,274

Percentage of Total

1934	100	13.1	12.6	54.1	—	3.5	9.6	—	2.1	5.0
1935	100	13.4	15.0	50.6	—	5.5	8.4	—	1.6	5.5
1936	100	16.0	18.0	40.8	—	9.1	8.9	0.5	1.5	5.3
1937	100	18.9	19.0	32.9	4.5	5.4	8.4	5.2	1.1	4.6
1938	100	18.3	18.9	26.5	10.1	5.9	4.9	10.6	0.9	4.0
1939	100	15.6	17.3	28.4	11.3	5.4	4.6	12.4	1.0	4.1
1940	100	13.9	16.3	28.7	12.2	5.2	4.8	12.5	0.9	5.5
1941	100	15.2	22.1	27.8	10.1	4.4	4.0	9.7	0.7	6.2
1942	100	21.2	31.3	22.5	7.9	2.8	2.4	7.3	0.7	4.0
1943	100	25.9	38.1	16.3	6.0	1.8	1.2	4.9	1.3	4.5
1944	100	41.2	30.8	10.0	3.7	1.1	0.9	2.8	1.7	7.9
1945	100	36.7	30.2	12.5	3.6	1.3	0.7	2.5	2.0	10.6
1946	100	37.1	27.2	16.1	3.9	1.5	1.0	2.3	2.1	8.8
1947	100	41.0	19.7	16.6	4.7	1.8	1.1	2.3	1.3	11.6
1948	100	42.6	21.3	16.2	5.3	2.0	0.9	2.2	1.0	8.6
1949	100	37.4	26.9	18.0	6.0	1.9	0.9	2.4	1.0	5.5
1950	100	38.5	25.5	18.4	7.0	1.7	1.0	2.7	1.1	4.1
1951	100	40.5	26.4	16.2	7.4	1.3	1.1	2.6	1.0	3.5
1952	100	41.0	31.2	13.0	6.7	1.2	0.8	2.1	0.7	3.2
1953	100	42.1	29.7	13.8	7.0	1.2	0.8	1.9	0.6	2.8
1954	100	41.2	29.5	13.9	7.6	1.3	0.8	1.7	0.6	3.4
1955	100	42.4	26.3	13.5	9.2	1.4	0.9	1.7	0.7	4.1
1956	100	41.8	27.1	12.9	9.4	1.5	0.9	1.7	0.6	4.2
1957	100	43.4	25.8	12.8	9.2	1.7	0.9	1.9	0.6	3.9
1958	100	42.4	24.5	13.0	10.5	1.7	1.0	1.8	0.6	4.6
1959	100	45.0	21.2	13.0	10.7	1.6	1.1	2.1	0.6	4.7
1960	100	42.8	22.6	12.3	11.6	1.7	1.2	2.3	0.5	5.0
1961	100	42.5	21.5	12.2	12.8	1.9	1.0	2.5	0.5	5.0
1962	100	44.7	20.1	12.3	12.3	2.0	1.1	2.7	0.5	4.2
1963	100	43.4	19.7	12.0	13.5	2.0	1.1	2.7	0.5	5.1
1964	100	42.2	20.3	11.9	14.6	2.1	1.1	2.6	0.4	4.8
1965	**100**	**40.8**	**21.3**	**12.2**	**14.1**	**2.3**	**1.2**	**2.5**	**0.4**	**5.2**

Sources: 1934–55: Worksheets of the Bureau of the Budget and the Treasury Department; 1956–65: *The Budget of the United States Government, 1967*, p. 439.
Note: Receipts are net after refunds.

TABLE C-4. Relationship of Direct and Indirect Taxes in Nine Countries to Gross National Product and to Total Tax Yield, 1961

Tax	United States	Canada	Germany	Italy	Japan	Netherlands	Sweden	United Kingdom	France
				Percentage of Gross National Product					
Direct Taxes									
Individual	8.6	5.0	6.9	3.4	4.2	8.9 }	17.9	10.9	4.8
Corporate	4.4	4.1	2.4	0.6	5.6	3.4 }		1.2	2.0
Death and gift	0.5	0.4	0.1	0.2	0.1	0.4	0.2	1.0	0.2
Social insurance[a]	1.8	1.3	4.7	1.9	1.3	5.2	2.5	2.3	2.3
Other	0.1	0.3	3.4	1.5	—	1.4	0.1	—	0.5
Subtotal, direct	15.3	11.1	17.5	7.6	11.2	19.2	20.7	15.4	9.7
Indirect Taxes									
Consumption	5.5	8.4	10.4	13.0	6.1	7.1	10.2	10.1	11.8
Customs	0.2	1.5	1.0	1.1	0.8	2.4	1.2	0.6	2.8
Property	3.5	3.6	0.6	—	1.2	0.2	—	2.9	0.3
Social insurance[b]	2.0	1.1	4.8	8.2	1.3	3.5	1.7	1.8	6.3
Other	0.2	0.1	0.7	0.4	0.3	—	0.1	—	1.7
Subtotal, indirect	11.4	14.6	17.4	22.7	9.6	13.2	13.1	15.3	22.9
Total, all taxes	26.8	25.8	34.9	30.3	20.8	32.4	33.8	30.7	32.6
				Percentage of Total Yield					
Direct Taxes									
Individual	32.2	19.5	19.7	11.3	20.3	27.4 }	52.8	35.5	14.7
Corporate	16.3	16.1	6.9	2.1	26.8	10.4 }		4.0	6.0
Death and gift	1.8	1.5	0.2	0.7	0.5	1.2	0.5	3.2	0.7
Social insurance[a]	6.7	4.9	13.5	6.3	6.4	16.2	7.4	7.3	6.9
Other	0.4	1.2	9.7	4.9	—	4.2	0.4	—	1.5
Subtotal, direct	57.3	43.2	50.1	25.2	54.0	59.3	61.2	50.0	29.8
Indirect Taxes									
Consumption	20.7	32.6	29.8	42.8	29.2	22.0	30.1	32.8	36.1
Customs	0.7	5.6	2.9	3.7	3.9	7.3	3.7	1.8	8.7
Property	13.2	14.2	1.6	—	5.7	0.5	—	9.5	1.0
Social insurance[b]	7.5	4.1	13.7	27.1	6.0	10.9	4.9	5.9	19.3
Other	0.6	0.3	1.9	1.2	1.2	—	0.2	—	5.1
Subtotal, indirect	42.7	56.8	49.9	74.8	46.0	40.7	38.8	50.0	70.2
Total, all taxes	100.0	100.0	100.0	100.0	100.0	100.0	100.0	100.0	100.0

Source: Jacob A. Stockfisch, "International Comparisons on Direct and Indirect Taxes," *Excise Tax Compendium*, Compendium of Papers on Excise Tax Structure Submitted to the Committee on Ways and Means for discussion on June 15–16, 1964, pp. 117–18.

[a] Contribution by employees.

[b] Contribution by employers.

TABLE C-5. Distribution of Taxes and Other Revenues[a] by Major Source and Level of Government, Selected Years, 1902–64

Fiscal Year	Income	Consumption	Property	Payroll	Other	Total
Amount (millions of dollars)						
Federal						
1902	—	259	—	—	299	558
1927	2,220	491	—	—	1,414	4,125
1938	2,629	1,870	—	645	984	6,128
1948	30,276	7,337	—	3,878	1,456	42,947
1958	52,793	10,535	—	10,955	2,502	76,785
1964	71,958	13,873	—	23,588	4,178	113,597
State and Local						
1902	—	28	706	—	245	979
1927	162	470	4,730	—	1,793	7,155
1938	383	1,794	4,440	—	1,811	8,428
1948	1,174	3,861	5,838	—	3,361	14,234
1958	2,719	8,671	13,499	—	8,174	33,063
1964	5,295	13,779	21,349	—	11,603	52,026
All Levels						
1902	—	287	706	—	544	1,537
1927	2,382	961	4,730	—	3,207	11,280
1938	3,012	3,664	4,440	645	2,795	14,556
1948	31,450	11,198	5,838	3,878	4,817	57,181
1958	55,512	19,206	13,499	10,955	10,676	109,848
1964	77,253	27,652	21,349	23,588	15,781	165,623
Percentage Distribution						
Federal						
1902	—	46.4	—	—	53.6	100
1927	53.8	11.9	—	—	34.6	100
1938	42.9	30.5	—	10.5	16.1	100
1948	70.5	17.1	—	9.0	3.4	100
1958	68.8	13.1	—	14.3	3.3	100
1964	63.3	12.2	—	20.8	3.7	100
State and Local						
1902	—	2.9	72.1	—	25.0	100
1927	2.3	6.6	66.1	—	25.1	100
1938	4.5	21.3	52.7	—	21.5	100
1948	8.2	27.1	41.0	—	23.6	100
1958	8.2	26.2	40.8	—	24.7	100
1964	10.2	26.5	41.0	—	22.3	100
All Levels						
1902	—	18.7	45.9	—	35.4	100
1927	21.1	8.5	41.9	—	28.4	100
1938	20.7	25.2	30.5	4.4	19.2	100
1948	55.0	19.6	10.2	6.8	8.4	100
1958	50.5	17.5	12.3	10.0	9.7	100
1964	46.6	16.7	12.9	14.2	9.5	100

Sources: 1902, 1927, and 1938: Bureau of the Census, *Historical Statistics of the United States, Colonial Times to 1957* (1960), pp. 720–30; 1948, 1958, and 1964: Worksheets of the Office of Business Economics, and *Governmental Finances in 1963–64.* Figures are rounded and will not necessarily add to totals.

[a] Revenues are defined as receipts in the national income accounts, less contributions for social insurance other than federal payroll taxes.

TABLE C-6. Number and Amount of Standard and Itemized Deductions, Taxable and Nontaxable Federal Individual Income Tax Returns, 1944–63

Year	Total Number of Returns (Millions)	Standard Deduction		Itemized Deductions		Total Deductions	
		Number[a] (Millions)	Amount (Billions of dollars)	Number (Millions)	Amount (Billions of dollars)	Amount (Billions of dollars)	Percentage of Adjusted Gross Income
1944	47.1	38.7	8.0	8.4	4.8	12.8	11.0
1945	49.9	41.5	8.1	8.5	5.5	13.6	11.3
1946	52.8	44.1	8.9	8.8	6.3	15.2	11.3
1947	55.1	44.7	9.8	10.4	7.8	17.6	11.8
1948	52.1	43.2	11.5	8.8	7.9	19.4	11.9
1949	51.8	42.1	11.1	9.7	8.8	19.9	12.4
1950	53.1	42.7	12.0	10.3	9.9	21.9	12.2
1951	55.4	43.9	13.3	11.6	11.9	25.2	12.5
1952	56.5	43.7	13.7	12.8	13.6	27.3	12.7
1953	57.8	43.4	14.2	14.4	15.6	29.8	13.0
1954	56.7	41.0	13.3	15.7	17.4	30.7	13.4
1955	58.3	41.4	13.6	16.9	20.0	33.6	13.5
1956	59.2	40.7	13.8	18.5	22.6	36.4	13.6
1957	59.8	39.7	13.8	20.2	25.7	39.5	14.1
1958	59.1	38.3	13.2	20.8	27.5	40.7	14.5
1959	60.3	37.8	13.4	22.5	32.0	45.4	14.9
1960	61.0	36.9	13.1	24.1	35.3	48.4	15.3
1961	61.5	36.2	12.9	25.3	38.4	51.3	15.6
1962	62.7	36.3	13.1	26.5	41.7	54.8	15.7
1963	63.9	35.8	13.1	28.2	46.1	59.2	16.1

Source: *Statistics of Income, Individual Income Tax Returns.* Figures are rounded and will not necessarily add to totals.
[a] Includes a small number of returns with no adjusted gross income and no deductions.

TABLE C-7. Federal Individual Income Tax Liabilities, Prepayments, Final Balances of Tax Due and Overpayments, 1944–63

(In billions of dollars)

Year	Tax Liabilities			Prepayments		Final Balances	
	Total	Income Tax	Self-employment Tax	With-holding	Declara-tion Payments	Tax Due	Over-payments
1944	16.2	16.2	—	9.6	5.5	2.4	1.4
1945	17.1	17.1	—	10.5	6.0	2.4	1.8
1946	16.1	16.1	—	9.2	6.0	2.7	1.9
1947	18.1	18.1	—	11.2	5.8	3.0	2.0
1948	15.4	15.4	—	10.6	5.3	2.2	2.7
1949	14.5	14.5	—	9.6	4.7	2.1	2.0
1950	18.4	18.4	—	11.8	5.6	3.1	2.1
1951	24.4	24.2	0.2	16.6	6.6	3.7	2.5
1952	28.0	27.8	0.2	20.3	7.1	3.6	2.9
1953	29.7	29.4	0.2	22.6	7.0	3.4	3.3
1954	27.0	26.7	0.3	20.5	7.2	3.0	3.7
1955	30.1	29.6	0.5	22.7	7.2	3.8	3.6
1956	33.3	32.7	0.5	25.2	7.9	4.1	4.0
1957	35.0	34.4	0.6	27.4	8.2	3.9	4.5
1958	34.9	34.3	0.6	27.6	8.0	4.1	4.8
1959	39.3	38.6	0.7	30.8	8.6	5.1	5.1
1960	40.3	39.5	0.8	32.7	8.6	4.7	5.7
1961	43.1	42.2	0.8	34.4	9.0	5.7	6.0
1962	45.8	44.9	0.9	37.4	9.3	5.6	6.6
1963	49.2	48.2	1.0	40.2	9.7	6.3	6.9

Source: Statistics of Income, Individual Income Tax Returns. Figures are rounded and will not necessarily add to totals.

TABLE C-8. Number of Federal Individual Income Tax Returns by Type of Final Settlement, 1944–63

(In millions)

Year	Total Number of Returns	Returns with		No Over-payments or Balances Due
		Tax Due	Overpayments	
1944	47.1	22.6	22.9	1.6
1945	49.9	14.5	33.5	1.9
1946	52.8	13.6	34.4	4.8
1947	55.1	15.3	33.0	6.7
1948	52.1	8.1	38.4	5.6
1949	51.8	13.8	30.2	7.9
1950	53.1	14.3	32.0	6.8
1951	55.4	18.6	31.0	5.8
1952	56.5	19.3	32.1	5.1
1953	57.8	19.0	32.7	6.2
1954	56.7	16.6	35.2	5.0
1955	58.3	18.7	35.4	4.2
1956	59.2	19.4	36.1	3.7
1957	59.8	18.6	37.6	3.6
1958	59.1	18.1	37.4	3.6
1959	60.3	19.1	38.4	2.8
1960	61.0	18.1	39.4	3.5
1961	61.5	18.6	40.0	2.9
1962	62.7	18.7	40.9	3.1
1963	63.9	19.3	41.4	3.3

Source: *Statistics of Income, Individual Income Tax Returns.* Figures are rounded and will not necessarily add to otals.

TABLE C-9. Distribution of Taxable Federal Individual Income Tax Returns and Tax Liabilities, 1941 and 1963

Income Class[a] (Dollars)	Taxable Returns		Tax Liabilities	
	Number (Thousands)	Percentage of Total	Amount (Millions of dollars)	Percentage of Total
	1941[b]			
Under 3,000	14,473	82.3	781	20.0
3,000– 5,000	2,165	12.3	409	10.5
5,000– 10,000	637	3.6	406	10.4
10,000– 25,000	243	1.4	683	17.5
25,000– 50,000	50	0.3	574	14.7
50,000–100,000	15	0.1	463	11.8
100,000 and over	5	c	591	15.1
Total	17,588	100.0	3,908	100.0
	1963			
Under 3,000	10,564	20.6	1,632	3.4
3,000– 5,000	10,968	21.4	4,278	8.9
5,000– 10,000	21,693	42.3	17,305	35.9
10,000– 25,000	7,344	14.3	14,852	30.8
25,000– 50,000	593	1.2	4,755	9.9
50,000–100,000	132	0.3	2,920	6.1
100,000 and over	29	0.1	2,460	5.1
Total	51,323	100.0	48,204	100.0

Source: *Statistics of Income, Individual Income Tax Returns.* Figures are rounded and will not necessarily add to totals.
[a] For 1941, data are classified on a net income basis; for 1963, on an adjusted gross income basis.
[b] Includes taxable fiduciary returns in 1941.
[c] Less than 0.05 percent.

TABLE C-10. Influence of Various Provisions on Effective Rates of Individual Income Tax, Taxable Returns, 1964 Act

(In percentages)

Total Income[a] Class (Dollars)		Nominal Tax[b]	Reduction Due to				Actual Tax[d]
			Personal Exemptions	Deductions[c]	Capital Gains Provisions	Income Splitting	
600–	1,000	14.5	9.4	4.4	—	—	0.8
1,000–	1,500	14.8	7.5	3.6	—	—	3.8
1,500–	2,000	15.3	6.9	3.1	—	—	5.3
2,000–	2,500	15.9	6.8	2.9	—	—	6.2
2,500–	3,000	16.4	6.5	2.7	—	—	7.1
3,000–	3,500	16.8	6.8	2.7	—	0.1	7.1
3,500–	4,000	17.1	6.8	2.8	—	0.1	7.2
4,000–	4,500	17.5	6.9	2.8	—	0.2	7.5
4,500–	5,000	18.0	7.0	2.9	—	0.3	7.7
5,000–	6,000	18.6	7.1	3.1	0.1	0.4	7.8
6,000–	7,000	19.3	7.2	3.2	0.1	0.6	8.1
7,000–	8,000	20.1	6.8	3.4	0.1	0.8	8.9
8,000–	9,000	20.8	6.5	3.5	0.1	1.0	9.5
9,000–	10,000	21.6	6.1	3.7	0.1	1.3	10.3
10,000–	11,000	22.4	5.9	3.9	0.1	1.6	10.8
11,000–	12,000	23.2	5.8	4.0	0.2	1.8	11.3
12,000–	13,000	24.0	5.5	4.2	0.3	2.1	11.9
13,000–	14,000	24.9	5.5	4.4	0.3	2.3	12.4
14,000–	15,000	25.8	5.5	4.6	0.3	2.6	12.7
15,000–	20,000	28.0	5.2	5.2	0.7	3.2	13.6
20,000–	25,000	32.2	4.7	6.0	1.2	4.6	15.4
25,000–	50,000	39.0	3.7	7.1	2.1	6.7	19.2
50,000–	100,000	49.6	2.2	8.8	5.2	7.2	26.1
100,000–	150,000	57.9	1.3	10.4	11.5	5.5	28.8
150,000–	200,000	61.6	0.9	10.9	16.3	4.0	29.1
200,000–	500,000	65.0	0.5	10.9	22.3	2.4	28.6
500,000–	1,000,000	67.8	0.2	10.0	29.0	0.9	27.3
1,000,000 and over		69.3	0.1	8.0	34.1	0.2	26.7
Total		23.8	6.0	4.1	0.9	1.7	10.9

Source: Based on a special file of about 100,000 federal tax returns for 1962 to which rates in effect on January 1, 1965, were applied.
[a] Total income is the sum of adjusted gross income, excluded portion of net realized capital gain, excludable sick pay, and excludable dividends.
[b] Rate schedule for single persons applied to total income.
[c] Personal deductions plus dividend exclusion, sick pay exclusion, and moving expense deduction.
[d] Actual tax after the dividends received credit and foreign tax credit, which are not shown separately.

TABLE C-11. Itemized Deductions as a Percentage of Adjusted Gross Income, by Adjusted Gross Income Classes, Federal Individual Income Tax Returns with Itemized Deductions, 1962

Adjusted Gross Income Class (Dollars)	Total	Contributions	Interest	Taxes	Medical	Other
Nontaxable Returns						
Under 1,000[a]	82.3	9.6	12.5	20.5	31.9	7.7
1,000– 3,000	45.2	6.4	6.2	11.3	17.8	3.5
3,000– 5,000	40.2	5.4	9.2	8.8	12.7	4.2
5,000 and over	55.9	9.2	12.7	9.4	13.2	11.5
Subtotal, nontaxable	46.7	6.7	9.1	10.1	15.0	5.8
Taxable Returns						
600– 1,000	21.4	6.4	0.9	6.2	5.2	2.7
1,000– 3,000	24.7	4.9	2.9	6.6	6.9	3.3
3,000– 5,000	22.2	3.9	4.2	6.2	5.1	2.7
5,000– 10,000	19.7	3.2	5.5	6.1	2.8	2.1
10,000– 25,000	17.2	3.1	4.6	5.9	1.7	1.9
25,000–100,000	15.5	3.6	2.9	5.7	1.2	2.1
100,000 and over	20.7	8.8	3.1	5.5	0.6	2.8
Subtotal, taxable	18.8	3.4	4.7	6.0	2.5	2.1
Total, all returns	19.6	3.5	4.8	6.1	2.9	2.2

Source: *Statistics of Income, Individual Income Tax Returns, 1962.*
[a] Excludes returns with no adjusted gross income or deficit.

285

TABLE C-12. Comparison of Federal Individual Income Tax Liabilities of Single Persons and Married Couples, 1965-66

(In dollars)

Taxable Income	Tax Liabilities		Difference	
	Single Persons	Married Couples	Amount	Percentage of Single Person's Tax
1,000	145	140	5	3.4
2,000	310	290	20	6.5
5,000	910	810	100	11.0
10,000	2,190	1,820	370	16.9
15,000	3,940	3,010	930	23.6
20,000	6,070	4,380	1,690	27.8
24,000	8,030	5,660	2,370	29.5
25,000	8,530	6,020	2,510	29.4
30,000	11,150	7,880	3,270	29.3
50,000	22,590	17,060	5,530	24.5
75,000	38,490	30,470	8,020	20.8
100,000	55,490	45,180	10,310	18.6
125,000	72,990	60,780	12,210	16.7
150,000	90,490	76,980	13,510	14.9
175,000	107,990	93,780	14,210	13.2
200,000	125,490	110,980	14,510	11.6

Source: Computed from Table 4-2.

TABLE C-13. Schedule of Transition to the Current Payment System for Corporations

(In percentages)

Income Year	Income Year				Following Year				Total
	April	June	September	December	March	June	September	December	
1949	—	—	—	—	25	25	25	25	100
1950	—	—	—	—	30	30	20	20	100
1951	—	—	—	—	35	35	15	15	100
1952	—	—	—	—	40	40	10	10	100
1953	—	—	—	—	45	45	5	5	100
1954	—	—	—	—	50	50	—	—	100
1955[a]	—	—	5	5	45	45	—	—	100
1956[a]	—	—	10	10	40	40	—	—	100
1957[a]	—	—	15	15	35	35	—	—	100
1958[a]	—	—	20	20	30	30	—	—	100
1959[a]	—	—	25	25	25	25	—	—	100
1960[a]	—	—	25	25	25	25	—	—	100
1961[a]	—	—	25	25	25	25	—	—	100
1962[a]	—	—	25	25	25	25	—	—	100
1963[a]	—	—	25	25	25	25	—	—	100
1964[a]	1	1	25	25	24	24	—	—	100
1965[a]	4	4	25	25	21	21	—	—	100
1966[a]	12	12	25	25	13	13	—	—	100
1967[a] and later years	25	25	25	25	—	—	—	—	100

Sources: 1949–65: *The Federal Tax System*, p. 266 (See Table A-1); 1966 and later years: *Tax Adjustment Act of 1966*, H. Report 1285, 89 Cong. 2 sess. (1966), p. 29.

[a] Applicable only to tax liability in excess of $100,000. The first $100,000 of a corporation's tax liability is paid in equal installments in March and June of the following year.

TABLE C-14. Selected Ratios Relating to the Corporate Sector, 1929-64

Year	National Income Originating in Corporate Business as Percentage of Income Originating in Business	Corporate Gross Product as Percentage of Business Gross Product	Corporate Gross Saving as Percentage of Gross National Product	Property Income as Percentage of Corporate Gross Product Less Indirect Taxes[a,c]	Dividends as Percentage of Corporate Cash Flow[b,c]
	(1)	(2)	(3)	(4)	(5)
1929	58.2	n.a.	7.3	n.a.	45.6
1930	58.1	n.a.	5.5	n.a.	77.3
1931	55.6	n.a.	2.4	n.a.	118.7
1932	53.4	n.a.	−0.3	n.a.	218.2
1933	53.6	n.a.	0.1	n.a.	52.6
1934	57.8	n.a.	3.1	n.a.	47.9
1935	56.6	n.a.	4.4	n.a.	43.9
1936	59.6	n.a.	4.0	n.a.	55.3
1937	59.8	n.a.	4.7	n.a.	53.8
1938	57.9	n.a.	5.2	n.a.	46.4
1939	59.4	n.a.	5.4	n.a.	39.8
1940	61.4	n.a.	6.8	n.a.	36.7
1941	62.5	n.a.	6.0	n.a.	30.5
1942	62.1	n.a.	6.1	n.a.	27.3
1943	62.9	n.a.	6.0	n.a.	26.5
1944	62.2	n.a.	5.8	n.a.	26.9
1945	58.7	n.a.	4.8	n.a.	30.2
1946	56.5	56.5	4.5	24.9	28.3
1947	60.4	59.4	6.0	27.0	24.6
1948	61.2	60.8	8.0	29.7	24.3
1949	61.7	60.4	8.2	29.4	28.0
1950	63.1	61.4	7.0	31.0	26.0
1951	63.8	61.7	6.7	30.6	27.7
1952	63.6	61.8	6.8	28.4	28.7
1953	64.7	62.6	6.5	27.2	27.3
1954	64.0	62.0	7.1	27.5	26.5
1955	65.7	63.8	8.1	29.6	23.9
1956	66.2	64.9	7.7	27.8	24.9
1957	66.2	64.8	7.6	27.3	25.2
1958	64.5	63.1	7.3	26.7	26.2
1959	66.5	64.9	8.0	28.3	24.0
1960	66.6	65.0	7.6	27.1	25.8
1961	66.0	64.7	7.6	27.2	25.2
1962	66.6	65.1	8.3	28.1	24.1
1963	66.8	65.3	8.2	28.2	24.2
1964	67.4	65.9	8.5	28.6	23.3

n.a. Not available.

Sources: Col. (1): Worksheets of the Office of Business Economics. Col. (2): Corporate gross product from *Survey of Current Business* (September 1965), p. 52; business gross product from Worksheets of the Office of Business Economics. Col. (3): *Survey of Current Business* (August 1965), pp. 24 and 40. Col. (4): 1946–64: *Survey of Current Business* (September 1965), p. 52. Col. (5): 1929–45: Worksheets of the Office of Business Economics; 1946–64: *Survey of Current Business* (September 1965), p. 53.

[a] Property income includes corporate profits before tax and inventory valuation adjustment, net interest, and corporate capital consumption allowances.

[b] Cash flow is net corporate profits after taxes plus corporate capital consumption allowances.

[c] Excludes amounts originating in the rest of the world.

TABLE C-15. Rates of Return Before and After Federal Income Tax, Manufacturing Corporations, 1927-41 and 1948-61

(In percentages)

Year	On Equity Capital[a] Before Tax	On Equity Capital[a] After Tax	On Total Capital[b] Before Tax	On Total Capital[b] After Tax	Debt-Capital Ratio[c]	General Corporation Income Tax Rate
1927	7.5	6.5	7.6	6.7	15.1	13.5
1928	9.1	8.0	9.0	8.0	15.6	12.0
1929	9.9	8.8	9.6	8.7	14.9	11.0
1930	2.1	1.5	2.9	2.4	15.3	12.0
1931	−1.6	−2.0	−0.4	−0.6	15.4	12.0
1932	−3.9	−4.2	−2.3	−2.5	15.5	13.75
1933	0.5	0.0	1.3	0.9	15.5	13.75
1934	2.4	1.8	2.8	2.3	13.7	13.75
1935	4.8	3.9	4.9	4.1	14.9	13.75
1936	9.5	8.0	8.8	7.5	14.2	15.0
1937	9.2	7.6	8.6	7.3	15.4	15.0
1938	3.9	3.0	3.9	3.2	15.4	19.0
1939	8.5	7.0	7.9	6.6	14.9	19.0
1940	12.2	8.7	11.1	8.1	14.4	24.0
1941	22.3	11.7	19.6	10.6	14.9	31.0
1948	22.4	14.0	19.5	12.4	15.7	38.0
1949	16.4	10.1	14.5	9.2	14.7	38.0
1950	25.4	14.0	22.2	12.5	14.8	42.0
1951	24.5	10.5	21.2	9.5	17.3	50.75
1952	18.9	8.3	16.2	7.5	19.2	52.0
1953	19.1	8.3	16.2	7.5	19.1	52.0
1954	15.6	7.1	13.4	6.5	18.9	52.0
1955	20.6	10.3	17.5	9.2	18.2	52.0
1956	18.1	9.1	15.5	8.2	20.0	52.0
1957	15.9	7.9	13.6	7.2	20.5	52.0
1958	12.2	6.0	10.7	5.7	20.4	52.0
1959	15.8	7.9	13.6	7.3	20.4	52.0
1960	13.4	6.5	11.7	6.2	20.6	52.0
1961	13.0	6.4	11.4	6.1	20.6	52.0

Sources: 1935–58: Marian Krzyzaniak and Richard A. Musgrave, *The Shifting of the Corporation Income Tax* (Johns Hopkins Press, 1963), p. 73; other years: *Statistics of Income, Corporation Income Tax Returns.*

[a] Equity capital is average of book value of stock and undistributed surplus at the beginning and end of the year.
[b] Profits plus interest paid as percentage of average equity capital plus debt capital at the beginning and end of the year.
[c] End of year.

TABLE C-16. Sources and Uses of Funds, Nonfarm Nonfinancial Corporate Business, 1960–65

(In billions of dollars)

Sources and Uses	1960	1961	1962	1963	1964	1965
Sources, total	47.3	54.5	61.0	63.6	68.5	88.7
Internal sources	34.4	35.6	41.8	44.3	49.9	55.3
Undistributed profits	10.0	10.2	12.4	13.8	17.3	21.9
Corporate inventory valuation adjustment	0.2	−0.1	0.3	−0.4	−0.3	−1.6
Capital consumption allowances	24.2	25.4	29.2	31.0	32.9	34.9
External sources	12.9	18.9	19.2	19.3	18.6	33.4
Stocks	1.6	2.5	0.6	−0.3	1.4	0.3
Bonds	3.5	4.6	4.6	3.9	4.0	5.4
Mortgages	0.7	1.7	2.9	3.4	3.4	3.5
Bank loans[a]	1.3	b	2.4	2.8	3.4	9.9
Other loans	1.0	0.3	0.7	0.5	1.3	1.2
Trade debt	3.2	6.7	3.8	5.3	2.4	6.7
Profits tax liability	−2.2	1.7	0.4	1.8	0.2	2.0
Other liabilities	3.9	1.4	3.8	1.9	2.5	4.5
Uses, total	42.5	52.1	56.0	60.5	64.3	83.9
Purchases of physical assets	36.7	34.9	42.0	43.6	49.6	59.6
Nonresidential fixed investment	32.5	31.1	34.3	35.7	41.3	49.0
Residential structures	1.2	2.3	3.0	3.7	3.7	3.8
Change in business inventories	3.0	1.5	4.7	4.2	4.6	6.9
Increase in financial assets	5.8	17.2	14.0	16.9	14.7	24.3
Liquid assets	−4.1	3.3	2.4	3.0	0.5	0.3
Demand deposits and currency	−0.5	1.6	−2.3	−1.9	−2.6	−3.3
Time deposits	1.3	1.9	3.7	3.9	3.2	5.0
U. S. Government securities	−5.4	−0.3	0.2	0.4	−1.5	−2.1
Finance company paper	0.6	0.1	0.8	0.7	1.5	0.7
Consumer credit	0.2	0.1	0.9	0.7	1.0	1.2
Trade credit	6.3	9.4	7.8	8.0	8.9	13.5
Other financial assets	3.5	4.4	2.9	5.2	4.3	9.3
Discrepancy (uses less sources)	−4.8	−2.4	−5.0	−3.1	−4.2	−4.8

Sources: 1960–63: *Economic Report of the President*, January 1966, p. 287; 1964–65: Board of Governors of the Federal Reserve System.

[a] Loans not elsewhere classified.

[b] Less than $50 million.

TABLE C-17. Assets of Selected Federal Trust Funds, Fiscal Years 1937-65

(In billions of dollars)

June 30	Old-Age and Survivors Insurance	Disability	Unemployment Insurance	Railroad Retirement
1937	0.3		0.3	
1938	0.8		0.9	0.1
1939	1.2		1.3	0.1
1940	1.7		1.7	0.1
1941	2.4		2.3	0.1
1942	3.2		3.2	0.1
1943	4.3		4.4	0.2
1944	5.4		5.9	0.3
1945	6.6		7.3	0.5
1946	7.6		7.4	0.7
1947	8.8		7.9	0.8
1948	10.0		8.3	1.4
1949	11.3		8.2	1.8
1950	12.9		7.4	2.2
1951	14.7		8.1	2.5
1952	16.6		8.7	2.9
1953	18.4		9.3	3.2
1954	20.0		9.0	3.4
1955	21.1		8.5	3.5
1956	22.6		8.8	3.7
1957	23.0	0.3	9.1	3.7
1958	22.8	1.1	7.8	3.7
1959	21.5	1.7	6.7	3.6
1960	20.8	2.2	6.7	3.9
1961	20.9	2.5	5.8	3.8
1962	19.6	2.5	5.8	3.8
1963	19.0	2.4	6.3	3.8
1964	19.7	2.3	6.9	3.9
1965ᵖ	20.2	2.0	7.9	4.0

ᵖ Preliminary.
Sources: 1937–55: U. S. Treasury Department, *Annual Reports of the Secretary of the Treasury;* 1956–65: U. S Treasury Department, *Treasury Bulletin* (November 1965).

TABLE C-18. Number of Estate Tax Returns, Value of Estates, and Amount of Tax, by Gross Estate Classes, 1963[a]

(Classes in dollars; other dollar amounts in millions)

Gross Estate Classes	Number of Returns	Gross Estate	Economic Estate[b]	Taxable Estate	Estate Tax Before Credits	Tax Credits	Estate Tax After Credits
Nontaxable returns, total	23,186	$ 2,294	$ 2,070	—	—	—	—
Taxable returns, total	55,207	14,714	14,059	$7,071	$2,087	$247	$1,841
$ 60,000– 100,000	14,782	1,197	1,170	207	16	c	16
100,000– 150,000	13,415	1,669	1,618	513	73	2	71
150,000– 200,000	8,704	1,504	1,443	523	97	5	92
200,000– 300,000	7,941	1,924	1,831	843	186	12	174
300,000– 500,000	5,483	2,091	1,985	1,103	283	24	259
500,000– 1,000,000	3,157	2,154	2,049	1,292	374	40	334
1,000,000– 2,000,000	1,115	1,528	1,452	985	323	42	281
2,000,000– 3,000,000	287	690	658	455	168	25	144
3,000,000– 5,000,000	190	714	679	443	182	28	154
5,000,000–10,000,000	101	666	622	409	199	34	165
10,000,000–20,000,000	24	335	316	168	98	17	80
20,000,000 and over	8	242	235	130	88	17	71
Grand total	78,393	17,007	16,129	7,071	2,087	247	1,841

Source: *Statistics of Income, Fiduciary, Gift, and Estate Tax Returns, 1962,* pp. 60–63. Figures are rounded and will not necessarily add to totals.
[a] Returns are classified by year in which they were filed.
[b] Economic estate is gross estate less debts (including mortgages).
[c] Less than $500,000.

TABLE C-19. Number of Gift Tax Returns, and Amounts of Gifts and Gift Tax, by Taxable Gift Classes, 1963[a]

(Classes in dollars; other dollar amounts in millions)

Taxable Gift Classes	Number of Returns	Total Gifts of Donor, Current Year	Taxable Gifts			Gift Tax
			Current Year	Prior Years	All Years	
Nontaxable returns, total	65,091	$1,248	—	$ 981	$ 981	—
Taxable returns, total	20,598	1,402	$790	2,004	2,794	$183
Under $3,000	5,873	136	7	368	375	1
$ 3,000– 10,000	5,329	150	31	277	308	3
10,000– 20,000	3,154	127	45	178	223	5
20,000– 50,000	3,318	200	103	286	389	14
50,000– 100,000	1,487	174	104	298	401	18
100,000– 250,000	939	195	143	214	357	31
250,000– 500,000	282	122	98	166	264	25
500,000–1,000,000	138	113	96	112	208	27
1,000,000–2,000,000	47	82	70	53	123	23
2,000,000–3,000,000	20	55	46	31	77	17
3,000,000–4,000,000	5	16	16	6	22	6
4,000,000–5,000,000	2	9	9	1	10	3
5,000,000–6,000,000	2	10	10	5	15	5
6,000,000 and over	2	13	12	10	22	6
Grand total	85,689	2,650	790	2,985	3,775	183

Source: *Statistics of Income, Fiduciary, Gift, and Estate Tax Returns, 1962,* p. 41. Figures are rounded and will not necessarily add to totals.
[a] Returns are classified by year in which they were filed.

TABLE C-20. General Expenditure of State and Local Governments, by Major Function, Fiscal Years 1954 and 1964

(Dollar amounts in millions)

Function	Amount		Increase 1954–64		
	1954	1964	Amount	Percentage Distribution of Increase	Percentage Increase
Total State and Local					
Total general expenditure[a]	$30,701	$69,302	$38,601	100.0	125.7
Education	10,557	26,533	15,976	41.4	151.3
Highways	5,527	11,664	6,137	15.9	111.0
Public welfare	3,060	5,766	2,706	7.0	88.4
Health and hospitals	2,409	4,910	2,501	6.5	103.8
Police and fire	1,783	3,588	1,805	4.7	101.2
Natural resources	762	1,835	1,073	2.8	140.8
Sewerage and sanitation	1,058	2,267	1,209	3.1	114.3
Housing and community redevelopment	611	1,142	531	1.4	86.9
General control and financial administration	1,375	2,567	1,192	3.1	86.7
Interest on debt	718	2,356	1,638	4.2	228.1
Other	2,841	6,674	3,833	9.9	134.9
State					
Total general expenditure[a]	10,109	24,275	14,166	100.0	140.1
Education	1,715	5,711	3,996	28.2	233.0
Highways	3,254	7,850	4,596	32.4	141.2
Public welfare	1,548	2,796	1,248	8.8	80.6
Health and hospitals	1,276	2,464	1,188	8.4	93.1
Police and fire	130	315	185	1.3	142.3
Natural resources	563	1,185	622	4.4	110.5
General control and financial administration	419	871	452	3.2	107.9
Interest on debt	193	765	572	4.0	296.4
Other	1,011	2,318	1,307	9.2	129.3
Local					
Total general expenditure[a]	20,593	45,027	24,434	100.0	118.7
Education	8,842	20,822	11,980	49.0	135.5
Highways	2,272	3,814	1,542	6.3	67.9
Public welfare	1,512	2,970	1,458	6.0	96.4
Health and hospitals	1,133	2,446	1,313	5.4	115.9
Police and fire	1,653	3,273	1,620	6.6	98.0
Natural resources	199	650	451	1.8	226.6
Sewerage and sanitation	1,058	2,267	1,209	4.9	114.3
Housing and community redevelopment	609	1,125	516	2.1	84.7
General control and financial administration	956	1,697	741	3.0	77.5
Interest on debt	525	1,590	1,065	4.4	202.9
Other	1,834	4,373	2,539	10.4	138.4

Sources: 1954: Bureau of the Census, *Historical Statistics on Governmental Finances and Employment*, Census of Governments, 1962, Vol. VI, No. 4, 1964: Bureau of the Census, *Government Finances in 1963–64*. Figures are rounded and will not necessarily add to totals.

[a] Excludes insurance trust, liquor store, and public utility expenditures. Includes federal grants-in-aid.

TABLE C-21. General Revenue of State and Local Governments, Fiscal Years 1954 and 1964

(Dollar amounts in millions)

Source	Amount 1954	Amount 1964	Increase 1954–64 Amount	Increase 1954–64 Percentage Distribution of Total Increase	Increase 1954–64 Percentage Distribution of Revenue from Own Sources
Total State and Local					
General revenue[a]	$29,012	$68,443	$39,431	100.0	
Revenue from federal government[b]	2,966	10,002	7,036	17.8	
General revenue from own sources	26,046	58,440	32,394	82.2	100.0
Taxes	22,067	47,785	25,718	65.2	79.4
Property	9,967	21,241	11,274	28.6	34.8
Sales and gross receipts	7,276	15,762	8,486	21.5	26.2
Individual income	1,127	3,791	2,664	6.8	8.2
Corporation income	778	1,695	917	2.3	2.8
Other	2,918	5,296	2,378	6.0	7.3
Charges and miscellaneous	3,979	10,655	6,676	16.9	20.6
State					
General revenue[a]	15,299	37,648	22,349	100.0	
Revenue from federal government[b]	2,668	9,046	6,378	28.5	
General revenue from own sources	12,417	28,184	15,767	70.5	100.0
Taxes	11,089	24,243	13,154	58.9	83.4
Property	391	722	331	1.5	2.1
Sales and gross receipts	6,573	13,957	7,384	33.0	46.8
Individual income	1,004	3,415	2,411	10.8	15.3
Corporation income	772	1,695	923	4.1	5.9
Other	2,349	4,454	2,105	9.4	13.4
Charges and miscellaneous	1,328	3,942	2,614	11.7	16.6
Local					
General revenue[a]	19,562	44,084	24,522	100.0	
Revenue from federal government[b]	298	956	658	2.7	
General revenue from own sources	13,629	30,256	16,627	67.8	100.0
Taxes	10,978	23,542	12,564	51.2	75.6
Property	9,577	20,519	10,942	44.6	65.8
Sales and gross receipts	703	1,806	1,103	4.5	6.6
Individual income	122	376	254	1.0	1.5
Other	576	841	265	1.1	1.6
Charges and miscellaneous	2,651	6,714	4,063	16.6	24.4

Sources: *Historical Statistics on Governmental Finances and Employment, Governmental Finances in 1963–64* (see Table C-20). Figures are rounded and will not necessarily add to totals.
[a] Excludes revenue from publicly operated utilities, liquor stores, and insurance trust systems.
[b] Includes in addition to direct grants-in-aid, shared revenues, amounts received from the federal government for contractual services, and payments in lieu of taxes. Excludes grants in kind (distribution of commodities, technical assistance, etc.) and net loans and repayable advances.

TABLE C-22. State and Local Government Debt, Fiscal Years 1954–64

End of Fiscal Year	Debt Outstanding	
	Amount (Millions of dollars)	Index 1954=100
1954	38,931	100.0
1955	44,267	113.7
1956	48,868	125.5
1957	53,039	136.2
1958	58,187	149.5
1959	64,110	164.7
1960	69,955	179.7
1961	75,023	192.7
1962	81,278	208.8
1963	87,451	224.6
1964	92,222	236.9

Sources: 1954–61: *Historical Statistics on Governmental Finances and Employment*, p. 52; 1962–64: *Governmental Finances in 1963–64*, p. 21.

TABLE C-23. Use of Major Tax Sources by the States, September 1, 1966

State	Tax Sources					
	Sales	Individual Income	Corporation Income	Motor Fuel	Cigarette	Alcoholic Beverages
Alabama	x	x	x	x	x	x
Alaska	—	x	x	x	x	x
Arizona	x	x	x	x	x	x
Arkansas	x	x	x	x	x	x
California	x	x	x	x	x	x
Colorado	x	x	x	x	x	x
Connecticut	x	—	x	x	x	x
Delaware	—	x	x	x	x	x
Florida	x	—	—	x	x	x
Georgia	x	x	x	x	x	x
Hawaii	x	x	x	x	x	x
Idaho	x	x	x	x	x	x
Illinois	x	—	—	x	x	x
Indiana	x	x	x	x	x	x
Iowa	x	x	x	x	x	x
Kansas	x	x	x	x	x	x
Kentucky	x	x	x	x	x	x
Louisiana	x	x	x	x	x	x
Maine	x	—	—	x	x	x
Maryland	x	x	x	x	x	x
Massachusetts	x	x	x	x	x	x
Michigan	x	—	—	x	x	x
Minnesota	—	x	x	x	x	x
Mississippi	x	x	x	x	x	x
Missouri	x	x	x	x	x	x
Montana	—	x	x	x	x	x
Nebraska	—	a	a	x	x	x
Nevada	x	—	—	x	x	x
New Hampshire	—	—	—	x	x	x
New Jersey	x	—	x	x	x	x
New Mexico	x	x	x	x	x	x
New York	x	x	x	x	x	x
North Carolina	x	x	x	x	—	x
North Dakota	x	x	x	x	x	x
Ohio	x	—	—	x	x	x
Oklahoma	x	x	x	x	x	x
Oregon	—	x	x	x	x	x
Pennsylvania	x	—	x	x	x	x
Rhode Island	x	—	x	x	x	x
South Carolina	x	x	x	x	x	x
South Dakota	x	—	—	x	x	x
Tennessee	x	—	x	x	x	x
Texas	x	—	—	x	x	x
Utah	x	x	x	x	x	x
Vermont	—	x	x	x	x	x
Virginia	x	x	x	x	x	x
Washington	x	—	—	x	x	x
West Virginia	x	x	—	x	x	x
Wisconsin	x	x	x	x	x	x
Wyoming	x	—	—	x	x	x
Total	**42**	**33**	**37**	**50**	**49**	**50**

Source: The Advisory Commission on Intergovernmental Relations.
a Passed by the state legislature subject to approval by a general referendum.

TABLE C-24. Top Bracket State Individual and Corporation Income Tax Rates Before and After Allowing for Federal and State Deductibility, as of September 1, 1966

State	Individual Income Tax Rates (Percentages)		Corporation Income Tax Rates (Percentages)	
	Maximum Nominal Rates	Rates After Allowing for Deductibility	Maximum Nominal Rates	Rates After Allowing for Deductibility
Alabama[b]	5.0	0.5	5.0	1.4
Alaska[ag]	14.6	4.4	9.4	4.9
Arizona[b]	5.9	0.6	6.6	1.8
Arkansas[a]	5.0	1.5	5.0	2.6
California[a]	7.0	2.1	5.5	2.9
Colorado	8.0	0.8[b]	5.0	2.6[a]
Connecticut[d]	—	—	5.25	2.6
Delaware[a]	11.0	3.3[e]	5.0	2.6
Georgia[a]	6.0	1.8	5.0	2.6
Hawaii	11.0	3.0[d]	6.435	3.3[a]
Idaho	9.0	0.9[b]	6.0	3.1[a]
Indiana[a]	2.0	0.6	2.0	1.0
Iowa[b]	4.5	0.4	4.0	1.1
Kansas[b]	6.5	0.6	4.5	1.2
Kentucky[b]	6.0	0.6	7.0	2.0
Louisiana[b]	6.0	0.6	4.0	1.1
Maryland[a]	3.0	0.9	5.0	2.6
Massachusetts	7.38	0.6[e]	6.765	3.3[d]
Minnesota[b]	12.0	1.2	9.3	2.6
Mississippi[a]	3.0	0.9	3.0	1.6
Missouri[b]	4.0	0.4	2.0	0.5
Montana	7.9	0.8[b]	5.25	2.7[a]
New Jersey[a]	—	—	1.75	0.9
New Mexico[e]	6.0	0.5	3.0	0.8
New York[a]	10.0	3.0	5.5	2.9
North Carolina[a]	7.0	2.1	6.0	3.1
North Dakota[b]	11.0	1.1	6.0	1.7
Oklahoma[e]	6.0	0.5	4.0	1.1
Oregon	9.5	0.9[b]	6.0	3.1[a]
Pennsylvania[d]	—	—	6.0	2.9
Rhode Island[a]	—	—	6.0	3.1
South Carolina[a]	7.0	2.1[e]	5.0	2.6
Tennessee[d]	—	—	4.0	2.0
Utah[b]	6.5	0.6	6.0	1.7
Vermont[d]	7.5	2.1	5.0	2.5
Virginia[a]	5.0	1.5	5.0	2.6
West Virginia[a]	5.5	1.6	—	—
Wisconsin[d]	10.0	2.7	7.0	3.4[f]

Source: Nominal rates from Commerce Clearing House, *State Tax Guide.*

[a] State tax deductible against federal tax.

[b] State tax deductible against federal tax and federal tax deductible against state tax.

[c] State tax deductible against federal tax, federal tax deductible against state tax, and state tax deductible against state tax.

[d] State tax deductible against federal tax, and state tax deductible against state tax.

[e] South Carolina and Delaware limit the amount of federal tax deductible against state taxes to $500 and $300, respectively. They are treated in this table as if no deductibility were allowed, since the calculations apply to the highest tax bracket.

[f] Wisconsin limits the deductibility of federal corporation taxes to 10 percent of corporate net income before federal tax. In this calculation, the tax is treated as if the federal tax is not deductible.

[g] Alaskan individual and corporation income taxes are levied at the rate of 16 percent and 18 percent of federal individual and corporation income taxes that would be payable at rates in effect on December 31, 1963. This is equivalent to tax rates of 14.6 percent and 9.4 percent on federal taxable income.

298

Bibliographical Notes

Chapter 1.   Introduction

Among standard textbooks in public finance devoting considerable space to federal taxation are the following: James M. Buchanan, *The Public Finances,* 2nd ed., Richard D. Irwin, 1965; John F. Due, *Government Finance,* 3rd ed., Richard D. Irwin, 1963; Harold M. Groves, *Financing Government,* 6th ed., Holt, Rinehart & Winston, 1964; and Earl R. Rolph and George F. Break, *Public Finance,* Ronald Press, 1961.

A concise treatment may be found in Otto Eckstein, *Public Finance,* Prentice-Hall, 1964. The most authoritative advanced treatise is by Richard A. Musgrave, *The Theory of Public Finance,* McGraw-Hill, 1959. Much of the ground covered in this book is discussed by Dan Throop Smith in *Federal Tax Reform,* McGraw-Hill, 1961. The most outstanding articles in the history of taxation are reprinted in Richard A. Musgrave and Alan T. Peacock, eds., *Classics in the Theory of Public Finance,* Macmillan, 1958; and in Richard A. Musgrave and Carl S. Shoup, eds., *Readings in the Economics of Taxation,* Richard D. Irwin, 1959. A convenient reference for information and statistics about the major elements of the federal tax structure is provided by U.S. Congress, Joint Economic Committee, *The Federal Tax System: Facts and Problems, 1964,* 88 Cong. 2 sess. (1964).

Chapter 2.   Taxes and Economic Policy

The role of taxation in economic policy is discussed in some detail in David J. Ott and Attiat F. Ott, *Federal Budget Policy,* Brookings Institution, 1965, Chapters 5, 6, and 7. Wilfred Lewis, Jr., in *Federal Fiscal Policy in the Postwar Recessions,* Brookings Institution, 1962, measures the quantitative impact of the automatic stabilizers and discretionary actions taken during the four postwar recessions and recoveries. The concept of the "full employment surplus" and current economic thinking on the role of tax policy in economic decisions are ably and lucidly presented in *Economic Report of the President* (1962), pp. 70-84. The concept is integrated into the analysis of saving and investment in *Economic Report of the President* (1966), pp. 42-44. Also worth reading are: the rationale for the 1964 tax cut in *Economic Report of the President* (1963), pp. 66-83; and the discussion of the Employment Act on its twentieth anniversary in *Economic Report of the President* (1966), pp. 170-86.

CED's budget policy was first presented in Committee for Economic Development, Research and Policy Committee, *Taxes and the Budget: A Program for Prosperity in a Free Economy,* a statement on national policy, CED, 1947. A shorter version of the policy is given in CED's pamphlet, *The Stabilizing Budget Policy, What it is and How it Works,* CED, 1950. For a discussion and critique of this policy, see Walter W. Heller, "CED's Stabilizing Budget Policy After Ten Years," *American Economic Review,* Vol. 47, September 1957 (reprinted in National Bureau of Economic Research, *Readings in Business Cycles,* Richard D. Irwin, 1965, pp. 696-702).

The role of taxation in promoting economic growth is explained by Herbert Stein and Edward F. Denison in "High Employment and Growth in the American Economy," *Goals for Americans: The Report of the President's Commission on National Goals,* Prentice-Hall, 1960. An analysis of the impact of tax policy on economic growth in Western Europe and Japan during the 1950's appears in a conference report of the National Bureau of Economic Research and the Brookings Institution, *Foreign Tax Policies and Economic Growth,* Columbia University Press, 1966.

For a discussion of national debt policy, see Marshall A. Robinson, *The National Debt Ceiling,* Brookings Institution, 1959. The latest thinking on the "burden" of the national debt is summarized in James M. Ferguson, ed., *Public Debt and Future Generations,* University of North Carolina Press, 1964.

Criteria for evaluating government expenditures are discussed in Francis M. Bator, *The Question of Government Spending,* Harper & Row, 1960; Jesse Burkhead, *Government Budgeting,* John Wiley, 1956; and Robert Dorfman, ed., *Measuring Benefits of Government Investments,* Brookings Institution, 1965.

Chapter 3.   The Tax Legislative Process

The standard work on the tax legislative process is Roy Blough, *The Federal Taxing Process,* Prentice-Hall, 1952. In addition to the discussion of legislative procedures, this book examines in detail the interest and pressure groups involved in tax legislation, and also reviews the considerations relating to the level and distribution of taxes.

The reader will obtain a good insight into the intricacies of the legislative process by reviewing the tax messages, hearings, and committee reports relating to any one of the major tax bills enumerated in Table 3-1. The Revenue Act of 1964 left the most voluminous official history, including the following U.S. Congress publications: (1) *President's 1963 Tax Message,* Hearings, House Ways and Means Committee, 88 Cong. 1 sess. (1963), 7 volumes; (2) *Revenue Act of 1963,* House Committee on Ways and Means, House Report 759, 88 Cong. 1 sess. (1963); (3) *Revenue Act of 1963,* Hearings, Senate Finance Committee, 88 Cong. 1 sess. (1963), 5 volumes; (4) *Revenue Act of 1964,* Senate Finance Committee, Senate Report 830, 88 Cong. 2 sess. (1964); (5) *Revenue Act of 1964,* Conference Report, House Report 1149, 88 Cong. 2 sess. (1964); (6) *Public Law 88-272,* 78 Stat. 19; (7) *Revenue Estimates Relating to the House, Senate, and Conference Versions of H.R. 8363, The Revenue Bill of 1964,* Joint Committee on Internal Revenue Taxation, 88 Cong. 2 sess. (1964). An interesting analysis of the decision-making process in connection with the enactment of the Revenue Act of 1964 is given in Edward S. Flash, Jr., *Economic Advice and Presidential Leadership: The Council of Economic Advisers,* Columbia University Press, 1965, Chapter 5.

The congressional method of conducting responsible and thorough reviews of federal tax issues is best illustrated by the 1955 inquiry of the Joint Committee on the Economic Report and the 1959 inquiry of the House Ways and Means Committee. In each case, a set of papers by leading experts was first published and hearings on these papers were later held to permit the committee members to interrogate the experts. See the U.S. Congress publications: Joint Economic Committee for the Economic Report, *Federal Tax Policy for Economic Growth and Stability,*

84 Cong. 2 sess. (1955), 2 volumes; and House Ways and Means Committee, *Tax Revision Compendium,* Compendium of Papers on Broadening the Tax Base, Volumes 1-3, and *Income Tax Revision,* Hearings, 86 Cong. 1 sess. (1959).

Chapter 4.   The Individual Income Tax

The latest, and most authoritative, treatise on this tax is Richard Goode, *The Individual Income Tax,* Brookings Institution, 1964. A scholarly analysis of the arguments for and against progression will be found in Walter J. Blum and Henry Kalven, Jr., *The Uneasy Case for Progressive Taxation,* University of Chicago Press, 1952. The reader will also wish to consult the following two classics: Henry Simons, *Personal Income Taxation,* University of Chicago Press, 1938; and William Vickrey, *Agenda for Progressive Taxation,* Ronald Press, 1947.

The best empirical analyses of the impact of income taxation on economic incentives, based on interviews with individual taxpayers, are J. Keith Butters, Lawrence E. Thompson, and Lynn L. Bollinger, *Investments by Individuals,* Graduate School of Business Administration, Harvard University, 1953; George F. Break, "Income Taxes and Incentives To Work: An Empirical Study," *American Economic Review,* Vol. 47, September 1957, pp. 529-49; and James N. Morgan, Robin Barlow, and Harvey Brazer, *Economic Behavior of the Affluent,* Brookings Institution, 1966.

A quantitative measure of the erosion of the individual income tax base is provided by Joseph A. Pechman, "What Would a Comprehensive Individual Income Tax Yield," *Tax Revision Compendium* (1959), cited above, pp. 251-82. Two interesting books for the general reader on income tax erosion are Louis Eisenstein, *The Ideologies of Taxation,* Ronald Press, 1961; and Philip M. Stern, *The Great Treasury Raid,* Random House, 1962.

The major structural features of the individual income tax are discussed in detail in the following sources: Michael E. Levy, *Income Tax Exemptions,* Amsterdam: North-Holland, 1960; Harold M. Groves, *Federal Tax Treatment of the Family,* Brookings Institution, 1963; C. Harry Kahn, *Personal Deductions in the Federal Income Tax,* Princeton University Press, 1960; Lawrence H. Seltzer, *The Nature and Tax Treatment of Capital Gains and Losses,* National Bureau of Economic Research, 1951; David J. Ott and Allan H. Meltzer, *Federal Tax Treatment of State and Local Securities,* Brookings Institution, 1963.

Negative taxation in the form suggested in the text was first discussed by Milton Friedman in *Capitalism and Freedom,* University of Chicago Press, 1962, pp. 191-94. The philosophy and mechanics of negative taxation are discussed in somewhat more detail by Robert J. Lampman, "Approaches to the Reduction of Poverty," *American Economic Review,* Vol. 55, May 1965, pp. 521-29.

Senator Russell B. Long's plan to offer top bracket taxpayers a lower tax rate schedule if they elect to be taxed on their entire income is described in his statement in the *Congressional Record,* Vol. 110, Part 18 (October 2, 1964), pp. 23653-65.

Chapter 5. The Corporation Income Tax

Richard Goode's classic *The Corporation Income Tax,* John Wiley, 1951, provides a thorough analysis and appraisal of the role of the corporation income tax. A discussion of the merits of the corporation income tax in comparison with other taxes is given in a symposium volume of the Tax Institute of America, *Alternatives to Present Federal Taxes,* the Institute, 1964.

For a sample of the differing viewpoints on the incidence of the corporation income tax, see Marian Krzyzaniak and Richard A. Musgrave, *The Shifting of the Corporation Income Tax,* Johns Hopkins Press, 1963; Challis A. Hall, Jr., "Direct Shifting of the Corporation Income Tax in Manufacturing," *American Economic Review,* Vol. 54, May 1964, pp. 258-71; Arnold C. Harberger, "The Incidence of the Corporation Income Tax," *Journal of Political Economy,* Vol. 70, June 1962, pp. 215-40; Marian Krzyzaniak, ed., *Effects of Corporation Income Tax,* Wayne State University Press, 1966.

The treatment of dividends under the income taxes has been investigated thoroughly in two books by Daniel M. Holland, *The Income Tax Burden on Stockholders,* Princeton University, 1958, and *Dividends Under the Income Tax,* Princeton University Press, 1962. The influence of federal taxation on corporate financial policy is appraised in Dan Throop Smith, *Corporate Financial Policy,* Graduate School of Business Administration, Harvard University, 1952. John A. Brittain in *Corporate Dividend Policy,* Brookings Institution, 1966, measures the impact of the income taxes on dividend payout policy of corporations.

The basic article on the incentive effects of depreciation is by E. Cary Brown, "Business Taxation and Investment Incentives," *Income, Employment and Public Policy,* Essays in Honor of Alvin H. Hansen, W. W. Norton, 1948. Another useful article on investment incentives is Sam B. Chase, "Tax Credits for Investment Spending," *National Tax Journal,* Vol. 15, March 1962, pp. 32-52. The need for liberalized depreciation policies in taxation (before the adoption of these policies in recent years) was ably presented by George Terborgh in *Realistic Depreciation Policy*, Machinery and Allied Products Institute (MAPI), 1954. Terborgh has also provided a succinct summary of the effects of the investment credit and depreciation changes in 1962 on rates of return in *Incentive Value of the Investment Credit, The Guideline System, and the Corporate Rate Reduction*, MAPI, 1964.

Other structural features of the corporation income tax are discussed in Stephen L. McDonald, *Federal Tax Treatment of Income from Oil and Gas*, Brookings Institution, 1963; Lawrence B. Krause and Kenneth W. Dam, *Federal Tax Treatment of Foreign Income*, Brookings Institution, 1964; and U.S. Congress, Senate Finance Committee, *Treasury Department Report on Private Foundations*, February 2, 1965. The effect of the corporation income tax on export prices is analyzed by Robert Z. Aliber and Herbert Stein in "The Price of U.S. Exports and the Mix of U.S. Direct and Indirect Taxes," *American Economic Review*, Vol. 54, September 1964, pp. 703-10. A report of the National Bureau of Economic Research and the Brookings Institution, *The Role of Direct and Indirect Taxes in the Federal Revenue System*, Princeton University Press, 1964, discusses the effect of various taxes on the balance of payments.

Chapter 6.   Consumption Taxes

There are excellent treatises on the major general consumption taxes. John F. Due in *Sales Taxation*, University of Illinois Press, 1957, discusses the role of consumption taxes in the tax structure and evaluates the different forms and features of sales and value added taxes, taking the experience of various countries into account. A brilliant defense of, and plea for, the adoption of a graduated expenditure tax may be found in Nicholas Kaldor, *An Expenditure Tax*, George Allen & Unwin, 1955. The value added tax is explored by Clara K. Sullivan in *The Tax on Value Added*, Columbia University Press, 1965. Daniel C. Morgan, Jr., appraises the retail sales tax in the light of recent developments in economic analysis in *Retail Sales Tax: An Appraisal of New Issues*, University of Wisconsin Press, 1964. The relative merits of income and consumption taxes are examined in detail in *The Role of Direct and Indirect Taxes in the Federal Revenue System*, cited above.

In preparation for the Excise Tax Reduction Act of 1965, federal excise taxes were evaluated in a series of papers by some of the nation's leading tax experts in U.S. Congress, House Ways and Means Committee, *Excise Tax Compendium;* these papers were then discussed in the Hearings on June 15 and 16, 1964, *Federal Excise Tax Structure*, 88 Cong. 2 sess. (1964), Parts 1 and 2, respectively.

Chapter 7.   Payroll Taxes

There is no single volume devoted to the economic effects of payroll taxes; the literature on these taxes is an outgrowth of the discussions of financing the social security system. The most comprehensive overall analysis of payroll taxation is contained in Seymour Harris, *Economics of Social Security*, McGraw-Hill, 1941; Part II of this volume is devoted to the incidence of payroll taxes. The reader will also wish to refer to Margaret S. Gordon, *The Economics of Welfare Policies*, Columbia University Press, 1963; John J. Carroll, *Alternative Methods of Financing Old-Age, Survivors and Disability Insurance*, Institute of Public Administration, University of Michigan, 1960; and Richard A. Lester, *The Economics of Unemployment Compensation*, Industrial Relations Section, Princeton University, 1962.

Questions of financing are discussed in the annual reports of the Advisory Council on Social Security. The latest report, *Economic Policies of the Social Security Program and Recommendations* (1965), discusses the major current issues. U.S. Congress, Joint Economic Committee, *European Social Security Systems*, Economic Policies and Practices, Paper No. 7, 89 Cong. 1 sess. (1965), provides a comparative analysis of the social security programs in England, Sweden, the Common Market countries, and the United States.

Chapter 8.   Estate and Gift Taxes

An incisive historical review and analysis of the estate and gift taxes in the United States is Louis Eisenstein, "The Rise and Decline of the Estate Tax," *Federal Tax Policy for Economic Growth and Stability*, Joint Committee on the Economic Report, 1955, cited above, pp. 819-47. Robert J. Lampman provides estimates of the size distribution of wealth in the United States in *The Share of Top Wealth-Holders in National Wealth, 1922-1956*, Princeton University Press, 1962, largely based on data from federal estate tax returns.

The first estimates of the amount of gift and trust transfers were made on the basis of 1945 estate tax returns and prior gift tax returns of the same decedents. These estimates were presented by Secretary of the Treasury John S. Snyder in Exhibit 5 of his statement before the House Ways and Means Committee on February 3, 1950 and published in Vol. 1 of the Hearings, *Revenue Act of 1950*, 81 Cong. 1 sess. (1950), pp. 75-89. More recent data on gift and trust transfers and a thorough analysis of the major structural problems in estate and gift taxation may be found in Carl S. Shoup, *Federal Estate and Gift Taxes,* Brookings Institution, 1966. The use of trusts and methods of taxing them under the transfer taxes are explored in detail in Gerald R. Jantscher, *Trusts and Estate Taxation,* Brookings Institution, 1966.

G. S. A. Wheatcroft, ed., *Estate and Gift Taxation, A Comparative Study,* London: Sweet & Maxwell, 1965, provides an up-to-date comparative analysis of the transfer taxes in Great Britain, Australia, Canada, and the United States.

Chapter 9.   State and Local Taxes

The two best general sources on the state-local tax structure and the major issues in this area are: James A. Maxwell, *Financing State and Local Governments,* Brookings Institution, 1965; and Advisory Commission on Intergovernmental Relations, *Tax Overlapping in the United States, 1964,* ACIR, U.S. Government Printing Office, 1964.

The literature on the property tax is very large. Jens P. Jensen, *Property Taxation in the United States,* University of Chicago Press, 1931, provides an evaluation of this tax from the vantage point of the late 1920's and early 1930's. Dick Netzer, *The Property Tax,* Brookings Institution, 1966, is the most recent authoritative analysis of the economic impact of the tax and of its role in the U.S. tax system. The best analysis of recent developments in property tax administration is the ACIR staff information report, *The Role of the States in Strengthening the Property Tax,* U.S. Government Printing Office, 1963, 2 volumes.

Federal-state-local fiscal relations may be studied by referring to ACIR, *Measures of State and Local Fiscal Capacity and Tax Effort,* the Commission, 1962; James A. Maxwell, *Tax Credits and Intergovernmental Fiscal Coordination,* Brookings Institution, 1962; *The Role of Equalization in Federal Grants,* ACIR, 1964; Richard A. Musgrave, ed., *Essays in Fiscal Federalism,* Brookings Institution, 1965; George F. Break, *Intergovernmental Fiscal Relations in the United States,* Brookings Institution, 1966; Joseph A. Pechman, "Financing State and Local Government," in American Bankers Association, *Proceedings of a Symposium on Federal Taxation,* the Association, 1965 (reprinted as Brookings Reprint No. 103).

For more specific aspects of intergovernmental relations, see *Coordination of State and Federal Inheritance, Estate and Gift Taxes,* ACIR, 1961; *Federal-State Coordination of Personal Income Taxes,* ACIR, 1965; and U.S. Congress, House Committee of the Judiciary, Special Subcommittee on State Taxation of Interstate Commerce, *State Taxa-*

tion of Interstate Commerce, House Report 1480, 88 Cong. 2 sess. (1964), and House Reports 256 and 952, 89 Cong. 1 sess. (1965).

Numerous official state and city tax commission reports provide excellent sources of information and analysis on state-local tax problems. Among the best are *Report of the Governor's Minnesota Tax Study Commission, 1956,* Colwell Press, 1956; *Michigan Tax Study Staff Papers,* Lansing, Michigan, 1958; University of Wisconsin Tax Study Committee, *Wisconsin's State and Local Tax Burden: Impact, Incidence and Tax Revision Alternatives,* University of Wisconsin, School of Commerce, 1959; University of Maryland, College of Business and Public Administration, *Maryland Tax Study,* the University, 1965; and City of New York, Temporary Commission on City Finances, *Toward Fiscal Strength, Overcoming New York City's Financial Dilemma,* Second Interim Report, New York City, November 1965.

Appendix A.   Historical Notes

E. R. A. Seligman in "Taxation," *Encyclopedia of Social Sciences,* Macmillan, 1934, Vol. 7, pp. 626-39, traces income taxation in Europe and the United States up to the early 1930's. The reader may also wish to refer to the history of the development of progression in the British income tax in F. Shehab, *Progressive Taxation,* Oxford University Press, 1953. A history of taxation in this country through 1951 is provided in Randolph Paul, *Taxation in the United States,* Atlantic, Little & Brown, 1954. Lewis H. Kimmel analyzes the changes in American attitudes toward government taxing, spending, and borrowing in *Federal Budget and Fiscal Policy, 1789-1958,* Brookings Institution, 1959.

The *Annual Reports of the Secretary of the Treasury on the State of the Finances* summarize the major features of tax legislation enacted each year in a section entitled "Taxation Developments." Comprehensive summaries of tax rates are provided for the period 1913-40 in the 1940 Report (pp. 466-534); 1940-50 in the 1950 Report (pp. 251-80); and 1950-62 in the 1962 Report (pp. 370-402).

Index*

Ability to pay: acceptance of principle of, 50; income as the measure of, 62; tax distribution according to, 209

Accessions tax, 198-99. *See also* Estate taxes

ACIR. *See* Advisory Commission on Intergovernmental Relations

Adjusted gross income (AGI): defined, 52; nontaxable items in, 52; use of on tax returns, 52-53; derivation of from personal income, 255-57, *260;* comparison of personal income and (1939-64), *261;* total for U.S. compared with AGI on tax returns, *262*

Administrative budget, *18,* 19, 172, *274*

Advisory Commission on Intergovernmental Relations (ACIR): proposals of on estate and gift taxes, 215, 216; on state-local taxes, 220, 221, 306; on property assessment, 222; publications of, 306-7

Advisory Council on Social Security, 305

AFL-CIO, 35

Age 65 or over: personal exemptions for, 53, 84-85; nontaxable benefit payments, 84-85; medical-expenses deductions for, 85, 87; tax disadvantage to persons continuing to work, 86; concessions to in 1964 bill, 86-87; tax-exempt gains on sale of houses, 91. *See also* OASDHI; Social Security

AGI. *See* Adjusted gross income

Aids in financing public services. *See* Federal aid; State governments

Alaska, 205, 206

Alcoholic beverage taxes, 142, 144, 148, 205

Aliber, Robert Z., 304

Allocation. *See* Resources allocation

Arizona, 205, 206

Automobile taxes, 142, 151, 204, 239, 240

Averaging of income: to promote saving, 24; tax burden on fluctuating income in annual accounting periods, 95-96; technique of in 1964 Revenue Act, 96, 236

Balance of payments: monetary ease limited by, 23; corporation income tax and, 115-16; capital outflows through foreign branches of U.S. corporations, 131-32; potential effects on of a general consumption tax, 160

Barkley, Alben, 42

Barlow, Robin, 302

Bator, Francis M., 301

Benefit taxes: for highways, airways, and recreational activities, 160-61

Blind persons: exemptions for, 53, 85

Blough, Roy, 301

Blum, Walter J., 302

Bollinger, Lynn L., 302

Boulding, Kenneth E., 104

Brazer, Harvey, 302

Break, George F., 299, 302, 306

British Royal Commission on the Taxation of Profits and Income, 157

Brittain, John A., 303

Brown, E. Cary, 303

Buchanan, James M., 299

Budget (federal): current views on policy, 7, 9, 24; surpluses and deficits in programs of, 11, 16, *17, 18,* 19, 22-23; restrictive vs. expansionary, 16; concepts of, *18,* 19; full employment surplus in, 19-23; use of automatic rules for stabilization, 24-26; receipts, expenditures, and surpluses or deficits in, *274*. *See also* Fiscal policy

Built-in fiscal stabilizers: the individual income tax as the major stabilizer, 12, 14; transfer payments as, 12, 13; place of corporation income tax in, 12-13; effect of on surpluses and deficits, *13*, 14, 19; as moderators of business activity, 28-29

Bureau of the Budget, 34, 37, 42

Burkhead, Jesse, 301

Business activity: expenditures increased by tax cuts, 9; percentage of income originating in the corporate sector, *107, 288*

Business cycles: countercyclical measures in, 15, 16, 43, 46-48; yield of individual income tax in, 96; effect of corporation income tax on, 114

Butters, J. Keith, 302

California, 207, 224

Canada: personal exemptions in, 71; sales tax in, 142; tax percentage of the GNP in, *278*

Capital assets, 117, 120-21, 155

Capital consumption: depreciation allowances on corporate taxes, 3, 24, 64, 110, 111, 112; methods of amortizing asset costs, *118, 119;* "service life" of depreciable assets, 117, 119-20, 122; "reserve ratio test" for determining depreciation, 120, 123; investment credit deduction, 120-21; effect of investment credit on rate of return, *122*

Capital formation, 26; corporation income tax and, 108-10

Capital gains: preferential rates on long-term gains, 24, 63, 90-92, 100, 111, 113, 236; on sale of houses, 90-91; in gift or death cases, 91, 92; amortization of tax on, 91-92

Capital losses: deductibility of, 92-93; offsetting losses against gains, 93

Carnegie, Andrew, 179

Carroll, John J., 305

Cash budget (federal), *18*, 19, 172, 177

Casualty losses: part of allowed as deduction, 53, 76

CED. *See* Committee for Economic Development

Ceylon: expenditure tax in, 141

Charitable contributions: allowed as deduction, 53, 236; ratio of to income, 76; desirability of questioned, 77; revision of deduction for, 78

Charitable foundations, 195-97

Chase, Sam B., 303

Child care: deduction for, 78

Cigarettes. *See* Tobacco taxes

Cities: adoption of income and sales taxes in, 203; revenue sources of, 207; denial of appropriate grants to in rural-dominated state legislatures, 225; needs of for blighted areas, 232

Civil Rights Act: need of compliance with in general purpose grants, 229

Civil War: use of individual income tax in, 235; excise taxes in, 238-39

Colorado, 154, 205

Commercial banks: tax treatment of, 129

Commissioner of Internal Revenue, 31

Committee for Economic Development (CED), 24, 35; publications of, 300

Commodity tax in foreign countries, 115

Compliance: with U.S. income tax laws, 51, 211; in interstate commerce taxation, 217, 219; benefited by unitary administration of taxes, 221, 223-24

Conference Committee of U.S. Congress, 41-42, 48

Congress: "power to lay and collect taxes," 30, 236; mentioned, 59, 81, 82, 84, 92, 93, 95, 98, 123, 125, 144, 173, 186, 200, 214, 215, 216, 217, 221, 227

Consolidated cash budget, *274*

Constitution of the United States: taxing power given to Congress in, 30; the Sixteenth Amendment, 236

Consumer durable equipment loans: interest on, 77, 79

Consumer expenditures: increased by

tax cut, 9, 10-11

Consumer price index, 25, *68n*

Consumption: dependence of on disposable income, 12, 13; effect of tax rate changes on, 14-15; in family budget, 83

Consumption taxes: compared with income tax, 62-63; percentage of GNP in selected countries, *142;* inequities of, 143, 161; pyramiding of, 143, 161; state-local yield from, 143; allocation of between federal-state-local governments, 144, 161; a general consumption tax as substitute for federal income taxes, 158-60, 161. *See also* Consumption; Excise taxes; Expenditure tax; Sales taxes; Value added tax

Cooperatives: tax treatment of, 130-31

Corporation income tax: effect of tax rate changes in, 14; compared with personal income tax, 64; history of, 98-99, 235, 237-38; incidence of, 99-100, 103-4; impact of on the economy, 100; capital gains and losses provisions in, 100-1; deductions for research and development, 101; intercorporate dividends, 101-2; foreign earnings, 102; partnership treatment of, 102; organizations exempted from, 102; rates of, 102-3, 237, *245;* method of payment, 103; shifting mechanism of, 104-14 *passim;* criticism of, 109-16, 139; general and effective rate of on profits (1946-65), 110, *111;* built-in flexibility of, 114-15; comparison of declines in with GNP, *115;* value added tax as substitute for, 115-16; ratio of to GNP, 116; investment credit allowance, 120-21; burden of on corporate income, *133, 134. See also* Income tax bases

Corporations: intercorporate affiliations, 98-99; dividend policy of, 100, 111-12, 114; output and prices, 105-7, 113; profits, 105, 108, 114; rates of return and debt-capital ratio, *108, 289;* property income share in

gross product of, *109;* investment incentives, 110-12, 114; increase of gross corporate saving (1929-65), 112; income from foreign subsidiaries of, 131-32; current payment system for, *287;* funds of nonfarm, nonfinancial business, *290*

—debt financing of: deduction allowance for interest payments, 112; interest rates, 112; ratio of to total capital, *108,* 113

—equity financing of: nonallowance for dividends paid out, 112; cost of compared with debt financing, 113

Council of Economic Advisers, 34, 35

Counties: state aid to, 225

Credit: access to and restraints on, 23

Current tax payment: individuals, 56-58, *281, 282;* corporations, 103, *287*

Customs duties: percentage of GNP in selected countries, 141, *142;* U.S. policy on, 143

Dam, Kenneth W., 304

Death taxes (federal): tax avoidance on capital gains, 92; *inter vivos* transfer of property, 178; effects of on economic incentives, 179; views on distribution of wealth by, 179, 180; credit against federal tax for state tax on, 242. *See also* Estate taxes (federal); State governments

Debt. *See* National debt

Debt financing. *See* Corporations

Declaration of estimated tax, 57-58

Deductibility of taxes: provisions in federal income tax, 74, 77, 79; in state income taxes, 211-14

Deductions. *See* Itemized deductions; Minimum standard deduction; Standard deduction

Denison, Edward F., 300

Dental expenses as deduction, 53, 85

Dependents: per capita exemptions for, 53; credit allowance for, 72, 236

Depletion allowances. *See* Minerals industries

Depreciation. *See* Capital consumption

Dillon, C. Douglas, 36
Direct taxes: categories of, *278*
Disability insurance, 163, 167
Disposable personal income: spending in changes of, 11, 12, 114; effect of tax change on, 14; budget policy effects on, 26; fluctuations in, 28; stabilized by individual income tax, 61
District of Columbia, 221
Dividends: information return by payers of, 59-60; exclusion allowances, 238. *See also* Corporations; "Double tax"
Domestic workers, 57; failure of to file, 256
Dorfman, Robert, 301
"Double tax" on dividends: diversity of views on, 132, 157: burden in low income classes, 133-34; integrating corporation and individual income tax, 134-38; dividend received credit as alternative, 134-35, *135;* dividend paid deduction as alternative, 135-36, *136;* withholding dividend received at the source, 136-37, *137;* dividend exclusion as alternative, 137-38; impracticality of partnership method, 138. *See also* Value added tax
Due, John F., 299, 304

Earned income: expenses of earning, 78, 88; views on allowance for, 87-88; savings deduction for self-employed, 89
Earned income credit, 88-89
Eckstein, Otto, 299
Economic Development Act of 1965, 176
Economic growth: basis of, 9, 21-24; effect of federal expenditures on, 11; impact of tax rates on, 15, 21-24; full employment factor in, 16-21; relation of the national debt to, 26-28; stimulated by capital gains treatment, 91. *See also* Stabilization policy
Economic policy: role of taxation in, 9, 51, 60-64, 300-1; saving and investment promoted by, 23-24; use of automatic budget rules for flexibility,

24-26; fiscal and monetary actions in, 28, 29
Education and research: government outlays for, 23; federal grants-in-aid for, 203
Eisenhower, Dwight D., 147
Eisenstein, Louis, 302, 305
Employment: increase in by state and local governments, 202. *See also* Full employment; Unemployment
Employment Act of 1946, 46
Equity financing. *See* Corporations
Equity of tax levies: vertical, 5; horizontal, 5, 64, 65, 80, 149; progressive distribution, 5-6, 49; analyses of by the Treasury, 34; discriminatory effects, 95-96
Erosion of the individual income tax, 64-65, 302; measurement of, *284*
Estate and gift taxes (federal): avoidance of, 91, 92, 192, 196, 199; incorporation in income tax, 179; revenues from, 179-80, 183, 186, 199, 200; calculation of, 180-81; tax base of, 182-83, 258-59; value of reported on returns, 183, 195, 196; distribution of estates by gifts, 187-91; tax differences in transfers during life or death, *188;* proposals for integration of, 190-91; generation-skipping, 191-95; effect of on trust transfers, 191-95; use of private foundations, 195-97; history of, 242, *253;* exemptions and exclusions in, *254. See also* Estate taxes; Gift taxes; Property transfers
Estate taxes (federal): components in base of, 180, 181; deductions, exemptions, and rates, 181, 242, *252;* in interspousal transfers, *185;* estate splitting as benefit to the wealthy, 187-88; small business and, 197; accessions tax as substitute for, 198-99; rates for computing state tax credits, *252;* returns on and percentage of deaths, *269;* tax before and after credits, *270, 292;* distribution of estates by rate brackets, *271. See also* Trusts; Estate and gift taxes
Excess profits tax, 237, 238

Excise Tax Reduction Act of 1965, 37, 150, 158, 160, 304

Excise taxes: nonallowance as deductions, 77; on particular commodities, 142; consumer burden of, 144-46, 149; economic effects of, 145-46, 161; federal revenue from, *145;* in wartime, 146-47; levies of on business, 149-51; effective rates of and customs, *150;* history of, 238-40; earmarked for special categories, 239, 240; rates on selected items, *246-49.* *See also* Sumptuary taxes; Use taxes

Exclusions from taxable income: specific items excluded, 52. *See also* Estate and gift taxes

Exemptions. *See* Personal exemptions

Expenditure tax as a possibility: defined, 141; collected from the consumer, 141, 157; as replacement of the income tax, 157; compliance and administrative problems of, 158, 161. *See also* Consumption taxes

Export-import prices: effect of on balance of payments, 115-16

Families: size of as exemptions factor, 50, *69,* 81, 84; use of income in budget of, *70,* 83; husband-wife income splitting, 81-84; burden of excise taxes on, 149

Farm workers, 57

Farmers and fishermen, 58, 88

Federal aid to state-local governments: for specific services, 203, 225; conditional grants-in-aid, 225-27; rise of federal grants (1902-64), *226;* general purpose grants, 227-30; in relation to state-local revenue, *228;* alternative methods of, 230-31

Federal expenditures: effect of changes in, 7, 9, 20, 22, 47; influence of on spending, 10; economic potency of, 11; deficits or surpluses resulting from, 11; national need as basis for, 14; versus tax adjustments, 14-16; ratio of taxes to, 29; and state-local expenditures, *202*

Federal Highway Trust Fund, 147

Federal receipts: amount and percent of GNP (1929-65), *2;* by source, *4, 98, 276-77;* revenue losses in tax-exempt state-local bonds, 93; by type of tax, *279*

Federal-state-local receipts, *275*

Federal-state-local tax system: deductibility of state taxes from federal income tax, 74, 77, 79, 205, 210, 211-14; tax coordination, 214-21; overlapping estate and gift taxation, 215; cooperative tax administration, 220-21; distribution of receipts by type of tax, *279*

Federal tax system: reliance of on income taxes, 1, 3; changes in structure of, 3; goals of, 5-6; origin of, 235

Ferguson, James M., 300

Finance Committee, U. S. Senate, 30, 31, 39-40

Financial institutions: problems in taxing of, 126-29; types of, 127-29

Fire and casualty insurance companies: special formulas for deferring taxation, 128-29

Fiscal drag: defined, 20; retarding effect of on economy, 25, 26

Fiscal policy: objectives of, 9, 45; impact of on income and output, 10; monetary policy as aid to, 12; as basis for increasing investment rate, 22. *See also* Budget; Built-in fiscal stabilizers

Flash, Edward S., Jr., 301

Flat rate taxes, 102, 143, 237

Florida, 218, 224

Fluctuating incomes. *See* Averaging of income

Foreign income. *See* Corporations

France: tax percentage of the GNP in, 1, *278;* income splitting principle in, 81; effect of commodity tax rebates on balance of payments, 115; value added tax in, 141, 155

Friedman, Milton, 303

Fringe benefits, 52

Full employment: defined, 9; and economic growth, 16-21; budget surpluses at, 22, 23; relation to potential GNP, 9

Gasoline taxes: as a deduction, 77, 78; deduction of as burden on general taxpayer, 79; purpose of, 142; burden of on consumer, 144; extensive use of, 205

General fund: use of for financing future OASDHI benefit increases, 172, 174-75; reliance of on progressive taxes, 175

Georgia, 218

Germany (West): tax percentage of the GNP in, 1, *278;* income splitting principle in, 81; effect of commodity tax rebates on balance of payments, 115; value added tax in, 154

Gift taxes (federal): computation of, 181-82; value reported on returns, 183; effect of gift splitting, 185; rates of, 188, 242; failure to use gifts to maximum tax-saving advantage, 189-90, *189;* exemptions in, 242; donee exclusions in, 242; statistics of on returns, *272, 293;* distribution of gifts by rate brackets, *273. See also* Estate and gift taxes

GNP. *See* Gross national product

Goode, Richard, 104, 302, 303

Gordon, Margaret S., 305

Government saving: effect of social insurance system on, 171-72

Government transfer payments: unemployment and welfare payments, 12, 52, 72; old-age insurance, 13; provided by public debt, 26; exclusion of from AGI, 52; increase of, 54

Graduated taxes, 84, 178, 237

Grants-in-aid. *See* Federal aid; State governments

Great Britain: personal exemptions in, 71; allowance for working wives in, 89; corporation income tax in, 137; sales tax in, 142; estate tax in, 191, 193, 195. *See also* United Kingdom

Gross national product (GNP): actual and potential, *8,* 16; dependence of on total spending, 9; increase and reduction of, 10-14; automatic adjustments as moderators of, 12; effect of tax rate changes on, 15; percentage increase of (1929-65), 112; relation of federal-state-local government receipts to, *275;* relation of taxes to, *278;* mentioned, 20, 25, 28, 114, 116, 203, 207

Groves, Harold M., 299, 302

Hall, Challis A., Jr., 303

Harberger, Arnold C., 104, 303

Harris, Seymour, 305

Hart, M. C., *250n*

Hawaii: credit against the income tax for sales taxes paid, 154, 205; income taxes adopted in (1901), 205

Head of household, 55, 58, 84

Health programs: outlays for, 23; federal grants-in-aid for, 203

Heller, Walter W., 300

High income classes: moderating influence of income tax on, 51-52, 159; advantage to of tax-exempt bonds, 93

Highway taxes, 3, 150

Highway Trust Fund, 239

Holland, Daniel M., 303

Hospital and medical insurance: for age 65 and over, 85, 163, 165, 167; employee and self-employed tax liability for, *168;* financing of, 173

House Banking and Currency Committee, 196

House Committee on Ways and Means. *See* Ways and Means Committee

House of Representatives: revenue bills originated in, 35-36; Ways and Means Committee procedures, 36-38, 47; public hearings on tax bill, 36, 37, 44; Rules Committee approval, 39; floor action, amendments, and final vote, 39, 48

Housewives. *See* Working wives

Illinois, 207

Incidence. *See* Shifting and incidence; Excise taxes; Payroll taxes

Income: defined, 52, 65; earned vs. unearned, 87-88; economic definition of, 90; inequalities in distribution of, 236

Income splitting: benefits of, 55, *56,* 65; provision for, 81-84, 236; tax rates in, 82-83; advantage of to married couple, *82;* as a tax burden to single persons, 83

Income Tax Act of 1894, 179

Income tax bases: definitions of, 53, 64

—for personal income: erosion of, 49, 64, *65,* 80; definition of, 53, 64; deductions in from AGI, 53-55; ratio of to income, *54;* increases in income and base compared, *55;* derivation of, *55, 255-57, 263;* defects of base, 63; concepts of, 255-57; distribution by rate brackets, 257, *265;* comparison of income and base (1939-64), *264*

—for corporation income: reconciliation of before-tax profits, compiled net profits, and tax base, 257-58, *266;* comparison of profits and tax base, *267;* distribution by rate brackets, 258, *268*

India: expenditure tax in, 141

Indiana, 154, 205

Indirect taxes: categories of, *278*

Individual income tax (federal): economic efficiency of, 14, 52, 57, 60-64; percentage of federal receipts from, 50; adoption of, 51, 235; uses of AGI in computation of, 52-55; graduated rates of, 55-56; methods of payment, 56-59; built-in flexibility of, 60-61, 97; effects of on saving and consumption, 61-63; impact of on work and investment incentives, 63-64; nominal vs. effective rates of, *66, 284;* exemptions compared with family income, *69;* exemptions and family budgets, *70;* fairness of, 97; history of, 235-37; rate schedules (1944-64), *244;* tax liabilities, prepayments, and overpayments, *281, 282, 283;* tax of single persons and married couples compared, *286. See also* Deductions; Income tax bases; Itemized deductions; Personal exemptions; Standard deductions

Inflation: counteracted by tax adjustments, 15-16

Interest income: information return by payers of, 59-60

Interest paid by taxpayer: allowed as deduction, 53, 76, 77; on business vs. consumer durable goods loans, 79

Interest rates: effects of rise or reduction in, 12, 23

Internal Revenue Code: as the vehicle of tax collection and filing, 31, 32; definition of taxable income in, 255

Internal Revenue Service, 33, 38, 43, 51, 58, 119, 120, 130, 221

Interstate commerce: state taxation of activities in, 216-19; "destination" principle in, 219; need of tax uniformity between states, 219

Investment, private: incentives for, 22, 23, 24, 62, 64; monetary policy for increase of, 23; future services yielded by, 26; credit restraint on, 28; in state and local bond issues, 52, 93-95; effect of corporation tax on, 104-9, 113-14; in corporation securities, 109-12; capital consumption allowances and, 121-23

Investment, public: use of national resources in, 22; components of, 23-24; future yield of, 26

Investment credit: to stimulate investment by business firms, 3, 24, 64, 123, 140; effect of, 110; allowance for qualified assets, 101, 120-21. *See also* Capital consumption

Iowa, 218

Italy: tax percentage of the GNP in, 1, *278;* turnover tax in, 142

Itemized deductions: expenditures allowed, 53; at different income levels, *74, 75;* resultant tax savings, 75; purpose and kinds of, 76-78; proposals for revision of, 78-81; amounts of on returns, 257, *280;* as percentage of AGI, *285*

Jantscher, Gerald R., 306

Japan: tax percentage of the GNP in, *278*

Jefferson Administration, 238

Jensen, Jens P., 306

Johnson, Lyndon B., 47, 48, 147, 176

Joint Committee on the Budget: proposal for, 46

Joint Committee on Internal Revenue Taxation, 31, 34, 37, 38, 41, 44, 46, 48
Joint Economic Committee, 46, 299, 301
Joint Federal-State Action Committee: on tax coordination, 214
Joint returns, 53, 55, 58

Kahn, C. Harry, 302
Kaldor, Nicholas, 304
Kalvin, Henry, Jr., 302
Kennedy, John F., 33, 47, 86, 92, 131, 147, 176
Kimmel, Lewis H., 307
Korean War, 51, 147, 201, 236-39 *passim*
Krause, Lawrence B., 304
Krzyzaniak, Marian, 104, *289n*, 303

Lampman, Robert J., 303, 305
Land: tax on income from, 236
Legislative counsels of the House and Senate. *See* Tax legislation
Lester, Richard A., 305
Levy, Michael E., 302
Lewis, Wilfred, Jr., *13n*, 300
License fees: as nontax revenue of local governments, 207
Life insurance companies: taxation history of, 127-28; present method of taxing, 128
Local governments: property tax revenue of, 206-7; sales and income taxes in, 207; nontax revenues of, 207; public services performed by, 221; limits to taxation freedom of, 223-24; state grants-in-aid to, 224-25; needs of cities and counties, 225, 232
"Locking-in" of securities: effect of on mobility of capital, 91
Long, Russell B., 80, 303
Low income classes: burden of taxes on, 56-57, 159; lack of taxpaying capacity of, 67, 83; personal exemptions and, 67; inadequacy of aid to, 72-73; negative income tax and, 73-75

McDonald, Stephen L., 304
Manpower Development and Training

Act of 1962, 176
Married couples, 53, 55, 58, 67, 71, *82, 83*
Maryland, 87
Massachusetts, 87
Maxwell, James A., *222n*, 306
Medical expenses: portion of allowed as deduction, 53, 75, 76, 79, 85, 87
Meltzer, Allan H., 302
Michigan: value added tax in, 155; yield of sales tax in, 210
Minerals industries: depletion allowance for exhaustion of deposits, 123-25, 140; depletion claimed on tax returns (1958-60), *124*
Minimum standard deduction: as a correction of personal exemption inadequacy, 69-70, 71-72
Mississippi: local government sales taxes in, 207
Monetary policy: role of in stabilization, 11-12; and private investment, 23; on growth of national debt, 26
Morgan, Daniel C., Jr., *150n*, 304
Morgan, James N., 302
Mortgage-financed homeownership: deductions for interest payments on, 75, 76-77
Moving expenses: in connection with new job, 88
Musgrave, Richard A., 104, *150n, 289n*, 299, 303, 306
Mutual financial institutions, 102, 127, 140
Myers, Robert J., *250n*

National Association of Manufacturers, 35
National Bureau of Economic Research, 300, 302, 304
National debt: public concern over, 26, 28; interest payments on, 26, *27*, 28; net federal debt defined, *27n;* and the GNP, *27*, 28; monetary restraint on, 28
National economy. *See* Economic policy
National income accounts budget, *18, 19, 274*

Natural resources: efficient uses of for economic growth, 22; user charges for depletion of, 143, 147

Nebraska, 205, 211

Negative income tax: proposal for, 72-75, 302

Netherlands: tax percentage of the GNP in, 1, *278*

Netzer, Dick, 306

Nevada, 206

New Hampshire, 211

New York State: yield of income tax in, 210

OASDHI. *See* Old-age, survivors, disability, and health insurance

Ohio, 207

Old age. *See* Age 65

Old-age, survivors, disability, and health insurance (OASI, OASDI, OASDHI): benefit payments, 52, 85, 165-74 *passim;* financed by payroll taxes, 162-63; tax rates for, 163, 165, *167;* employee contributions, 163, 167-68; employer contributions, 163, 167; coverage, 165, 166; administered through trust funds, 165-66; pattern of tax incidence in, 166-70 *passim;* regressivity of, 166-68; illustrative tax liabilities, *168;* history of tax rates, *250. See also* Payroll taxes

Oregon: tax withholding adopted in (1948), 206

Orshansky, Mollie, *70n*

Ott, Attiat F., 300

Ott, David J., 300, 302

Overpayment of tax, 59

Owner-occupied houses: imputed rental value of, 52; tax deductions on, 76, 79; tax treatment of gains on sale of, 90-91

Paul, Randolph, 307

Payment of tax: current payment system, 57, 59-60; requirements for those not subject to withholding, 58; final tax reconciliation, 58-59

Payroll taxes: increases in rates of, 3, 177; "earmarked" for social insurance, 162, 172, 176; percentage of in federal receipts, *163;* employee contributions, 163, 167-68, 240; employer contributions, 163, 169-70, 240; impact of on the economy, 166, 169; regressive features of, 166-68, 173; built-in flexibility of, 168-69; incidence of, 167, 169-71, 176; effect of on prices, employment, and wages, 169-71; and personal saving, 171; and government saving, 171-72; history of, 240-42; coverage, 241. *See also* OASDHI

Peacock, Alan T., 299

Pechman, Joseph A., *66n,* 302, 306

Pennsylvania: inheritance tax adopted in (1825), 206; local income taxes in, 207

Pensions: plans paid by employer excluded from AGI, 52; industrial plans, 85, 89, 171; self-employed retirement plans, 89. *See also* Railroad employees

Personal exemptions: amounts for specific persons, 53; importance to low income groups, 65, 67; history of, 65-67, 236-37, *243;* standards of for different family sizes, 67, 69; inadequacies in, 69-71; per capita system vs. variable exemptions, 70-71; revenue losses incurred by increases in, 71; tax credits in lieu of, 72; total amounts of in 1963, 257. *See also* Estate and gift taxes; Negative income tax

President of the United States: proposal to provide discretionary tax authority to, 16, 47-48; tax recommendations of, 30, 33; annual budget message and economic report, 35, 46, 47, 48, 300; *1963 Tax Message,* 124, 301

Progressive taxation, 5-6, 141, 149, 166, 209; virtues of, 50, 60; personal exemptions contributing to, 67; violated by state-local tax-exempt securities, 94-95

Property: recipients of income from, 58

Property tax: as deduction from taxable income, 53, 77, 79; revenue from, 206-7; administration of, 221-23; assessment of values, 221-23, *222,* 231

Property transfers: in estate and gift taxation, 178-91 *passim;* use of by married couples, 183-87, *185;* in community and noncommunity property systems, 184-86; proposals for tax reforms on, 186-87; influence on of the trust device, 192-95
Proportional taxes, 141, 154, 161, 166
Prosperity: budget policy and, 7
Public assistance payments. *See* Government transfer payments
Public services: growth in demand for, 3, 201; federal activities in, 129; types of performed by local governments, 221; unequal local capacity to pay for, 227

Railroad employees: pensions not taxed at age 65, 85; unemployment insurance tax rates, 165, 242, *251;* retirement tax rates, 241, *250*
Railroad retirement benefits, 85, 86
Recessions: effect of built-in stabilizers on, 13, 60; President's proposal for combatting, 47; corporation profits in, 114; insurance against in the tax system, 159; OASDI tax increases effected in along with benefit increases, 168-69
Refunds to taxpayers: total paid each year, 31; reasons for great numbers of, 59
Regressivity of taxes, 65, 94, 143, 149, 150, 154, 159, 161, 166-68, 176, 202, 213
Regulatory taxes, 148-49
Religious organizations: tax-exempt status of, 129-30; not subject to "unrelated business income" tax, 130
Renters: unfairness to as against homeowners, 79
Resources allocation: distorted by tax-exempt securities, 93-94; between corporate and noncorporate sectors, 113, 114, 139; effect of on the economy, 114; distorted by special treatment of mineral products, 125; effect of excise taxes on, 145, 146
Retirement income: credit against, 85, 86

Revenue Acts: of 1942, 184; 1943, 42; 1948, 42, 184; 1950, *32n,* 130, 237, 239, 305; 1951, 41, 127; 1962, 41, 110, 119, 121, 132; 1963, 131, 301; 1964, 9, 37, 40, 41, 43, 45, 61, 96, 121, 126, 138, 237, 301
Revenue sharing. *See* Federal aid to state-local governments; State and local governments
Robinson, Marshall A., 300
Rolph, Earl R., 299
Roosevelt, Franklin D., 42
Royalties: capital gains rates on, 91

Sales taxes: allowed as deduction, 53, 77; collected from the seller, 141; turnover tax, 142, 143, 151, 156; single- and multi-stage types of, 142, 151-52; burden of on the poor, 143; wholesalers' and manufacturers' taxes, 151, 152, 156, 161; on goods and consumer services at the retail level, 151, 153-54, 161, 205; pyramiding effects under wholesalers' tax, 152, 153; burden of on the retailer, 211
Saving, corporate, 112
Saving, personal: tax measures as incentives for, 24; exclusion from AGI of life insurance income on, 52; tax on income produced by, 61-62; in family budget, 83; influences on, 171-72. *See also* Government saving
Savings and loan associations, 127
Self-employed persons: earned and unearned incomes of, 88-89; savings deduction of for retirement plan, 89; OASDHI tax rates for, 165; tax payments by for OASDHI, 168
Seligman, E. R. A., 307
Seltzer, Lawrence H., 302
Senate in the tax legislative process: bill sent to after House passage, 39; Finance Committee's consideration and report, 39-40, 47; amendments proposed on the floor, 40, 48; reasons for long debate, 40-41; pressure from the administration, 41; vote on the bill, 41; House action on Senate amendments, 41
Separate returns, 53, 58, 82

Service life. *See* Capital consumption

Shehab, F., 307

Shifting and incidence: short-run shifting of corporation tax, 103-6, 110, 113; long-run shifting of corporation tax, 106, 107-8, 110; excise taxes, 144-46; payroll taxes, 169-71

Shoup, Carl S., 299, 306

Simons, Henry, 302

Single persons: smaller responsibility of, 50, 84; tax rate range for, 55; unfairness to in tax system, 69, 83-84; taxes of compared with taxes of married couples, 82-83, *286. See also* Head of household

Smith, Dan Throop, 299, 303

Snyder, John S., 305

Social Security: benefits, 85, 86, 163, 166, 240; tax rates for, 163, 165; coverage, 165, 173, 174, 241; earnings subject to tax, 165, 174, 240; effect of on government saving, 171-72

—financing methods: the contributory system, 172-75; proposal for increases in earnings base, 173-74, 177; proposal for payroll-income tax integration, 174, 177; proposal for using general fund receipts, 174-75, 177

—social insurance programs, 162-66; characteristics of, *164*

Social Security Act of 1935, 162, 235, 240; Act of 1965, 167-72

Stabilization policy: impact on of expenditure and tax changes, 10-12; role of monetary policy in, 11-12; role of income taxes in, 12-13, 15, 51; built-in stabilizers, 12-14, *13;* expenditure vs. tax adjustments, 14-16

Standard deduction: in lieu of itemized deductions, 53, 75, 80, 81; amounts of on returns, *280*

Standards of living: income needed on low-cost and economy levels of, 67, *69*

State governments: sales tax relief measures in, 154, 205, 231; inheritance and death taxes in, 178, 198, 215-16; reliance of on consumption taxes, 202, 205; withholding of state taxes in, 203, 206; deduction for federal taxes in, 205, 211, 213, 231; individual and corporate income taxes in, 205-6, 217, 231; estate and gift taxes in, 206, 215-16; merits of income vs. sales taxes, 209-11; tax liabilities in an income tax and a sales tax state, *210;* deductibility features in, 211-14, *212;* interstate commerce taxation by, 216-19; taxation of nonresidents, 219-20; grants-in-aid to local governments, 224-25, *226;* tax sources of each of the states (1966), *297;* top-bracket rates of on individual and corporate income taxes, 298

State and local governments: receipts of as percentage of GNP (1929-65), *2;* rise of tax rates in, 3; sources of revenue, *4, 204, 295;* tax-free interest on bonds of, 52, 93-95; federal deductions on tax payments to, 53, 77; community property laws in, 82; mounting needs of, 93, 94, 159, 231-32; federal aid to, 94, 225-31; consumption taxes in, 142, 143, 153; rising expenditures of, 201, *202,* 203; per capita revenue of, 207-8, *208;* fiscal performance, capacity, and effort of, 207-8, 227-28; fiscal relations between, 221-25; tax supplements, sharing, and credits, 223-24, 230; expenditures of by functions, *294;* debt outstanding (1954-64), *296. See also* Property tax

State Taxation of Interstate Commerce Subcommittee of the House Judiciary Committee, 216, 306

State of the Union Message, 35

Stein, Herbert, 300, 304

Stern, Philip M., 302

Stockfisch, Jacob A., *278n*

Sullivan, Clara K., 304

Sumptuary and regulatory taxes: purposes of, 148-49, 161; "interest equalization tax" on foreign securities, 149, 249; retained in 1965 law, 240

Supreme Court decisions, 82, 98, 99, 216, 218, 236

Surtax exemptions for corporations: for

helping small firms, 125; abuses of in formation of subsidiary firms, 125-26, 140

Survivors insurance, 163

Sweden: tax percentage of the GNP in, 1, *278*

Tax Adjustment Act of 1966, 59, *145n*, 151

Tax Analysis Office, 33

Tax avoidance, 31, 91, 92, 131-32, 192, 196, 199, 218; on interest and dividends, 60

Tax base. *See* Income tax bases

Tax credits: for state sales taxes, 3; in lieu of exemptions, 72, 236

Tax deficiency notices served, 31

Tax-exempt income: specific items of excluded in money income, 52. *See also* Personal exemptions

Tax-exempt organizations: types of, 102, 129; revenue loss from exemptions, 129; "unrelated business income" of, 130; property lease-back as abuse of exemption, 130; tax status of cooperatives, 130-31; estate taxes and charitable foundations, 195-97

Tax legislation: proposals for by the President, 30, 33, 34; congressional committees in enacting tax law, 30, 36-38, 39-40; the Treasury Department's role, 30-41 *passim;* staff of experts in law and economics, 31; drafting of bill by legislative counsels, 31, 33, 38; history of bills enacted, *32;* preparation of bill by the executive branch, 33-35; outside consultants, 33, 34; the President's budget message and economic report, 35; the tax bill in the House, 35-39; the tax bill in the Senate, 39-41; the Conference Committee's reconciliation of two versions, 41-42; the President's action, 42-43; regulations on new law issued by the Treasury, 43; criticisms of the legislative process, 43-48; improvements proposed, 44-48; publications on the legislative process, 301; congressional inquiries and reports, 301-2. *See also* House of Representatives; Senate; and titles of Acts, Codes, agencies, etc., mentioned in Chapter 3

Tax payment: methods of for personal income, 56-60; for corporations, 103, 287

Tax rates: bracket system of, 55, *56;* schedules of, 56, *244, 245, 246-49, 252, 253;* state income tax rates, 205-6, 298; present maximum individual rate, 236

—changes in: economic potency of cuts, 9, 10, 15, 61; deficits or surpluses resulting from, 11; stabilization effects of, 14-15, 20; multiplier effect of, 15; time handicap in legislation for, 16

Tax returns: number of filed, 31; reconciliation on between tax liability and prepayments, 58-59; filing requirements, 256

Tax Revision Compendium (1959), 45

Tax yields: stability of, 60, 143; differences in between various tax forms, 62; during business cycles, 96; effect of social insurance system on, 171-72

Taxable income. See Income tax bases

Taxation: effect of on work and investment incentives, 63

Taxpayers: preference of for overwithholding in current payment system, 59; pressure from for special benefits, 65

Teeters, Nancy H., *21n*

Telephone taxes, 151, 239, *248*

Terborgh, George, 304

Theft losses, 53

Thompson, Lawrence E., 302

Thrift institutions: tax on retained earnings of, 127; reserves of for bad debts, 127

Tobacco taxes, 142, 144, 148, 205, *246*

Trade Expansion Act of 1962, 176

Transfers. *See* Government transfer payments

Treasury Department, 33, 63, 93, 124, 126, 157, 189, 218, 221

Truman, Harry S., 42, 125

Trusts: use of, 191-92; property transfers in trust by millionaires, *193, 194;* alternative methods of taxing transfers in, 198-99

Trust funds for social insurance: in cash budget statements, *18;* "earmarked" in payroll taxes, 162; economic stability promoted by, 169; assets of, 171, *291;* effect of on federal saving, 172; views on continuance of, 173, 177

Turnover taxes. *See* Sales taxes

Unemployment: counteracted by government policies, 26

Unemployment compensation trust funds, 166, 169, 175

Unemployment insurance: benefit payments, 13, 52, 166, 169, 175, 176; a federal-state system, 162; financing of, 163, 175-76; tax rate on employers, 165, 175, 241; coverage, 165, 175, 241; "experience rating" system of, 169, 175, 241

United Kingdom: tax percentage of the GNP in, 1, *278;* earned income allowance in, 87. *See also* Great Britain

United States Chamber of Commerce, 35

United States tax system: compared with other countries, 1; stabilizing effect of on income and spending, 5; saving and investment promoted by, 24; contribution of to the nation's welfare, 49; advantages of current payment system of, 73; relationship of to GNP and tax yield, *278*

Use taxes: in interstate commerce, 216, 218, 219; general categories of, 240

User charges: burden of on general taxpayer, 79, 147; on persons benefiting from public services, 142, 147; resistance to, 148; in state-local taxation, 204; reduction of in 1965 law, 240

Utah, 207, 224

Value added tax: as substitute for corporation income tax, 115-16, 138-39, 161; collected from the seller, 141; levied on the difference between a firm's sales and purchases, 141, 155; forms of, 155; advocated for use in stabilization policy, 155; economic effects of, 156; versus the retail sales tax, 156-57

Vanishing exemption, 72

Vickrey, William, 302

Vietnam conflict: expenditures for, 9

Virginia, 224

Voorhees, E. M., 104

War of 1812, 238

Ways and Means Committee, U. S. House of Representatives, 30-48 *passim,* 301, 302

Wealth: transferred by gift, *189;* transferred in trust, *193*

Welfare programs: traditional methods of, 72-73; relation to income tax system, 73; government's responsibilities for, 129; federal grants-in-aid for, 203

Wheatcroft, G. S. A., 306

Whisky Rebellion of 1794: revolt by farmers against tax, 238

Wisconsin: retail sales tax of, *150;* regressivity of sales tax in, 154; individual and corporate taxes adopted in 1911, 205; inheritance tax adopted in 1903, 206; revenue from income and sales taxes in, 209

Withholding of tax: a means of making speedy tax rate changes, 14; on wages and salaries, 57; inclusion of interest and dividends proposed, 59-60

Working wives: allowance for, 89-90; household expenses of, 90

World War I, 236-42 *passim*

World War II, 3, 13, 14, 28, 51, 53, 56, 59, 63, 82, 103, 110, 111, 114, 140, 149, 157, 160, 180, 192, 201, 224, 236, 237, 238, 239, 256, 257

Wyoming, 205

Yield. *See* Tax yields